FOOD CULTURE

Research Methods for Anthropological Studies of Food and Nutrition

Published in Association with the Society for the Anthropology of Food and Nutrition (SAFN) and in Collaboration with Rachel Black and Leslie Carlin

Volume I
Food Research: Nutritional Anthropology and Archaeological Methods
Edited by Janet Chrzan and John Brett

Volume II
Food Culture: Anthropology, Linguistics, and Food Studies
Edited by Janet Chrzan and John Brett

Volume III
Food Health: Nutrition, Technology, and Public Health
Edited by Janet Chrzan and John Brett

Food Culture

Anthropology, Linguistics, and Food Studies

Edited by
Janet Chrzan and John Brett

Published in 2017
Berghahn Books
www.berghahnbooks.com

© 2017, 2019 Janet Chrzan and John Brett
First paperback edition published in 2019

All rights reserved.

Except for the quotation of short passages for the purposes
of criticism and review, no part of this book may be reproduced
in any form or by any means, electronic or mechanical,
including photocopying, recording, or any information
storage and retrieval system now known or to be invented,
without written permission of the publisher.

Library of Congress Cataloging-in-Publication Data

Names: Chrzan, Janet, editor. | Brett, John A., editor.
Title: Food culture : anthropology, linguistics and food studies / edited by Janet Chrzan and John A. Brett.
Other titles: Food culture (Berghahn Books : 2017)
Description: New York : Berghahn Books, 2017. | Series: Research methods for anthropological studies of food and nutrition ; volume II | Includes bibliographical references and index.
Identifiers: LCCN 2016047921 (print) | LCCN 2016048830 (ebook) | ISBN 9781785332890 (hardback : alk. paper) | ISBN 9781785332906 (E-book)
Subjects: LCSH: Nutritional anthropology—Research—Methodology. | Food habits—Research—Methodology. | Anthropological linguistics—Research—Methodology.
Classification: LCC GN407 .F6595 2016 (print) | LCC GN407 (ebook) | DDC 394.1/20721--dc23
LC record available at https://lccn.loc.gov/2016047921

British Library Cataloguing in Publication Data

A catalogue record for this book is available from the British Library.

ISBN 978-1-78533-289-0 hardback
ISBN 978-1-78920-524-4 paperback
ISBN 978-1-78533-290-6 ebook

Contents

Introduction to the Three-Volume Set *Research Methods for Anthropological Studies of Food and Nutrition* 1
  Janet Chrzan

Introduction to *Food Culture: Anthropology, Linguistics, and Food Studies* 7
  Janet Chrzan

Research Ethics in Food Studies 15
  Sharon Devine and John Brett

Section IV. Socio-Cultural Approaches

Chapter 1. The Anthropology of Food and Food Anthropology: A Sociocultural Perspective 31
  Geraldine Moreno-Black

Chapter 2. Interviewing Epistemologies: From Life History to Kitchen Table Ethnography 47
  Ramona Lee Pérez

Chapter 3. Studying Body Image and Food Consumption Practices 58
  Nicole Taylor and Mimi Nichter

Chapter 4. Visual Anthropology Methods 70
  Helen Vallianatos

Chapter 5. On the Lookout: The Use of Direct Observation in Nutritional Anthropology 81
  Barbara A. Piperata and Darna L. Dufour

Chapter 6. Participant-Observation and Interviewing Techniques 92
  Heather Paxson

Chapter 7. Focus Groups in Qualitative or Mixed-Methods Research 101
  Ramona L. Pérez

Chapter 8. Studying Food and Culture: Ethnographic Methods in the Classroom
   Appendix 1: Food Ethnography Course Syllabus
   Appendix 2: Food Ethnographies   112
   Carole Counihan

Section V. Linguistics and Food Talk

Chapter 9. Introduction to Linguistic Anthropology Food Research Methods   131
   Jillian R. Cavanaugh and Kathleen C. Riley

Chapter 10. Food Talk: Studying Foodways and Language in Use Together   143
   Jillian R. Cavanaugh and Kathleen C. Riley

Chapter 11. An Introduction to Cultural Domain Analysis in Food Research: Free Lists and Pile Sorts   159
   Ariela Zycherman

Chapter 12. Food and Text(ual) Analysis   170
   Kathleen C. Riley

Chapter 13. Analysis of Historic Primary Sources   183
   Ken Albala

Section VI. Food Studies

Chapter 14. Introduction to Food Studies Methods   197
   Amy B. Trubek

Chapter 15. Meaning-Centered Research in Food Studies   204
   Lucy M. Long

Chapter 16. Food and Place   218
   William Woys Weaver

Chapter 17. Sensory Ethnography: Methods and Research Design for Food Studies Research   228
   Rachel E. Black

Chapter 18. Methods for Examining Food Value Chains in Conventional and Alternative Trade   239
   Catherine M. Tucker

Chapter 19. The Single Food Approach: A Research Strategy in Nutritional Anthropology   253
   Andrea S. Wiley and Janet Chrzan

Index   270

Introduction to the Three-Volume Set *Research Methods for Anthropological Studies of Food and Nutrition*

Janet Chrzan

These three volumes provide a comprehensive examination of research design and methods for studies in food and nutritional anthropology. Our goal is to provide a resource that bridges the biocultural or biological focus that traditionally characterized nutritional anthropology and the broad range of studies widely labeled as the anthropology of food, and food studies. The dramatic increase in all things food in popular and academic fields over the last two decades, accompanied by vast changes in technology, has generated a diverse and dynamic set of new methods and approaches to understanding the relationships and interactions people have with food. Earlier methods books tended toward the biocultural perspective of nutritional anthropology (e.g., Pelto, Pelto, and Messer 1989; Quandt and Ritenbaugh 1986) while more recent volumes have focused on food studies (e.g., MacBeth and MacClancy 2004; Belasco, 2008; Miller and Deutsch 2009) and applied work (e.g., den Hartog, Van Staveren and Brouwer 2006). The rapidly evolving field of food studies has generated a host of new perspectives and methods from a wide variety of academic backgrounds, many of which include anthropological theories and research designs. Because of the expansion of the field and the recent rise of food studies, we saw a need for a comprehensive reference volume to guide design and research across the full spectrum of food, diet, and nutrition studies.

The set has eight sections, each of which can almost stand alone as a food methods volume for a particular subdiscipline of anthropology. Just as nutritional anthropology and studies in the anthropology of food benefit from a four-field, contextualized approach, this volume assumes that research in food systems and nutrition relies upon four subdisciplines in order to effectively study the importance of food within human societies. Therefore, in addition to sections covering biological/nutritional, sociocultural, linguistic, and archeological anthropology methods, we have included sections on public health/applied nutrition, food studies, technology, and statistics. Each section is anchored by an introductory chapter that chronicles the history of the study of food within that area of research or practice and provides a comprehensive discussion of previous studies that have helped to define current work. By examining where we have been in relation to what we are doing and where we are going, each section seeks to define how current and future research can choose, adopt, and adapt the best methods to ensure high-quality outcomes. Each section is designed to provide readers with the background sources necessary for a fully comprehensive understanding of the use of methods for that area of study—a "pointing to" of studies and practitioners that have defined the field so that the reader has a good understanding of what is necessary to conduct respectable food research using methods germane to that area of anthropology. The individual chapters provide case studies and examples of how these methods have been used by other social scientists.

    The chapters within each section form a complementary packet covering most of the major methods generally used by practitioners within each subdiscipline. We have included what might be called standard methods in the various subdisciplines (e.g., participant observation, ethnographic interviewing, excavation techniques, site surveying, etc.) but have expanded this focus with specialized techniques and approaches that have emerged or become popular more recently, such as digital storytelling, GIS, bone chemistry, and the use of biomarkers. The authors write about the methods and research design for their topics from their own research experience, outlining how they thought through their research questions, designs, data collection, and in some cases analysis. These volumes are meant to be a primary resource for research about food for not only the beginning student but also graduate students as well as research and teaching professionals who desire a better understanding of how their peers have tackled specific questions and problems. Each author follows a similar outline, with a short introduction to the method and its antecedents (covering key background/historical literature and essential readings where applicable) followed by current discussions and uses of the method, including the gray literature where applicable (e.g., material from the FANTA projects, FAO, Gates Foundation, etc.) and then discussion of analysis and research design considerations, concluding with the references cited and further readings. The sections on further reading include key historical volumes, reviews, monographs, software links, and so on for background or more in-depth exploration.

The eight sections were divided into three volumes by clustering areas of anthropological research that are linked conceptually and methodologically. The first volume contains ethics, nutritional anthropology and archeological methods, studies that are often biological in focus. The second volume is mostly sociocultural, covering classic social anthropology, linguistic anthropology, and food studies. We felt that research in food studies was more frequently rooted in social processes and disciplines such as history, journalism, and sociology and thus belonged amongst the allied anthropological fields. The final volume folds the more applied research paradigms together with public health anthropology and finishes with a section on technology and statistical analysis. Clearly, this last volume could be paired with one or the other volumes to provide a comprehensive overview of allied methods, as applied anthropology and technology are utilized in biological/archeological fields as well as socio-cultural, linguistic, and food studies research and practice. By breaking these three volumes into sections we hope to provide a comprehensive overview of methods related to food research, one that allows faculty, students, and researchers to purchase the volume(s) best suited to their subdiscipline and research interests.

A final word concerns research design. These volumes have no chapter dedicated to research design for two reasons: one, the topic is far too large to be adequately covered in one or even two chapters, and two, each chapter includes some aspect of research design. Clearly, research design will differ between biological and sociocultural studies, even if the philosophy of each is derived from classic anthropology theory. However, each author was asked to provide foundational examples of research design in their field in order to create a comprehensive core bibliography for research design and methods in food and nutritional anthropology and food studies. That bibliography is given here, along with a second bibliography for Rapid Assessment Procedures and Focused Ethnographic Studies.

Food/Nutritional Anthropology and Food Studies: Research Design and Methods

Albala, Ken, ed. 2013. *Routledge Handbook to Food Studies.* New York: Routledge.
Axinn, William, and Lisa Pearce. 2006. *Mixed Method Data Collection Strategies.* Cambridge: Cambridge University Press.
Belasco, Warren. 2008. *Food: The Key Concepts.* New York and Oxford: Berg.
Bernard, H. Russell. 2011. *Research Methods in Anthropology: Qualitative and Quantitative Approaches,* 5th ed. Lanham, MD: AltaMira Press.
den Hartog, Adel P., Wija A. van Staveren, and Inge D. Brouwer. 2006. *Food Habits and Consumption in Developing Countries.* Wageningen, The Netherlands: Wageningen Academic Publishers.
Dufour, Darna L., and Nicolette I. Teufel. 1995. Minimum Data Sets for the Description of Diet and Measurement of Food Intake and Nutritional Status. In *The Comparative Anal-*

ysis of Human Societies: Toward Common Standards for Data Collection and Reporting, ed. Emilio F. Moran, 97–128. Boulder, CO: Lynne Rienner.
Edge, John T. 2013. *The Larder: Food Studies Methods from the American South*. Athens, GA: University of Georgia Press.
Gibson, Rosalind. 2005. *Principles of Nutritional Assessment*, 2nd ed. Oxford: Oxford University Press.
Johnston, Francis, ed. 1987. *Nutritional Anthropology*. New York: Alan R. Liss.
Kedia, Satish, and John van Willigen. 2005. *Applied Anthropology: Domains of Application*. Westport, CT: Praeger.
Kiefer, Christie W. 2006. *Doing Health Anthropology: Research Methods for Community Assessment and Change*. New York: Springer.
Macbeth, Helen, and Jeremy MacClancy. 2004. *Researching Food Habits: Methods and Problems*. New York: Berghahn Books.
Margetts, Barrie, and Michael Nelson. 1997. *Design Concepts in Nutritional Epidemiology*, 2nd ed. Oxford: Oxford University Press.
Mead, Margaret. 1945. *Manual for the Study of Food Habits*. Washington, DC: National Research Council.
Miller, Jeff, and Jonathan Deutsch. 2009. *Food Studies: an Introduction to Research Methods*. Oxford and New York: Berg.
Murcott, Anne, Warren Belasco, and Peter Jackson, eds. 2013. *The Handbook of Food Research*. London and New York: Bloomsbury.
Pellett, P. L. 1987. Problems and Pitfalls in the Assessment of Human Nutritional Status. In *Food and Evolution: Toward a Theory of Human Food Habits,* ed. Marvin Harris and Eric Ross, 163-180. Philadelphia: Temple University Press.
Pelto, Gretel, Pertti Pelto, and Ellen Messer. 1989. *Research Methods in Nutritional Anthropology*. Tokyo: United Nations University.
Pelto, Pertti. 2013. *Applied Ethnography: Guidelines for Field Research*. Walnut Creek, CA: Left Coast Press.
Pelto, Pertti, and Gretel Pelto. 1978. *Anthropological Research: The Structure of Inquiry*. Cambridge: Cambridge University Press.
Quandt, Sara, and Cheryl Ritenbaugh, eds. 1986. *Training Manual in Nutritional Anthropology*. Washington, DC: American Anthropological Association.
Scrimshaw, Susan C. M., and Elena Hurtado. 1987. *Rapid Assessment Procedures for Nutrition and Primary Health Care: Anthropological Approaches to Improving Programme Effectiveness*. Tokyo: United Nations University and New York: UNICEF.
Shamoo, A., and D. Resnik. 2009. *Responsible Conduct of Research*, 2nd ed. New York: Oxford University Press.
Sobo, Elisa J. 2009. *Culture and Meaning in Health Services Research*. Walnut Creek, CA: Left Coast Press.
Sutton, Mark Q., Kristin D. Sobolik, and Jill K. Gardner. 2010. *Paleonutrition*. Tucson: University of Arizona Press.
Thursby, Jacqueline S. 2008. *Foodways and Folklore*. Westport, CT: Greenwood Folklore Handbooks.
Ulijaszek, Stanley. 2005. *Human Energetics in Biological Anthropology*. Cambridge Studies in Biological and Evolutionary Anthropology 16. Cambridge: Cambridge University Press.

Ulijaszek, Stanley, and S. S. Strickland. 1993. *Nutritional Anthropology: Biological Perspectives.* Littlehampton: Smith-Gordon.

VanderWerker, Amber M., and Tanya M. Peres. 2010. *Integrating Zooarchaeology and Paleoethnobotany: A Consideration of Issues, Methods and Cases.* New York: Springer.

Weiss, William, and Paul Bolton. 2000. *Training in Qualitative Research Methods for NGOs and PVOs: A Trainer's Guide to Strengthening Program Planning and Evaluation.* Baltimore, MD: Center for Refugee and Disaster Studies, Johns Hopkins University School of Public Health. http://www.jhsph.edu/research/centers-and-institutes/center-for-refugee-and-disaster-response/publications_tools/publications/_pdf/TQR/tg_introduction.pdf.

Rapid Assessment Procedures and Focused Ethnographic Studies

Beebe, James. 2001. *Rapid Assessment Process: An Introduction.* Lanham, MD: AltaMira Press.

———. 2014. *Rapid Qualitative Inquiry: A Field Guide to Team-Based Assessment.* Lanham, MD: Rowman and Littlefield.

Blum L., P. J. Pelto, G. H. Pelto, & H. V. Kuhnlein. 1997. *Community Assessment of Natural Food Sources of Vitamin A.* Boston: International Nutrition Foundation.

Catholic Relief Services. n.d. *Rapid Rural Appraisal/Participatory Rural Appraisal Manual.* http://www.crsprogramquality.org/storage/pubs/me/rrapra.pdf.

Catley, Andrew, John Burns, Davit Abebe, and Omeno Suji. 2008. Participatory Impact Assessment: A Guide for Practitioners. Feinstein International Center, Friedman School of Nutrition Science and Policy, Tufts University (in English, Spanish, or French). http://fic.tufts.edu/assets/Part_Impact_10_21_08V2.pdf.

Chaiken, Miriam S. 2011. Using Qualitative Methods in Save the Children Programs and Research: A Training Manual. Washington, DC: Save the Children.

Chaiken, Miriam S., J. Richard Dixon, Colette Powers, and Erica Wetzler, 2009. Asking the Right Questions: Community-Based Strategies to Combat Hunger. *NAPA Bulletin* 32(1): 42–54.

GERANDO: *Community Based Disaster Risk Management; Facilitator's Manual.* 2011. http://www.wvi.org/disaster-risk-reduction-and-community-resilience/publication/gerando-community-based-risk-reduction.

Gittelsohn, J., P. J. Pelto, M. E. Bentley, K. Bhattacharyya, and J. Russ. 1998. *Ethnographic Methods to Investigate Women's Health.* Boston: International Nutrition Foundation.

Gove, S., and G. H. Pelto. 1994. Focused Ethnographic Studies in the WHO Programme for the Control of Acute Respiratory Infections. *Medical Anthropology* 15: 409–24.

Pelto, Gretel H., and Margaret Armar-Klemesu. 2014. *Focused Ethnographic Study of Infant and Young Child Feeding 6–23 Months: Behaviors, Beliefs, Contexts and Environments. Manual for Conducting the Study, Analyzing the Results, and Writing a Report.* Global Alliance for Improved Nutrition (GAIN). http://www.hftag.org/resources/all-resources/ (select "Demand Generation for Home Fortification", then "Focused Ethnographic Study").

Pelto, G. H., M. Armar-Klemesu, J. Siekmann, and D. Schofield. 2013. The Focused Ethnographic Study: Assessing the Behavioral and Local Market Environment for Improving the Diets of Infants and Young Children 6 to 23 Months Old and Its Use in Three Countries. *Maternal & Child Nutrition* 9: 35–46.

Pelto, G. H., and S. Gove. 1994. Developing a Focused Ethnographic Study for the WHO Acute Respiratory Infection Control Programme. In *Rapid Assessment Procedures: Qualitative Methodologies for Planning and Evaluation of Health Related Programmes,* ed. N. S. Scrimshaw and G. R. Gleason, 215–26. Boston: International Nutrition Foundation.

Scrimshaw, Nevin S., and Gary R. Gleason, eds. 1992. *Rapid Assessment Procedures: Qualitative Methodologies for Planning and Evaluation of Health Related Programmes.* Boston: International Nutrition Foundation for Developing Countries (INFDC). http://archive.unu.edu/unupress/food2/UIN08E/UIN08E00.HTM.

Scrimshaw, S., and E. Hurtado. 1987. *Rapid Assessment Procedures for Nutrition and Primary Health Care.* Tokyo: UNU.

Smith, Madeleine, Geoff Heinrich, Linda Lovick, and David Vosburg. 2010. *Livelihoods in Malawi: A Rapid Livelihoods Assessment Using the Integral Human Development Conceptual Framework.* http://www.crsprogramquality.org/storage/pubs/general/Malawi-Assessment-low.pdf.

Introduction to *Food Culture: Anthropology, Linguistics, and Food Studies*

Janet Chrzan

Introduction, Research Design and Ethics

This volume, the second in the set *Research Methods for Anthropological Studies of Food and Nutrition,* begins with a discussion of the volume followed by a chapter on research ethics by Sharon Devine and John Brett. Their chapter will be reproduced in all three volumes because ethics must be understood by all researchers, and a consideration of the ethics of methods used to collect, analyze, store, and publish must be an essential and initial element of the planning of any project. In their chapter they expand the idea of research ethics beyond publication and permissions to include the ethics of study design, recruitment, enrollment, and obtaining informed consent. They present a brief history of the research problems that led to the current ethics regulation requirements as well as a primer on the principles that guide ethical research: respect for persons, beneficence, and justice. They conclude with two short case studies highlighting application of these ethical principles in hypothetical food studies.

Volume and Section Overviews: Volume Two, Sections IV through VI

Section IV: Sociocultural Anthropology

Section IV examines sociocultural anthropology methods to understand how they work within a food and nutrition framework. This section captures many of the perspectives and approaches within an anthropological framework but is not explicitly biocultural in orientation. Topics include interviewing techniques, body image studies, direct observation, visual anthropology, participant-observation, focus groups, life histories, and use of food ethnography in sociocultural classroom settings. Geraldine Moreno-Black introduces the section with an overview of methods typically used in sociocultural studies, an analysis of best-case examples from previously published studies and manuals, a discussion of the commonalities between these methods and those used by biocultural researchers, and an overview of research design with a focus on developing research questions within appropriate theoretical frameworks. Her chapter introduces the reader to a broader history of how anthropologists have used food to study human relations and understand patterns of behavior within and between cultures, and how the study of human systems has relied on analysis of food production, distribution, and use.

Anthropological studies using sociocultural methods are what most lay people think of when they hear about our field of study: it is the Radcliff-Browns and the Margaret Meads who come to mind—intrepid researchers who venture deep into the "bush" alone to find out how other peoples live and think. Many students might be told that the first anthropologist to explicitly study food was Audrey Richards, who used a biocultural model to understand food and nutrition among the Bemba of Sub-Saharan Africa. She was primarily a social anthropologist, however, and most of her methods for understanding food production and use were drawn from social and cultural anthropology. Many others studied food during the early days of anthropology, but for most of these researchers the study of food was part of a broad descriptive agenda of early ethnography rather than something to be studied as a focal point. The remaining chapters in Section IV document the authors' use of specific methods to study food use as a central element in the construction and daily functioning of social systems, rather than as a result of social organization. Ramona Lee Pérez uses what she terms "kitchen table ethnography" to elucidate life histories of food use among women in Mexico and the U.S. borderlands. She is particularly interested in how researchers can use verbal interactions to elicit life stories and how the investigator must prepare for a truly reflexive and effective interview experience that is respectful of the people interviewed.

Nicole Taylor and Mimi Nichter have contributed a chapter on body image studies that provides a comprehensive overview of techniques used to understand how body image can be included in anthropological studies. Beginning with an overview of which disciplines have examined body image and where and how they have done so, the authors move into a discussion of specific methods used by anthropologists and other researchers. They provide examples of studies that can be accessed for further information about the topic, cover issues of confidentiality and ethics, and discuss a number of case studies. Readers will find that their chapter and Pérez's together provide an excellent background to thinking through research about difficult topics in a one-to-one setting.

The next chapter, by Helen Vallianatos, explores methods in visual anthropology, a topic briefly touched upon by Taylor and Nichter. Vallianatos presents an in-depth history of the technique as used by anthropologists, but references how visual methods can be used by food studies in general. She also chronicles the history of visual techniques, from recording and analysis to more recent collaborative work with study populations and individuals. She discusses visual methods in film, photography, drawing and newer digital and multimedia tools, supplying case studies of each, and references particularly effective examples of research. Most importantly she covers the ethics of image collection—currently a hot topic in anthropology and media of all sorts—and finishes with a step-by-step outline of how to think through a visual project from initial research query to final written report.

The chapter that follows is a biocultural review of another form of seeing—that of direct observation in anthropological studies. The authors, Barbara Piperata and Darna Dufour, focus on applying these methods in biocultural or nutritional anthropology research. Echoing themes discussed by Ramona Lee Pérez, they emphasize the importance of "being there" when observing study groups. They provide an analysis of the essential literature, a thorough discussion of several examples of direct observation studies, and then outline how a biocultural anthropologist can best use these methods, either with other structured data collection methods or to help construct accurate and effective data instruments, including qualitative/quantitative mixed-methods questionnaires. Relying on examples from their own extensive research, they also discuss how careful observation of activities and mindful listening can lead the investigator into new areas of research that strengthen the outcomes of their studies.

Moving back into the sociocultural realm, the rest of this section focuses on classic methods and ends with a discussion on using ethnographic techniques in the classroom. Heather Paxson contributes a robust examination of participant observation and interviewing techniques that complements and extends the earlier discussions about related methods. She first discusses the history and theory behind participant observation, continues with a description of how to "do" this method, and explains how it differs from and augments other forms of observational studies. She also tackles the difficulty of doing actual "participant" observation, given the observer status of the researcher, and provides examples of how she used "inquisitive fieldwork" to study cheesemakers and their worlds even though she could not directly make cheese with them. Finishing with a section on how to arrange and analyze interviews, she ends with a point-by-point outline of how to conduct such a project from initial interesting idea to final write-up and ethics considerations.

Ramona L. Pérez follows with another key sociocultural method, one that is often used by researchers in other disciplines: the focus group. Her chapter contains information about where focus groups are appropriate, how to use them to gather data prior to designing a comprehensive study, when (and when not) to use a group, and how to manage the groups during research. She backs this with examples from her own research and includes a discussion about the history of the method and its limitations, finishing with a detailed examination of how to begin such work. The two classic methods of participant observation and focus groups are standard in anthropology, and Paxson's and Pérez's chapters provide an updated view of how to use them in food research.

In the section's final chapter, Carole Counihan describes how these ethnographic methods can be incorporated into classroom work and teaching protocols. Counihan illustrates this with the example of her course on foodways, which is offered as a methods course. The class guides students through all phases of a fieldwork project, from initial idea through research design, IRB review, data-gathering and analysis, write-up, and oral presentation, and is designed to ensure that all students master research methods. In combination with the other chapters in this section, this final chapter presents a 'soup to nuts' finale on the conceptualization, implementation, analysis and reporting of a sociocultural foodways project.

Section V: Linguistics and Food Talk

Linguistic Anthropology offers many methods for examining food-related behavior, including the language of food, food and cognition, recipes, and other food-related discourse. This section explores the range of methods available, how anthropologists have used them, and how they overlap with Food Studies frameworks. It is a natural successor to the previous section on sociocultural anthropology, since linguistic data collection often relies on similar methods and the two subdisciplines share theoretical understandings. Specific chapters cover the essentials of a linguistic analysis: cultural domain analysis—especially the use of free lists and pile sorts—historical sources, food talk, and food texts. The section begins with an overview by Kathleen Riley and Jillian Cavanaugh that provides a four-field approach to linguistic anthropology, giving examples of how anthropologists of all subdisciplines have studied food use through language and the connections between food and language use. They approach this as "an emergent field, joined both by the materiality of language and food as experienced via the body, but also by the symbolic properties and potentials of both." More importantly they explain the solid theoretical grounding for anthropologists' and others' reading of semiotic texts of all sorts—from the written or spoken words to material culture remains—in order to make sense of human communications about food.

From theory, Riley and Cavanaugh move to an overview of methods used to explore the semiotics of food, paying particular attention to how field notes created during research—a form of meta-text—can also be understood as a food text of importance. They discuss the standard anthropological toolkit in relation to data collection for linguistic studies (participant observation, detailed field notes, photographs, interviews, focus groups, audio-recording, and video-recording) and elucidate how they can be "used to investigate what people say when engaged in food-related activities, and how food is made meaningful through discourse and interaction." After discussing the chapters in Section V, they conclude with a list of key texts for understanding methods in the semiotics of food. Perhaps the most valuable aspect of this chapter is the authors' explanation of how the standard toolkit can be used for linguistic studies and provide further tools for "thinking through" the design and implementation of a research project.

Riley and Cavanaugh follow their introduction with an in-depth chapter about "food talk," which they define as "how language and food meaningfully co-occur within specific sociocultural contexts." In this chapter they detail how to plan and execute studies using participant observation, contextualized interviews and focus groups, and audio/video-recording and transcription, as well as how to examine documents. They divide such studies into research-elicited data, such as interviews and focus groups, and free-living or naturally occurring use of language about food. Particularly valuable is their discussion of the ethnography of communication, a topic that cuts across multiple subdisciplines of anthropology and food studies. They also comprehensively cover how to analyze talk during mealtimes and how language socialization channels food use. They conclude with a discussion of the future of food talk research and a list of resources.

In the next chapter, Ariela Zycherman explores methods in cultural domain analysis (CDA), focusing on free lists and pile sorts. She begins with a discussion about CDA and how it can be used in food research, from elucidating how people organize types of foods to understanding how they link food types and food meanings. She is particularly interested in how cultures link foods to social structures (situations, social categories, etc.) and how that affects how food is used. From there, she explains methods for identifying food domains, focusing on pile sorts and free listing. Perhaps one of the most valuable aspects of CDA is its capacity to get at the emic understanding of how people think about, classify, and use food substances, as well as the relatively low cost (and ease of analysis) of such approaches. They provide a means to quickly identify areas of cultural knowledge that may require greater investigation, or to identify obvious culturally determined connections that would otherwise be obscure. Zycherman concludes with a section on "thinking through" how to do CDA, along with examples of good research practice.

The next chapter in this section is also written by Kathleen Riley, this time tackling a topic often feared by students and established researchers alike: text analysis. She points out that for many in academia, the "text" has expanded from words and speech to all manners of communicative discourse, both intentional (speech, writing, visual media) and incidental (gestural, placement, gustatory, tactile, etc.). Adding to this confusion is the expansion of the readership as well as who might be considered a creator of texts. Finally, these methods have increasingly been used to analyze metatexts, defined as cultural analysis of textual discourse, which adds another layer of complexity. Riley thoroughly discusses the history and theory of text analysis, also explaining current examples of such research and descriptions of the actual methods (how to collect code and analyze data). She concludes with a list of available resources and tools—digital and otherwise—for examining texts.

Next, Ken Albala describes how to use primary historical sources to study food use in the past. Although this may seem to require a more established, conventional set of methods, Albala points out that history and anthropology overlap in many areas, particularly in the need to explore the context of an historical document. Words on a page are not immutable symbols that indicate meaning, but like all other systems of meaning are negotiated and contextualized by their time and place, as well as by how the author(s) chose to convey meaning. After discussing different types of historical documents, Albala provides the reader with a roadmap on how to think through the study of a document to best understand how it represents its time and place and contributes to our knowledge of food. Together these five chapters provide the reader with a brief but very comprehensive overview of how a study about food and food use can incorporate cultural analysis of text of all sorts to better understand the emic worlds of the peoples being studied.

Section VI: Food Studies

This last section of broadly sociocultural methods travels somewhat outside of traditional anthropology to embrace other disciplines' research about food. The recent popularity of food studies, broadly (and contentiously) defined as cross- or interdisciplinary examinations of food culture, often utilizes anthropological methods in conjunction with theory and methods from other areas of academic study. Rather than being simply an example of "anthropology-lite," food studies are more accurately thought of as the wilder shores of research, a potentially rocky harbor where dragons congregate to eat the unwary, poorly prepared student researcher. Like the last sentence, food studies practitioners sometimes mix metaphors and methods blithely, taking an "Oooh, look! Something Shiny!" approach to research theory and design. Aiming to dispel these bugbears and dragons, this section emphasizes how anthropologists and students can best use established methods to conduct viable research in fields broadly labeled "food studies" with the goal of describing how such methods contribute to strong research projects, independent of disciplinary labeling.

The seven chapters in this section were written by anthropologists, historians, and folklorists, and each author displays a fearless willingness to describe and discuss methods that either are relatively new and untested, or are established but used in new ways or in combination with methods from other disciplines. There are a few texts that describe methods in food studies, including *Food Studies* (Jeff Miller and Jonathan Deutsch, 2009), *Food: the Key Concepts* (Warren Belasco, 2008), and *The Larder: Food Studies Methods from the American South* (edited by John T. Edge, 2013). However, because food studies is interdisciplinary or cross-disciplinary, the methods used are often derived from other established academic traditions. One question that anthropologists must ask, therefore, is how far afield we can effectively travel in search of the means to conduct "food studies," or how we can use established anthropological methods in order to produce effective interdisciplinary work in food. These chapters endeavor to answer these questions. Given that scholars from other disciplines utilize anthropological methods, this section is designed to provide them (as well as other anthropologists) with examples of how to use these methods effectively.

Amy Trubek begins the section with a chapter that examines food studies methods in general, and how anthropologists have used anthropological and other methods to design food-related research. In addition to discussing the chapters that follow, she points out that food studies scholars use methods and theories from various disciplines, and that many researchers in health and environmental fields are increasingly incorporating mixed methods into their own research about food use. Additionally, research in food studies is often driven by issues and problems rather than research question or design; as Trubek points out: "food studies scholarship tends to focus on 'an issue' or 'a problem' within the larger system and therefore the researcher needs to adopt a holistic approach. The discipline of anthropology has always been interested in problems that emerge from the field and also has adopted holism as an axiom." This acknowledges that the central question shifts from "what methods are best used given the theory that underlies my research question?" to "what is the core problem or issue, and what methods can I use to better understand its processes, functions, and solutions?" It would be too simplistic to assert that the first is deductive and the second inductive, but these two approaches do demonstrate different ways to think through and implement research. A similar fluidity is shown by the remaining authors in this section, who bravely outline how they have implemented some rather revolutionary methods and combinations of methods in their own research.

Lucy Long takes just such an "issues" approach in her chapter, which explores how food meanings can be studied using a variety of methods from anthropology, folklore, and linguistics. She separates what food "means" into two broad categories—meaning as symbol or reference, and meaning as signifier. In the first, food stands for something else or represents a relationship between cultural categories, and in the second, food has personal or cultural meanings that are emotionally or intellectually important. Of course these categories are fluid and can overlap, so the methods and theories needed to understand how they work within human systems are necessarily flexible and wide-ranging.

Similarly, William Woys Weaver takes on another difficult and rather nebulous issue: food and "place." He provides examples from his own research in Pennsylvania as well as discussion of other work that studies how place and foodways are connected historically, geographically, and ideationally. Central to this question is the appropriate establishment of boundaries in both place and time. Also essential is knowing the right questions to ask to understand how something as seemingly insubstantial as a sense of place can inform food use, and how food can help to create culture from location.

Rachel Black tackles yet another difficult issue, that of food and the senses, and describes how one can study such connections and use them to teach about food, culture, and perception. Sensory anthropology requires ethnographers to use their senses just as surely as they query how others experience their world through sensory input. The differing senses—sight, taste, smell, touch, hearing—all play important roles in food production, processing, and use, so exploring how people operate within their sensory worlds can reveal much about their culture and food systems. Black concludes with examples from her research and teaching that demonstrate how sensory input can be used to explore various meanings in food and consumption.

In the following chapter, Catherine Tucker explores food commodity chains or value chains, defined as "the set of processes and linkages that connect disparate activities and relationships, and build value that culminates in a final product." This farm- (and even "before-the-farm-") to-table approach traces all of the processes, materials, and human connections that a food item requires, up to—and beyond—ingestion. She points out the special challenges of following a chain in a globalized world and outlines methods used to bridge space, time, and language barriers to understand how our food arrives on our plates.

Finally, Andrea Wiley and Janet Chrzan describe many of these methods in their chapter on the study of single foods. Such an issue—a single food item—ranges across time, meaning, and space. One of the most critical elements in writing about a single food, they contend, is choosing an approach and following it thoroughly. Studies of single foods can be inductive (stemming from a description of the food and its relation to other areas of cultural life) or deductive (starting with an issue and then following how the food relates to the problem). These approaches are not exclusive, and when they interact can provide a "thick description" of food use and culture. Such an agenda allows for a four-field methodology but can lead to an overload of information. The authors discuss how they covered their own single food studies—of milk and alcohol—using an explicitly biocultural perspective to link cultural actions to biological and health outcomes. In many ways, the study of single foods illustrates the plethora of theoretical and methodological approaches available to food studies because it allows for interdisciplinary research across cultures, time, and space.

Research Ethics in Food Studies
Sharon Devine and John Brett

Why Ethics Are Important

Imagine that someone approaches you at a shopping center and asks if you would mind answering a few questions about what you eat. You answer the questions—what time you usually eat; how many meals you typically eat in a day; the types of foods you eat; and whether you consider yourself of average weight. Later you find out a research study has published your answers together with your photograph. The analysis suggests that you are overweight and that your nutritional intake could explain your deviation from ideal weight. Most people in this situation would be surprised and perhaps angry that by answering a few generic questions they wound up enrolled in a research study, and that personally identifiable information was in the public domain as a result.

Our research results are only as good as the information provided by those we study, and a trusting and respectful relationship is the basis for obtaining in-depth and nuanced information. Therefore compliance with ethical principles and the regulatory structures that support them should be a professional virtue of researchers (DuBois 2004). The question is, how do we ensure that research is conducted ethically? First, we must be aware of the historical background of ethical lapses that led to the development of principles embodied in research regulations. Second, we must incorporate ethical principles into our research designs from the very beginning.

History of Ethical Lapses in Research

A lengthy history of research studies raising ethical concerns led up to the adoption of federal regulations for protection of human subjects in the United States.

A favorite argument of social scientists is that federal regulations governing research were designed to curb biomedical researchers (Heimer and Petty 2010; Hammersley 2009; Hamilton 2005). However, the impetus for ethical principles and regulations is not solely a result of ill-advised medical studies. A brief description of key episodes in the history of ethical lapses makes clear that ethical concerns apply as much to social science as to medical studies. Each of the examples described in this chapter has been explored in depth, and at the end of the chapter references are provided for those who wish to learn more. In hindsight concerns with these studies might appear obvious, but the facts, context, and nuances of each are often complex, sometimes contradictory, and documentation may be sketchy or lost to history. The purpose of this list is not to condemn so much as to present a number of studies, done over a long period of time, from which lessons for contemporary ethics have been extracted.

- Reed Commission/Yellow Fever (1900–1901). This research occurred as part of the U.S. occupation of Cuba after the Spanish-American War. Yellow fever was devastating occupation forces at the time, and it was unclear how it was transmitted. Suspected modes included contact with an infected person, contact with infected objects such as clothing or blankets, and transmission via mosquitoes. Army personnel and other volunteers were offered $100 in gold to participate in the study and be exposed to blankets used by infected persons, transfused with blood from an infected person, or bitten by mosquitoes. The study was carefully designed and implemented at great expense. Notes of Major Walter Reed, who conducted the study, state that written informed consent was obtained from the volunteers (Lederer 2008; Baxby 2005).
- Tuskegee Syphilis Study (1932–1972). The U.S. Public Health Service, working with the Tuskegee Institute, investigated the natural history of syphilis to justify treatment programs for blacks. Six hundred men volunteered for the study: 399 with syphilis, 201 without. The volunteers were poor, most were illiterate, and none knew anything about syphilis. The study included routine blood tests, spinal taps, as well as autopsies. The men were told they were being treated for "bad blood." They were offered free hot meals, clinic visits, and burial insurance, which was of great importance to this group. In 1943 penicillin was accepted as curative for syphilis, but it was not offered to the men in the study, which continued to observe the study participants without treating them until 1972 (Katz and Warren 2011; Reverby 2009; Jones 1993).
- Radiation Experiments (1944–1994). People were intentionally exposed to fallout from nuclear bomb testing events and told that the fallout was not harmful, even though scientists involved in the testing knew differently.

In some instances people were injected with plutonium to see what would happen (U.S. Department of Defense 1994a, 1994b).
- Willowbrook Study (1956). Willowbrook was a school for the intellectually challenged. Healthy children were injected with a virus causing hepatitis to study the natural history of the disease and eventually test a vaccine. Parental consent was obtained (Robinson and Unruh 2008; Rothman 1982).
- Milgram Obedience Study (1961). Milgram wanted to investigate the psychology of people who follow the directions of an authority figure, even when they are told to do cruel and unethical things. Participants were told the study was investigating learning and memory. They were asked to give what appeared to be increasingly harmful electric shocks to a fake "subject" if the subject performed incorrectly on a memory test. Participants were not told the real purpose of the study (how long people would follow orders) or that the shocks were fake until their participation was over. At this debriefing, many experienced extreme psychological distress (Nicholson 2011; McArthur 2009).
- Tearoom Trade Study (1970). A graduate student conducted a study of homosexual behavior in public restrooms. While functioning as a "watch queen" outside the restroom to sound the alert at any police presence, he recorded car license numbers to locate names and addresses of subjects. He then went to their homes and misrepresented himself to interview subjects about their lives (Warwick 1973).
- Zimbardo Prisoner Study (1971). College students were recruited for a two-week experiment to determine whether personality or situational differences cause conflict between guards and prisoners. The students took the California Personality Inventory and interviewed with the study team. The most normal, average, and healthy students on all dimensions were invited to participate and divided into guards and prisoners. The guards met for a general orientation and to formulate rules for proper prisoner behavior. The prisoners were arrested by the local police and brought to the site in handcuffs. The study was stopped after six days when the simulation seemed real and the guards became abusive. About half of the prisoners left the study before it ended due to severe emotional or cognitive reaction (McLeod 2008; Savin 1973; Zimbardo 1973).
- Havasupai Origins Study (1990–2003). Members of the Havasupai tribe provided DNA samples to researchers from Arizona State University beginning in 1990 for studies of diabetes. Other researchers at the university later used these samples to study mental illness and theories about the tribe's geographical origins. The results of the study about origins conflicted with the tribe's origin beliefs. The scope of the informed consent was disputed. Ultimately unused samples were returned to the tribe, and the university

paid $700,000 to settle a lawsuit brought by the tribe (Garrison and Cho 2013; Reardon and TallBear 2012).

Types of Ethical Concerns in Food Studies

Many involved in food studies might argue that ethical concerns, especially of the type that led to the creation of the regulations applicable to human subject research, are unlikely to arise in their work. And yet, because food is so central to life—and in many cases to our sense of identity and place in the world—study topics can easily raise ethical issues if they are not appropriately addressed.

- Stigma can attach to studies of overweight, obesity, and eating disorders, as noted in the scenario that introduces this chapter.
- Belief systems of certain groups of people may conflict with the taking of blood samples or body measurements.
- Cultural norms may be offended by judgments about body image.
- Communities may be negatively impacted by studies of action anthropology such as advocating breastfeeding or studies of food security.

In short, almost any study can raise ethical issues. Therefore, ethical principles should be the foundation of the design and operation of all studies so as to minimize ethical lapses, protect human subjects, and obtain valid research results.

What Makes a Study Ethical?

Nuremberg Code

The Nuremberg Code and the Helsinki Declaration are international statements of aspirational principles for ethical research. The Nuremberg Code was proposed as a result of the war crimes trials held in Nuremberg, Germany, after the end of World War II (Nuremberg Military Tribunals 1949). The trial verdict against one of the doctors accused of unlawfully conducting medical experiments during the war incorporated ten principles that were later labeled the Nuremberg Code. These ten principles address the record in the trials of experiments done on captives who were not able to consent to or dissent from participation in experiments, many of which had little if any scientific value when weighed against the risk to subjects. A common defense was that the experimenter was following orders of superiors. The ten principles in the code are:

1. Each subject must give voluntary consent, based on comprehension of the study, its procedures, and the risks associated with participation in the

experiment. This is a personal duty of any researcher involved in obtaining informed consent—it cannot be delegated.
2. The experiment should be designed to produce results for the good of society and not be random or unnecessary.
3. The experiment should be based on scientific knowledge and previous animal studies, if appropriate.
4. The experiment should avoid unnecessary physical and psychological suffering and injury.
5. No experiment should be done if there is reasonable belief that death or disabling injury would occur.
6. The degree of risk should never exceed the potential humanitarian benefit.
7. Researchers must prepare for and provide facilities to address even remote possibilities of injury, disability, or death.
8. Only scientifically qualified persons may conduct experiments on humans.
9. A human subject must have the liberty to refuse to continue with an experiment.
10. The scientist in charge of the experiment must terminate any experiment, at any stage, if the scientist has probable cause to believe that the experiment might lead to injury, disability, or death of any human subject.

Declaration of Helsinki

In 1947, representatives of twenty-seven medical associations from around the world created the World Medical Association, an open forum for discussions about medical ethics, medical education, and socio-medical topics with the purpose of reaching international consensus and guidance. In 1964, the World Medical Association adopted the Declaration of Helsinki—Ethical Principles for Medical Research Involving Human Subjects (World Medical Association 1964). It incorporates the same principles as the Nuremberg Code and adds others that broaden interests to be protected and provide procedural safeguards:

1. It is the right of human subjects to protect their privacy and confidentiality of private information.
2. Research proposals should address funding, sponsors, institutional affiliations, conflicts of interest, and incentives to subjects.
3. Research proposals must be reviewed and monitored by an independent committee.
4. Research on a vulnerable population or community may be justified only if it is responsive to the needs and priorities of the population or community and there is a reasonable likelihood that the vulnerable group stands to benefit from the results of the research.

5. Clinical trials must be registered in a publicly accessible database before recruitment of any subject.
6. Ordinarily, subjects must consent to collection, analysis, storage, or reuse of identifiable human materials or data. Waiver of consent may be granted only by the independent review committee.
7. The welfare of animals used for research must be respected.
8. Research must respect harm to the environment.
9. Authors, editors, and publishers have ethical duties regarding the publication of results of human subjects research.

Belmont Report and Federal Regulations

Certain states and countries adopted the Nuremberg Code into law, but neither it nor the Declaration of Helsinki has the authority of federal law in the United States. However, in 1974, prompted largely by revelations about the Tuskegee Syphilis Study, Congress authorized the National Commission for the Protection of Human Subjects of Biomedical and Behavioral Research, as part of the National Research Act, to recommend ethical principles for research with human subjects. In 1979, the predecessor of the Department of Health and Human Services published the report of the national commission. Called the Belmont Report, this document organizes its discussion of ethics in research around three principles: respect for persons, beneficence, and justice (U.S. Department of Health and Human Services 1979). It draws heavily from both the Nuremberg Code and the Declaration of Helsinki. These principles were embodied in federal regulations in the 1980s. In 1991, fourteen other federal agencies adopted the same federal regulations, codified as 45 C.F.R. Part 46 and known today as the "Common Rule" (U.S. Department of Health & Human Services 2009, n.d. [List]). The regulations also established a requirement for independent review by an institutional review board (IRB) in many circumstances. A study may need permission from multiple IRBs—university, tribe, and country (or regional IRBs if the study is international). IRBs in the United States apply the regulations that are based on the Belmont Report and any other regulations applicable to the study under review. All researchers should use the Belmont principles as their touchstone for ethical research whether or not they are required to get approval from an IRB.

Respect for persons

Respect for persons requires that research involving human subjects must protect their autonomy, privacy, and confidentiality; avoid coercion; and provide additional protection for vulnerable populations. Autonomy demands that a person be in control of her or his life and not suffer from diminished self-worth and independence as a result of participating in research. Thus respect requires that human subjects provide informed consent to research that is not obtained through coercion or undue influence. This principle of respect requires that subjects receive sufficient information about a study—its purpose, why they are being recruited, what they will be asked to do, potential harms, potential benefits, alternatives to being in the study, and information about confidentiality—so that they can understand what is being asked and their consent is truly voluntary. Although these elements of informed consent are usually embodied in a document, informed consent is a process. Different methods of communication may be used and should accommodate subjects' levels of understanding. The informed consent process should include methods to test each subject's comprehension of the study.

Respect for persons requires that any compensation for study participation be compensatory for the time of participation and not unduly influence the decision to participate. If the payment constitutes an inducement, then consent is not voluntary. Therefore payment is not considered a benefit for participation in a study and may not be considered in the analysis of risk and benefit.

Consent may be waived by the IRB if full waiver of consent is necessary to accomplish the goals of the research, risks are no more than minimal, and there is an adequate plan to debrief subjects if appropriate, including when deception is involved (45 CFR 46.116). The regulations require a showing that the waiver is necessary for the validity of the research; waivers are not granted simply because it is inconvenient or more expensive to obtain informed consent. Waiver of consent may be appropriate for the review of pre-existing medical records when it is impracticable to reach all subjects to ask for their consent or when study design requires information from consecutive medical records. Waiver of signature may be appropriate in cultures where signing a document is culturally inappropriate under the circumstances, when the signature is the only link identifying the subject to the study and identification of participation in the study could increase risk, or when the study collects information for which written consent is not normally obtained (45 CFR 46.117).

Some individuals may have diminished autonomy and therefore receive additional protections against coercion or undue influence. Certain groups are specifically addressed as "vulnerable" in the federal regulations: minors (45 CFR 46.401–409); pregnant women, fetuses, and neonates (45 CFR 46.201–207); and prisoners or other institutionalized persons (45 CFR 46.301–306). Other groups that may be considered vulnerable to coercion include decisionally challenged persons and those in other situations subject to coercion or undue influence. Situational and institutional coercion can occur when someone is asked to be in a study by their treating physician or professor, or when a person feels obligated to participate because the community feels that participation is important. There are mechanisms for obtaining consent from appropriate third parties when the subject is not capable of giving his or her own consent. These mechanisms, such as parental consent, legally authorized representatives, and proxies, can be complex because they are governed by federal regulation and sometimes also by state law.

Protection of privacy and confidentiality originates in the concept of respect for persons. The harm that results from an invasion of privacy or breach of confidentiality is a social harm because it can compromise reputation, financial status, employability, or insurability. Although often conflated, privacy and confidentiality address different concepts. Privacy is the desire to control access to oneself and comes into play when considering methods to contact and recruit subjects, the research setting, and methods of data collection. Confidentiality applies to the way information is handled, managed, and stored once a person is enrolled in a study. Here researchers should consider how information is protected, what limitations affect access to information, and how to collect the least amount of information necessary for the study.

Beneficence

Ethical research maximizes benefits and minimizes risks, as researchers have an obligation to protect subjects from harm. The principle of beneficence comes from the Hippocratic Oath: "I will do no harm or injustice." Harm in the context of research includes not just physical harm, but also psychological and social harm, which may apply to the individual or the community. Brutal or inhumane treatment of human subjects is never morally justified.

Application of the principle of beneficence requires an assessment of potential risks and benefits to assure that the balance is always in favor of potential benefits. Subjects may participate in studies that will provide no direct or immediate benefit to them so long as the risks are minimal and there is the potential for societal benefit. The higher the risk and the more remote the benefit, the harder the questions of balancing risks and benefits. When assessing risk, it is important to consider both probability and magnitude of risk. A risk may be common but low or very uncommon but very damaging. Studies need not be risk free, but researchers should design their studies to minimize risk. The principle of beneficence necessarily implicates study design. A poorly designed study that is unlikely to generate data to answer the research question posed has no benefit to subjects or to society. Researchers should always consider whether human subjects are necessary. And if the study proposes to include vulnerable subjects, the researcher should justify why they are necessary for the study.

Justice

The principle of justice requires that the benefits and burdens of research be distributed equitably in society. Injustice occurs when one group is unduly burdened with research risks and another group receives benefits. One of the reasons prisoners are identified as a vulnerable population and given additional regulatory protections, aside from the potential for coercion as a captive population, is that historically they have borne unequal burdens of research with no prospect of enjoying the benefits. Selecting classes of subjects because they are convenient, compromised, marginalized, or easily manipulated raises questions of justice. Injustice also occurs when one group is denied access to benefits to which they are entitled, as in the Tuskegee Syphilis Study. Another example of injustice includes the groups of people who are selected for study. For many years most pharmaceutical research was conducted using Caucasian males. Women and people of color were not routinely included in research. Today federally funded studies prohibit researchers from excluding subjects on the basis of gender, race, or ethnicity unless exclusion is required based on the question being studied, so that benefits of the research may accrue to all groups.

Other Sources of Ethical Principles and Rules

The Common Rule, as embodied in federal regulations, is not the only source of ethical rules for research. The Department of Health and Human Services administers the Health Insurance Portability and Accountability Act (HIPAA) (U.S. Department of Health and Human Services n.d. [Health Information Privacy]), which protects personal health information. HIPAA is complex and applies to "covered entities." The Food and Drug Administration, Department of Veterans Affairs, Department of Education, and Department of Defense all have regulations governing aspects of research under their auspices (U.S. Department of Health & Human Services n.d. [List]). In addition, many professional associations, such as the American Anthropological Association (American Anthropological Association 2012), Society for Applied Anthropology (Society for Applied Anthropology n.d.), and the American Sociological Association (American Sociological Association n.d.), have codes of conduct that include ethical standards for research. In general, all of these bodies apply principles consistent with or based on the principles in the Belmont Report, but they may have more protective requirements or specific processes that apply to research within their domains. Researchers should familiarize themselves with all applicable sources of ethical principles before designing their studies.

Application of Principles

There is usually little disagreement on the ethical principles for research, but their application in practice is often much more nuanced than a mere recitation of the rules. The following two case studies raise various ethical questions. Each is followed by a brief identification of ethical issues and considerations.

Case 1

Researchers wish to study the dietary practices of a community of Native Americans living on a tribal reservation in the United States. The study is designed to identify attitudes and understanding of the healthfulness of foods in the diet; journal actual consumption by individuals and families; collect weight, height, and medical histories; and correlate the findings with concerns about BMI and diabetes. Some information will be confirmed by comparing it with Indian Health Service medical records of subjects. The study is exploratory and will inform interventions designed to reduce obesity and diabetes among those living on the reservation. The tribal council is enthusiastic about the study and wants it to be in the nature of community-based participatory research including the use of tribal research assistants, data collectors, and analysts.

Issues

Respect for persons
- There is the potential for coercion of individuals in light of tribal support. Can individual members safely exercise their autonomy and say no? Will the tribal council demand to know who has agreed to participate and who has not? What if the tribe has a long history of communal decision making that binds the group? Do you impose Western ideals of individual autonomy? First, it is important to understand the cultural values of the tribe or group and discuss all proposed procedures with the community and the IRB to identify any nuances in their application. Then consider whether you need to institute procedures to reduce the potential for coercion. For example, researchers might make clear that they will not provide any information about the identity of those who enroll or decline to participate to the tribal council to protect the privacy of individual participants.
- There is the potential for inadvertent release of confidential information. As part of the community-based approach, research assistants and data collectors will be members of the community. Procedures to train assistants and data collectors should emphasize the need for absolute confidentiality of information obtained. Personally identifiable data should be entered immediately into encrypted databases and recorded in such a way that data cannot be linked back to individuals or coded in a way that makes identification without the code very difficult. Any paper records should be destroyed as soon as possible.

Beneficence
- All researchers should be trained in cultural sensitivity, including respect for cultural norms around body image to assure appropriate interaction with

subjects and reporting of findings in a nonjudgmental, nonstigmatizing manner.

Justice
- Concerns about justice could arise if there is divergence of understanding about the scope of the research between the researchers and the community. For example, the community may expect that interventions will be immediately forthcoming while researchers understand that the current study is a pilot and that there is no funding for interventions at this time.

Process
- There may be multiple IRB stakeholders: researchers' institutions, the tribe, and the Indian Health Service. HIPAA may apply. Community-based research is, by definition, fluid and dynamic, requiring lots of work, time, and patience to manage the review process.

Case 2

Researchers wish to conduct action research into breastfeeding in a lesser-developed country. The study wishes to catalog women's decision making around breastfeeding to identify cultural norms and tie breastfeeding to infant and child health outcomes. The community where this is to occur is poor and has a variety of breastfeeding practices. Women come to live with their husband's family; the culture is strongly patriarchal.

Issues

Respect for persons
- When looking at women's decision making, the very process of getting informed consent may influence choices. If women choose not to breastfeed, they may not want to discuss it or may feel that they are "bad mothers." In this situation, researchers might consider requesting permission from the IRB to engage in minor deception, for example by describing the study as one of infant/child heath generally, without mentioning that the focus of the study is breastfeeding (technically, this is a request to waive consent to omit the true purpose of the study). This type of waiver for minor deception is justifiable if telling people about the focus of the study would tend to skew the results.
- In a patriarchal society it may be appropriate to assure that men understand and approve of the research, even if men will not be subjects. Knowing the culture and its norms is key.

Beneficence
- Women who face or have experienced sexual abuse may have strong emotional attitudes, unknown to the researcher. As with all research, it is important to know the culture and its norms so that appropriate probes and safeguards can be used to protect vulnerable subjects, so as not to cause additional harm from participation in the study.
- If it is reasonable to expect that the researcher may identify cases of neglect from inadequate or inappropriate breastfeeding, the team should consider how to handle such instances in advance.

Sharon Devine, PhD, JD is Research Assistant Professor at the University of Colorado Denver, where she teaches, conducts research, and co-chairs the social and behavioral panel of the Colorado Multiple Institutional Review Board. Before joining academia, she practiced corporate and compliance law.

John Brett is retired faculty in the Department of Anthropology, University of Colorado Denver. He received his PhD from the Joint Program in Medical Anthropology at the University of California San Francisco and Berkeley in 1994. His primary research interests focus on food systems, food security and food justice, and microfinance as a development enterprise.

References

45 C.F.R. 46.116.
45 C.F.R. 46.117.
45 C.F.R. 46.201–207.
45 C.F.R. 46. 301–306.
45 C.F.R. 46.401–409.
American Anthropological Association. 2012. AAA Statement on Ethics-Principles of Professional Responsibility. http://ethics.aaanet.org/category/statement/. Accessed 30 August 2016.
American Sociological Association. n.d. ASA Code of Ethics. http://www.asanet.org/about/ethics.cfm. Accessed 30 August 2016.
Baxby, Derrick. 2005. Walter Reed and Yellow Fever. *Epidemiology & Infection* 133(Supp. 1): S7–8.
DuBois, James M. 2004. Is Compliance a Professional Virtue of Researchers? Reflections on Promoting the Responsible conduct of Research. *Ethics & Behavior* 14(4): 383–395.
Garrison, Nanibaa' A., and Mildred K. Cho. 2013. Awareness and Acceptable Practices: IRB and Researcher Reflection on the Havasupai Lawsuit. *American Journal of Bioethics Primary Research* 4(4): 55–63.
Hamilton, Ann. 2005. The Development and Operation of IRBs: Medical Regulations and Social Science. *Journal of Applied Communication Research* 33(3): 189–203.
Hammersley, Martyn.2009. Against the Ethicists: On the Evils of Ethical Regulation. *Journal of Social Research Methodology* 12(3): 211–225.

Heimer, Carol A., and JuLeigh Petty. 2010. Bureaucratic Ethics: IRBs and the Legal Regulation of Human Subjects Research. *Annual Review of Law and Social Science* 6: 601–626.

Jones, James H. 1993. *Bad Blood: The Tuskegee Syphilis Experiment.* New York: Free Press.

Katz, Ralph V., and Reuben Warren, eds. 2011. *The Search for the Legacy of the USPHS Syphilis Study at Tuskegee.* Lanham: Lexington Books.

Lederer, Susan E. 2008. Walter Reed and the Yellow Fever Experiments. In *Oxford Textbook of Clinical Research Ethics,* ed. Ezekiel J. Emanuel and Christine Grady et al., 9–18. Oxford: Oxford University Press.

McArthur, Dan. 2009. Good Ethics Can Sometimes Mean Better Science: Research Ethics and the Milgram Experiments. *Science and Engineering Ethics* 15: 69–79.

McLeod, Saul. 2008. Zimbardo-Stanford Prison Experiment. *Simply Psychology.* http://www.simplypsychology.org/zimbardo.html. Accessed 30 August 2016.

Nicholson, Ian. 2011. "Torture at Yale": Experimental Subjects, Laboratory Torment and the "Rehabilitation" of Milgram's "Obedience to Authority." *Theory & Psychology* 21(6): 737–761.

Nuremberg Military Tribunals. 1949. Trials of War Criminals before the Nuremberg Military Tribunals under Control Council Law No. 10, V.2, 181–182. https://history.nih.gov/research/downloads/nuremberg.pdf. Accessed 30 August 30 2016.

Reardon, Jenny, and Kim TallBear. 2012. "Your DNA Is *Our* History": Genomics, Anthropology, and the Construction of Whiteness as Property. *Current Anthropology* 53(S5): S233–S245.

Reverby, Susan M. 2009. *Examining Tuskegee: The Infamous Syphilis Study and Its Legacy.* Chapel Hill: University of North Carolina Press.

Robinson, Walter M., and Brandon T. Unruh. 2008. The Hepatitis Experiments at the Willowbrook State School. In *Oxford Textbook of Clinical Research Ethics,* ed. Ezekiel J. Emanuel and Christine Grady et al., 80–85. Oxford: Oxford University Press.

Rothman, David J. 1982. Were Tuskegee & Willowbrook "Studies in Nature"? *Hastings Center Report* 12(2): 5–7.

Savin, H. B. 1973. Professors and Psychological Researchers: Conflicting Values in Conflicting Roles. *Cognition* 2(1): 147–149.

Society for Applied Anthropology. n.d. Statement of Ethics and & Professional Responsibilities. http://www.sfaa.net/about/ethics/. Accessed 30 August 2016.

U.S. Department of Defense. 1994a. Report on Search for Human Radiation Experiment Records 1944-1994, V.1. http://archive.defense.gov/pubs/dodhre/Narratv.pdf. Accessed 30 August 2016.

U.S. Department of Defense. 1994b. Report on Search for Human Radiation Experiment Records 1944-1994, V.2. http://archive.defense.gov/pubs/dodhre/Volume2.pdf. Accessed 30 August 2016.

U.S. Department of Health and Human Services. 1979. Ethical Principles and Guidelines for the Protection of Human Subjects Research (The Belmont Report). http://www.hhs.gov/ohrp/humansubjects/guidance/belmont.html. Accessed 30 August 2016.

———. 2009. Federal Policy for the Protection of Human Subjects ("Common Rule"). 45 C.F.R. 46. http://www.hhs.gov/ohrp/humansubjects/guidance/45cfr46.html. Accessed 30 August 2016.

———. n.d. Health Information Privacy. http://www.hhs.gov/ocr/privacy/hipaa/understanding/index.html. Accessed 30 August 2016.

———. n.d. List of U.S. federal agencies that have signed onto the Federal Policy for the Protection of Human Subjects ("Common Rule"). http://www.hhs.gov/ohrp/humansubjects/commonrule/index.html. Accessed 30 August 2016.

Warwick, Donald P. 1973. Tearoom Trade: Means & Ends in Social Research. *Hastings Center Studies* 1(1): 27–38.

World Medical Association. 1964, as amended. WMA Declaration of Helsinki-Ethical Principles for Medical Research Involving Human Subjects. http://www.wma.net/en/30publications/10policies/b3/. Accessed 30 August 2016.

Zimbardo, Philip G. 1973. On the Ethics of Intervention in Human Psychological Research: With Special Reference to the Stanford Prison Experiment. *Cognition* 2(2): 243–256.

SECTION
IV

Socio-Cultural Approaches

CHAPTER 1

The Anthropology of Food and Food Anthropology
A Sociocultural Perspective

Geraldine Moreno-Black

Method is about choice.
—H. Russell Bernard, *Handbook of Methods in Cultural Anthropology*

Another nice thing about methods is that disciplines cannot own them.
—H. Russell Bernard, *Handbook of Methods in Cultural Anthropology*

Introduction

Food as a topic of study has deep roots and a long history in anthropology; some suggest it is probably as old as the discipline itself (Mintz and Dubois 2002; Murcott 1998; Ulijaszek and Strickland 1993). Food represents an integral part of human culture, livelihood, and biology, so the study of food has relevance for all subfields of anthropology—sociocultural anthropology, biological anthropology, archaeology, and linguistics. During past decades, the development of food- and nutrition-focused scholarship in anthropology has raised fundamental challenges to the way many anthropologists formulate hypotheses, collect and analyze data, and develop theories. In this chapter, I present an overview of sociocultural anthropology methods as a way to introduce more specific sections on what methods cultural anthropologists employ to understand food use and how they "work" within a food and nutrition framework.

Review of Extant Methods Manuals

Although food as a theme can integrate aspects of all of the subfields of anthropology, the development of work on food and nutrition issues in the field has been consistently uneven. Like the subdisciplines themselves, research focusing on food and nutrition in anthropology stems from branches of anthropology that have separated and converged over the course of the past decades. The origin of the more formal focus on food and nutrition in anthropology can be traced back to 1974 when the Committee on Nutritional Anthropology (CNA) was formed as a group within the Society for Medical Anthropology. The purpose of the organization at that time was "to bring together all persons interested in various aspects of the relationship between nutrition and anthropology from a biocultural perspective, irrespective of their specialty in archeology, physical or biological anthropology, sociocultural anthropology, or linguistics" (Katona-Apte 1975: 8).

Almost three decades later, the CNA executive board proposed a name change that the CNA membership voted on and approved in the 2004 elections. Thus the CNA became the Society for the Anthropology of Food and Nutrition (SAFN) in order to "more fully engage the spectrum of theoretical and methodological perspectives of individuals AAA-wide" (SAFN 2013). Despite this name change, anthropological studies of food continue to be divided into two discernible approaches: nutritional anthropology, which predominantly focuses on biocultural theory and methods; and the anthropology of food, which is dominated by more qualitative methods and a cultural, behavioral, and ideological core.

Seven research methods manuals focusing on food-related research were published in the period from 1986 through 2009:

- *Training Manual in Nutritional Anthropology*, by Sara Quandt and Cheryl Ritenbaugh (1986);
- *Rapid Assessment Procedures For Nutrition and Primary Health Care: Anthropological Appoaches to Improving Programme Effectiveness*, by Susan Scrimshaw and Elana Hurtado (1987);
- *Research Methods in Nutritional Anthropology*, by Gretel Pelto, Perti Pelto, and Ellen Messer (1989);
- *Researching Food Habits: Methods and Problems*, by Helen MacBeth and Jeremy MacClancy (2004);
- *Food Habits and Consumption in Developing Countries: Manual for Field Studies*, by A. P. den Hartog, Wije A. van Staveren, and Inge Brouwer (2006);
- *Food Studies: An Introduction to Research Methods*, by Jeff Miller and Jonathan Deutsch (2009).

I first reviewed the introductory sections written by the editors or authors of these texts. I chose to focus my attention on these sections in the texts because they consistently contained discussions of the writers' theoretical perspectives, as well as explanations of the choice of topics and organization of the manuals. I used the technique of content analysis to determine the presence of specific words or concepts within introductory sections. I specifically looked for words, phrases, sentences, or themes that pertained to the orientation of the editors and authors, and explanations for inclusion of specific topics. I did not begin with set categories or codes. Instead, I focused on uncovering emerging themes or conceptual categories in order to make inferences about the messages in the texts.

Second, I reviewed all the chapters in each of the texts in order to examine the types of methods that were included and the frequency of the types. Since this chapter is specifically focused on methods in sociocultural anthropology, I only touch briefly on the nutritional/biocultural manuals and in my discussion focus specifically on their applicability to sociocultural anthropology (for a more detailed discussion of biocultural anthropology methods see Dufour and Piperata). Lastly, I reviewed each of the chapters focusing on the methods specifically aimed at sociocultural anthropology (Anthropology of Food) using the same content analysis approach described above.

Nutritional Anthropology Manuals: A Sociocultural Gaze

Two of the methods manuals written for food-related research specifically focus on the theme of nutritional anthropology. These manuals clearly state this orientation in their titles: (1) *Training Manual in Nutritional Anthropology* (Quandt and Ritenbaugh 1986), and (2) *Research Methods in Nutritional Anthropology* (Pelto et al. 1989). A third, *Rapid Assessment Procedures for Nutrition and Primary Health Care: Anthropological Approaches to Improving Programme Effectiveness* (Scrimshaw and Hurtado 1987) implies this by highlighting both nutrition and health care in the title. The biocultural theme is clearly seen in the discussion provided in the introduction section of these manuals:

> This training manual was designed as a starting point for practitioners of nutritional anthropology. The biocultural, ecological perspective is emphasized. (Quandt & Ritenbaugh 1986: 2)

> This book is intended for both anthropologists and nutritionists who are pursuing community nutrition studies in either industrialized or developing countries. It provides solid information on the development and application of anthropological methodologies for studying key aspects of the nutrition of individuals, families, and communities. (Pelto et al. 1989: vii)

> This guide is intended for use by persons already trained in anthropological or related field methods. Consequently, it does not provide detailed descriptions of basic anthropological techniques. It does, however, suggest appropriate topics for data collection on health-seeking behaviors. (Scrimshaw and Hurtado 1987:1)

These three manuals afford sociocultural anthropologists an interesting window into nutritional anthropology and the biocultural approach. They provide an overview of the theoretical orientations used by nutritional anthropologists as well as a perspective on how nutritional anthropologists (or the cultural anthropologists they chose to include) view and utilize "traditional" methods of cultural anthropology (Goode 1989, Messer 1989, Messer and Kuhnlein 1986). A close read of the material in these manuals reveals an ecological approach in which such variables as socioeconomic status, gender, sensory characteristics of food, cultural classifications of food, and symbolic dimensions of food should be considered as important to food intake patterns. All of these texts include reference to, and some explanation of, cultural methods such as interviewing, participant observation and focus group interviews. This can be seen in the introductory section of Pelto et al (1989):

> All of the chapters in this book were written with the assumption that specific kinds of quantified data would be gathered against a background of general ethnographic information. In this context, ethnography may be regarded as field-based data gathering carried out for the purpose both qualitative and quantitative descriptive information in a community, region or other research site. Participant observation, as well as open-ended and structured interviewing, are typically part of the ethnographic process. [p. xi]

In particular, Scrimshaw and Hurtado (1987) provide a clear, albeit brief, overview of basic methods with diagrams of field notes and file organization.

Additionally, these texts provide insightful discussions into the qualitative-quantitative methodology debate. The general consensus is that qualitative methods are needed to provide the type of information for hypothesis testing, especially in relation to nutritional status and health. Consequently, most of the manuals contain sections that indicate strong qualitative information (usually ethnographic) is at the core of the quantitative research. Examples of the melding of qualitative and quantitative research to address nutritional health issues can be seen in the recent literature. For example, Weaver and Hadley's (2009) extensive review of the literature on food insecurity and mental health concludes:

> Future studies in this realm should employ rigorous definitions of food insecurity and longitudinal, mixed-methods designs with representative samples. Given the current global food crisis and the recent upsurge of interest in global mental health, such work is timely and crucial. [p. 280]

Another example of the mixed method approach used in nutritional/applied research is seen in the development of the concept of a focused ethnographic study (FES) discussed by Pelto et al. (2013). The mixed-method FES approach draws from a variety of ethnographic methods such as open-ended questions, formal ethnographic cognitive mapping techniques, survey questions, visual information, and participatory mapping in order to answer questions posed about nutrition and health interventions (Pelto et al. 2013)

Food Anthropology, the Anthropology of Food and Anthropologies of Food: Manuals With A Sociocultural Gaze.

The sociocultural enquiry into the topic of food is large, diverse and evolving. Consequently, it encompasses a wide range of methods and perspectives. Two recent manuals focus on the sphere of food from a more sociocultural perspective than the manuals on nutritional anthropology. The first, *Researching Food Habits: Methods and Problems* (Macbeth and MacClancy 2004) aims to cover a wide range of approaches to exemplify the diversity of food anthropology (p. 8). The editors indicate "interdisciplinarity" was a central theme for the development of the volume: "… members of the International Commission on the Anthropology of Food (ICAF) thought it worthwhile to edit a book which brought together into one volume a cross-disciplinary selection of relevant research methods" (p. ix). The editors also suggest: "one aim of this volume is to aid new researchers in their choice of which research methods can best answer cross-disciplinary questions" (p.x). They also acknowledge that there is a multitude of ways to practice interdisciplinarity and that it is not a requirement of food anthropology, thus not all researchers choose to use a multidisciplinary approach.

Given the core theme of the manual, the contents are varied and range from broad discussions of research issues to chapters focusing on specific methods. The broad discussions include chapters on interdisciplinarity (de Garine 2004), the utilization of a comprehensive research approach that melds qualitative and quantitative methods (Hubert 2004), the realities of conducting fieldwork (Mars and Mars 2004); and relationships between the researcher and participant (Medina 2004). The more specific methodological chapters include a wide range of topics including, but not limited to, ethnobotany; taste and hedonic response research; dietary intake; and energy balance.

Given the wide range of topics, it is to be expected that the specific methods discussed would also be broad. A review of the specific techniques discussed throughout the chapters revealed a number of common methods. Not surprisingly, given the sociocultural focus, participant observation and interviews were the most commonly discussed methods. Interview methods were wide ranging and included a variety of techniques such as open ended conversations, semi-structured and structured questionnaires, dietary intake and hedonic interviews were the most frequent. Other methods such as using documents, media, photography; and laboratory research were also discussed.

Miller and Deutsch (2009) provide another methods manual, *Food Studies. An Introduction to Research Methods,* that is of interest to sociocultural anthropologists, although the disciplinary center is food studies not anthropology per se. Their focus for the book is "the study of people's relationships with food" (p. 4) or put another way: "the relationships between food and the human experience" (p. 3). Another central theme guiding the text is their proposition that food, a worthy topic of study, can be used to gain insight into other issues such as gender relationships, identity and politics (personal, national and global). From the anthropological perspective the book offers a valuable discussion about methods, with examples from food focused research. They also provide a window into how the study of food can be used to enhance methods such as the extension of the interview method in Abarca's *charlas culinarias* (culinary chats) (Miller and Deutsch: 9). Similarly, Marte (2007) uses food mappings as a methodology to research spatial-temporal aspects of food relations from the cultural perspectives of people in specific communities.

Miller and Deutch (2004) organized their book into two main sections. The first section provides "an overview of the research process" (p. 9) which includes a discussion of the definition of research, why research is done and an overview of the paradigms of quantitative, qualitative and mixed methods. They also provide information about the mechanics of the research process including human subjects protection review and the literature review process. All of this, and the methods section that follows are written with what they identify as a "food studies spin" (p. 9). The second section of the book highlights specific methods interspersed with "conversations" with specific researchers who have either pioneered or utilized the method in question. The main categorical divisions they utilize include historical, quantitative, observational, and material culture methods.

All of the material included in the manual can provide useful information for sociocultural anthropologists as well as insight into food studies perspectives and how anthropology overlaps and diverges from it. As seen in other volumes, the main methods discussed by Miller and Deutsch (2004) include ethnographic at methods such as participant observation, interviews, questionnaires, and document analysis for both historical projects and those involving analysis of material objects in food research.

In conclusion, it is clear that thoughtful reading of all of the previously published methods manuals on nutritional anthropology and the anthropology of food can be a valuable place to begin any inquiry into food-focused research by a sociocultural anthropologist. They provide a wide range of possibilities and support Bernard's observation:

> While Anthropology has always been an eclectic discipline with regard to methods, the adoption by anthropologists of the full range of social research methods has accelerated since 1970. [Bernard 1998:17]

Study Design in Sociocultural Anthropology of Food

I begin this section of the chapter with an insightful diagram (Figure 1.1) adapted from Smith's book "How to be an Explorer of the World (2008). In many ways it provides a guide for developing and designing a food focused study. The manuals reviewed above also provide valuable sections to assist researchers develop their project. Additionally, a number of general texts that are invaluable resources, such as Fetterman's *Ethnography* (2010), H. Russel Bernard's *Handbook of Methods in Cultural Anthropology* (1998) and Muchison's *Ethnography Essentials* (2010).

In this section I provide an brief overview of two core elements of research design, developing the research question and selecting a theoretical approach, with some examples from the food anthropology literature. I draw from a broader field of literature since anthropological theory and methods often spill over into other disciplines and anthropology similarly often draws from other fields. The chapters that follow include some of this material (for example see Counihan, this volume) and provide more detailed discussion of specific methods used by food anthropologists.

> **How to Be a Food Researcher (or Study Anything Else)** *
>
> 1. Observe: Always look at the world around you. Pay attention!
> 2. Reflect on everything – animate & inanimate: it all is noteworthy.
> 3. Be curious & remember what you see determines what you miss.
> 4. Look again; Look Closer.
> 5. Choose a path and then change your course. Do this often.
> 6. Things are happening all around you – take them in.
> 7. Make connections & find patterns.
> 8. Taste the food.
> 9. Notice smells and textures.
> 10. Watch food being made. Catch the details. Cooking is important.
> 11. Listen to the food stories – they are all around you.
> 12. Create a dialogue with the world around you. Everything is pertinent.
> 13. Find the food origins.
> 14. Ask questions.
> 15. Record everything. Make notes in a variety of forms.

Figure 1.1. A Research Guide For Studying Food.

*Adapted from K. Smith How to Be an Explorer of the World.

Choosing a Research Question or Problem: Start by Starting

"Everything must have a beginning ... and that beginning must be linked to something that went before" *(Mary Shelly: Frankenstein 1994: viii)*

Research projects usually start as a question or problem. I often think that the origin of a research question springs from an inner source—something inside ourselves that inspires the way we look at the world. Perhaps though, the process of research question development can be seen as stemming from questions that arise from observing the world around us, our personal interest or experiences, what Wollcot (2005) refers to when he says: "relying on oneself as the primary research instrument (p. 45). Often the research question is based on our background and exposure to the field. Murchison (2010) advises "… you should also read widely to gain a good sense of potential topics (p. 22). Similar advice is found in most methods manuals such as Fetterman (2010), Miller and Deutsch (2009).

Selecting a good topic may not be easy. It is important to keep a topic focused enough to be interesting, yet broad enough to find adequate information. Above all, it is important to choose or develop a topic that touches you personally, something you will enjoy focusing on and doing. Miller and Deutsch (2009) aptly say " Choosing a research topic outside your areas of true interest is a guanteed prescription for agony" (p. 26).

While it may be difficult to find examples of research where the deep underlying motivation for the project is clarified, most researchers are clear in their discussion of their research question. For example Jarosz (2011) states:

> The purpose of this study is not to count how many women share these particular motivations, but to focus ethnographically upon how women talk about what motivates them to take up and to continue small-scale farming that is comprised of very hard work and little monetary gain. [p. 307]

A less direct explanation of the research question, but one that reveals much about how an anthropologist formulates a topic and focuses a project can be seen in Black's (2007) discussion of her research on foraging and hunger in her chapter: "Eating Garbage":

> This paper looks at the practice of foraging for food in urban refuse, focusing on the social and cultural aspects of 'eating garbage.' What is rubbish and what is good to eat is often culturally determined, but this paper will argue that what is considered edible is often shaped by economic circumstances in the Western World. [p. 41]

Calling on examples from the food industry, as well as other service industries, Fuentes-Mayorga (2011) clarifies her research question for the reader when she states:

> These ethnographic accounts from two New York City restaurants help support the main argument of this article: that rapid growth in small services sector establishments disproportionately benefits newer Mexican immigrants at the expense of native and Black immigrant workers within rapidly changing minority neighborhoods. [p. 107]

Additionally, it is important to think about whether the research project focuses on a particular place, group or event. Any of these can form the core of a study and each brings with it a specific set of issues that need to be considered. Clarifying the focus of the project is an important step since it leads to not only identifying where the project is located but also how the project will be conducted.

Steps in the proces of defining a research topic:

1. Brainstorm for ideas
2. Read background information
3. Define the project as a focused question
4. Read more literature
5. Refine your question or topic

Selecting and Identifying the Theoretical Approach that Speaks to You and Your Topic

> "Whether you can observe a thing or not depends on the theory which you use. It is the theory which decides what can be observed." (attributed to Albert Einstein)

> "In theory, theory and practice are the same. In practice, they are not." (Albert Einstein)

Theory, which can be thought of as a group of general propositions used as principles of explanation and prediction, is a guide that helps define a problem as well as the methods to answer it. Fetterman also suggests theory is a guide to practice and that it is impossible to conduct a study without an underlying model (2010: 5). In terms of theory guiding the selection of methods, Gailey (1998) suggests:

> Theory informs method and method shapes theory. What is distinctive is how method and theory are related: The bridges between the two are ontology (the set of assumptions that underlies one's research design) and epistemology (how one knows what one thinks one knows, the basis for knowledge claims) (p. 204).

Cheyney and Moreno-Black (2010) provide an example of the linkage between theory and method their study focusing on health practitioners' prenatal nutrition advice:

> For the purposes of this study, we utilized a modified grounded theory approach following the methodology proposed by Charmaz (1990, 2000). In classical grounded theory assessment (Glaser and Strauss, 1967), researchers ask a series of open-ended questions and look for common or recurring themes

> in interview narratives. Research is therefore "grounded" in the participants' experiences, as interviewees' responses, and not the researchers' preconceived expectations, dictate the categories evaluated. In keeping with grounded theory approaches, we began with two basic research questions: How do obstetricians and midwives view and transmit prenatal nutrition recommendations to their patients/clients? Are there differences between the perceptions and practices of midwives and physicians? [p. 5]

Anthropology includes a wide number of theories such as feminist, ecological, interpretive, symbolic, grounded theory, embodiment, and political economy to name a few. Usually researchers lean toward a theoretical approach because of its explanatory power as well as appropriateness for the research project topic. It is increasingly common, especially when focusing on a complex topic such as food, for researchers to rely on more than one theoretical approach. It is important to remember that when multiple theories inform a study, they need to be linked and integrated not simply superimposed on each other.

This type of combining of approaches is evident when Cherry, Ellis and DeSoucey (2011) discuss their fieldwork on three different consumption movements centered on food production:

> Our reliance on feminist and symbolic interactionist methodological literatures lays crucial groundwork for exploring how a focus on *practices* complements a focus on *identity* when studying lifestyle and consumption movements (p. 234).

Their work is also important because of their use of reflexivity to highlight the way their own "consumption identities" affected their data collection, analyses, and the article. Through their reflection about the performance of their own food habits during their fieldwork, they acknowledged that they brought personal, political and social stances about what they ate to the project. The act of doing fieldwork on food consumption patterns sometimes challenged their own food preferences leading them to rethink their own choices. Additionally, the type of food they ate or did not eat when they were with the participants of the study both enhanced and potentially jeopardized rapport.

As indicated above, theory and method are linked and inform each other. Different theoretical approaches lend themselves to certain types of methods. The relationship between theory and method has often led to the tension between qualitative and quantitative paradigms since each is rooted in a researcher's epistemological position. Quantitative research provides explanations of experiences about food through numerical data while qualitative research focuses on thick descriptions of experiences people have about food. Neither approach is necessarily the correct or true one; instead, one may be better suited to answer a specific question than the other. Consequently, the methods used in a research study are rooted in the theoretical approach. Sometimes researchers will find a mixed method approach, that is combining both qualitative and quantitative approaches, provides invaluable insights because sometimes a single approach cannot answer the research question. For example, in their study of food security in the UK, Dowler et al. (2011) used an online quantitative survey and a series of qualitative, deliberative workshops, to evaluate UK consumers' understanding of, and reactions to, changing food prices and food security. The quantitative survey led to the identification of trends in consumer behavior and the qualitative workshops explored in-depth thinking about, and responses to, rising food prices as well as food insecurity.

Conclusion

In this chapter, I have briefly reviewed the current manuals that focus on anthropology and food. I approached the review primarily from the perspective of the content and issues that are of interest to cultural anthropologists. Other chapters in this book pay more close attention to other subfields of anthropology that address and focus on food. I also highlighted two important aspects of research design in food anthropology—choosing research topics and the relationship of theory to research project design.

The chapters that follow focus on some of the specific methods used by sociocultural anthropologists when they are doing anthropology of food. Pérez aptly discusses the application of core ethnographic methods of interviewing, life histories and narratives to the anthropological study of food. In so doing she calls attention to the importance of considering the politics of representation when using these methods. Emphasizing the reliance on feminist ethnography and Chicana/Latina feminist theory she draws attention to the way food is a powerful voice and "kitchen table ethnography" as a research method privileges the voices and experiences of individual women. Taylor and Nichter provide an extensive discussion of the key methods such as interviews, visual prompts for discussion, diaries and participant observation, available to anthropologists interested in body image research.

In her chapter on Visual Anthropology Methods Vallianatos provides a discussion of both traditional and newly reimagined approaches and techniques for studying food through visual data. She includes such topics as food in film, the use of photographs and videos for eliciting information about food and food habits, food maps and mapping and digital storytelling. Vallianatos also calls attention to the growing interest in the larger issue of the sensory issue of knowledge related to food and the embodied nature of food experiences and knowledge. Piperata and Dufour focus on recent examples from the anthropological literature to examine direct observation methods. They highlight both the use of direct observation in the context of participant observation as well as in combination with quantitative data collection. Counihan's chapter, Studying Food and Culture: Ethnographic Methods in the Classroom ties many of the themes and concepts together as she examines and describes her use of ethnography on the classroom as an educational experience. She discusses how she explores the use of participant-observation, interview, life history, photography, map-making, and informant documentation in a course on ethnographic methods that specifically focuses on food and culture. She also discusses how she uses a required ethnographic food focused project in the class to amplify the readings and provide personal experience with doing this type of ethnographic fieldwork. Paxson presents a discussion of the ethnographic methods of participant observation/inquisitive observation and open-ended interviewing. She underscores the concept that participant observation/inquisitive observation often generate research questions more than answering them and provide insights into the lives of others. Using her personal research experience she provides interesting insights into the research methods and also presents valuable lists of tips for doing participant observation and interviewing.

In the chapter on Focus Groups in Qualitative or Mixed Methods Research, Pérez provides insights into how the technique of the focus group interview as a source of data for research offers deep insight into a group's shared practices and ideologies. Using examples from her own research as well as the literature, she provides information about how to create and manage focus group interviews as well as their limitations. Riley's chapter on food and textual analyses first discusses the range of texts which include or touch on food-related topics. This diverse body of material can include items such as the bible, poems, Platonic dialogues, books, television programs and even legislative material. She reviews current thoughts on ways to "read" and code the variety of food text material and in her section on making meaning of the material includes important discussion of the ethics involved in the collection, analysis, and publication of food textual data, Additionally she highlights the way some food researchers using texts seek to transform our thoughts and practices involving food.

There is much left uncovered in this introductory chapter—such as a discussion of ethics in research as well as the challenges, both positive and negative, that are encountered when doing field work. I touched only briefly on reflexive and collaborative research and hope that the morsels I provided stimulate you to read further and delve deeply into these topics. Given the array of anthropological approaches and the complexity of the field, sociocultural anthropologists are well positioned to contribute a wealth of nuanced and in-depth information about food and the human experience.

Geraldine Moreno-Black is a Senior Research Associate at Oregon Research Institute/ Community Evaluation Services (ORI/CES) and Professor Emerita at the University of Oregon. Her research is located at the intersection of nutritional anthropology and biocultural anthropology. She is engaged in a four year public health project to develop and evaluate the implementation of a county wide school-based BMI monitoring program with county elementary schools. She has been involved in CBPR research focusing on child obesity and has done food research in Thailand, Ecuador and the United States. Her previous research in northeastern Thailand focused on the relationships among gender, cultural and economic transformation, and food habits, including the reliance on wild food. Her research has been funded by numerous granting agencies including Trillium, the National Science Foundation, Wenner-Gren Foundation, Medical Research Foundation of Oregon, the Social Science Research Council, Fulbright Hayes and published in a variety of journals including, *J. School Health; Pediatric Obesity; Human Organization, Voices*. She worked on the development and founding of the Lane County Food Policy Council (LCFPC), participated in a local food assessment committee and served as co-chair of the LCFCP. She has been a councilor for the Agriculture, Food and Human Values Society since 2010.

References Cited

Bernard, H. Russell. 1998. *Handbook of Methods in Cultural Anthropology*. Altamira Press: CA.

Black, Rachel. 2007. "Eating Garbage: Socially Marginal Food Provisioning Practices". In *Consuming the Inedible: Neglected Dimensions of Food Choice*. Jeremy MacClancy, C. J. K. Henry, Helen M. Macbeth, eds. 141–150. Berghahn Books: Oxford.

Cherry, Elizabeth, Colter Ellis and Michaela DeSoucey. 2011. "Food for Thought, Thought for Food: Consumption, Identity, and Ethnography". *Journal of Contemporary Ethnography* 40: 231–258.

Cheyney, Melissa and Geraldine Moreno-Black. 2010. "Nutritional Counseling in Midwifery and Obstetric Practice". *Ecology of Food and Nutrition* 49:1–29.

Dowler, Elizabeth, Moya Kneafsey, Hannah Lambie, Alex Inman and Rosemary Collier. 2011. "Thinking About 'Food Security': Engaging with UK Consumers". *Critical Public Health* 21(4): 403–416.

Fetterman, David. 2009. *Ethnography: Step-by-Step*. Thousand Oaks, CA: Sage, 3rd edition.

Fuentes-Magora, Norma. 2007. "Sorting Black and Brown Latino service workers in gentrifying New York neighborhoods". *Latino Studies* 9:106–125.

Gailey, Christine W. 2007. "Feminist Methods". In *Handbook of Methods in Cultural Anthropology*. H. Russel Bernard, ed, 203–233. Altamira Press: CA.

Garine, I. de. 2004. "Anthropology of Food and Pluridisciplinarity". In *Researching Food Habits: Methods and Problems*. Helen MacBeth and Jeremy MacClancey, eds, 15–28. New York: Berghahn Books.

Goode, Judith. 1989. "Cultural Patterning and Group-shared Rules for the Study of Food Intake". In *Research methods in Nutritional Anthropology*. Gretl Pelto, et al. eds, 126–161. Tokyo: United Nations Publications.

Hartog, A. P. den, Wija A. van Staveren and Inge D. Brouwer. 2006. *Food Habits and Consumption in Developing Countries: Manual for Social Surveys*. Wageningen Academic Pub. The Netherlands.

Hubert, Annie. 2004. "Qualitative Research in the Anthropology of Food: A Comprehensive Qualitative/Quantitative Approach". In *Researching Food Habits: Methods and Problems*. Helen MacBeth and Jeremy MacClancey, eds, 42–54. New York: Berghahn Books.

Jarosz, Lucy. 2011. "Nourishing women: Toward a feminist political ecology of community supported agriculture in the United States". *Gender, Place & Culture: A Journal of Feminist Geography* 18:307–326.

Katona-Apte, Judit. 1975. "Nutritional Anthropology". *Medical Anthropology Newsletter* 6 (2):8.

Mars, Gerald and Valarie Mars. 2004. "Doing it Wrong: Why Bother to do Imperfect Research?" In *Researching Food Habits: Methods and Problems*. Helen MacBeth and Jeremy MacClancey, eds, 75–86. New York: Berghahn Books.

Marte, Lydia. 2007. "Foodmaps: Tracing Boundaries of 'Home' Through Food Relations". *Food and Foodways*, 15 (3):261–289.

Macbeth, Helen and Jeremy MacClancy. 2004. *Researching Food Habits: Methods and Problems*. New York: Berghahn Books.

Medina, F. Xavier. 2004. "'Tell me what you eat and you tell me who you are': Methodological Notes on the Interaction between Researcher and Informants in the Anthropology of Food". In *Researching Food Habits: Methods and Problems*. Helen MacBeth and Jeremy MacClancey, eds, 55–62. New York: Berghahn Books.

Messer, Ellen. 1989. "Methods for Studying Determinants of Food Intake". In *Research methods in Nutrtional Anthropology*. Gretl Pelto, et al eds, ix–xvi. Tokyo: United Nations Publications.

Messer, Ellen and Harriet Kuhnlein. 1986. "Traditional Foods". In *Training Manual in Nutritional Anthropology*, Sara Quandt and Cheryl Ritenbaugh eds, 66–81. Washington D.C.: American Anthropological Association 20.

Miller, Jeff and Jonathan Deutsch. 2009. *Food Studies An Introduction to Reseach Methods*. Berg: NY.

Mintz, Sidney and Du Bois, Christine. 2002. "The Anthropology of Food and Eating". *Annu. Rev. Anthropol*. 31:99–119.

Murcott Anne. 1998. *The Nation's Diet: the Social Science of Food Choice*. London: Longman.

Murchison, Julian. 2010. *Ethnography Essentials: Designing, Conducting, and Presenting Your Research*. San Francisco: Jossey-Bass.

Pelto, Gretl. 1989. "Introduction: Methodological Directions in Nutritional Anthropology". In *Research Methods in Nutritional Anthropology*, Gretl Pelto, et al eds, ix–xvi. Tokyo: United Nations Publications.

Pelto, Gretel H, Pelto, Perti J, Messer, Ellen. 1989. *Research Methods in Nutritional Anthropology*. Tokyo: United Nations Publications.

Pelto, Gretl, Margaret Armar-Klemesut, Jonathan Siekmann and Dominic Schofield. 2013. "The focused ethnographic study 'assessing the behavioral and local market environment for improving the diets of infants and young children 6 to 23 months old' and its use in three countries." *Maternal and Child Nutrition* 9 (Suppl.1):35–46.

Quandt, Sara and Cheryl Ritenbaugh. 1986. *Training Manual in Nutritional Anthropology*. Washington D.C.: American Anthropological Association 20.

Scrimshaw, Susan C. and Elana Hurtado. 1987. *Rapid Assessment Procedures for Nutrition and Primary health Care, Anthropological Approaches to Improving Programme Effectiveness*. Tokyo: The United Nations University.

SAFN (Society for the Anthropoloy of Food and Nutrition). 2013. "2004 Name Change". http://foodanthro.com/about-safn/ (accessed 8/2013).

Shelly, Mary. 1994. "Author's Introduction". In *Frankenstein*. Dover Publications, Inc: NY.
Smith, K. 2008. *How To Be An Explorer of The World: Portable Life Museum*. New York: A Perigee Book (Published by the Penguin Group).
Ulijasek, Stanley, J. and Simon S. Strickland. 1993. *Nutritional Anthropology. Prospects and Perspectives*. London: Smith-Gordon & Co. Ltd.
Weaver, Lesley Jo and Craig Hadley. 2009. "Moving Beyond Hunger and Nutrition: A Systematic Review of the Evidence Linking Food Insecurity and Mental Health in Developing Countries". *Ecology of Food and Nutrition*, 48:263–284.
Wolcott, Harry F. 2005. *Ethnography: A Way of Seeing*. New York: Altamira Press.

Online resources for methods

World Food Habits Bibliography
    http://lilt.ilstu.edu/rtdirks/
Food and Nutrition Center
    http://fnic.nal.usda.gov/
World Health Organization
    http://www.who.int/topics/nutrition/en/
    http://www.who.int/topics/diet/en/
Medical Research Council: Dietary Assessment:
    http://dapa-toolkit.mrc.ac.uk/dietary-assessment/
Qualitative Data Analysis Software Comparison (Boston University):
    http://www.bu.edu/tech/services/support/desktop/distribution/nvivo/comparison/
National Cancer Institute (Data Analysis Tools & Methods) See:
    Diet Section
    http://appliedresearch.cancer.gov/resource/analysis.html
    Data Collection Instruments (Diet)
    http://appliedresearch.cancer.gov/resource/collection.html
USDA Food Surveys Research Group
    http://fnic.nal.usda.gov/food-composition/ars-food-surveys-research-group
FoodRisc Resource Center
    http://resourcecentre.foodrisc.org/mixed-methods-research_185.html
Democratizing Food Research in West Africa
    http://www.excludedvoices.org/democratising-agricultural-research-food-sovereignty-west-africa
Food Vision (Food Maping)
    http://www.foodvision.cieh.org/pages/food-mapping
FAO: Choosing a method for poverty mapping
    http://www.fao.org/docrep/005/y4597e/Y4597E04.htm

Other Resources

American Museum of Natural History: Our Global Kitchen Additional Resources:
    http://www.amnh.org/exhibitions/past-exhibitions/our-global-kitchen-food-nature-culture/additional-resources

Lunch Love Community: On Line Documentary Project:
   http://www.lunchlovecommunity.org/
MIT Food & Culture Open Course: *Food and Culture, Spring 2011*
   Paxson, Heather. *21A.265*. (MIT OpenCourseWare: Massachusetts Institute of Technology), http://ocw.mit.edu/courses/anthropology/21a-265-food-and-culture-spring-2011 (Accessed 12 Jul, 2014). License: Creative Commons BY-NC-SA
The New York Food Museum
   http://www.nyfoodmuseum.org/
The Institute for Food and Development Policy (Food First)
   http://foodfirst.org/
International Food Policy Research Institute
   http://www.ifpri.org/
Food Research and Action Center (FRAC)
   http://frac.org/
Food and Agriculture Organization
   http://www.fao.org/home/en/

CHAPTER 2

Interviewing Epistemologies
From Life History to Kitchen Table Ethnography

Ramona Lee Pérez

Despite its importance in ethnographic circles, life history remains elusive. A review of recent food studies literature reveals a burgeoning genre of food autobiography by chefs and celebrity foodies reflecting on their own lives, but little in terms of food-based life history of everyday people. More analytical than biography but less structured than qualitative research, life history engages people in narrating their own perspectives. Preferably conducted over an extended time span and often covering decades of personal experience, it rests on inscribing person-focused (rather than research-focused) data. Life history rests on what the researcher can elicit, not so much through formal questioning but rather through deliberate listening. Once interviews are completed, analysis focuses on reconstructing the arc of an individual's development throughout the life cycle and exploring that personal history as an example of embodied ideologies, evidence of cultural practices, and the ways these relate to patterns of personal and social change.

One of the most humanistic of research methods, life history hinges on putting others at ease, getting them to trust you, and convincing them that you really care, that their stories are important. Why does this matter? To answer that question, I use a term that often arose during my research in the Mexico-U.S. borderlands: *confianza*. Encompassing the principles of trust, rapport, and intimacy, *confianza* means you would feel safe putting your life into another person's hands. That, essentially, is what we are asking of life history participants. We are asking that they entrust us with important details of their hard-earned personal experience. We are asking for permission to sift through their memories. They are risking that we will alter the significance of their lives, or even worse, that we will find them lacking. Finding people willing to participate in life history research and respectfully executing the process is an exercise in profound trust and great hope.

For food studies research, taking a life history approach does not just mean that each person with whom you speak is the expert on his/her own experience. Since everyone eats, each person is also an expert on food as it relates to his or her life. By screening your interlocutors for their relationship to and expertise on your specific research topic, you can gather a variety of perspectives and in-depth case studies along a range of personal practice. The further you develop each life history, the more the focus shifts away from academic theories and research models toward what people really think and feel. Ultimately, life history is about how people tell their own stories. During my first major research project, the most important findings arose not out of my own questions, but out of my interlocutors' concerns. After releasing my hold on a prefabricated agenda (and my own ego) and allowing myself to be redirected by the concerns of whoever sat in front of me, I dropped into the flow of conversation and learned the contours of the person: wisdom, flaws, humor, hurts, concerns, preferences, complaints, insights, blind spots. Moreover, I learned my own. Despite this reflexive promise, life history remains underutilized. This chapter promotes use of the method by detailing its potential and limitations for food studies research.

Life History and the Food Voice

No scholar has done more to promote life history as a key method for the study of food habits than Carole Counihan. As she writes in *Around the Tuscan Table*, "This book emerges out of a quarter-century of exploration of how ethnographic interviews centered on food can be a way for people to talk about history, culture, relationships and identity" (2004: 223). Her earlier work highlights the stories of Florentine women grappling with the impact of wage-labor employment on domestic nurturance (Counihan 1988), while later articles explore the role of food in mediating intergenerational relationships (1999a) and individual food cravings (1999b). Finally, her ethnographic monograph (2004) integrates extensive quotations from interview transcripts to address topics ranging from gender differences in productive and reproductive food labor to the historical origins of and contemporary changes in the Florentine diet. Counihan has also collected food-centered life histories from U.S. college students (1992), and Mexican American women for a long-term study in southern Colorado (2002, 2005, 2006, 2008, 2009).

Annie Hauck-Lawson's concept of the "food voice" (1992, 1998, 2004), a result of her ethnographic study of the meanings of food among Polish-American families in New York (1991), is another landmark in the theory and method of food-based ethnography. Rather than incidental gathering of verbal anecdotes on food habits, Hauck-Lawson's deliberate oral history shows that actions can speak louder than words as people procure, prepare and consume their food. What and how they eat, and conversely what they avoid, reveals volumes about individual and cultural identity, just as do their stories about these activities.

Both Counihan and Hauck-Lawson have influenced scholars interested in studying foodways via interviewing and life history (Abarca 2001, 2006, 2007; Deutsch 2004, 2005; Harris-Shapiro 2006; R. Pérez 2004, 2009). Asking, "How do they shop, cook, and eat? How do they feel about what they are doing? How and why do they choose to cook? What issues do they face with regard to their identity as men, and how does this influence their food choices, cooking, and eating?" Deutsch finds that firefighters exhibit multiple versions of masculinity and an apparent conflict between their food voices and spoken voices (2005: 91; see also 2004). Meanwhile, Harris-Shapiro (2006) posits the food narratives of her respondents as opposition to and reformulation of normative American Jewish culture. Finally, Abarca (2001, 2006) and Ramona Lee Pérez (2004, 2009) draw on extensive food-based informal interviews not only as ethnographic data but to articulate a theory of informant-driven research.

Is Life History Right for Your Project?

The decision to use life history hinges on several critical criteria that the researcher(s) must evaluate when formulating the methodological strategy. These criteria cluster around the focus and scope of the project as well as the temperament of the researcher(s). Below is a checklist of issues to consider when determining whether a life history approach is appropriate to your research.

First, assess the focus of the project. Life history is well suited for studying food habits over time, as well as ideology and patterns of cultural change. It is best utilized with those who have already engaged in some degree of personal reflection about their own lives, although past ruminations need not necessarily have been about food habits. What is important is the person's cognitive capacity to tell stories about her- or himself, which typically means that the best life history interviews will be with adult, often elderly, research subjects. The method works to a lesser extent in creating verbal snapshots of specific moments by getting people to reflect during or shortly after a relevant activity. However, this can be difficult to execute as participants frequently lose the thread of conversation. Recording talk in the midst of activity or in the company of others can be a rich source of data often revealing unanticipated findings and is definitely worthwhile with any research sample, but it is advisable to employ a backup method, such as photography, videography, focused participant-observation, and/or surveys. Conversely, life history is not recommended when the project requires a large sample size or must be conduced on a tight time frame. Thus, it is not an appropriate tool for solving an immediate crisis (e.g., in the midst of a famine), although it can document the personal testimony of those involved and help identify long-term factors precipitating the crisis in the first place. In this regard, life history is underutilized as a tool for influencing public policy. Legislators are often inspired to action by the powerful testimony of "real people" speaking about topics that impact their lives.

Another element to consider is the scope of your project. Life history requires considerable time and energy. Ample time is needed to screen, befriend, and engage candidates, drawing out their unique perspectives through active listening. Key to success is the researcher's commitment to conduct multiple interviews with selected participants, as is the patience to understand that not everyone with whom time is invested during initial sessions will become a suitable long-term candidate. Also, gently guiding conversation toward your research topic while allowing conversation to flow according to the speaker's interest and expertise requires just as much patience as identifying and interacting with initial prospects.

Beyond the time required to orchestrate contacts and to collect data, even more time-consuming is the persistence necessary to transcribe and analyze completed interviews. Transcription and coding software continues to improve, but this process remains a tedious (though eminently productive) aspect of the life history venture. Given that the life history interviews are best conducted over a stretch of time, the researcher and subject are likely to form some degree of personal relationship over the span of research. Analysis will be easier once the researcher establishes some degree of emotional distance from the data. To facilitate this process, consider engaging an assistant to complete transcriptions and coding. The lead researcher(s) will need to approve written data, listening to recordings to check the accuracy of transcripts and reviewing lists of recurrent themes to be sure that coding includes all major topics of conversation. This supervisory role allows the researcher to begin distinguishing analytical patterns from the personal relationships of the research process.

The final group of criteria to consider when assessing your methodological approach is the personality of the researcher. Requisite character traits include the ability to empathize with other people and patiently listen to them. If you cannot stay quiet for extended periods of time, letting your own opinions take a back seat and asking only clarifying questions while others expound their points of view, then this may not be the right method for you. That said, active listening can be learned, but recognize that your first interviews may be spotty until you learn to be comfortable with your own silence and develop the ability to encourage the flow of conversation, rather than structuring it according to your research questions.

When I first began conducting life history interviews, immediately following each session I would listen to the recordings without trying to transcribe them, simply to assess my own performance and identify topics for follow-up interviews. I was embarrassed by my initial attempts—by how much I was talking versus listening, how often I cut people off, glossed over a meaningful moment, or insisted on my own agenda rather than hearing what they were trying to say. This reflexive assessment in the midst of research helped me retrain myself, focusing my ear, stilling my tongue, and fostering an ability to focus on the experience of others rather than my own agenda. Such a reflexive component, whether conducted as mutual evaluations among the research team or through periodic self-assessment, will radically improve research skills and data collection, and may result in an emotional intimacy between researcher and subject that is uncommon in many other methodological approaches. Again, assess whether the personality of your research team matches, or can be trained to match, the depth of the data that you hope to collect, and carefully consider how you will match interviewers to prospective subjects.

Tips for Successful Food-Based Life History

In life history methodology, getting started begins, as most studies do, with recruiting likely candidates. Depending on the population to be studied, you may post notices requesting volunteers or gather contacts via snowball sampling, collecting personal referrals from each new participant. Try to choose people who balance each other's perspectives, with varied access to material resources, different sizes and types of families and social networks, different ethnic/identity categories, and different career histories. Despite your best efforts, it is a general truism in life history research that busy people are difficult participants. Choose people who have the time and temperament to sit with you and ponder. Most successful interviews are conducted with elders or other people past child-rearing and full-time employment.

Once you have a group of potential subjects, plan to book one to three hours for each session, initially shorter and lengthening as you get to know each person. Collecting a life history from someone you already know typically requires three to a half-dozen sessions to build rapport, and recording conversations with people you see infrequently can take several months to many years. To prevent burnout while maintaining a working relationship, attempt to visit your candidates no more than once a week and no less than once a month, bringing small food gifts for each visit in order to show thanks. Interviews are best set in the context related to your topic: if home cooking, then the kitchen; if farming or community gardening, then on or near the cultivated land; if about the eating habits of seniors, then the local community center. To break the conversational ice in earlier sessions, bring along favorite foods to share, commenting on what you prefer and why, and then asking about their food preferences. Show engagement by using culturally appropriate body language and facial expression. It often helps to dress down but with respect to local standards in order to be unobtrusive (e.g. working casual wardrobe in neutral colors). Remember to consistently exhibit respect and show ample gratitude for their time and attention. Early sessions are important for building rapport and may not yield significant data. Rather, the goal is to create a sense of mutual investment in the research process and a context for sharing personal recollections.

After rapport is established or if you already have a strong relationship, remember to set a tone of commensality by sharing food or drink before each session. Begin with general questions from everyday conversation (e.g., likes and dislikes, key memories). Prompts to guide speakers through major stages in the life cycle (childhood, adulthood, old age) are best left for follow-up sessions. Once speakers begin, they commonly warm up to the subject and have plenty to say. After establishing strong rapport, questions can shift to more intimate topics, (e.g. food-related expenses, health issues, and how important relationships are mediated by food). Keep in mind that sometimes speakers will feel the need to talk about off-topic issues before addressing the research topic. When this occurs, spend interview time discussing their immediate concerns in order to build rapport, and then assess whether this is a respondent you can work with on a consistent basis. Some degree of drop-off during life history research is common. Be prepared with back-up candidates, accept that you may not cover all the questions that interest you within your given time frame, and be content to focus the majority of your energies on a handful of enthusiastic speakers. With life history data, fewer respondents and greater depth of talk is far better than dozens of interviews that only skim the surface.

In terms of equipment, a pad and paper to jot down key phrases and a good audio or video recorder are crucial. However, it is best to wait until rapport is strong and consent forms are signed before bringing recording equipment to your sessions. Many good candidates can be scared silent by technology, while others will find their tongues loosened. Watch your interlocutors and wait until it feels comfortable to begin recording, if at all. Understanding how to operate your equipment and ensuring adequate pickup from the microphones and minimal ambient noise are also important. Whatever your level of technical prowess, ultimately your best tools during life history are good eye contact and the ability to sit down after the session is over and produce detailed notes. Finally, during both interviews and analysis, remember that your role resembles that of a biographer, but instead of simply recording the story of one person's life, you are looking for patterns in how their lives compare to others and how they represent larger cultural patterns. Having explored the practicalities of life history methodology, I now turn to its epistemological ramifications.

Food-Centered Life History and Culinary Chats as Testimonial Literature

Many food studies ethnographers conduct interviews or collect oral histories, but only a few express explicit concern with the politics of knowledge production

(Abarca 2001, 2006; Counihan 2004, 2006, 2008, 2009; R. Pérez 2004, 2009). Working within the trope of "food-centered life history," Counihan (2004: 1–2) first articulated her motivations in *Around the Tuscan Table*:

> For many people, food is a powerful voice, especially for women, who are often heavily involved with food acquisition, preparation, provisioning and cleanup. Food-centered life histories have fit my desire to use ethnography to give voice to traditionally muted people—people not part of the economic or intellectual elite.

She later theorized the method as a way to express the perspectives of those who are otherwise marginalized (2006, 2008; cf. Sandoval 1991 on oppositional consciousness). In *A Tortilla Is Like Life,* Counihan (2009: 7–8) describes her ethics and research style:

> Before doing interviews I established informed consent…I asked for their permission to tape-record, explaining that I wanted to have their verbatim comments about their culture, but I also told them they could turn the tape recorder off at any time and decline to answer any questions, which people did on occasion…Interviews were conversations with their own momentum and wandered into many nonfood topics.

Meredith Abarca's *charlas culinarias,* or informal culinary chats, similarly intertwine personal narrative, testimonial autobiography, and culinary memoir (2001, 2006). Employing feminist approaches from literary criticism, geography, and anthropology, Abarca shows how participants demonstrate agency, reveal diverse subjectivities, articulate sensual knowledge, and transform domestic space into a site of power and creative expression. My notion of "kitchen table ethnography," as outlined below and in other works (R. Pérez 2004, 2009), operates in a similar vein.

Life history research, however, is not simply an issue of methods while in the field; one must also consider the politics of representation (see Deutsch 2004; cf. Patai 1988). Counihan (2009: 8–9) comments on how she addressed this issue:

> I gave respondents copies of their verbatim interview transcriptions so that they could request corrections or deletions and keep them for posterity…at the urging of participants I have edited the transcriptions to achieve readability while staying as close to their original language as possible…I grappled with issues of balance as I tried to forge my own voice and simultaneously to keep participants' voices as prominent and authentic as possible.

Abarca (2001: 136) likewise states that she "reseason[ed] my academic training so that I will not conceptualize and frame my subject of research with hierarchical and binary paradigms." She expands this discussion in her book *Voices in the Kitchen* (Abarca 2006: 9):

> *Charlas* are about vertical thinking, not horizontal, meaning that researcher and women in the field are intellectually on the same plane. The praxis of this methodological paradigm, the analysis, focuses on thought-provoking moments that illustrate the gaps within master narratives of patriarchal and capitalist ideologies, where these women *do* speak and theorize about their own lives.

To achieve our methodological, theoretical and political aims, Counihan, Abarca, and I have all built on feminist ethnography (e.g., Behar and Gordon 1995), Chicana/Latina feminist theory (e.g., Sandoval 1991) and *testimonio* literature (e.g., LFG 2001), a genre that emerged from both from colonial era *relaciones* or reports to the king (e.g. de las Casas 1542) and Latin American liberation movements (e.g. Menchú and Burgos-Debray 1984), as the framework motivating our use of life history as epistemological intervention. Abarca adds the notion of "decolonizing" scholarship (Alarcón 2002; E. Perez 1999; Smith 1999), adapting the work of Spivak (1988) to ask "*how* does the subaltern speak?" and advocates "talking back" (Castillo 1992; hooks 1989) to structures of knowledge and power. My vision of "kitchen table ethnography" utilizes a similar model with additional emphasis on reflexive epistemology (Bourdieu and Wacquant 1992) and "theorizing from the flesh" (LFG 2001). Counihan, Abarca, and I all have "learned to speak with…rather than to" (Abarca 2006: 8) our interlocutors, "listen[ing] to what [they] wanted to say and not worry[ing] about following a preconceived methodological research agenda" (ibid.).

Kitchen Table Ethnography: Fleshy Theory and Reflexive Epistemology

To complete this discussion of life history methods for food studies, I present my own model of "kitchen table ethnography," a method I have worked with over the past fifteen years. Invented during research on food habits in the Mexico-U.S. borderlands and later refined in projects with local food activists in New York City, I gradually shifted away from questionnaires and structured interviews in favor of casual talk about food, personal history, and social significance. Over the course of this work, I discovered that sharing about my own life improved the depth of our exchange; learning how to hold the stories I was given led to rich discourses on food and related subjects.

The "kitchen table" truly is the heart of the home and the greater community, yet it is not only a literal space but also a conceptual one emphasizing informal talk and interpersonal relationships. Offering refuge from an unending cycle of domestic tasks and social struggle, the kitchen table is a place where the talk is flavorful, just like the food. At table with willing speakers, I got tips on where to find the best local foods, shared stories about health and family, and received advice on how to manage my household or how to organize a community campaign. I received cooking lessons and parenting tips, learned about home-based businesses, and whiled away hours in games and conversation. More than anything, though, kitchen table ethnography taught me the eloquence of silence and the power of simply listening. Between menu planning and favorite television shows, one evening a key informant mourned the death of her eldest son. Cold, quiet tears rolled down her cheeks as she spoke. Sitting with her at the kitchen table, I thought to myself, I am not trained for this! I am not a grief counselor! But all I could do was wait and listen as we mused over our tea.

That moment taught me the power of being fully present with my research participants, but it was a different relationship that showed me the epistemological insights of the method. During my borderlands project, I was frequently in the kitchen with a middle school Spanish teacher, enjoying her delicious cooking, learning her special recipes, and perturbing her young son by insistently serving him vegetables. It was in this context that she critiqued my eating habits after dinner one evening. "*Sabes que* [you know]," she said, "It's fun eating with you. You might be skinny but you sure can enjoy a good meal." As usual, she got me thinking, this time about the nature of appetite and its relationship to body shape. Her comment sounded quite like what the authors of *Telling to Live: Latina Feminist Testimonios* call "theorizing from the flesh." Upon reflection, I realized that she, like other hosts, was determined to fatten me up until I was "rich and juicy," rather than looking like a stick-skinny New York type. It became her personal mission to take me to every hole-in-the-wall restaurant in three different counties, then take me home and feed me again. She was literally reshaping the ethnographer, refocusing my body, my attention, and the nature of the research project through her focus on my appetite.

Food is a powerful voice, and kitchen table ethnography seeks to emphasize individual subjectivity. Rather than extracting data to fit a preconceived research agenda, it demands a reflexive consciousness and seeks to destabilize hierarchies of knowledge. Following decolonial, liberatory, and embodied theory, the method regards all interlocutors as intellectual peers. Rather than informant and scholar, participants become co-conspirators in a collective research agenda. Central to the project are careful documentation of instances of "talking back" or challenges to dominant cultural models—including the legitimacy of the scholarly endeavor—as they can redirect the scope of our inquiry and understandings. Looking back at my path toward this methodology, I am immensely grateful for my good fortune and am once again reminded that the most fruitful ethnography is often the discovery of the unexpected.

Ramona Lee Pérez teaches anthropology and Latin American and Latino Studies at Queens College, City University of New York. Her interests include food and the senses, gender and kinship, borderlands, and feminist research methods. Her publications include "Livin' *la vida sabrosa*: Savoring Latino New York" in *Gastropolis*, "*Cocinas Públicas*: Food and Border Consciousness" in the journal *Food and Foodways*, and "*Las fronteras del sabor*: Taste as Consciousness, Kinship, and Space in the Mexico-U.S. Borderlands" in the *Journal of Latin American and Caribbean Anthropology*.

References Cited

Abarca, Meredith E. 2001. Los Chilaquiles de Mi 'amá: The Language of Everyday Cooking. In *Pilaf, Pozole, and Pad Thai: American Women and Ethnic Food*, ed. Sherri A. Inness, 119–144. Amherst: University of Massachusetts Press.

———. 2006. *Voices in the Kitchen: Views of Food and the World from Working-Class Mexican and Mexican American Women*. College Station: Texas A&M University Press.

———. 2007. *Charlas Culinarias*: Mexican Women Speak from Their Public Kitchens. *Food and Foodways* 15(3–4): 183–212.

Alarcón, Norma. 2002. Anzaldúa's *Frontera*: Inscribing Gynetics. In *Decolonial Voices: Chicana and Chicano Cultural Studies in the Twenty-First Century*, ed. J. Arturo Aldama and Naomi H. Quiñonez, 113–126. Bloomington: Indiana University Press.

Behar, Ruth, and Deborah Gordon, eds. 1995. *Women Writing Culture*. Berkeley: University of California Press.

Bourdieu, Pierre, and Loïc J. D. Wacquant. 1992. *An Invitation to Reflexive Sociology*. Chicago: University of Chicago Press.

Castillo, Debra. 1992. *Talking Back: Toward a Latin American Feminist Literary Criticism*. Ithaca: Cornell University Press.

Counihan, Carole M. 1988. Female Identity, Food, and Power in Contemporary Florence. *Anthropological Quarterly* 61(2): 51–62.

———. 1992. Food Rules in the United States: Individualism, Control, and Hierarchy. *Anthropological Quarterly* 65(2): 55–66.

———. 1999a. Food as Tie and Rupture: Negotiating Intimacy and Autonomy in the Florentine Family. In *The Anthropology of Food and Body: Gender, Meaning and Power*, 156–177. New York: Routledge.

———. 1999b. The Body as Voice of Desire and Connection in Florence, Italy. In *The Anthropology of Food and Body: Gender, Meaning and Power*, 178–194. New York: Routledge.

———. 2002. Food as Women's Voice in the San Luis Valley of Colorado. In *Food in the USA: A Reader*, ed. Carole Counihan, 295–304. New York: Routledge.

———. 2004. *Around the Tuscan Table: Food, Family and Gender in Twentieth-Century Florence*. New York: Routledge.

———. 2005. The Border as Barrier and Bridge: Food, Gender, and Ethnicity in the San Luis Valley of Colorado. In *From Betty Crocker to Feminist Food Studies: Critical Perspectives on Women and Food*, ed. A. Avakian and B. Haber, 200–217. Amherst: University of Massachusetts Press.

———. 2006. Food as Mediating Voice and Oppositional Consciousness for Chicanas in Colorado's San Luis Valley. In *Mediating Chicana/o Culture: Multicultural American Vernacular*, ed. Scott Baugh, 70–84. Cambridge, England: Cambridge Scholars Press.
———. 2008. Mexicanas' Food Voice and Differential Consciousness in the San Luis Valley of Colorado. In *Food and Culture: A Reader Revised Edition*, ed. Carole Counihan and Penny Van Esterik, 354–368. New York: Routledge.
———. 2009. *A Tortilla Is Like Life: Food and Culture in the San Luis Valley of Colorado*. Austin: University of Texas Press.
de las Casas, Bartolomé; commentary by José Miguel Martínez-Torrejón. 2006 [1552]. *Brevísima relación de la destrucción de las Indias*. Alicante: Universidad de Alicante.
Deutsch, Jonathan. 2004. "Eat Me Up": Spoken Voice and Food Voice in an Urban Firehouse. *Food, Culture and Society* 7(1): 27–36.
———. 2005. "Please Pass the Chicken Tits": Rethinking Men and Cooking in an Urban Firehouse. *Food and Foodways* 13(1–2): 91–114.
Harris-Shapiro, Carol. 2006. Bloody Shankbones and Braided Bread: The Food Voice and the Fashioning of American Jewish Identities. *Food and Foodways* 14(2): 67–90.
Hauck-Lawson, Annie S. 1991. Foodways of Three Polish-American Families. Doctoral dissertation. New York: New York University.
———. 1992. Hearing the Food Voice: An Epiphany for a Researcher. *Digest: An Interdisciplinary Study of Food and Foodways* 12(1–2): 6–7.
———. 1998. When Food is the Voice: A Case Study of a Polish-American Woman. *Journal for the Study of Food and Society* 2(1): 21–28.
———. 2004. Introduction: The Food Voice. *Food, Culture and Society* 7(1): 14–15.
hooks, bell. 1989. *Talking Back: Thinking Feminist, Thinking Black*. Boston: South End Press
LFG (Latina Feminist Group). 2001. *Telling to Live: Latina Feminist Testimonios*. Durham, NC: Duke University Press.
Menchú, Rigoberta, and Elisabeth Burgos-Debray. 1984. *I, Rigoberta Menchú: An Indian woman in Guatemala*. London: Verso Press.
Patai, Daphne. 1988. Constructing a Self: A Brazilian Life Story. *Feminist Studies* 14: 143–166.
Perez, Emma. 1999. *The Decolonial Imaginary: Writing Chicanas into History*. Bloomington: Indiana University Press.
Pérez, Ramona Lee. 2004. Kitchen Table Ethnography and Feminist Anthropology. Conference Paper. 14th Annual Joint Conference of the Association for the Study of Food and Society and the Agriculture, Food and Human Values Society: Hyde Park, NY.
———. 2009. Tasting Culture: Food, Family and Flavor in Greater Mexico. Doctoral dissertation. New York: New York University.
Sandoval, Chela. 1991. U.S. Third World Feminism: The Theory and Method of Oppositional Consciousness in the Postmodern World. *Genders* 10(1): 1–24.
Smith, Linda Tuhiwai. 1999. *Decolonizing Methodologies: Research and Indigenous Peoples*. New York: Zed Books.
Spivak, Gayatri Chaktravorty. 1988. Can the Subaltern Speak? In *Marxism and the Interpretation of Culture*, ed. Cary Nelson and Lawrence Grossberg, 271–314. Urbana-Champaign: University of Illinois Press.

CHAPTER 3

Studying Body Image and Food Consumption Practices

Nicole Taylor and Mimi Nichter

Studies of body image have been numerous over the past three decades, with scholars from multiple disciplines investigating the meaning and lived experience of this concept across contexts. Body image needs to be understood as a multidimensional phenomenon that includes perceptual, attitudinal, affective, and cultural components (Streigel-Moore and Franko 2002). A cursory look at the literature reveals multiple ways body image has been defined, including body weight concerns, feelings about one's body shape, body esteem, body schema, weight dissatisfaction, and body image disorder, to name but a few (Cash and Pruzinsky 2002).

Psychologists have developed a range of assessment tools to measure attitudes, perceptions, and behaviors regarding the body and body image (e.g., Cash 2012; Cash and Smolak 2011; Grogan 2008). Cultural anthropologists (as well as feminist theorists) have tended to frame body image as a project of the self situated in a particular cultural (or subcultural) context (e.g., Anderson-Fye 2004, 2010, 2012; Nichter 2000; Nichter and Nichter 1991; Nichter and Vuckovic 1994; Taylor 2011a, 2015; and Trainer 2012). Other researchers, including sociologists, have explored how individuals construct and manage their weight-related identities in everyday social situations (e.g., Sobal and Maurer 1999; Sobal, Hanson, and Frongillo 2009).

Of particular importance has been a consideration of the media environment, specifically advertisements, which are populated with directives of how one should look and what one should consume, including food. One's sense of how their body "fits in" to culturally idealized notions of beauty is central to an understanding of body image. From an early age, girls learn what their bodies should look like and that having a culturally appropriate body shape is linked to femininity. Indeed, body image issues and bodywork are prominent across women's lives and food often becomes a focal point. Dissatisfaction with self at the site of the body ("negative" body image) can result in dieting, watching what one eats, guilt around eating, and engaging in exercise strategies to change one's body shape.

Body image studies have traditionally focused on girls and women. However, as pressures for boys and men to achieve a certain body type have increased in recent years, researchers have begun to explore how males feel about the way they look, how they talk with each other about body image and tease each other about their bodies, and what types of behaviors they engage in to achieve the ideal look (e.g., Gill, Henwood, and McLean 2005; Grogan and Richards 2002; Kehler and Atkinson 2010; Ryan and Morrison 2009; Taylor 2011a, 2011b, 2015). Although studies of male body image have increased over the past decade, it is still a relatively new area of inquiry, and there is a need for ongoing research.

Studies of body image disorders, including anorexia nervosa and bulimia nervosa, are numerous. For example, anthropologist Gremillion (2003) conducted an ethnographic study of an eating disorders clinic that included participant observation in various settings and individual interviews with patients, parents, staff, and clinicians. Other anthropologists have examined the effects of Western media exposure and increasing globalization on body image, dieting practices, and eating disorder prevalence in developing nations (e.g., Anderson-Fye 2004; Becker 2004).

On the opposite end of the spectrum, researchers have examined various aspects of obesity, including social and built environments that contribute to sedentary lifestyles, physical activity levels and food consumption behaviors in various populations, and obesity stigma and its social, economic, and psychological consequences (e.g., Brownell and Horgen 2004; Brownell et al. 2010; Kwan 2009; Puhl and Brownell 2001; Taylor 2011a, 2011b, 2015). In particular, anthropologists have examined different meanings of obesity cross-culturally, often showing that the large body size demonized by Western cultures as a medical problem is acceptable and/or desired in some non-Western societies (Anderson-Fye 2010; Brewis 2011; McClure 2012; Popenoe 2004).

In this chapter we explore methodologies for studying body image and food consumption practices, including participant observation, key informant interviews, semi-structured open-ended interviews, visual aids as prompts for discussion, focus groups, diary data, quantitative surveys, and measurement of body mass. While issues of body image are salient across the lifespan, many of our examples are drawn from studies of adolescents and emerging adults, as much of the research in this area has focused on youth, particularly young women.

Participant Observation

Participant observation is sometimes referred to as the hallmark of ethnographic research (de Munck 1998; Spradley 1980). A form of *experience near* research, it involves observations of naturally occurring events by a social scientist who is not merely watching, but is interacting with those being studied. This requires some degree of cultural competence learned over time and the establishment of an identity that is acceptable to others. Ethnographers are their own research instruments and can view interactions through multiple theoretical lenses.

One of the rationales for observing behavior rather than simply asking people what they do is that what people say they do and what they actually do often differs. For example, Taylor (2011a, 2015) found that teens tended to "play it cool" when being teased about their bodies by peers, often laughing along with everyone else. During individual interviews, however, some teens admitted that being teased about the way they look and their body size made them feel bad about themselves. Participant observation coupled with interviews allows the researcher to gain insight into how a particular behavior is actually practiced, with or toward whom, and what the ramifications are.

Participant observation is a useful method for learning about the ways in which discourse and social networks affect food consumption behaviors and ideas about body image. Whereas interviews yield meta-discursive data about body image and food discourse, observation allows the researcher to observe firsthand how participants actually change their food consumption practices in relation to issues of body image (sharing food with friends, abstaining from eating, etc.). This is important because participants may not be willing to articulate these practices in an interview.

Participant observation also affords the researcher an opportunity to observe performative aspects of talk about the body as well as eating practices that may reveal such things as gender differences in food consumption. For example, it was through participant observation that Nichter (2000) and Taylor (2011b, 2015) learned how adolescent girls discursively displayed personal responsibility for eating fattening foods and preempted possible verbal censure from others by stating, "I'm so fat" or "I shouldn't be eating this" before consuming the food item in question.

Participant observation provides an important means of building rapport with potential participants, which can aid in recruitment and gathering meaningful information through interviews and focus groups. Particularly when researching a sensitive topic such as body image, the importance of rapport should not be underestimated. It takes time for people to feel comfortable around a stranger who wants to learn about their lives and ask questions about how they feel about their body. Importantly, conducting ethnographic research on obesity and body image in a school setting necessitates building rapport with students. In order to engender rapport, Taylor (2015) built relationships with students by participating alongside them in physical education classes, eating lunch with them, and hanging out on campus all day, every day. Eventually students began to trust her, at which point she was able to collect sensitive and personal data on body image.

Participant observation can be an important first step to gaining the degree of cultural sensitivity necessary for developing or refining other research instruments. For example, Nichter (2000) observed that high school girls engaged in "fat talk," a popular discourse where a girl exclaimed, "I'm so fat" and her friends replied, "No, you're not." This observation led to the development of interview and focus group questions among her research group and the development of measures and experimental studies among social and clinical psychologists (Arroyo and Harwood 2012; Clarke, Murnen, and Smolak 2010; Corning and Gondoli 2012; Salk and Engeln-Maddox 2011; Tucker et al. 2007)

Detailed note-taking to record your observations, as well as your own thoughts and feelings about what you have observed, is very important. Sometimes the patterns that emerge through daily note-taking would otherwise have gone unnoticed. For this reason, you will want to review your field notes on a regular basis to determine whether there are emergent patterns worth further exploration.

Key Informant Interviews

Key informants can be thought of as community advisers who help the researcher better understand what is occurring in a particular local setting. A relationship with a key informant develops over time, usually over the course of several interviews. Key informants are provided with a deeper sense of the study's purpose than participants are and may be able to introduce the researcher to other individuals in the community who may want to participate in the study.

Typically, initial interviews are loosely structured and require the development of trust and rapport with the key informant, who acts like a guide to his or her lifeworld. Ideally, the researcher selects three to four individuals who are cultural experts, meaning they are insightful and articulate about their community. These individuals serve several roles in the research process, helping to clarify and elaborate on what a researcher has seen and heard, assist in the development of appropriate questions, and suggest other areas to explore. Dressler, Santos, and Balieiro (1996), for example, used key informant interviews to test a set of cultural domains, including lifestyle, social support, family life, national identity, and food, as part of an effort to develop a model of how culture shapes the body in Brazil.

Semi-structured Open-Ended Interviews

Open-ended interviews are typically conducted face-to-face, allowing the researcher to establish rapport with a participant during the interview. This can be particularly important when discussing sensitive topics like body image. The topics these interviews focus on are first explored with key informants to determine their appropriateness, and interview guides are pretested to check for clarity, comprehensibility, and the appropriate ordering of questions. The interviews can provide in-depth information about how participants perceive their ideal body image, how they feel about their body, what sorts of body-related practices they engage in or want to engage in to look better, and what barriers they perceive to attaining their body ideals, including an inability to change how they eat.

Individual interviews can complement other forms of data collection, such as surveys, focus groups, and participant observation. Ethnographic findings can contribute to improving the validity of a survey instrument or help in the identification of new survey questions. For example, Nichter (2000) learned through interviews that many teenaged girls were not so much dieting as "watching what they ate." Drawing on this finding, Nichter's research team developed several survey questions to allow for quantification of this concept in a larger sample. Results showed that many girls were engaged in the healthy behavior of "watching," defined as avoiding "junk food" and eating more fruits and vegetables.

Interviews are also a good forum for further exploration of patterned behaviors or interactions observed during the course of participant observation. For example, Taylor (2011b, 2015) observed that groups of two or three girls would share one food item, such as a piece of pizza or a serving of French fries, and learned that girls shared junk food in order to limit the amount they consumed because they were concerned about weight gain. When this prompted her to ask what other types of behaviors girls engage in to limit the amount of calories consumed, the responses revealed that girls also refrained from bringing lunch money to school to avoid being able to purchase junk food. This led on to an exploration of gender differences in food consumption ("Do guys share food?") and concerns with junk food consumption ("Are guys concerned with eating too much junk food at school?").

Whenever possible, interviews should be recorded (if the participant agrees to this and institutional review board approval has been obtained) and later transcribed. Particularly when interviewing about a sensitive topic like body image, it is important to give participants the chance to have the digital recorder turned off at certain points, if they so desire. Targeted notes taken either during or immediately after each interview that include important highlights and commentary on the quality of the interview can serve as a useful reference as well. Typically, more sensitive questions are asked after rapport has been developed with a participant. To this end, it may be desirable to have more than one interview as part of your research design.

Visual Aids as Prompts for Discussion

Photographs or magazine advertisements can be used during individual and group interviews to prompt discussion (Collier 1967; Laver 1994). Participants can be shown numerous photos of individuals as a springboard for a discussion of preferred body types and ideas about personhood in relation to body size. For example, Daniels (2009) showed media-generated photos of female athletes and models to adolescent girls and college women and asked each participant to record her responses in various ways, including (1) writing a paragraph describing the woman in the photograph and how the photograph made the respondent feel about her own body; (2) giving the photo a title that captured the theme of the photograph; and (3) making up twenty statements about herself after viewing the photographs. Daniels used these methods to examine how the images impacted girls' and women's tendency to objectify themselves.

Another visual approach that can be used in individual interviews is to present a participant with line drawings of body silhouettes and to ask that person to select one that most resembles her or his current size, as well as one representing the respondent's preferred body shape. This can be followed up with questions about why these choices were made. For more information on issues to think through when using body silhouettes as a method, see Gardner, Friedman, and Jackson (1998).

Also, given the ubiquity of cell phones, participants could be asked to take pictures of their food consumption practices (both alone and with friends) to be shared in later interviews or discussion groups. This method could serve as an alternative or complement to food diary data.

Focus Groups

Focus group interviews are a useful way to further explore themes that emerge from individual interviews and participant observation. Focus groups allow researchers to facilitate an exchange of opinions in a carefully selected subject area, which may include such topics as a response to advertisements, alternative ideas for an "eat healthy" or healthy body image program, or even the meaning and wording of a body image instrument being pretested.

There is no exact formula for choosing focus group participants, as the right mix of people will depend on your research design and your research community. At the same time, the size and composition of a focus group are key to its success. Too few participants may not generate sufficient discussion, whereas too many participants can result in chaotic simultaneous talking. A group that is too large may also make some participants feel shy and self-conscious about talking candidly. A focus group of five to eight participants is typically a good size.

It is also important to choose participants who know and trust each other and you, especially when exploring a sensitive topic like body image. In research among adolescent girls, Nichter and colleagues learned that putting together a group of girls to talk about their bodies required knowing who would talk freely with others. Initial experiences in focus groups were problematic as some girls did not want to share intimate details in the presence of others who were not their friends. For this reason, it may be best to hold focus group interviews at a later stage in the research project when you have already built rapport with participants and are able to choose individuals to participate in groups that will generate good discussion.

There are several methods for choosing focus group participants. In purposive sampling, the most common method, researcher chooses participants based on their potential contributions. It is important to choose a sample of participants that will reflect your overall research community in terms of gender, ethnicity, socioeconomic status, and other relevant variables. If your study design includes examining the relationship between ethnic differences and body image, then you may want to group participants according to self-identified ethnic categories so that participants will feel more comfortable speaking openly about their beliefs, experiences, and practices.

For example, in interviews with African-American high school students, Parker and colleagues (1995) found that these girls expressed greater acceptance of their bodies at heavier weights than did their white peers. In selecting focus group participants it was important to have only African-American girls, as these girls displayed a high level of bicultural competency. The researchers sensed that in a mixed ethnic focus group, their cultural appreciation of women who had a heavier ("fuller") body shape might not have been openly discussed. What emerged from these focus groups was the cultural importance of "looking good," a concept that entailed "makin' what you got work for you" and "styling," which was considered far more important than one's body weight.

Similarly, Rubin, Fitts, and Becker (2003) conducted focus groups with Latina and African-American women to examine relationships among ethnicity, body image ideals, and self-representation. For the interviews, participants were grouped according to self-identified ethnicity, which meant having separate Latina and African-American focus groups. The researchers found that both African-American and Latina participants embraced a set of body ethics related to care and presentation of the body rather than adhering to a specific, narrowly defined ideal body size and type.

The composition of the focus group will greatly impact the data you are able to collect. For example, a group of six women who do not know each other well may be more likely to speak about body image abstractly than to share personal experiences or feelings. It may be difficult to elicit rich data on body image from an all-male focus group, regardless of their relationship with one another, because men may be more reluctant to talk about sensitive issues among their male peers. There are, however, ways to break the ice and encourage participants to speak more openly about this topic.

Grogan and Richards (2002) recruited volunteers for all-male focus groups on body image with participants ranging in age from eight to twenty-five. Participants were grouped according to age, and the researchers encouraged them to open up by first engaging them in informal chat. Once participants seemed relaxed and comfortable with each other, the researchers turned on the audio recorder and began asking questions. The authors reported that focus groups lasted about thirty minutes and ended when the conversation naturally "dried up."

For her research project on body image and obesity among youth, Taylor (2015) identified participants who were particularly insightful during individual interviews and who expressed interest in participating in a focus group. She asked these individuals to recruit three or four close friends for the group. Teen boys' choice of participants tended to result in mixed gender focus groups, whereas teen girls' choices tended to result in all-girl focus groups. The all-girl focus groups generated more focused and in-depth data about body image than the mixed gender focus groups. With mixed gender focus groups, however, Taylor got to see examples of how friends teased each other about the way their bodies look, a phenomenon she had learned about in individual interviews but had rarely observed firsthand.

A focus group has to be run by a skilled moderator who can lead a group of participants to discuss a particular topic—even as they drift into side conversations—and draw out the opinions of all members of the group, avoiding domination by a vocal few. It is important to audio record and possibly even videotape focus group discussions, depending on the type of analysis you will do. Video recording is useful for linguistic anthropologists who want to observe nonverbal communication in conjunction with verbal interaction. Either way, having an audio and/or video recording of focus group interviews will allow you to transcribe them at a later date.

Diaries

As an alternative to individual or focus group interviews, you can ask participants to write down their thoughts, feelings, and experiences that relate to body image. Greenhalgh (2012) found this to be an effective method for eliciting deeply personal stories about body image from undergraduate students. As Greenhalgh notes (ibid., p. 475), it can be easier for people to write about topics that evoke strong emotion rather than discuss them.

The benefit of this method compared to others is that the researcher is not required to build such a strong foundation of trust and rapport in order to gather data. Greenhalgh was able to quickly and easily gather the type of information that it would take months to obtain via interviews. The downside to this method as a one-time data collection tool is that the researcher cannot ask follow-up questions or delve further into interesting topics that emerge through interviews or focus groups. Diaries could be particularly effective when used in conjunction with interviews and/or focus groups where the researcher could further probe ideas and themes that emerge from the diaries.

Quantitative Surveys

Surveys allow researchers to gather larger data sets that are generalizable to the broader community. Surveys can provide general information about preferred body types, dieting practices, and levels of body dis/satisfaction, which can be disaggregated according to various demographic markers, including gender, ethnicity, and age. Anthropologists sometimes use surveys in conjunction with interviews, focus groups, and participant observation to situate rich ethnographic accounts from a small sample within a larger social context. For example, Anderson-Fye (2004) utilized participant observation and individual interviews in conjunction with a number of questionnaires, including the Eating Attitudes Test, Body Shape Preferences, and a demographic information survey to examine beauty ideals in Belize.

Measuring Body Mass

Calculating body mass index (BMI) among participants using a simple equation that takes height, weight, and gender into account is another method for gathering data on body image. As this method has been somewhat controversial among researchers, it is important to think about why you want to collect this information and how you will use it before incorporating it into your research design. In other words, is measuring body fat and/or classifying your participants as "underweight," "normal weight," "overweight," or "obese" absolutely necessary to answer your research questions? How will your participants feel about your taking their measurements?

In the United States, BMI is used by medical professionals and insurance companies as an indicator of individual health risks. Brewis (2011) argues that BMI is an imprecise, one-size-fits-all method that cannot accurately measure body fat cross-culturally in populations that have different average body shapes and overall age structures. Brewis suggests that other measures, such as fat distribution and waist-to-height ratio, may be better indicators of health risks than overall fat levels. Measuring BMI can have important ethical implications for research and draw greater attention to overweight and obese individuals, thereby perpetuating their stigmatized status in the community.

In Taylor's (2011a, 2015) research on body image and obesity among youth, some participants self-reported height and weight information during interviews; however, this information was neither systematically collected nor solicited. For participants who volunteered height and weight information, Taylor calculated

BMI and body size classifications using the Centers for Disease Control and Prevention's online BMI calculator for children and teens. These data provided insight into participants' self-perceptions of body size within the context of weight-based teasing. For example, Taylor found that many female participants whose peers had criticized them for displaying too much body fat self-reported height and weight within the normal BMI range. This is one example of how BMI can be used in body image research.

Conclusion

Anthropological methods, which are designed to gather rich, in-depth data from within particular communities and cultural contexts, have provided valuable insights into the study of body image. Anthropologists are uniquely positioned to gather meaningful, nuanced data on body image that can unpack and explain information collected via large-scale surveys. To date, the vast majority of body image studies have been quantitative in nature. Body size is becoming increasingly politicized and medicalized due to panic over obesity in the United States and heightened attention to body size and body weight in low- and middle-income countries. As such, continued anthropological research on this topic is critical.

Mimi Nichter is Professor in the School of Anthropology at the University of Arizona, where she holds joint appointments in the Norton School of Family and Consumer Sciences and the College of Public Health. She is the author of *Fat Talk: What Girls and Their Parents Say About Dieting* and *Lighting Up: The Rise of Social Smoking on College Campuses.*

Nicole Taylor is Associate Professor in the Department of Anthropology at Texas State University. She is the author of *Schooled on Fat: What Teens Tell Us About Gender, Body Image, and Obesity.*

References Cited

Anderson-Fye, E. 2004. A "Coca-Cola" Shape: Cultural Change, Body Image, and Eating Disorders in San Andrés, Belize. *Culture, Medicine, and Psychiatry* 28: 561–595.

———. 2010. Body Images in Non-Western Cultures. In *Body Image: A Handbook of Theory, Research, and Clinical Practice,* ed. T. Cash and L. Smolak, 244–252. New York: Guilford Press.

———. 2012. Anthropological Approaches to the Study of Body Image and Human Appearance. In *Encyclopedia of Body Image and Human Appearance,* ed. T. Cash et al., 15–22. New York: Elsevier Press.

Arroyo, A., and J. Harwood. 2012. Exploring the Causes and Consequences of Engaging in Fat Talk. *Journal of Applied Communication Research:* 40(2): 167–187.

Becker, A. 2004. Television, Disordered Eating, and Young Women in Fiji: Negotiating Body Image and Identity During Rapid Social Change. *Culture, Medicine, and Psychiatry* 28: 533–559.

Brewis, A. A. 2011. *Obesity: Cultural and Biocultural Perspectives*. New Brunswick, NJ: Rutgers University Press.

Brownell, K. D., and K. B. Horgen. 2004. *Food Fight: The Inside Story of the Food Industry, America's Obesity Crisis, and What We Can Do about It*. New York: McGraw-Hill.

Brownell, K. D., R. Kersh, D. S. Ludwig, R. C. Post, R. M. Puhl, M. B. Schwartz, and W. C. Willett. 2010. Personal Responsibility and Obesity: A Constructivist Approach to a Controversial Issue. *Health Affairs* 29(3): 379–387.

Cash, T. F., ed. 2012. *Encyclopedia of Body Image and Human Appearance*. Amsterdam: Academic Press.

Cash, T. F., and T. Pruzinsky, eds. 2002. *Body Image: A Handbook of Theory, Research and Clinical Practice*. New York: The Guilford Press.

Cash, T. F., and L. Smolak, eds. 2011. *Body Image: A Handbook of Science, Practice, and Prevention*, 2nd ed. New York: The Guilford Press.

Clarke, P. M., S. K. Murnen, and L. Smolak. 2010. Development and Psychometric Evaluation of a Quantitative Measure of "Fat Talk." *Body Image: An International Journal of Research* 7: 1–7.

Collier, J. 1967. *Visual Anthropology: Photography as a Research Method*. New York: Holt, Rinehart and Winston.

Corning, A. F., and D. M. Gondoli. 2012. Who Is Most Likely to Fat Talk? A Social Comparison Perspective. *Body Image: An International Journal of Research* 9: 528–531.

Daniels, E. 2009. Sex Objects, Athletes, and Sexy Athletes: How Media Representations of Women Athletes Can Impact Adolescent Girls and College Women. *Journal of Adolescent Research* 24(4): 399–422.

De Munck, V. C. 1998. Participant Observation: A Thick Explanation of Conflict in a Sri Lankan Village. In *Using Methods in the Field: A Practical Introduction and Casebook*, ed. V. C. De Munck and E. J. Sobo, 37–52. Walnut Creek, CA: Altamira Press.

Dressler, William W., J. Santos, and M. Balieiro. 1996. Studying Diversity and Sharing in Culture: An Example of Lifestyle in Brazil. *Journal of Anthropological Research* 52: 331–353.

Gardner, R., B. Friedman, and N. Jackson. 1998. Methodological Concerns When Using Silhouettes to Measure Body Image. *Perceptual and Motor Skills* 86: 387–395.

Gill, R., K. Henwood, and C. McLean. 2005. Body Projects and the Regulation of Normative Masculinity. *Body and Society* 11(1): 37–62.

Greenhalgh, S. 2012. Weighty Subjects: The Biopolitics of the U.S. War on Fat. *American Ethnologist* 39(3): 471–487.

Gremillion, H. 2003. *Feeding Anorexia: Gender and Power at a Treatment Center*. Durham, NC: Duke University Press.

Grogan, S. 2008. *Body Image: Understanding Body Dissatisfaction in Men, Women, and Children*. New York: Routledge.

Grogan, S., and H. Richards. 2002. Body Image: Focus Groups with Boys and Men. *Men and Masculinities* 4(3): 219–232.

Kehler, M., and M. Atkinson, eds. 2010. *Boys' Bodies: Speaking the Unspoken*. New York: Peter Lang.

Kwan, S. 2009. Individual versus Corporate Responsibility: Market Choice, the Food Industry, and the Pervasiveness of Moral Models of Fatness. *Food, Culture, and Society* 12(4): 478–495.

Laver, S. M. L. 1994. Picture Codes as Discussion Starters in AIDS Education. *World Health Forum* 15: 39–41.
McClure, S. 2012. Body Image Among African-Americans. In *Encyclopedia of Body Image and Human Appearance,* ed. T. Cash et al., 89–94. New York: Elsevier.
Nichter, M. 2000. *Fat Talk: What Girls and Their Parents Say About Dieting.* Cambridge and London: Harvard University Press.
Nichter, M., and M. Nichter. 1991. Hype and Weight. *Medical Anthropology* 13(3): 249–284.
Nichter, M., and N. Vuckovic. 1994. Fat Talk: Body Image among Adolescent Girls. In *Many Mirrors: Body Image and Social Relations,* ed. N. Sault, 109–131. New Brunswick, NJ: Rutgers University Press.
Parker, S., Mimi Nichter, Mark Nichter, N. Vuckovic, C. Sims, and C. Ritenbaugh. 1995. Body Image and Weight Concerns among African-Americans and White Adolescent Females: Differences Which Make a Difference. *Human Organization* 54(2): 103–114.
Popenoe, R. 2004. *Feeding Desire: Fatness, Beauty, and Sexuality among a Saharan People.* London: Routledge.
Puhl, R., and K. Brownell. 2001. Bias, Discrimination, and Obesity. *Obesity Research* 9(12): 788–805.
Rubin, L., M. Fitts, and A. E. Becker. 2003. "Whatever Feels Good in My Soul": Body Ethics and Aesthetics among African-American and Latina Women. *Culture, Medicine and Psychiatry* 27(1): 49–75.
Ryan, T. A., and T. Morrison. 2009. Factors Perceived to Influence Young Irish Men's Body Image Investment: A Qualitative Investigation. *International Journal of Men's Health* 8(3): 213–234.
Salk, R., and R. Engeln-Maddox. 2011. "If You're Fat then I'm Humongous!" Frequency, Content, and Impact of Fat Talk among College Women. *Psychology of Women Quarterly* 35(1): 18–28.
Sobal, J., K. Hanson, and E. A. Frongillo. 2009. Gender, Ethnicity, Marital Status, and Body Weight in the U.S. *Obesity* 17: 2223–2231.
Sobal, J., and D. Maurer, eds. 1999. *Weighty Issues: Fatness and Thinness as Social Problems.* Piscataway, NJ: Aldine Transaction.
Spradley, J. 1980. *Participant Observation.* New York: Holt, Rinehart and Winston.
Streigel-Moore, R. H. and D. Franko. 2002. Body Image Issues among Girls and Women. In *Body Image: A Handbook of Theory, Research and Clinical Practice,* ed. Cash and Pruzinsky, 183–191. New York: The Guilford Press.
Taylor, N. 2011a. "Guys, She's Humongous!": Gender and Weight-Based Teasing in Adolescence. *Journal of Adolescent Research* 26(2): 178–199.
Taylor, N. 2011b. Negotiating Popular Obesity Discourses in Adolescence: School Food, Personal Responsibility, and Gendered Food Consumption Behaviors. *Food, Culture and Society* 14(4): 587–606.
Taylor, N. 2015. *Schooled on Fat: What Teens Tell Us About Gender, Body Image, and Obesity.* New York: Routledge (Innovative Ethnographies).
Trainer, S. 2012. Negotiating Weight and Body Image in the UAE: Strategies among Young Emirati Women. *American Journal of Human Biology* 24(3): 314–324.
Tucker, K. L., D. M. Martz, L. A. Curtin, D. G. Bazzini. 2007. Examining "Fat Talk" Experimentally in a Female Dyad: How Are Women Influenced by Another Woman's Body Presentation Style? *Body Image* 4: 157–164.

CHAPTER 4

Visual Anthropology Methods

Helen Vallianatos

Introduction

Visual anthropology can be defined as the study of visual culture, including art and material culture as well as kinesics and proxemics, and the use of visual data to answer anthropological questions. Fadwa El Guindi (2004: 17) emphasizes that visual anthropology is "not confined to the visible or the material. Cultural and social relations can be visually manifested, and invisible domains, including underlying rules and hidden premises, are part of the visual anthropology project." Underlying much of visual anthropology research is the concept that the visual is socioculturally constructed (see, e.g., Edwards and Bhaumik 2008), and what is an "image" is culturally mediated (Belting 2011). Visual anthropology methods are well suited to conducting collaborative, participatory research; see the photo-video voice chapter in Volume Three of this set for an example.

Visual anthropology is most commonly associated with ethnographic film and photography. Although use of photography and film was arguably an important tool from the early years of the discipline, the use of visual methods to investigate anthropological concepts did not flourish until the post–World War II period. Marcus Banks and Jay Ruby (2011) divided this history into three phases: (1) the mid-nineteenth to mid-twentieth century, when photographs and film were used to support theoretical schemas or to document the fieldwork context (e.g., Margaret Mead and Gregory Bateson's photographic and film record, exemplified in Bateson and Mead 1942); (2) the 1960s to 1980s, when ethnographic film production proliferated and reassessment of the photographic archive and questions of representation arose (e.g. Jacknis 1988); (3) the 1990s to the present, when interdisciplinary collaboration and influence flourished, new media forms (digital) were utilized, and efforts to incorporate and include all the senses (not just visual elements) began (e.g., Milne, Mitchell, and De Lange 2012; Pink 2007, 2009). Coinciding with these phases were methodological shifts from producing visual materials to study people and societies, to examining pre-existing visual materials in order to learn about sociocultural issues and individual experiences, to collaborating with others in the creation of visual representations (Banks 1995).

This chapter begins with a discussion of film and photography, the two main types of visual data. This is followed by brief discussions of other kinds of visual recordings and productions. An exploration of possible future directions in visual methods provides readers with ideas to consider as new projects are developed. Finally, this chapter considers issues in knowledge dissemination through visual means.

Film

Ethnographic film is arguably the dominant form of study for visual anthropologists. This is evident in the seminal text *Principles of Visual Anthropology*, edited by Paul Hockings (2003), in which the majority of chapters focus on the use and analysis of film. Examples of such films about food include films that focus on the food acquisition process, such as Karl Heider's (1974) *Dani Sweet Potatoes*, John and Naomi Bishop's (1997) *Himalayan Herders* and Lina Fruzzetti and colleagues' (1995) *Seed and Earth*. Many others critique the contemporary industrial food system (e.g., *Food, Inc., Our Daily Bread*). Whereas some scholars equate ethnographic film and documentary film, others demarcate differences between them. El Guindi (2004: 79–84) summarizes this divergence by identifying two genealogies in visual anthropology: one pathway includes cinematic and documentary films, such as John Marshall's (1957) *The Hunters*; the other includes scientific and ethnographic films exemplified by Timothy Asch and Napolean Chagnon's (1970) *The Feast*. More examples can be found at the websites Culture Unplugged (www.cultureunplugged.com/documentaries/watch-online/filmedia/index.php), Ethnographic Video Online (search.alexanderstreet.com/anth), and Ethnographic Video for Instruction and Analysis (www.eviada.org/).

Another element of film and food studies is the examination of the role of food in movies, television, and other media. Such work includes examination of the visible and invisible role of food to understand how, through food, cultures are represented and social values portrayed. In film, food very often serves as a prop, where the food item or meal is hidden or the actors are never actually seen eating it. Food is frequently used as a transition, exemplified by a shot of the actor beginning and then ending a meal, and as a tool to symbolically illustrate an element of the story or a character trait. Finally, food stars in its own right in food genre films, in which food items and meals are aesthetic centerpieces in the film, and people are actually shown eating (Zimmerman and Weiss 2005; see also Bower 2004; Keller 2006). Examples of food genre films include *Eat, Drink, Man, Woman, Babette's Feast,* and *Chocolat*. Examining intersections of class, gender, ethnicity, and the role of food in films from different cultures provides insight into social values and understandings of self/other.

Photography

A seminal work in the use of photographs in visual anthropology is *Visual Anthropology: Photography as a Research Method* (Collier and Collier 1986). In a later work, John Collier (2003) identified archaeological use of photography as illustrative of the ways photographs can be used to construct scientific knowledge (through measuring, counting, and comparing). He described how photographs are essential in documenting the excavation, capturing the interrelationships amongst objects as they emerge from the soil. Collier equates this with photographic records of places as a way of mapping relationships between buildings, fields, rivers, and so on. Inventorying through photography is a way to capture variation in type or condition of the object of interest (e.g., homes) and collect useful data (social status, economic condition, etc.) for later analysis. Finally, Collier also discussed the use of photographs of people, individually and in groups, in studies of proxemics and kinesics (especially when a series of images is captured). As with film, issues of authorship, representation, choice of content (i.e., what is included in the image and what is silenced), and interpretation have been debated by scholars.

Food scholars have used photographs to elicit information during interviews. A number of different styles and terminologies exist, such as photo elicitation (Clark-Ibáñez 2004; Harper 2002), auto-driving (Clark 1999), visual narrative inquiry (Bach 2007), photo novella, and photovoice (Wang and Burris 1994, 1997). The reader is referred to the chapter on photo-video voice in Volume Three, for further information on this methodology.

One line of anthropological research with photographs concerns the examination of photographs taken in the past as a means to better understand and possibly reframe past peoples and cultures. Such efforts are exemplified by Elizabeth Edwards' (1992) edited volume examining issues of representation and construction of ethnographic knowledge using photographs taken in the late nineteenth and early twentieth centuries. Other work uses postcards consisting of "authentic," "ethnographic" images of people, places, and things to question the construction of authenticity, and constructions of self/other (e.g., Albers and James 1990; Burns 2004; Edwards 1996; Poole 2005). Related work in food studies examines the images used in cookbooks, marketing (e.g., posters, advertisements), and media (e.g., television) to examine social values in both past and contemporary cultures (e.g., de Solier 2005; Henderson and Kelly 2005; Holden 2005; Pollay 1985; Wright 2013).

Drawing

A plethora of studies have used mapping and GIS technologies to document food access and distribution across space (e.g., Hemphill et al. 2008; Raja, Ma, and Yadav 2008; Schafft, Jensen, and Hinrichs 2009). Some scholars use hand-drawn diagrams and maps as a way to engage with participants during the research process. An excellent example of this is the work of Lidia Marte (2007), who used immigrant participants' mappings of food to trace their spatial and temporal connections. She proposed the concept of "foodmaps" as a specific tool to use in research with immigrants, where boundaries are created and crossed through food practices. This kind of mapping is aimed at charting relationships that are both immediate and stretched across space and time. They are "perceptual models of how people experience the boundaries of local home through food connections…that pays attention to the way people relate to food in the interaction of senses, emotions, and environments" (ibid.: 262–263).

Drawing has also been used in research with children, as a means of grasping children's experiences and ideas. This method may offer a way for children to articulate ideas that are otherwise difficult to express. For example, Ephrat Huss, Roni Kaufman, and Avril Siboni (2013), who used drawing to explore children's psychological and phenomenological experiences of food insecurity, suggest that this method is empowering for child participants, giving them an opportunity to voice their ideas and be heard.

Drawing may be conceived as part of a larger approach to research known as arts-based methodology (Knowles and Cole 2008; Leavy 2009). Participants may use drawing or other kinds of art to express their thoughts, feelings, and experiences. Ephrat Huss (2008) has explicitly connected drawing with arts-based research in his work with Bedouin women. There is close overlap here with arts-based therapy; a number of studies working on health and recovery have found art therapy to be a useful tool (e.g., Coad 2007; Stuckey and Nobel 2010). An interesting resource illustrating the intersections of art and anthropological research is the website Artpologist; for a food example see the project "The Borrowed Kazan" (artpologist.com/projects/borrowed-kazan).

On a different tangent, building on ideas of art as a technical practice—as a system of actions embedded in a dynamic social matrix or a network of intentionalities (Gell 1996, 1998)—Joy Adapon (2008) presents cooking as a creative process that requires technical expertise. She equates the cook with an artist who creatively builds upon a culinary repertoire based on traditional recipes but modified according to the dictates of personal taste, pragmatics (i.e., availability of particular food items), and consideration of the intended recipient(s). Central to Adapon's application of Gell's theory of art is that both artists and art have agency in the production of social relations. The cook and artist use their culinary crafts to structure spatiotemporal relations within families and communities. Food can be viewed as an art object that has social agency in turn, affecting both producers and consumers.

Digital/Multimedia

The prevalence of digital media in everyday life makes them a fruitful area for research and exploration in food studies. Furthermore, this format provides a platform for social justice and advocacy work that reaches beyond local places and interactions, though of course issues of cost and training in these technologies shape access and opportunities for interactive engagement. Peter Biella (2009) presents a basic introduction to software that is comparatively readily accessible, and evaluates the software in terms of characteristics that would affect applications in research and in collaboration with stakeholders. Digital storytelling is a method that allows for interactive collaboration. Defined as use of digital tools to share narratives, it has been used in research across disciplines (e.g., Alexandra 2008; Gubrium and Difulvio 2011). Further information on this methodology can be found in the digital storytelling chapter in Volume Three.

New Directions

Future methodological innovations center on incorporating new and emerging technologies into the research process, and on expanding visual ethnographic approaches to explicitly incorporate other senses. For example, Gunnar Iversen and Jan Simonsen (2010) point out that although sound is an important component of ethnographic film, there has been little work on aural analysis and issues in aural representations. This links to other scholars' calls for a sensory ethnography that explicitly moves analysis of the visual materials beyond the focus on sight and seeing (e.g. Pink 2006, 2009). The sensory, embodied nature of knowledge can be developed by utilizing digital media that allow for development of interactive research and dissemination (e.g. Wright 2008).

Food studies is ripe for applying academic interests in sensory scholarship. Both Paul Stoller's (1989) book on how the taste of food illustrates social relations and Nadia Seremetakis' (1994) text on food and memory are founding works in sensory ethnographic research. Key here is that the researcher is attuned not only to the sensory knowledge that participants share, but also to their own embodied experiences (see Stoller 1997). Sarah Pink (2004) used video—not for dissemination, but as a data collection tool while conducting interviews with participants in their homes. In the process of recording and walking through the homes, the sensory aspects of what makes a house a home came to the fore.

Thus, audiovisual or other technological tools may be useful at different stages of the research process, and care must be taken to choose tools that are ethically and culturally appropriate (e.g., Rowe 2011; Wiles, Clark, and Prosser 2011). An array of affordable, easy-to-use technological options is currently available. For example, photovoice projects that may have used disposable cameras in the past may instead use cheap digital cameras, or participants who can use their own camera phones may do so. One place to acquire up-to-date information on camera and software tools is Digital Photography Review (www.dpreview.com). Commonly used, accessible software to work with still images includes Adobe Photoshop or Apple Aperture; for video editing, iMovie, Windows MovieMaker, and WeVideo (which can be saved on one's Google drive, and thus particularly useful for collaborative projects) are available.

This overview highlights the diversity of ways the visual can be constructed and used in research projects. Regardless of tools or aspects of the visual that is focused on, shared steps ought to be tracked when designing a project (see Table 1). Ethical considerations are critical. For example, who is the author of the images, and has the researcher obtained the author's permission to use these images in research dissemination? Are there copyright issues? Who is captured in the images, and have these subjects given permission for their inclusion? Not only must researchers be aware of the legal and ethical regulations of their home institutions

Table 4.1. Checklist of issues to consider when designing and conducting a visual anthropology project.

Research Question	Is community consultation necessary or preferable during development of research objectives?
Technology Tools	What tools would be most effective in answering the research question? Note other concerns that may impact tool choice— cost, accessibility, etc. If conducting participatory research, discuss with community partners.
Research Ethics	University ethics board + any country or organizational permissions
Data Collection	Regular check-ins with participants are required if they are the ones collecting images.
Data Analysis	For participatory research, share preliminary findings and elicit feedback from participants on emergent themes.
Dissemination	For participatory research, collaborative community venues, both virtual and emplaced, ought to be part of the dissemination strategy. For all research, both academic and non-academic avenues for sharing findings ought to be pursued, so as to reach diverse audiences (including policymakers).

and countries, but they must also consider the cultural appropriateness and ethics of conducting this kind of research in a foreign place. In some countries, visual images captured in public places (e.g., a park) are legally allowable but may not be appropriate. Protection of the participants' anonymity must also be considered (e.g., blurring faces, altering voices and names). Thus, before beginning the study, researchers must not only obtain ethics approval, but also learn the local mores surrounding the appropriateness of capturing and sharing visual data.

As in any research project, analysis of the data is dependent on the research question and theoretical standpoint. Analysis of images will depend on whether the images are viewed as records of reality or constructs of a reality, reflecting the values, ideologies, or beliefs of whoever created the image (or both). The unit of analysis must also be defined—a single image or a collection of images (note that film is a collection of images). A decision must be made on whether the focus of analysis is the content of the image or its context, revealed through accompanying interviews or other sources. Finally, the researcher needs to determine whether it is the image producer's or the audience's (viewer's) perspectives that are analyzed. An excellent source with examples of different kinds of analysis and projects is *The Handbook of Visual Analysis* (van Leeuwen and Jewitt 2001).

Disseminating Knowledge

Another key aspect to the study and use of visual materials is sharing knowledge with various audiences, including participants and their communities, the larger public, policy makers, media, and so on. All the visual forms included here—film, photography, digital—can be utilized in the knowledge translation process. In fact, it can be argued that visual information is at times far more evocative than text in sharing findings and agitating for change. An excellent source presenting the varied ways anthropologists work with visual materials is Mary Strong and Laena Wilder's (2009) text.

Computer software programs have both been vilified and extolled as tools for knowledge translation. PowerPoint slide presentations, though widely used in a variety of settings, have been criticized for their format of minimal information typically displayed using bullet points, a presentation style that fails to capture the complex interactions between the various factors that have led to those summary points (Tufte 2003). Meanwhile, other visual scholars call for a strategic use of such software to creatively disseminate findings to a wide audience. Fadwa El Guindi (2004: 49–58) provides a detailed explanation of the process and method of developing a PowerPoint presentation for public consumption. More recently, some scholars have utilized other software, such as Prezi, to illustrate the interconnectedness of concepts better than does the linear presentation typically offered by PowerPoint.

Conclusion

Simply put, visual anthropology "is the exploration of the visual in the process of cultural and social reproduction" (Morphy and Banks 1997: 17). Key academic journals holding further examples of research studies and analysis include *Visual Anthropology, Visual Anthropology Review, Visual Ethnography, AnthroVision,* and *Visual Studies,* as well as visual journals in other disciplinary fields. An excellent source for further information on visual research methods is the *Handbook of Visual Research Methods* (Margolis and Pauwels 2011). A variety of visual methods and forms of dissemination are available to researchers to creatively engage with and share findings with academic and non-academic audiences. Visual media may be an ideal means to perform an engaged, public anthropology that is relevant for contemporary audiences.

Helen Vallianatos is Associate Professor of Anthropology and Associate Dean, Office of the Dean of Students at the University of Alberta, Canada. Her research and teaching focuses on the topics of food, gender, body, and health. Examples of her research include her early work on food consumption during pregnancy in New Delhi, India, examining how a confluence of individual, community, and political-economic factors shaped women's food practices and nutritional health status (*Poor and Pregnant in New Delhi, India,* available through Left Coast Press), and recent and ongoing collaborative interdisciplinary research on family food practices (*Acquired Tastes: Why Families Eat The Way They Do,* available through University of British Columbia Press*),* the ways place shapes health practices and behaviors, and the food and health experiences and needs of various immigrant communities. Much of this collaborative work involves use of photo elicitation and photovoice methods.

References

Adapon, Joy. 2008. *Culinary Art and Anthropology.* Oxford: Berg.
Albers, Patricia C., and William R. James. 1990. Private and Public Images: A Study of Photographic Contrasts in Postcard Pictures of Great Basin Indians, 1898–1919. *Visual Anthropology* 3: 343–366.
Alexandra, Darcy. 2008. Digital Storytelling as Transformative Practice: Critical Analysis and Creative Expression in the Representation of Migration in Ireland. *Journal of Media Practice* 9: 101–112.
Bach, Hedy. 2007. Composing a Visual Narrative Inquiry. In *Handbook of Narrative Inquiry: Mapping a Methodology,* ed. D. Jean Clandinin, 280–307. Thousand Oaks, CA: Sage.
Banks, Marcus. 1995. Visual Research Methods. *Social Research Update* 11.
Banks, Marcus, and Jay Ruby. 2011. Introduction. In *Made to Be Seen: Perspectives on the History of Visual Anthropology,* ed. Marcus Banks and Jay Ruby, 1–18. Chicago: University of Chicago Press.

Bateson, Gregory, and Margaret Mead. 1942. *Balinese Character: A Photographic Analysis.* New York: New York Academy of Sciences.
Belting, Hans. 2011. *An Anthropology of Images.* Princeton: Princeton University Press.
Biella, Peter. 2009. Elementary Forms of the Digital Media: Tools for Applied Action Collaboration and Research in Visual Anthropology. In *Viewpoints: Visual Anthropologists at Work,* ed. Mary Strong and Laena Wilder, 363–387. Austin: University of Texas Press.
Bower, Anne L., ed. 2004. *Reel Food: Essays on Food and Film.* New York: Routledge.
Burns, Peter M. 2004. Six Postcards from Arabia: A Visual Discourse of Colonial Travels in the Orient. *Tourist Studies* 4: 255–275.
Clark, Cindy D. 1999. The Autodriven Interview: A Photographic Viewfinder into Children's Experiences. *Visual Sociology* 14: 39–50.
Clark-Ibáñez, Marisol. 2004. Framing the Social World with Photo-Elicitation Interviews. *American Behavioral Scientist* 47: 1507–1527.
Coad, Jane. 2007. Using Art-Based Techniques in Engaging Children and Young People in Health Care Consultations and/or Research. *Journal of Research in Nursing* 12: 487–497.
Collier, John. 2003. Photography and Visual Anthropology. In *Principles of Visual Anthropology,* ed. Paul Hockings, 235–254. 3rd ed. Berlin: Mouton de Gruyter.
Collier, John, and Malcolm Collier. 1986. *Visual Anthropology: Photography as a Research Method.* Rev. and exp. ed. Albuquerque: University of New Mexico Press.
de Solier, Isabelle. 2005. TV Dinners: Culinary Television, Education and Distinction. *Continuum: Journal of Media and Cultural Studies* 19: 465–481.
Edwards, Elizabeth, ed. 1992. *Anthropology and Photography, 1860–1920.* New Haven: Yale University Press.
Edwards, Elizabeth. 1996. Postcards: Greetings from Another World. In *The Tourist Image: Myth and Myth-Making in Tourism,* ed. Tom Selwyn, 197–221. Chichester: John Wiley & Sons.
Edwards, Elizabeth, and Kaushik Bhaumik, eds. 2008. *Visual Sense: A Cultural Reader.* Oxford: Berg.
El Guindi, Fadwa. 2004. *Visual Anthropology: Essential Method and Theory.* Walnut Creek, CA: AltaMira Press.
Gell, Alfred. 1996. Vogel's Net: Traps as Artworks and Artworks as Traps. *Journal of Material Culture* 1: 15–38.
———. 1998. *Art and Agency: An Anthropological Theory.* Oxford: Clarendon.
Gubrium, Aline C., and Gloria T. Difulvio. 2011. Girls in the World: Digital Storytelling as a Feminist Public Health Approach. *Girlhood Studies* 4: 28–46.
Harper, Douglas. 2002. Talking about Pictures: A Case for Photo Elicitation. *Visual Studies* 17: 13–26.
Hemphill, Eric, Kim Raine, John C. Spence, and Karen E. Smoyer-Tomic. 2008. Exploring Obesogenic Food Environments in Edmonton, Canada: The Association between Socioeconomic Factors and Fast-Food Outlet Access. *American Journal of Health Promotion* 22: 426–432.
Henderson, Vani R., and Bridget Kelly. 2005. Food Advertising in the Age of Obesity: Content Analysis of Food Advertising on General Market and African American Television. *Journal of Nutrition Education and Behavior* 37: 191–196.
Hockings, Paul, ed. 2003. *Principles of Visual Anthropology.* 3rd ed. Berlin: Mouton de Gruyter.

Holden, T. J. M. 2005. The Overcooked and Underdone: Masculinities in Japanese Food Programming. *Food and Foodways* 13: 39–65.

Huss, Ephrat. 2008. Shifting Spaces and Lack of Spaces: Impoverished Bedouin Women's Experience of Cultural Transition through Arts-Based Research. *Visual Anthropology* 21: 58–71.

Huss, Ephrat, Roni Kaufman, and Avril Siboni. 2013. Children's Drawings and Social Change: Food Insecurity and Hunger among Israeli Bedouin Children. *British Journal of Social Work* advance access: doi:10.1093/bjsw/bct034.

Iversen, Gunnar, and Jan K. Simonsen, eds. 2010. *Beyond the Visual: Sound and Image in Ethnographic and Documentary Film*. Höjbjerg, Denmark: Intervention Press.

Jacknis, Ira. 1988. Margaret Mead and Gregory Bateson in Bali: Their Use of Photography and Film. *Cultural Anthropology* 3: 160–177.

Keller, James R. 2006. *Food, Film and Culture*. Jefferson, NC: McFarland.

Knowles, J. Gary, and Ardra L. Cole. 2008. *Handbook of the Arts in Qualitative Research*. Thousand Oaks, CA: Sage.

Leavy, Patricia. 2009. *Method Meets Art: Arts-Based Research Practice*. New York: Guilford Press.

Margolis, Eric, and Luc Pauwels, eds. 2011. *Handbook of Visual Research Methods*. London: Sage.

Marte, Lidia. 2007. Foodmaps: Tracing Boundaries of "Home" Through Food Relations. *Food and Foodways* 15: 261–289.

Milne, E.-J., Claudia Mitchell, and Naydene De Lange, eds. 2012. *Handbook of Participatory Video*. Lanham, MD: AltaMira.

Morphy, Howard, and Marcus Banks. 1997. Introduction. In *Rethinking Visual Anthropology*, ed. Marcus Banks and Howard Morphy, 1–35. New Haven, CT: Yale University Press.

Pink, Sarah. 2004. *Home Truths*. Oxford: Berg.

———. 2006. *The Future of Visual Anthropology: Engaging the Senses*. London: Routledge.

———. 2007. *Doing Visual Ethnography*. 2nd ed. London: Sage.

———. 2009. *Doing Sensory Ethnography*. London: Sage.

Pollay, Richard W. 1985. The Subsiding Sizzle: A Descriptive History of Print Advertising, 1900–1980. *Journal of Marketing* 49: 24–37.

Poole, Deborah. 2005. An Excess of Description: Ethnography, Race, and Visual Technologies. *Annual Review of Anthropology* 34: 159–179.

Raja, Samina, Changxing Ma, and Pavan Yadav. 2008. Beyond Food Deserts: Measuring and Mapping Racial Disparities in Neighborhood Food Environments. *Journal of Planning Education and Research* 27: 469–482.

Rowe, Jeremy. 2011. Legal Issues of Using Images in Research. In *Handbook of Visual Research Methods*, ed. Eric Margolis and Luc Pauwels, 707–723. London: Sage.

Schafft, Kai A., Eric B. Jensen, and C. Clare Hinrichs. 2009. Food Deserts and Overweight Schoolchildren: Evidence from Pennsylvania. *Rural Sociology* 74: 153–177.

Seremetakis, C. N. 1994. *The Senses Still*. Chicago: University of Chicago Press.

Stoller, Paul. 1997. *Sensuous Scholarship*. Philadelphia: University of Pennsylvania Press.

———. 1989. *The Taste of Ethnographic Things: The Senses in Ethnography*. Philadelphia: University of Philadelphia Press.

Strong, Mary, and Laena Wilder. 2009. *Viewpoints: Visual Anthropologists at Work*. Austin: University of Texas Press.

Stuckey, Heather L., and Jeremy Nobel. 2010. The Connection between Art, Healing and Public Health: A Review of Current Literature. *American Journal of Public Health* 100: 254–263.

Tufte, Edward R. 2003. *The Cognitive Style of PowerPoint*. Cheshire: Graphics Press.

Van Leeuwen, Theo, and Carey Jewitt, eds. 2001. *The Handbook of Visual Analysis*. London: Sage.

Wang, Caroline, and Mary Ann Burris. 1994. Empowerment through Photo Novella: Portraits of Participation. *Health Education Quarterly* 21: 171–186.

———. 1997. Photovoice: Concept, Methodology, and Use for Participatory Needs Assessment. *Health Education and Behavior* 24: 369–387.

Wiles, Rose, Andrew Clark, and Jon Prosser. 2011. Visual Research Ethics at the Crossroads. In *Handbook of Visual Research Methods*, ed. Eric Margolis and Luc Pauwels, 685–707. London: Sage.

Wright, Christopher. 2013. *The Echo of Things: The Lives of Photographs in the Solomon Islands*. Durham, NC: Duke University Press.

Zimmerman, Steve, and Ken Weiss. 2005. *Food in the Movies*. Jefferson, NC: McFarland.

Filmography

Babette's Feast. Gabriel Axel. Orion Classics, 1987.

Chocolat. Lasse Hallstrom. Miramax Films, 2000.

Dani Sweet Potatoes. Karl Heider. DER Documentary, 1974.

Eat, Drink, Man, Woman. Ang Lee. Samuel Goldwyn Company, 1994.

Feast, The (part of the *Yanomamo* series). Timothy Asch and Napoleon Chagnon. DER Documentary, 1970.

Food, Inc. Robert Kenner. Magnolia Pictures, 2008.

Himalayan Herders. John and Naomi Bishop. DER Documentary, 1997.

Hunters, The (part of the *!Kung* series). John Marshall. DER Documentary, 1957.

Our Daily Bread. Nikolaus Geyrhalter. First Run Icarus Films, 2005.

Seed and Earth. Lina Fruzzetti, Alfred Guzzetti, Ned Johnston, and Ákos Östör. DER Documentary, 1995.

CHAPTER 5

On the Lookout
The Use of Direct Observation in Nutritional Anthropology

Barbara A. Piperata and Darna L. Dufour

Introduction

Russell Bernard tells us to "spend lots of time studying a culture, learn the language, hang out, do all the everyday things that everyone else does, become inconspicuous by sheer tenaciousness and stay aware of what's really going on" (1999: 319). This is participant observation, the method that has allowed anthropologists to gain insight into complex cultural phenomenon for over a hundred years. Our goal in this chapter is to demonstrate how anthropologists use participant observation, as well as some of the more structured direct observation methods, to understand the relationship between humans and their food. These methods can be thought of as falling along a continuum, from those that rely solely or primarily on unstructured participant observation to those that are highly structured and incorporate systematically collected, often quantitative data on dietary practices and/or the time people expend to secure and process food. Regardless of where a particular methodological approach falls along this continuum, we argue that it is the rich contextual data gathered through direct observation that sets anthropological studies of food apart from those of other disciplines. Moving along this continuum, we demonstrate ways that direct observation methods can be used, highlight the types of information they can provide and consider some of the advantages and disadvantages associated with their use in nutritional anthropology.

Essential Literature

As direct observation is ubiquitous in nutritional anthropology, a comprehensive list of noteworthy readings on the topic would be quite large. Therefore, we limit our list of "essential readings" to some classic studies, a few methodological discussions, and some newer research that relies heavily on observations. In terms of classic ethnographically grounded research focused on humans and their food, we recommend Richards' (1932) *Hunger and Work in a Savage Tribe*, Firth's (1959) *Social Change in Tikopia*, Weismantel's (1988) *Food, Gender, and Poverty in the Ecuadorian Andes*, and Dewalt's (1983) *Nutritional Strategies and Agricultural Change in a Mexican Community*, as well as Lee's (1979) *The ¡Kung San: Men, Women, and Work in a Foraging Society*. In addition to demonstrating the use of direct observation in understanding dietary practices, Dettwyler's *Dancing Skeletons* (1993) is also very useful in teaching students about the advantages of such methods. Finally, a more recent study, *Uncertain Tastes* by Holtzman (2009), illustrates the critical role that "being there" played in understanding the use and meaning of food among the Sambura of Kenya. Several edited volumes are also useful for gaining a sense of the breadth of nutritional anthropology work that relies on direct observation, for example Counihan and Van Esterik (2012), Dufour, Goodman, and Pelto (2013), and Watson and Caldwell (2005).

In terms of discussions of direct observation methods, we want to point out a few pieces that illustrate the range of information a researcher can gather using these techniques, as well as pieces that outline how the methods should be used and potential problems and limitations associated with them. Several chapters in the edited volume by MacBeth and MacClancy (2004) make a strong case for the integration of qualitative and quantitative methods, including direct observation, in nutritional anthropology. Other valuable chapters draw attention to possible pitfalls and challenges those planning such research should carefully consider. The edited volume by Pelto, Pelto, and Messer (1989) is also very useful. The introduction by Gretel Pelto emphasizes the critical role participant observation and other less structured methods, such as open-ended interviews, play in collecting essential background data required to guide research questions and hypothesis formulation, and in evaluating methods for the collection of quantitative data on intake or time allocation in food production and processing (see also Dufour and Teufel 1995; Mead 1945). Other chapters focus on specific methods that integrate direct observation, including methods for the collection of data on food intake and energy expenditure. The chapter by Ellen Messer (1989) centers on time allocation research and provides a thorough overview of many classic studies including Johnson's (1975) work among the Machinguenga, Lee's work among the Kung (1979) and Rappaport's (1968) study among the Tsembaga. For those interested in designing food-related time allocation studies, we highly recommend Altmann (1974), Bernard and Killworth (1993), and Johnson (1975).

Our intention is to not repeat the valuable work of those cited above. Instead, we hope to add to these discussions by using more recent research in nutritional anthropology to show how direct observation methods are used and what kinds of valuable information they provide. The examples we use illustrate what are, we argue, some of direct observation's most critical contributions to nutritional anthropology research. They include (1) providing background and understanding needed to design a valid study and systematic data collection instruments; (2) the collection of more accurate data than can be achieved with other methods alone, given that people's dietary beliefs and patterns are often so ingrained that they are unable to recall them with accuracy; (3) insight into the relationship between, on the one hand, food preparation, taste, and consumption, and on the other hand embedded power structures that would likely be inaccessible using other techniques; (4) the development of research questions that could not be foreseen before getting into the field; and (5) allowing the researcher to more accurately interpret the meaning of data collected through using more structured methods.

The Use of Direct Observation: Across the Spectrum

Participant Observation

Participant observation is about being there, establishing rapport, and allowing the researcher to become the instrument of data collection and analysis. Any of the above-cited ethnographies centered on food will give the reader a strong sense of the sheer amount of time the researcher spent in the field conducting participant observation and the role it played in generating research questions and analyzing the significance of the data they collected. Here we highlight two rather recent studies in nutritional anthropology that rely on participant observation as the primary method of data collection to illustrate how the technique was used and the data it provided.

The first study, conducted in Japan by Anne Allison (1991), focused on the role of bento boxes—the traditional Japanese single-portion meal that mothers prepare for their young, pre–school-aged children—in transmitting state ideology. Allison's interest in bento box production derives from her personal experiences preparing them for her own child while temporarily living in Japan, making her a true participant-observer. In this way, participant observation led to the generation of her research question. Through participant observation, Allison was able to provide rich details on the preparation process and time she and other women invested in their children's lunches, as well as convey the pressure and scrutiny they were under and the anxiety they felt while preparing the appealing lunches their children were required to consume during the rigidly controlled lunch period. Drawing on these experiences and conversations she had with her Japanese female friends, Allison argues that bento box preparation is a form of ideological indoctrination of both mother and child. For the woman, the elaborate, precise preparation of the box is one way she fulfills her primary role in society—being a good mother—which demands that she ensure her child's academic and social success. For the child, finishing lunch during the timed lunch period conveys the importance of conformity and group membership. Besides leading to a research question, participant observation was critical in allowing Allison to uncover an embedded power structure that may not have been accessed using other methods, such as interviews.

The second study, conducted by Yunxiang Yan (2008), also relied in large part on participant observation. In this case, the method was used to address the already conceived research question of why American fast food restaurants were so popular in Beijing, China. This case illustrates how *being there* and directly observing human behavior allowed the researcher to challenge the dominant explanation of the success of American fast food—namely, its novelty, taste, price, and convenience. To collect his data, Yan "hung out" in and around American and Chinese fast food restaurants, as well as more traditional Chinese eateries. His keen observations led him to argue that the actual physical space and the experiences individuals had in American fast food establishments were at least as important as the food itself in explaining their popularity. Yan noted several aspects of these new environments that sharply contrasted with Chinese-owned traditional and fast food restaurants. For example, the American restaurants were very clean and bright; all individuals, regardless of class or gender, had the same ordering experience and thus, to some extent, power; staff were courteous; and people were under no pressure to eat quickly and leave. In a nontraditional eatery, the social context of eating was also transformed. Yan observed that instead of arriving in large patriarchal family groups, customers of American fast food establishments were mainly women with their children or groups of friends, including teenagers, who used the space as a hangout, lingering in "lovers' corners" for hours. Overall, Yan argues that the space allowed women and young people a greater sense of freedom and equality that was key to explaining the restaurants' popularity. Yan's direct observations broadened our understanding of the use and meaning of American fast food eateries in China, and one can easily see how such information would be critical in the development of a valid structured interview that asked respondents as much about the space as about the food.

Direct Observation Combined with Systematic Data Collection

Whereas the work cited above relied almost solely on direct observations, the work reviewed here combines direct observation with the more systematic collection of quantitative data on food gathering, processing and/or consumption. Thinking back to the idea of a continuum, these studies fall toward the center and right side of the spectrum. The studies reviewed highlight how direct observation can complement more structured data collection and allow nutritional anthropologists to address challenges inherent in the study of food. Worth mentioning is the fact that in such mixed-methods publications, the use of participant observation is often omitted from the methods section, obscuring its role. We hope that in drawing attention to its importance, we can provide those pursuing such research with a more complete guide to designing their studies.

Starting research in a new setting is always a challenge. No matter how much one reads on a topic, there are some things that simply cannot be known until you get there and have a look around. In this way direct observation, including participant observation, can provide basic information needed for generating more systematic data collection, help better define a research question or perhaps lead to the generation of a brand new question. Hubert (2004) provides a useful list of potential questions and topics a researcher can address with direct observations and explains how these can then be used to develop a questionnaire. For example, using direct observation one can gather critical data on (1) the utensils and techniques, as well as condiments and sauces used in serving and preparing food, (2) who eats in the home, which might include non-household members, (3) the patterning of food consumption and, (4) who makes decisions about, shops for and prepares food all of which will prove invaluable for designing any form of systematic dietary data collection protocol. In fact, the importance of direct observation in the development of instruments for systematic data collection was recognized and promoted by Margaret Mead when she was asked to assist the US government collect data on the dietary practices of the American people (Mead, 1945).

How direct observations can inform the development of a structured data collection protocol

Darna Dufour's work on manioc (cassava) processing serves as a good example of how direct observations made early on in the research process can aid in better defining a research question and designing a structured protocol to answer it. Dufour's (1988) research was the first to identify how food processing allowed Tukanoans, an indigenous group living in the northwest Amazon, to use the highly toxic root as their dietary staple. Her interest in the subject stemmed from careful observations of manioc processing she made while living in a Tukanoan village. She found it intriguing because women devoted so much time to processing it and were judged within the village on the quality of their manioc products, and because everyone said the raw unprocessed roots were toxic. She reasoned that if indeed the roots were toxic, then processing must be the key to detoxification. She completed some of the observations via participant observation, and some in conjunction with maintaining activity diaries. In the latter cases she detailed the steps and their timing as well as the amounts of roots processed and products produced.

These detailed observations proved important in a number of ways and were particularly useful in designing the precise protocol she used to systematically assess the toxicity of the roots and the effectiveness of processing, both of which were done experimentally in a lab at CIAT (Centro Internacional de Agricultura

Tropical) (Dufour 1988). To assess their toxicity, Dufour transported fresh roots from the Tukanoan villages to CIAT for analysis of cyanide content. In the lab analysis, the crucial specific observation concerned how Tukanoans peeled the roots. In most places peeling involves removing both the bark-like outer peel of the root and the smooth inner peel. Both these peel layers have high levels of cyanogenic glucosides (cyanide-containing compounds), so removing them reduces the cyanogen content of the edible portion. Tukanoans, however, removed only the outermost, bark-like peel. This seems counterintuitive, but further analysis in the lab demonstrated that the inner peel layer contained a high level of the enzyme responsible for degrading the principal cyanogenic glucoside, which meant that grating the root with the inner peel intact actually increased the effectiveness of processing.

Additional experiments at CIAT revealed the importance of another key observation made in the field: the amount of time the grated and washed root mash was allowed to stand before it was used to prepare bread (*casabe*), the final product. For Tukanoans the time lag was 48 hours, whereas in some neighboring groups it was much less. The significance of the time lag was twofold. First it allowed the cyanide (as HCN) to volatilize; hence, the longer the time lag, the less toxic the mash. This experimental fact dovetailed with the Tukanoan claim that feeding the fresh mash to chickens would kill them. Second, the long time lag allowed for fermentation, which gave the bread a tangier taste and a more bread-like texture—two culturally highly valued qualities that were a kind of ethnic marker in the region. Without the detailed direct observations, Dufour would not have had the insight needed to design the protocol that proved invaluable in discovering how Tukanaons detoxified their staple crop.

The Role of Direct Observation in Uncovering a New Area Of Inquiry

Direct observation can also lead to the development of entirely new areas of inquiry. So it was with Dufour's (1987) research on insect consumption in the Amazon. It all started one evening when Dufour stopped to visit with some Tukanoan women sitting in a patch of grass in front of their house, an unusual place to sit. It turned out that the women were foraging for leafcutter ants by poking long pieces of palm (the central rib of a fond) into the entrance holes of an ant nest, pulling out the probes and deftly, with thumb and fore finger, removing the ants that had embedded their mandibles in the probe in valiant defense of their nest. The women were eating the ants as they removed them from the probe and kindly offered some to Dufour, along with instructions to bite down on the ant's head first to keep them from biting the tongue.

Dufour was in the Tukanoan village working on an energy flow study that involved measuring both food energy intake and energy expenditure in food production. She had been focused on measuring the major source of food energy, cassava, and the major sources of dietary protein, fish. But then she saw people eating ants. Her observations that evening raised a whole series of new questions. Were these rather small creatures, the ants, actually a source of energy or even protein? Could they really be sources of energy and/or protein that mattered from a nutritional point of view, or were they instead a kind of condiment consumed to add variety to the diet? Though much larger than any ants she had ever seen before, they were still small for a human food. How could people ever collect enough ants for them to play a role in the diet? Did they consume other kinds of insects? How were they collected? Did men collect them also? Why did they even bother eating such small things?

With these questions in mind, Dufour continued to use participant observation to document the collection and consumption of insects. Initially these observations were opportunistic, but as the importance of insects in the diet became clearer, she sought out foraging opportunities to systematically document the ecological context and foraging method, as well as the amount of insect material collected per unit time, and by whom. To this she added systematic observations of any preparations or cooking prior to consumption, and the circumstances surrounding consumption. Given that she could not distinguish an ant from a termite, a bee from a wasp, or a weevil from a beetle, she also began collecting samples and storing them in alcohol for later identification. To answer the diet questions she used measurements of food intake (weighed food records) that had been planned as part of the larger energy flow study, coupled with actual nutrient analysis of samples she preserved in the field. Without participant observation, Dufour's understanding of the importance of insects in the diet would have been limited because (1) she would not even have known what questions to ask; (2) much of the consumption was in the form of easily forgotten snacks; and (3) many Tukanoans were reluctant to discuss insect consumption because of prejudices held by the local non-Indians.

The Importance of Direct Observation in Revealing Embedded Dietary Practices and Improving Accuracy

Regardless of where one studies, food is so ingrained in everyday life, and dietary practices are so often rote, that people are commonly unable to provide accurate information on their own intakes or the intakes of others in their household, and may not recognize potential biases in access to food. Gittelsohn, Thapa, and Landman's (1997) research in Nepal is an excellent example of how direct observation can be used to overcome these types of challenges. To explore their question, which centered on the relationship between energy and micronutrient sufficiency and intra-household variation in access to different foods (energy- vs. micronutrient-rich), they developed a novel instrument to guide their direct observations. Using this instrument, they collected both qualitative and quantitative data on food distribution and individual household members' consumption patterns in 105 Nepalese families during the midday meal. The data revealed gender bias in food distribution that affected the micronutrient more than the energy sufficiency of females' diets. Reliance on 24-hour recall, a commonly used method in nutrition research, or a more qualitative interview would likely have caused these subtleties in food distribution patterns, important for understanding health risks in these communities, to be overlooked. This is because study participants would probably not have been able to recall the dietary intake data with sufficient accuracy to uncover this bias and/or may not have reported highly normalized and potentially unrecognized food distribution patterns. The authors of this study also noted an important pitfall in using direct observation to collect dietary data: the presence of a researcher can influence people's eating behaviors. This should be taken into account when designing a study. But even though the presence of an outsider, even a local field worker, can distort data, it is generally true that the more time researchers spend in the field the less of a novelty they become, and the less likely their presence is to alter normal behavior.

Direct observation also has an important role in collecting accurate data on breastfeeding patterns, which can also be a challenge for nutritional anthropologists. In societies where mothers spend a great deal of time in close contact with their infants and where feeding is on-demand, breastfeeding patterns can be difficult for women to recall with accuracy. Such was the case in the rural Amazon, where Piperata conducted long-term fieldwork on maternal energetics during lactation. When asked how often they breastfed, women usually used the word "frequently," and when asked for how long, the most common response was one year. Using a detailed direct observation protocol developed by Vitzthum (1994), Piperata collected highly structured data on the number of times women breastfed and the length of each breastfeeding session for approximately eight hours a day from a sample of twenty-three women during early, peak, and late lactation (Piperata and Gooden-Mattern 2011). These direct observations revealed a significant degree of variation in breastfeeding patterns, both between women and over time, which challenged the rather homogenous responses women gave in interviews.

In addition, the duration of breastfeeding lasted far longer (~18 months) than most women had reported feeding their previous children. Direct observations proved important for understanding this discrepancy. In the communities there was consensus around the idea that at one year children were strong enough to consume almost all adult foods, including fish and game meat, which Piperata commonly observed them eating. It appeared that women, in recalling the duration of breastfeeding with previous children, associated it with this important transitory phase in their infants' lives. Direct observations, however, indicated that despite increased consumption of adult foods, the number of times infants breastfed at around one year of age did not differ significantly from the number of times they breastfed at three months of age. In this case, direct observation combined with detailed data collection following a published protocol provided Piperata with a clear picture of infant feeding practices and the ability to compare the data collected from Amazonian women with other published studies.

Conclusion

In this chapter we have argued that regardless of where direct observation falls along the methodological spectrum, the time invested in it can prove critical to understanding the relationship between humans and their food. Using a range of examples, we have demonstrated how incorporating direct observation techniques into the development of research questions and protocol designs, as well as into interpretation of data gathered using other techniques, strengthens nutritional anthropology research and often sets it apart from other disciplines with similar interests in food.

Barbara A. Piperata is Associate Professor of Anthropology at The Ohio State University. She has conducted field research on human reproductive energetics (dietary intake, energy expenditure, and body composition), child growth, and the nutrition transition in the eastern Brazilian Amazon, and on food security and maternal-child health in rural and urban communities in Nicaragua.

Darna L. Dufour is Professor of Anthropology at the University of Colorado, Boulder. She has conducted long-term field research on food and nutrition with Tukanoans in the northwest Amazon and economically disadvantaged women in urban Colombia. Her current research is on the nutrition transition in Latin America.

References

Allison, Anne. 1991. Japanese Mothers and Obentos: The Lunch-box as Ideological State Apparatus. *Anthropological Quarterly* 64(4): 195–208.
Altmann, Jeanne. 1974. Observational Study of Behavior: Sampling Methods. *Behaviour* 49(3): 227–267.
Bernard, Russell. 1999. *Handbook of Methods in Cultural Anthropology.* Walnut Creek, CA: Altamira Press.
Bernard, Russell, and Peter Killworth. 1993. Sampling in Time Allocation Research. *Ethnology* 32(2): 207–215.
Counihan, Carolyn, and Penny Van Esterik. 2012. *Food and Culture: A Reader.* New York: Routledge.
Dettwyler, Katherine. 1993. *Dancing Skeletons: Life and Death in West Africa.* Long Grove, IL: Waveland Press.

Dewalt, Kathleen Musante. 1983. *Nutritional Strategies and Agricultural Change in a Mexican Community.* Ann Arbor: University of Michigan Research Press.

Dufour, Darna L. 1987. Insects as Food: A Case Study for the Northwest Amazon. *American Anthropologist* 89(2): 383–397.

Dufour, Darna L. 1988. Cyanide Context of Cassava Cultivars (*Manihot esculenta, Euphorbiaceae*) used by Tukanoan Indians in the Northwest Amazon. *Economic Botany* 42(2): 255–266.

Dufour, Darna L., Alan Goodman, and Gretel Pelto. 2013. *Nutritional Anthropology: Biocultural Perspectives on Food and Nutrition.* Oxford: Oxford University Press.

Dufour, Darna L., and Nicolette I. Teufel. 1995. Minimum Data Sets for the Description of Diet and Measurement of Food Intake and Nutritional Status. In *The Comparative Analysis of Human Societies: Toward Common Standards for Data Collection and Reporting,* ed. Emilio F. Moran, 97–128. Boulder, CO: Lynne Rienner.

Firth, Raymond. 1959. *Social Change in Tikopia: A Re-study of a Polynesian Community after a Generation.* New York: MacMillan.

Gittelsohn, Joel, Meera Thapa, and Laura T. Landman. 1997. Cultural Factors, Caloric Intake and Micronutrient Sufficiency in Rural Nepali Households. *Social Science and Medicine* 44(11): 1739–1749.

Holtzman, Jon. 2009. *Uncertain Tastes, Memory and Ambivalence and the Politics of Eating Among the Samburu, Northern Kenya.* Berkeley: University of California Press.

Hubert, Annie. 2004. Qualitative Research in the Anthropology of Food. In *Researching Food Habits, Methods and Problems,* ed. Helen MacBeth and Jeremy MacClancy, 41–54. New York: Berghahn Books.

Johnson, Allen. 1975. Time Allocation in a Machiguenga Community. *Ethnology* 14(3): 301–310.

Lee, Richard. 1979. *The !Kung San: Men, Women and Work in a Foraging Society.* Cambridge: Cambridge University Press.

MacBeth, Helen, and Jeremy MacClancy. 2004. *Researching Food Habits: Methods and Problems.* New York: Berghahn Books.

Mead, Margaret. 1945. *Manual for the Study of Food Habits.* Washington, DC: National Research Council.

Messer, Ellen. 1989. The Relevance of Time-allocation Analyses for Nutritional Anthropology: The Relationship of Time and Household Organization to Nutrition Intake and Status. In *Research Methods in Nutritional Anthropology,* ed. Gretel Pelto, Perti Pelto, and Ellen Messer, 82–125. Tokyo: United Nations.

Pelto, Gretel H., Perti J. Pelto, and Ellen Messer, eds. 1989. *Research Methods in Nutritional Anthropology.* Tokyo: United Nations.

Piperata, Barbara A., and Lindsey Gooden-Mattern. 2011. Longitudinal Study of Breastfeeding Structure and Women's Work in the Brazilian Amazon. *American Journal of Physical Anthropology* 144: 226–237.

Rappaport, Roy A. 1968. *Pigs for the Ancestors.* New Haven: Yale University Press.

Richards, Audrey. 1932. *Hunger and Work in a Savage Tribe: A Functional Study of Nutrition among the Southern Bantu.* London: Routledge & Kegan Paul.

Watson, James, and Melissa Caldwell. 2005. *The Cultural Politics of Food and Eating.* Malden, MA: Wiley-Blackwell.

Weismantel, Mary. 1988. *Food, Gender and Poverty in the Ecuadorian Andes.* Philadelphia: University of Pennsylvania Press.

Vitzthum, Virginia J. 1994. Comparative Structure of Breastfeeding and Its Relation with Human Reproductive Ecology. *Yearbook of Physical Anthropology* 37: 307–349.

Yan, Yunxiang. 2008. Of Hamburger and Social Space: Consuming McDonald's in Beijing. In *Food and Culture: A Reader*, ed. Carole Counihan and Penny Van Esterik, 500–522. New York: Routledge.

CHAPTER 6

Participant-Observation and Interviewing Techniques

Heather Paxson

Sociocultural anthropology seeks to account not only for what people do, but also for what they think and feel about what they, and others around them, do. It is an interpretive science; analysis entails the researcher's synthetic interpretation of other people's experiences with, and interpretations of, a given set of conditions, events, and/or practices (Geertz 1973). In practice, the primary job of the ethnographic researcher is to "prod people to think about (and to talk about) the mundane aspects of their lives" (Bestor 2003: 326). Methodologically, participant observation and semi-structured interviewing go hand in hand.

Participant Observation

Participant observation has its roots in the early social and cultural anthropology of Bronislaw Malinowski, Franz Boas, and students of theirs who conducted "fieldwork" in far-flung, exotic settings in East Africa and the Pacific Islands, or in circumscribed "subcultures" of the United States such as Native American reservations, African-American communities in the rural South, and Hollywood. The motivating principle of classic participant-observation research is the understanding that in order to gain "insider" perspectives on social life and cultural meanings, a researcher cannot remain on the sidelines but must venture "off the veranda," as Malinowski famously put it, to participate in the activities of daily life. In the early decades of the discipline, this participation entailed living in native villages and—importantly for my discussion here—eating what the "natives" ate. Not surprisingly, then, anthropological accounts have long paid detailed attention to food and eating. Franz Boas's collaborator George Hunt famously collected scores of Kwakiutal fish recipes, while Audrey Richards pioneered the field of nutritional anthropology through her early fieldwork among the Bemba in (what was then) Northern Rhodesia (Richards 1939).

Participant observation is not to be reductively characterized as "going somewhere else to do research." Significant time, effort, openness, and—often—unforeseen opportunity is required to make an outsider a viable participant in the lifeworlds of others and to "gain rapport" in developing trusting relationships through which local knowledges may be shared (cf. Geertz 1973). Participant observation may entail a long-term research commitment in a particular place or with a particular community.

A wonderful example of ethnographic analysis drawn from participant observation surrounding foodways comes from Jane Cowan's study of everyday sociability as a gendered practice in northern Greece (1990: chapter 3, 1991). As part of a wider study on changes in gender relations, Cowan (1990: 64) analyzes the social event of coffee drinking "as a seemingly trivial pursuit in which gender is symbolically and practically realized (both comprehended and made real) with much pleasure and little ado." Cowan's analysis revolves around articulating five "voices" that express diverse, situated interpretations of the emergence of a new public space for coffee drinking, alternative to both feminine domesticity and the masculinity of the classic Greek *kafeneio*: namely, the modern *kafeteria*. In presenting five stances on the matter, Cowan gives a "thick description" (Geertz 1973) of gender ideology—and the sociability of coffee drinking—in northern Greece.

The "voices" do not come to us, via Cowan, through formal interviews. Rather, they were drawn from the dialogical interaction of participant observation. One "voice" belongs to Katina, a woman who had previously hosted Cowan in her home. During a social visit with Katina and her mother-in-law—quite probably over a cup of coffee—conversation turned to how "things are very different for young girls [today]...They go into the *kafeterias*," where all manner of bad things may happen to them. For Irene, the *kafeteria* is metonymic for the (to her mind, dangerous) expansion of women's social mobility more generally. Cowan draws other voices from a conversation about *kafeterias* that occurred in a *kafeteria*. She was there to hear a speech in honor of International Women's Day, but the speech was poorly attended; those women who were present blamed the sparse turnout on the speech's *kafeteria* location. Cowan sat down with two twenty-year-old women to interview them, with the tape recorder running, about their views of feminism. A man at an adjacent table eavesdropped before butting in, compelled to share his (critical) opinion, similarly articulated with reference to the social space of the *kafeteria*. Others joined in, and Cowan took copious notes. This is one way that participant observation works: Cowan put herself in a place and position to become witness to a miniature social drama. Moreover, she was able to draw significant data for interpretation from the encounter because she was awake to the potential of a side conversation—an interruption of a semiformal interview—to generate more data. Participant observation research is often opportunistic.

Top Tips for Participant Observation
- Read up before you go/begin. Know that you are not the first person to think about the questions that interest you. Build on knowledge that is already published. Keep an eye out for continuities as well as changes in what you observe compared with previous accounts; both are telling.
- Accept opportunities as they are presented, including accepting hospitality when it is offered. Be prepared to range beyond your "comfort zone" because this demonstrates respect and politeness and can also be instructive.
- Keep a field journal, apart from more formal notes from interviews and events attended. This is a place to take note of relevant news stories, impressions and working interpretations, and new questions to explore, as well as those quotidian and chance encounters that can add up to a comprehensive, if necessarily situated, "take" on a field site or community of practice.
- Observe with all your senses: smell, sound, touch, and of course taste are just as empirical as is sight.

As should be apparent, participant observation takes innumerable forms. A researcher might readily participate in the everyday life of sociability through coffee drinking or food sharing or market shopping or vending (Weiss 2011; Black 2012); be an observant attendee of a food festival, butchery class, tasting event, or conference (Sutton 2001; Meneley 2005; Weiss 2012; Paxson 2013); or gain insight as an active member of a CSA or other alternative food provisioning group (DeLind 1999; Markowitz 2008) or as a volunteer working in a soup kitchen (Caldwell 2004). Less evident is how one might "participate" in a professional kitchen or government food safety inspection. Opportunities for genuine participation on the part of a researcher may be severely limited. Ted Bestor, as he began fieldwork in Tokyo's Tsukiji fish market, soon realized that nobody "was going to let me carve a tuna or cast a casual bid into the auctions just so I could experience it myself" (2003: 319). Instead, Bestor worked formal and informal introductions to various players in the market network. "Snowball sampling" occurs when such referrals lead to the accumulation of interview subjects.

As an alternative to participant observation, Bestor has suggested the notion of "inquisitive observation" as a more accurate description of the sort of fieldwork he conducted by hanging out and interacting with people, commenting that "observation is too passive a term to describe the activity of constantly asking questions about what's going on" (2003: 317). The notion of inquisitive observation points to the dialogical nature of anthropological fieldwork; we do not interrogate "informants" to extract information so much as we converse with interlocutors to reach mutual comprehension.

Even the most engaged forms of participant observation are ultimately less about the fieldworker's own firsthand experience than about the insights gained thereby into the lives of others. As part of ethnographic research I conducted (episodically) between 2004 and 2011 on American artisanal cheese and the people who make it, I was fortunate to spend ten days on a sheep dairy farm in Vermont, helping in nearly all aspects of farmstead cheese making. I woke at dawn to help milk 180 sheep; I went out to the fields to help "make pasture," moving lengths of plastic fencing to create zones of fresh pasture for the sheep to nibble; I awkwardly held a ewe in my lap as the farmer reached into her birth canal to deliver recalcitrant twin lambs. In the cheese house, I helped on three different days to make three batches of cheese, spending other afternoons brushing and turning wheels of cheese in the "aging cave" to facilitate the formation of "natural" rinds. I accompanied the farmer to a farm-related state policy meeting as well as a public event that could be described as dairy boosterism. And there was much more. What did I gain from this intensive yet circumscribed experience that I could not have learned simply by interviewing my host?

In retrospect, what I primarily gained from this fieldwork experience—which occurred quite early in my research, even before I wrote a successful grant proposal—was a comprehensive overview of my research topic. I came to realize that the material properties of handmade cheese begin to form well before the milking parlor, in pastures and in the practices of animal husbandry. My screaming muscles—sore from lifting milk cans in and out of soapy water as I scrubbed and sterilized them as part of making cheese—kept me aware that artisan labor is physical labor. The sore muscles joined a shallow, persistent cough I had developed while working in the cave (an allergic reaction to the mold) to tell me that cheese making is a process of microbial control: all that washing and sterilizing we did, like our brushing of fungal filaments off of the surfaces of cheese wheels, served to weed out harmful or malodorous microbes and ensure proper fermentation and the development of protective and flavor-enhancing rinds. In other words, my participant observation generated rather than satisfied research questions. Working on a sheep dairy farm did not make me a cheese maker; it made me a better ethnographer of cheese making by preparing me to ask knowledgeable and unexpected questions of people who were cheese makers. Participant observation and interviewing inform one another in the practice of fieldwork.

Interviewing

Wayne Fife (2005) distinguishes three types of interviewing: unstructured, structured, and semi-structured. Unstructured interviewing refers to the sort of opportunistic questioning that is integral to participant observation—what Bestor terms inquisitive observation. At the other end of the spectrum, structured interviewing is essentially the oral administration of a formal survey. Its goal is to gather large sets of data that can be readily quantified, aggregated, and statistically rendered. Nutritionists might use structured interviewing to gather data on caloric intake ("How many servings of meat did you eat over the past week?") or household expenditures on food ("How much on average do you spend at the grocery store per week?"). Numerous responses to each question are averaged and cross-tabulated to generate generalizable knowledge about a population or phenomenon. To generate good quantitative data, it's important that each interviewee be asked the same questions in the same way so that the researcher can be confident of an equivalency among responses. If questions are posed—or interpreted—differently by different respondents, then the data's signal will be muddied by interpretive noise.

Semi-structured interviewing is what most sociocultural anthropologists mean when we talk about "interviewing." In contrast to structured interviewing, the interviewer does not run down a list of pre-scripted questions to be asked verbatim; instead, the interview is more conversational and dialogical—each interview proceeds uniquely as the researcher follows the conversational thread, pursuing interesting leads as they arise. Yet there remains some structure to the interview: throughout the conversation, the interviewer consults (mentally, if not also on paper) a pre-prepared schedule of questions or list of topics to ensure they are covered. Because data collected in this fashion are qualitative and not destined for quantitative aggregation (though comparison may well be possible), it is not necessary to pose precisely the same questions to each interviewee. In fact, a skillful interviewer refines the line of questioning as the research proceeds, building on what has been learned through previous interviews and from participant observation and other forms of research. Also known as "open-ended" interviewing, this method does not presume a range of responses from the outset but is instead crafted in such a way as to remain open to discovering what is important to the people being interviewed, from their perspective.

Interviewing may sound like a straightforward exercise: you want to learn about something, so you ask someone questions about it. In practice, though, interviewing can be anything but straightforward. Successful interviewing, which sheds light on what you wish to learn about, rests on a number of factors: knowing whom to interview, being able to interview desirable subjects, conveying your questions in an intelligible and appropriate way, eliciting honest and illuminating responses. It can be dumbfounding, not to mention frustrating, when an interview does not go well—when earnest questions are met with resistance or professed ignorance, or when an interview is simply boring. But when an interview goes well—when the conversation takes off, both parties are clearly gaining fresh insights while also enjoying themselves, and the interviewer records pithy, articulate quotations that are sure to make it into an eventual publication—there is nothing more invigorating, let alone validating, for a researcher.

When recruiting interview subjects, it is ethically as well as methodologically important to explain your project and why you are interested in speaking with someone. Unlike investigative journalists, ethnographers do not work "under cover"; we explain who we are, where we are coming from, and the uses to which the information we gather may be put. Is the intended outcome a doctoral thesis, crucial for launching an academic career? Is the intended outcome a series of scholarly articles or a monograph with "crossover" potential that might be widely read? As stipulated by university review boards, interviewees must be notified whether and how the researcher will protect the anonymity of interview subjects by using pseudonyms and other methods, or whether publications may identify the real names behind quotations drawn from interviews.

I used real names of persons and businesses in my ethnographic book *The Life of Cheese: Crafting Food and Value in America*. I opted against the use of pseudonyms for two reasons. First, the cheese community is fairly small, and many of the people I interviewed (as well as their business operations) could be readily identified by other cheese makers, retailers, and others in the cheese world. Internal confidentiality (internal, that is, to the population studied) did not seem a realistic possibility when I wanted to tell individual stories in addition to speaking generally. Second, many of the people I interviewed saw my research (and anticipated publications) as an opportunity for free publicity and wanted to be named. When seeking to quote people by name in reference to things said during an interview (as opposed to a public venue), it is standard practice among anthropologists to share draft passages with interviewees, giving them the opportunity to vet and even modify quotations associated with their names before going to print. As I had promised when seeking "informed consent" for my interviews, I sent relevant passages drawn from interviews (including the unstructured interviewing of inquisitive observation) to everyone I wished to quote by name. All but a couple gave their written consent (some after insisting on minor revisions). One interviewee never responded to numerous requests sent electronically as well as by snail mail; in the end, on the principle of "due diligence," I kept that person's name in the text in association with interview quotes that speak insightfully to the practice of artisanal cheesemaking, but I omitted some personal information from the passage. Another interviewee responded to my request for permission to quote him/her with a polite (though unexplained) request that I not include his/her name in the book. I accepted that request by anonymizing one comment ("one cheesemaker told me...") and entirely omitting a passage relating the origin story of this person's cheese-making business.

Top Tips for Interviewing (drawn from James Spradley [1979] and others who have written about interviewing method, as well as from my own experience):
- Begin informally, thanking interviewees for their time and chatting briefly to establish a conversational tone, reminding them why you are there. Do not

immediately launch into an interrogation. Give the people you are talking to some sense of the larger questions you hope to address through your research. If you explain not only what you are interested in, but also why you are interested in it, interviewees will likely be more forthcoming with their own analyses and interpretations.
- If you wish to record the interview for future transcription, you need written permission to do so. Explain what you plan to do regarding confidentiality. It is good practice to offer to switch off the recording device if the person being interviewed wishes at some point to say something "off the record."
- Ask a mix of direct (factual), open-ended (experiential, perspectival), and hypothetical (What would happen if…?) questions. Pose questions in such a way as to invite anecdotes, stories, explanations; avoid questions that could elicit yes-or-no answers. Ask not only about people's ideas and opinions but also about their practices, about what they do as well as what they think.
- Do not hesitate to ask about the apparently obvious or trivial, as things may not be so obvious after all and sometimes the smallest detail can illuminate larger concerns.
- Be an active listener. Express interest ("Oh, that's interesting") and confess ignorance ("Oh, I didn't know that") as a way of prompting the speaker to continue and to elaborate ("Can you say more?").
- Take conversational turns. Offer stories of your own, from your own life or from your research thus far (but take care not to dominate the discussion). You are aiming at the mutual construction of knowledge and understanding.
- Do not be afraid of silences or pauses in the conversation. Give people time to formulate their thoughts, to find the right words (after all, they may well realize they could be quoted in the future). Try not to interrupt.
- If you're working with an interpreter, be sure to explain your larger project to the interpreter as well as you can. Be sure to convey that you are interested not only in what the gist of an interviewee's response is, but also in how the response is phrased.
- Your last question should be something along the lines of, "Can you think of anything to add? What else do you think it's important that I know or understand?" about what you've been talking about.
- Thank interviewees for their help.
- Finally, be sure to take retrospective field notes on every interview encounter, even—or especially—if you have audio recorded the interview. Characterize the interview setting: was it in a professional office, or in someone's backyard with kids running around? Was the tone of the conversation comfortable or a little strained, was the person interviewed enthusiastic or reluctant? Did you both laugh a lot or did it feel like pulling teeth? Such a record can help you make better sense of an interview transcript months or (realistically) even years after an interview took place.

When writing up research results as dissertation chapters or article-length publications, scene-setting detail can contribute to a compelling ethnographic portrait. *Ethnography*, after all, means *writing* (about) culture. Just as tasty artisanal cheese begins with rich and flavorful milk given by healthy animals, well-written ethnographies begin with vivid, meticulous field notes drawn both from participant observation and interviewing.

Heather Paxson is William R. Kenan Jr. Professor of Anthropology at the Massachusetts Institute of Technology, where she teaches courses on food, gender, craft knowledge, and ethnographic research methods. She is the author of two books, including *The Life of Cheese: Crafting Food and Value in America* (University of California Press, 2013), which was awarded the 2013 Diana Forsythe Prize. Heather received her PhD from Stanford University.

Key Texts on Participant Observation and Interviewing

Angrosino, Michael V., ed. 2007. *Doing Cultural Anthropology: Projects in Ethnographic Data Collection*. 2nd ed. Long Grove, IL: Waveland Press.

Berg, Bruce L. 1998. *Qualitative Research Methods for the Social Sciences*. Boston: Allyn and Bacon.

Briggs, Charles. 1986. *Learning How to Ask: A Sociolinguistic Appraisal of the Role of the Interview in Social Science Research*. Cambridge: Cambridge University Press.

Emerson, Robert. M., Rachel I. Fretz, and Linda L. Shaw. 2011. *Writing Ethnographic Fieldnotes*. 2nd ed. Chicago: University of Chicago Press.

Fife, Wayne. 1995. *Doing Fieldwork: Ethnographic Methods for Research in Developing Countries and Beyond*. New York: Palgrave Macmillan.

Holstein, James A., and Jaber F. Gubrium. 1995. *The Active Interview*. Thousand Oaks, CA: Sage.

Lofland, John, David A. Snow, Leon Anderson, Lyn H. Lofland. 2005. *Analyzing Social Settings: A Guide to Qualitative Observation and Analysis*. 4th ed. Stamford, CT: Cengage Learning.

McCracken, Grant. 1988. *The Long Interview*. Thousand Oaks, CA: Sage.

Mishler, Elliott. 1986. *Research Interviewing: Context and Narrative*. Cambridge, MA: Harvard University Press.

Pawson, Ray. 1996. Theorizing the Interview. *British Journal of Sociology* 47(2): 295–314.

Spradley, James. 1979. *The Ethnographic Interview*. Belmont, CA: Wadsworth.

———. 1980. *Participant Observation*. Belmont, CA: Wadsworth.

Medecins Sans Frontieres. http://fieldresearch.msf.org/msf/bitstream/10144/84230/1/Qualitative%20research%20methodology.pdf

USAID: Qualitative Research Methods: A Data Collector's Field Guide. http://www.fhi360.org/sites/default/files/media/documents/Qualitative%20Research%20Methods%20-%20A%20Data%20Collector%27s%20Field%20Guide.pdf

References

Bestor, Theodore C. 2003. Inquisitive Observation: Following Networks in Urban Fieldwork. In *Doing Fieldwork in Japan*, ed. Theodore C. Bestor, Patricia G. Steinhoff, and Victoria Lyon Bestor, 315–334. Honolulu: University of Hawaii Press.

———. 2004. *Tsukiji: The Fish Market at the Center of the World.* Berkeley: University of California Press.

Black, Rachel E. 2012. *Porta Palazzo: The Anthropology of an Italian Market.* Philadelphia: University of Pennsylvania Press.

Caldwell, Melissa L. 2004. *Not By Bread Alone: Social Support in the New Russia.* Berkeley: University of California Press.

Cowan, Jane. 1990. *Dance and the Body Politic in Northern Greece.* Princeton, NJ: Princeton University Press.

———. 1991. Going out for Coffee? Contesting the Grounds of Gendered Pleasures in Everyday Sociability. In *Contested Identities: Gender and Kinship in Modern Greece,* ed. Peter Loizos and Evthymios Papataxiarchis, 180–202. Princeton, NJ: Princeton University Press.

DeLind, Laura. 1999. Close Encounters with a CSA: The Reflections of a Bruised and Somewhat Wiser Anthropologist. *Agriculture and Human Values* 16: 3–9.

Fife, Wayne. 2005. *Doing Fieldwork: Ethnographic Methods for Research in Developing Countries and Beyond.* New York: Palgrave-McMillan.

Geertz, Clifford. 1973. *The Interpretation of Cultures.* New York: Basic Books.

Markowitz, Lisa. 2008. Produce(ing) Equity: Creating Fresh Markets in a Food Desert. *Research in Economic Anthropology* 28: 195–211.

Meneley, Anne. 2005. Oil. In *Fat: The Anthropology of an Obsession,* ed. Don Kulick and Anne Meneley, 29–43. New York: Tarcher/Penguin.

Paxson, Heather. 2013. *The Life of Cheese: Crafting Food and Value in America.* Berkeley: University of California Press.

Richards, Audrey. 1939. *Land, Labor and Diet in Northern Rhodesia: An Economic Study of the Bemba Tribe.* London: Oxford University Press.

Spradley, James P. 1979. *The Ethnographic Interview.* Belmont, CA: Wadsworth.

Sutton, David. 2001. *Remembrance of Repasts: An Anthropology of Food and Memory.* Oxford: Berg.

Weiss, Brad. 2011. Making Pigs Local: Discerning the Sensory Character of Place. *Cultural Anthropology* 26(3): 438–461.

———. 2012. Configuring the Authentic Value of Real Food: Farm-to-Fork, Snout-to-Tail, and Local Food Movements. *American Ethnologist* 39(3): 614–626.

CHAPTER 7

Focus Groups in Qualitative or Mixed-Methods Research

Ramona L. Pérez

Introduction

During my long-term fieldwork in Mexico from 1995 to 1997, one of my favorite kinds of occasions was the formation of informal working groups that evolved as men and women came together to prepare for large festivals. In much of rural Mexico today, workaday life is punctuated by fiestas that celebrate life events such as baptism, marriage, and other major transitions in status, as well as communal celebrations of a saint's feast day that punctuate the mundane of everyday life. Fiestas can last for three days and usually begin at dawn on the first day, when women gathered to create an outdoor kitchen that would be used to prepare food for the guests. The women would form work groups that reflected their common bonds: age, marital status, and even the subtle yet important arena of sociopolitical rank. Each group would focus on a particular task in meal preparation. One group might sit together to prepare bushels of tomatoes for the sauces that would be served over the next three days. Others might focus on peeling kilos of garlic, washing and preparing corn for tortillas, chopping up whatever meat would form the base of the meal, or washing and sorting all of the dishes that would be used by the guests. The *cocinera*, or lead cook, would monitor each group and advise them on exactly what she needed and how she wanted it done. We spent hours together, moving from one task to the next. Here, in these informal groups, I learned much about the intimacies of life in the community. I also turned to these groups to resolve conflicting data or events. They were my informal focus groups comprised of representative community members who had intimate knowledge of whatever topic I introduced about the community and had no problem discussing any such topic at length. They taught me much about the symbolic elements of particular foods, ingredients, the relationship of food to health, and of course, whom to buy from and how to know if I was paying a decent price. They were also open to many other topics as far-reaching as gender roles, domestic violence, political structures, and migration. They did not always agree, and in many ways I learned just how diverse opinions can be, even in a small, rural community. I learned how they were coming to terms with changes in their worlds and which traditional practices or ideologies were less malleable than others.

Although many researchers believe that a focus group must be formally constituted, have a particular aim, and be regulated by time, just as many researchers in developing regions create focus groups according to decision-making models used by the local group. Paying attention to the ways in which culture groups create their own groups to discuss issues is an important aspect of focus group construction. Dawson, Manderson, and Tallo (1993: 2) caution readers that groups formed around kinship or activity may not provide a "range of attitudes and practices within a particular residential or cultural setting." All researchers need to understand that informal groups, when used as sources of data for research, must be recognized for their limitations as well as their strengths. Group composition should represent the larger population the researcher seeks to understand and consist of individuals who are able to openly communicate with each other. Kin groups, gender groups, clubs, and other such bonding arenas may be limited by intragroup power relations and enforcement of social mores that can hinder open discussion. The dynamic of open communication and group debate is what makes the focus group such an important element in qualitative research. The key to a successful focus group, then, is to bring together a group that has a strong relationship with the topic you wish to further understand or develop *and* with the group you intend to generalize about with the data.

Defining the Focus Group

Focus groups have been in use since the 1940s and were traditionally used by marketing firms seeking to better understand consumer groups and their use of particular products, technologies, and programs. Focus groups did not become a standard methodological option for scientific researchers until the 1980s, and their use remains limited primarily because they are labor-intensive and require as much work afterward as they do in their design and execution. Their use, however, can also save a researcher much time, expense, energy, and embarrassment over misunderstood meanings and practices.

Material on focus groups emerged in social science methods handbooks in the late 1980s and early 1990s (Morgan 1996; Krueger 2008) and now forms a part of most comprehensive handbooks. The multiplicity of uses and structures has also resulted in a series of handbooks dedicated to focus groups alone, many of them speaking directly to their use in a particular environment or discipline. Today, researchers and granting agencies view focus groups as an important methodological tool in qualitative and mixed-methods research design (Bernard 2000: 209).

To be effective, focus groups should be comprised of representative members of the group under study, be conducted in a place where participants are comfortable sharing their insights and perspectives, be focused on one particular issue, and allow sufficient time for each member to have a voice. There is much debate as to whether or not the members of a focus group should be acquainted with each other, whether the meeting should take place in an institutional setting or a natural setting for the participants, what degree of continuity should exist in the demographics of the participants, how the questions should be asked, and much more. I prefer that the social and cultural mores of the focus group mirror those of the larger group (see also Hennink 2007 for more discussion on focus groups in international settings) so that their responses and interactions reflect their comfort levels and the discussion achieves a level of intimate reflection that allows for difference among the members. Ultimately, the composition of the focus group, the setting, and the manner in which it is held should be governed by what the researcher is trying to achieve.

For instance, Crockett et al. (1990) wanted to develop a nutrition education intervention for seniors over age sixty in rural areas of North Dakota. In general, persons over sixty have been shown to have decreasing diversity in their diets and to eat less frequently; they may also have trouble correlating dietary restrictions made necessary by their changing health patterns (Learner and Kivett 1981; Lee and Frongillo 2001; O'Hanlon and Kohrs 1978; Posner et al. 1993). Crockett et al. first needed to know what healthy, active people within this age range were doing, and what this demographic might want to know, about nutrition. They also needed to get a better understanding of elders' attitudes and behaviors toward nutrition education (1990: 563) before embarking on an education and outreach program. They diversified their participants by seeking out sixty-eight men and women aged 60 to 80 who were from communities of less than 2,500 people and had varying levels of education. To assure ethnic and economic diversity, they formed focus groups in five geographic locations throughout the state of North Dakota. Because the age range is actually quite broad and they wanted all the participants to feel comfortable, they chose prominent public buildings such as a restaurant banquet room and community center (ibid.: 565). The environment, they noted, "should be relaxed and natural, to encourage informal discussion" (ibid.).

In my own research in creating a school lunch program for a rural community of migrant farm workers in Baja California, I had a different kind of research problem. I needed to focus not on what could be brought in to address a nutrition problem but rather what could be done with existing but scarce resources that were incompatible with the group. The community was extremely poor, and despite working on a corporate farm, people had very little access to fresh food. The municipal social services office (Desarrollo Integral de la Familia) provided the elementary school with random foodstuffs of very poor quality that were inconsistent with local dietary patterns. Meanwhile the school was charged with providing breakfast for three hundred children whose parents left for work several hours before the children left for school. My research team and I conducted an inventory of the foodstuffs that social services had dropped off the week we were in the community. They included strawberry-flavored soy milk, powdered eggs, very ripe and soft bananas, powdered nonfat milk, peanut butter, flour, sugar, vegetable oil, stale multigrain bread, margarine, and an assortment of wilted and rotting root vegetables. The questions we sought to answer through a focus group consisting of children who attended the school were simple. Would the children eat these kinds of meals, which did not taste or look like the food from their home? If not, why (taste, texture, form)? What could the children teach us about how they related to the food provided by the school? Ultimately, because we could not change the food resources that were provided, the goal was to learn how to make unknown foodstuffs palatable and as nutritionally complete as possible.

We set out to create five different meals that would be as nutritionally sound as we could make them. Utilizing other pantry ingredients in the school kitchen, we combined powdered eggs and milk with chopped vegetables and poured the mixture over the stale bread on large, rimmed cookie sheets to make a quiche that we simply called egg and vegetable pie (*pay de verdura y huevo*). Pancakes emerged from the strawberry soymilk and flour and were spread with peanut butter and rolled into *tacos de hotcake*. We blended bananas with powdered milk and a little powdered egg to make a thick smoothie or *licuado*. The remaining bread and powdered eggs became French toast (*tostadas francesas*), and for the last day we made a vegetable soup with egg dumplings (*sopa de verdura con pan de huevo*).

We assembled three groups of twelve children between six and ten years of age with an equal distribution of girls and boys. There was no need to screen for socioeconomic standing as all families were farm workers, had migrated from the southern states of Oaxaca or Guerrero, and identified as members of Mixtec or Triqui indigenous groups. The focus groups were held in a known and comfortable location, a classroom at the elementary school in which desks were arranged in a circle. We explained to the children that we needed their help in a nutrition program that would bring new meals to their school. We began by asking them to draw a picture of their favorite breakfast that they ate with their family. Then we asked them to draw a picture of their favorite breakfast at the school. This prompted a chorus of "yuck, there isn't any good breakfast at school," "the food is too gross to eat," and even "you just close your eyes and eat it to stop the noise in your tummy," which was followed by loud agreement.

Once we had them thinking about food at home and at school we introduced samples of the various foods we had prepared. We gave the children a worksheet with an image of each meal and a series of stickers including a happy face, a neutral face, and a sad face. As they tried each sample, we asked them to put a sticker next to the image to indicate their reaction. Older students were encouraged to write down any words that would help us understand what they did or did not like. After the first focus group we quickly realized that the boys were more experimental than the girls and that, based on their written and verbal comments, the idea of a square egg (the quiche) or egg-coated bread cut into strips prevented many from even trying them. We adjusted the presentation for the two subsequent groups by giving each meal sample a fun name such as Sponge Bob Square Pants eggs (*huevos de* Sponge Bob Square *Pantalones*), Sticky Finger Bread (*Dedos de Pan Pegajoso*), and Cloud Soup (*Sopa de Nubes*). Although girls remained more hesitant to eat the new foods, the renaming eliminated the hesitation among boys. Some foods, however, were simply rejected, such as peanut butter. Substituting the peanut butter with mashed banana flavored with juice from oranges or limes, however, worked great among the final group.

In this case, we modified each focus group in response to immediate hesitations and reactions. This worked because the research objective was to understand how to make a limited resource acceptable to the participants rather than what resources would be the most acceptable. The focus groups taught us that new food forms and tastes could be introduced but this would require active engagement with children's imaginations rather than correlations of new foods to known foods. We also learned that whereas the children could not articulate the reality of scarce resources endured by the school cook, they did understand that she was doing her best to address the insecurity surrounding food in the community. Thus, another benefit of the focus groups was the formation of a rotating student group who helped the school cook name the meals for each week and figure out what might work with the ingredients they had for that week.

Focus groups have also been used to acquire broad yet deep data on global food consumption in order to document normative dietary patterns for use by researchers across the globe (Samuda et al. 1998). The Network of Food Data Base Systems (INFOODS) was founded in 1984 and is managed through the United Nations Food and Agriculture Organization. These kinds of data serve as an important starting point for focus groups that can then flesh out changes to dietary patterns as well as local uses.

Managing the Focus Group

Focus groups can be a rich source of data. However, if the person moderating the group is working with questions or topics not easily understood by the group, is not skilled at controlling the dynamics that unfold in group settings, or does not establish a rapport that makes the group feel safe and appreciated, then it can quickly go awry. Developing the skills to conduct focus groups is an integral part of the methodological framework and should be discussed as part of the research design. As with any group, the diversity of personalities is sure to emerge in the focus group. The moderator should be sufficiently experienced in group interaction to be able to redirect a dominant personality to keep one person from controlling interaction, draw out the voice of the shy or reserved person, and allow dissension among participants that does not escalate into negative personal interactions. It is a good idea to begin each focus group by introducing guidelines that clearly indicate that each participant should respect each person's opinions, will have an opportunity to speak, and should understand that group members may not always agree and that the disagreement or differing opinions are just as important for the research as agreement.

The moderator should also be someone that the group views as neutral and respectful of them and their culture. For instance, in Hildebrand and Shriver's (2010) recent study on African-American fruit and vegetable consumption, they make clear that they did not personally conduct the focus groups because they did not believe the community would view them as neutral or impartial. Rather, they trained a graduate assistant who was more equipped to "establish rapport and trust between the researcher and focus-group participants and created a safe environment for the sharing of credible and dependable information" (2010: 713). Lang and Savirithi (2009: 218) argue that the moderator should preferably be from the culture group of the participants and trained in focus group facilitation. Though that is not always possible, great care should be taken in assuring that the moderator can manage group dynamics and will not negatively impact the group dynamics.

Of equal importance to the moderator is the observer, whose responsibility lies in taking field notes that aid in interpreting the data. The moderator and the observer should not be the same person. It is critically important that the moderator be seen as an active listener who acknowledges the contributions of each speaker, guides the participants into a natural discussion, and assures a sense of equal knowledge on the topic among the participants. The observer is charged with documenting whatever cannot be reproduced through the voice recording of the session and may also work with the moderator to assure that a topic is explored as deeply as possible.

Focus groups typically last one hour and should not exceed two hours, as fatigue and repetition can set in quickly and participants will start to "check out" and lose interest. A skilled moderator should be able to determine when the group has reached the point of saturation on a topic and when to move away from a topic in order to assure that the group has a chance to address each of the questions on the focus group guide. Focus groups should attempt to follow the group's normal communication pattern, allowing for the introduction of new conversation topics in order to keep the discussion lively and the participants interested. This, however, makes data analysis more complex because the participants are sure to jump between topics as they correlate an idea with a previous discussion. A word of warning: most experienced focus group researchers will tell you that for each hour of focus group discussion, you should commit five to six more hours for transcription, review of the observer's notes, and generalized discussion between the moderator and the observer on the interactions between participants and between the participants and the moderator before data analysis begins (Bernard and Ryan 2010; Dawson et al. 1990; Rabiee 2004).

The guide used by the moderator should be general enough to allow for exploration by the participants. Dawson et al. (1993: 08) argue that the guide should be "flexible enough to allow the group to take the discussion in any way it chooses, while providing enough structure and direction to stop the discussion [from] moving away from the original topic to be studied." The questions should be short and open-ended, allowing the group to define how they want to respond to the query. The question guide should include general questions that allow the group to bond and relax, broad introductory questions that help define the relationship of the topic to the group, transition questions that allow the moderator to move the group away from one topic and onto another, and summative questions that allow any final thoughts to be expressed.

Remember that whereas focus groups can offer insight into how a group understands a phenomenon, the social mores or attitudes about it, and even how it may be contested or flexible depending on context, focus groups cannot provide you with detailed knowledge on how the issue or phenomenon is played out. This kind of knowledge is best obtained through observation and in-depth interviews.

Limitations of Focus Groups

Like any research methodology, focus groups have distinct limitations. These can include a lack of intragroup cohesion, dominant participants who prevent others from expressing their opinions, the difficulty of forming a representative focus group, cultural standards that prevent the expression of individual opinion, and lack of adequate planning at each stage of implementation and analysis. Many of these issues have already been discussed, but it is critical to reiterate two areas: cultural standards and planning.

The decision to use qualitative research in a research design is usually predicated on the desire to better understand the mores, practices, ideologies, and dynamics of a particular group. It is critically important that the design, implementation, and analysis of focus groups be guided by a skilled practitioner in qualitative methods who has experience with the group. Many groups have social practices that must be respected in the process of forming a group and in the dynamics of expressing and interacting with each other. Issues of age, gender, status, culturally or socially restricted topics, and even the location of the focus group can be of vital importance and must be considered.

In my work with a community of farm laborers, household surveys on nutrition indicated that fresh vegetables had been an integral part of their diet prior to relocation to the Baja California area but were no longer consumed at the same levels. The household members' working hours were very long and left little time for individual interviews, leading us to use focus groups as a means of gathering information on this and other issues of dietary change. Once we were in the focus groups, however, the question of fresh vegetables produced very little discussion; in fact, great silence occurred. I tried backing into the question by asking about their favorite dishes from their home communities, what they missed in their new community, and what they would like to have available if there were no obstacles. I obtained much information on their favorite dishes and what they missed but could not get any information on why they lacked access to them here, especially since they literally worked in the fields that produced many of these resources.

I could tell that something other than the topic of vegetables was governing the silence, so I moved on to the other topics we wanted to cover. Then, over the next several days, individuals stopped me as I was working on other projects in the community or pulled me aside at events to whisper that the issue was the chemicals that were used in the fields: they all felt that they were dangerous. No one wanted to say it out loud in the focus groups because their employers had made it clear that they were never to discuss pesticides or fertilizers with any researchers who came into the community at the risk of losing their jobs. In this case, the focus group method could not produce all the data we needed to better understand their dietary issues because the subject was a socially restricted topic. Thankfully, the rapport I had with the community led to a deeper understanding of not only their refusal to eat what they perceived as contaminated foodstuffs but also the restrictions the research team would face in addressing a major health issue in the community—exposure to harmful chemicals.

The final limitation that must be considered is the amount of data produced in focus groups and the time needed to appropriately and adequately analyze the information. As I mentioned earlier, most experienced researchers estimate that for each hour of focus group interaction, an additional five to six hours are needed to transcribe the audio or video recordings, integrate the observer's notes, code emergent themes, and input this information into the chosen mode of analysis. This does not include time that may be needed to translate the transcriptions or resolve investigators' differences of interpretation or translation.

Thinking Through Your Focus Group

As noted earlier, focus groups have a distinct application. Do you need data that is based on local practices, understandings, or interpretations? Do you have sufficient rapport with the community to conduct the group, or do you have access to someone who does and can be trained in focus group management? Do you have the resources to convert the lengthy discussions into data sets (transcription, coding, and incorporation of observer notes)? If you can answer yes to each of these questions, then a focus group is likely one of the methods you will want to incorporate into your research. There are five basic components of a focus group design, and each has its own set of parameters:

1. Define the group you wish to target. Establish the parameters for inclusion and exclusion, the recruitment process, the best location for the meetings, and the time frame you have to obtain the necessary data.
2. Establish your guide for facilitation of the group, including the key issues or questions that frame your desired information. As a general guide, you will want to allow fifteen minutes for each topic, understanding that you may want to flesh out the responses of your group before moving on to the next topic. Remember that you do not want to take up more than ninety minutes of the group's time. You also will want to ensure that you end the focus group with one or two questions that bring closure to the group and allow for any last-minute thoughts.
3. Follow the cultural patterns of group cohesion as you select the facilitator/moderator, determine the location for the meeting, and create the appropriate environment, which may involve appropriate refreshments, gifting for their time, and inclusion of the observer or recording equipment. If you will rely on note-taking or wish to enhance the recording of the session, you will need someone other than the facilitator to take the notes.
4. Listen and be present, but do not participate in the responses either consciously or unconsciously. The group should feel confident that their opinions matter, but you should take care not to unduly influence the outcomes. Watch your facial expressions, body language, and other interactions. Much of this will be interpreted within local frames of social interaction, so you will want to be sure that you are fully aware of the social parameters of the group.
5. Take your time and ensure that your data captures not just the group's words but also its dynamic. Was there silence around a particular topic? Were some members excluded from responses? How did the group's body language influence the responses of others? Not all of this is important to each focus group, but the intention of the methodology is to determine the

intimacy and specificity of a topic that cannot be gleaned from individual responses alone. In other words, the group is as important as the responses.

Final Discussion

Focus groups can be an important research method for obtaining deeper insight into a group's shared practices, ideologies, and understandings of their worlds. They are an inexpensive methodology that can greatly enhance a research project, but they must also be appropriately managed before, during, and after the actual event. Their overall design should include information on why a focus group will be useful in terms of the kind of data needed; how the moderator will be chosen and, if necessary, how they will be trained; the locations of the focus groups and the relation of the location to the group; and finally, the method that will be used to transcribe, translate if necessary, code, and then analyze the data. When you are appropriately organized, focus groups can provide important and plentiful data for your research project.

Ramona L. Pérez is Professor of Anthropology and Director of the Center for Latin American Studies at San Diego State University. She has worked for more than twenty years on migration and health; lead poisoning and folk ceramic production in Mexico; the training of *promotoras* on nutrition and diabetes, maternal health, and infant and child nutrition in Oaxaca; and the formation of community among Oaxacan migrants in the United States. Her recent work focuses on binational youth identity and family composition, migrant youth in the context of deportation and survival, squatter settlements, and shifts in culinary food practices and nutrition.

References

Bernard, H. Russell. 2000. *Social Research Methods: Qualitative and Quantitative Approaches*. Thousand Oaks, CA: Sage.

Crockett, Susan J., Karen E. Heller, Joyce M. Merkel, and Jane M. Peterson. 1990. Assessing Beliefs of Older Rural Americans about Nutrition Education: Use of the Focus Group Approach. *American Dietetic Association* 90(4): 563–565.

Dawson, Susan, Lenore Manderson, and Veronica L. Tallo. 1993. *A Manual for the Use of Focus Groups: Methods for Social Research in Disease*. International Nutrition Foundation for Developing Countries (INFDC), Boston, MA.

Hennink, Monique M. 2007. *International Focus Group Research: A Handbook for the Health and Social Sciences*. Cambridge: Cambridge University Press.

Hildebrand, Deana A. and Lenka H. Shriver. 2010. A Quantitative and Qualitative Approach to Understanding Fruit and Vegetable Availability in Low-Income African-American Families with Children Enrolled in an Urban Head Start Program. *Journal of the American Dietetic Association* 110(5): 710–718.

Krueger, Richard A. and Mary Anne Casey. 2008. *Focus Groups: A Practical Guide for Applied Research*. Sage Publications: Thousand Oaks.

Lee, J. S., and E. A. Frongillo, Jr. 2001. Nutritional and Health Consequences Are Associated with Food Insecurity among US Elderly Persons. *Journal of Nutrition* 131(5): 1503–1509.

Learner, RM and VR Kivett. 1981. Discriminators of perceived dietary adequacy among the rural elderly. *Journal of the American Dietetic Association* 78(4): 330–337.

Leung, Fok-Han, and Ratnapalan Savithiri. 2009. Spotlight on Focus Groups. *Canadian Family Physician / Le Médecin de famille canadien* 55(February): 218–219.

Morgan, David L. 1996. *Focus Groups as Qualitative Research*. 2nd ed. Thousand Oaks, CA: Sage.

O'Hanlon, P., and M. B. Kohrs. 1978. Dietary Studies of Older Americans. *American Journal of Clinical Nutrition* 31: 1257.

Posner, Barbara Millen, Alan M. Jette, Kevin W. Smith, and Donald R. Miller. 1993. Nutrition and Health Risks in the Elderly: The Nutrition Screening Initiative. *American Journal of Public Health* 83(7): 972–978.

Samuda, Pauline M., Richard A. Cook, Cristanna M. Cook, and Fitzroy Henry. 1998. Identifying Goods Commonly Consumed by the Jamaican Population: The Focus Group Approach. *International Journal of Food Sciences and Nutrition* 49: 79–86.

United Nations International Network of Food Data Systems (INFOODS). http://www.fao.org/infoods/en/. Accessed 30 November 2013.

Additional Resources

Training Videos

Using Focus Groups. Boise State University, 2009.
http://www.youtube.com/watch?v=rt5W7tXvljo

Training Websites

US Department of Interior National Parks Focus Group Training, University of Idaho
About focus groups: http://psu.uidaho.edu/focusgroup/about.html
Managing focus groups: http://psu.uidaho.edu/focusgroup/evaluation/00.html
Moderator training: http://psu.uidaho.edu/focusgroup/moderator/00.html

Training Manuals

Omni Focus Group Training Manual
http://www.rowan.edu/colleges/chss/facultystaff/focusgrouptoolkit.pdf

University of Southern Florida Youth Focus Group Training Manual (1999)
http://health.usf.edu/nr/rdonlyres/544bc0a8-8995-43c7-8277-1a0e0a5cfe6e/0/youthfocusgrouptraining.pdf

A Manual for the Use of Focus Groups: Methods for Social Research in Disease. By Susan Dawson, Lenore Manderson, and Veronica L. Tallo, 1993, International Nutrition Foundation for Developing Countries.
http://www.seesac.org/sasp2/english/publications/7/5_Focus.pdf

CHAPTER 8

Studying Food and Culture
Ethnographic Methods in the Classroom
Carole Counihan

Introduction

Using ethnographic methods in the classroom is a heady experience. Students' learning is continuous and palpable, and they share the excitement of ongoing discovery. Learning is inevitable because students are doing fieldwork; in the practice of anthropology they learn what it is, what its challenges are, and what sorts of knowledge it creates. They learn collectively from each other as they share roadblocks, discoveries, and strategies. When used in teaching food studies, ethnography is a valuable tool in the interdisciplinary toolkit that informs the whole class about the local food scene. Using a food focus to teach ethnography unites the class around one large common theme while enabling students to specialize in a topic and build independent research to present at conferences.

Ethnography works as a productive teaching tool at both undergraduate and graduate levels. I used it in most of my courses in twenty-five years of teaching undergraduates at Millersville University, a public university of 8,000 in eastern central Pennsylvania. I have also used ethnography in an eighteen-hour Food Anthropology course for students pursuing master's degrees that I have taught since 2005 at the University of Gastronomic Sciences (UNISG) in Italy, and since 2011 in a semester-long course in the Gastronomy MLA Program at Boston University (BU), a private university of 32,000 in the heart of Boston. In this chapter I will use my BU graduate course "Food Ethnography" as a springboard to discuss using ethnography to teach food and culture.

Objectives

The overall goal of the course is to learn ethnography by doing it. I break this down on my course syllabus (see Appendix 1) into five specific objectives that the remainder of this chapter will discuss, showing how the course fulfills them through readings, class discussions, assignments, and student fieldwork.

Objective 1: Students Will Learn What Food Ethnography Is

To fulfill the goal of understanding food ethnography as a field, we use two strategies: readings and an ethnographic project (discussed below). The goals of the readings are several: first, to introduce the students to the fundamental anthropological concept of culture (e.g., Geertz 1966); second, to provide them with a short manual summarizing the ethnographic research process such as Fetterman (2009) (see also Angrosino 1996; Crane and Angrosino 1992; McCurdy, Spradley, and Shandy 2005; Murchison 2010); third, to have them read articles detailing other, more specialized methods; and fourth, to explore together critical reflections on the ethnographic process such as those posed in Cerwonka and Malkki's (2007) *Improvising Theory* or in Wolf's (1992) *Thrice Told Tale*.

I use Pink's *Doing Sensory Ethnography* (2009) to explore the sensory domains that are unique and highly informative in foodways research. An excellent review of the literature on the role of the senses in anthropology, Pink's book offers some suggestive hints about how to study people's sensory experiences. Her definition of "embodiment," which defines the body as "a source of knowledge and subsequently of agency" (24), pushes students to think about the role of the body—both the subject's and the researcher's—in learning about the world. Pink emphasizes the importance of commensal events as rich sites for studying the senses and encourages student ethnographers doing interviews to record not only the verbal utterances that are anthropology's standard fare, but also visual, auditory, olfactory, and gustatory stimuli.

As they develop their own projects, students read some food ethnographies to give them a sense of what ethnographers study, how they do it, what pitfalls they encounter, how they pull together their data, and how they write. Most recently, my students have read Glasser's (2010 [1988]) *More than Bread: Ethnography of a Soup Kitchen,* which is an insightful foray into the challenging environment of a church basement soup kitchen frequented by individuals suffering poverty, unemployment, ill health, loneliness, and physical and mental handicaps. The book raises issues of ethics, advocacy, subjectivity/objectivity, and the researcher's role and emotions in research and writing. Reading food ethnographies (see Appendix 2) can give students models for their own research and writing, enable them to explore issues and questions that arise during their work, and develop their understanding of food ethnography.

During the semester, students also read and discuss "think" texts to develop a critical perspective on the fieldwork process, for example Cerwonka and Malkki's (2007) *Improvising Theory*. This is a report and analysis of the email correspondence during 1994–1995 between Cerwonka, a political science PhD student doing ethnographic fieldwork in Melbourne, Australia, and Malkki, the anthropology professor on her dissertation committee. Their emails explore issues of multi-sited urban fieldwork, research ethics, the "anxiety and euphoria" of fieldwork, how personal lives affect research, and the process of interpretation based on constantly "tacking between theory and empirical data" (4). Another "think" text is Wolf's (1992) *Thrice Told Tale,* which recounts one central fieldwork episode as fieldnotes, as fiction, and as a classic scholarly article, pushing students to think about the role of writing in ethnographic understanding.

Objective 2: Students Will Learn How to Conduct an Ethnographic Research Project from Start to Finish; and Objective 3: Students Will Understand Fieldwork Ethics

Fulfillment of these objectives engages students in all phases of research, from the first idea through research design, institutional review board (IRB) approval, data collection, analysis, writing, and presentation. This process unfolds over the entire semester at a rapid pace, starting from the second week, when students come to class with a short (2–3 page) initial statement of their field site, study population, central question, and proposed methodology. In class we talk about each student's ideas, with all students participating in discussion of their own and others' projects. Students then have two weeks to refine their ideas, confer with the professor in person and by email, and write a complete research design and IRB proposal. In the intervening week, we have a presentation from a campus IRB representative who explains the ins and outs of the IRB process to students.

The syllabus mandates the necessary components of the research design. It describes the problem or topic under investigation, explains why it is important, and aims to "operationalize" it by showing how it can be addressed by obtaining certain kinds of data. The research design contains a short literature review describing briefly what others have written on the topic and the gaps in scholarship. It describes the field site, study population, and methods, linking them to the research question and data needed to address it. It includes a statement of research ethics, a sample consent form, and a complete IRB application.

Different universities differently interpret and apply IRB rules depending on whether professors, graduate students, or undergraduate students are involved; whether they have university funding; and whether their projects fit the definition of "research" as "a systematic investigation...designed to develop or contribute to generalizable knowledge" (OHRP 2008). In my BU course, all students go through the IRB to master the process and to be able in the future to present their work at conferences or publish it if they desire. Students and professor all go through the Collaborative Institutional Training Initiative (CITI) course and quiz (https://www.citiprogram.org/citiinfo.asp), whose successful completion confers a certification necessary (but not sufficient) to attain BU IRB approval. We read Katz's (2006) critical discussion of the IRB process, which outlines the problems it poses for ethnographers and "ethical escape routes."

We read the American Anthropological Association's (AAA 2012) code of ethics and highlight its most important principles, especially "do no harm." We discuss at length the kinds of inadvertent harm that might result from ethnography, for example, the pain of stirring up old memories, threats to the job of a subject who criticizes the workplace, and legal troubles that might stem from admitting to marginally lawful practices. A second key principle of the AAA code of ethics is determination of whether research subjects want to be anonymous or receive recognition, something researchers must work out with them. A third important principle is informed consent and the recognition that the informed consent process is "dynamic, continuous and reflexive." We discuss written and oral versions of informed consent, the awkwardness of getting written consent before people know what the interview is about, cases where written consent is essential, and others where oral consent suffices. A fourth important principal is that anthropologists are to acknowledge their debt to the people they study and to reciprocate when possible. We discuss how anthropologists do not usually pay informants because they do not wish to monetize the research relationship, and how reciprocity can nonetheless be expressed through recognition, gifts, and favors. Overall goals are for students to understand fieldwork ethics, their complexity, and their need for constant monitoring; to inform students about the importance, history, and current state of human subjects review; to enable them to pass IRB review quickly so they can complete their research in one semester; and to develop their critical thinking about the human subjects review process.

Objective 4: Students Will Learn and Use Several Ethnographic Methods

Methods explored in the course include participant observation, interview, life history, photography, map-making, and informant documentation. Students learn about these methods from reading about them, discussing them in class, and using them.

Participant observation
Participant observation is one of the fundaments of ethnographic research. Fetterman (2009: 35) teaches students to begin with an "informal strategy" of finding a field site, hanging around it, and getting a foot in the door. They are exhorted

to take notes, notes, and more notes. We cover practical considerations in taking field notes and discuss how style and mode depend on both the researcher's predilections and the research site. For example, when studying a coffee shop, researchers taking notes on a laptop fit in perfectly, but observing a busy restaurant kitchen may necessitate taking notes in cryptic shorthand in a small notebook while dodging frenetic fry cooks, and filling in details later. We discuss using photographs as "notes," for example, as a means to document material culture and practices, including menus, inventories, prices, signs, trademarks, cooking tools, and techniques. Discussing many possibilities in class helps students find the best ways to get the richest field notes possible in their unique field sites.

Interviews and food-centered life histories

Fetterman (2009: 40) claims that interviews are ethnography's "most important data-gathering technique." In their research designs, students define whom they plan to interview, the interview focus, and the questions, even as we discuss how the actual interview may wander and take on a life of its own. We discuss selection and sampling, including random, snowball, reality, convenience, and serendipity samples. We discuss structured, semi-structured, informal, and retrospective interviews, and nondirective or "grand tour" (Spradley 1979: 86) vs. directive or specific questions, generally agreeing on the value of starting with the most open-ended questions such as "tell me about…" to uncover informants' food culture, and then later probing for details. We discuss the value and use of one or a few key informants versus attaining a broader perspective from many informants.

To explore the power of interviews beyond the information they can provide, as well as their significant role in providing voice to ethnographic subjects, students investigate food-centered life histories (Counihan 2008), the food voice (Hauck-Lawson 1998), and *testimonios* (Gugelberger and Kearney 1991). Food-centered life histories are semi-structured recorded interviews on beliefs and behaviors surrounding food production, preparation, distribution, and consumption. They cover both material conditions like meal content, garden plantings, and family labor, and subjective feelings and memories about eating, nurturing, or household burdens. This method coheres with the work of other scholars of food as women's voice—particularly Abarca's (2006) "culinary chats" and Perez's (2009) "kitchen table ethnography."

Students expand their understanding of the value of insider accounts such as food-centered life histories by reading about *testimonios*: first-person accounts by participants who have witnessed events centered on "a story that *needs* to be told—involving a problem of repression, poverty, subalternity, exploitation, or simply survival" (Beverly 1993: 73). Their goal is "to rewrite and to retell…history and reality from the people's perspective" (Gugelberger and Kearney 1991: 11). For students, *testimonios* emphasize both the value of first-person life history–type accounts, and the need to ground these accounts in social, cultural, and political context, without which they fail to be anthropological.

Other course readings explore autoethnography (Vidal-Ortiz 2004; Wall 2006, 2008), which involves researchers' own personal experience drawn on as data about society and culture. Discussing autoethnography pushes students to think critically about how their own experience—just like that of the people they are studying—is inflected by cultural forces. This contributes to discussions of objectivity/subjectivity and provides students with a means for judicious use of their own relevant experiences as part of the anthropological record.

Photos, maps, and drawings
In ethnography, photography has long-standing utility for documenting material culture, people, practices, landscapes, emotional expressions, architecture, spatial relations, and other facets of culture (Bateson and Mead 1942; Collier and Collier 1986; Counihan 1980; Hockings 2003; Pink 2007; Sullivan 1999). Salazar, Feenstra, and Ohmart (2008), when using photographs to assess the composition and nutritional content of California children's salad bar meals, made the additional unexpected discovery in the photographs of a children's "food culture" distinct from that of adults. Salazar (2012) has explored using photography and new media in her study of middle schoolers' food networks, the pros and cons of giving cameras to adolescents, and the uses of photo-mapping.

Another highly productive method in food ethnography is Marte's (2007) food-mapping strategy. She discusses both researcher- and informant-generated food maps of kitchens, food acquisition or consumption networks, and key dishes and their ingredients. She has managed to show, for example, how Dominican immigrants to New York City forged rich transnational and local networks to gain access to key foods through gift, barter, and purchase. Students have come up with their own ideas about maps, drawing, for example, diagrams of restaurants or food stores, locations of food businesses relative to population type and density, recipe transmission across time and place showing evolution of ingredients, and maps of social interactions in bars. One student (Fitzmaurice 2012) plotted the Boston Food Truck program's prescribed parking spots on top of USDA-defined food deserts and found that the city's food truck program failed to fulfill one of its goals—combating food deserts—because there were no parking spots anywhere near them. Food-mapping is a highly flexible method that can offer diverse insights into food culture. It can also be an ice-breaker that gets students started on research as they gear up for interviews and participant observation.

Informant documentation
Informant documentation is material the ethnographic researcher acquires from the study subjects. It could be photos, letters, diaries, menus, postcards, scrap-

books, or other items of material culture. Students can take photographs of many forms of informant documentation that people do not want to part with, for example, a favorite skillet, wedding cake photo, or homemade recipe book.

Objective 5: Students Will Gain In-Depth Expertise about One Specific Facet of Their Local Food Culture

This objective, which builds on the previous four, is the result of the semester-long research project. The course structure mandates several checkpoints throughout the semester that keep students on track by having them report on the status of their project and uncover roadblocks in time to resolve them. Paper 1, the initial statement of research project, and Paper 2, the research design, were discussed above. The third checkpoint is Paper 3, the data report, which takes place mid-semester. Students give a ten- to fifteen-minute oral presentation of their paper's focus, data gathered so far, data still needed, a preliminary outline of the paper, and a bibliography. They also report changes to the project, pressing questions, problems, and challenges.

Finally, students write Paper 4, a first draft of the research paper, and Paper 5, the final paper. The research paper should contain an abstract, acknowledgments, introduction, literature review, findings, significance, problems, and conclusion. Students bring the first draft to class for peer review. They pair off, read each other's papers, and comment on argument, organization, data, writing style, and mechanics. Together we discuss questions that arise from reading each other's papers. Then they have a week to revise and prepare the final draft and their oral presentation.

The twelve- to fifteen-minute oral presentation mimics a conference presentation so as to give students practice with that format. The presentation also forces them to clarify their ideas and be synthetic about the crux of their project. Oral presentations are interesting to the entire class, as we learn about the local food scene and the process of doing ethnography from each other. The multi-staged two-draft paper and oral presentation process heightens learning and improves the final paper, which is gratifying for students and professor alike.

Conclusion

Use of ethnographic methods in the classroom produces a successful educational experience. Each student comes away with a complete research project that demonstrates competence in research methods and mastery of some part of the local food scene. Students can present their projects at conferences, use them as the basis of bigger thesis projects, and/or aim for publication. Students' ethnographic projects are generally of high quality, and their learning is obvious and gratifying.

Carole Counihan is Professor Emerita of Anthropology at Millersville University in Pennsylvania and editor-in-chief of the scholarly journal *Food and Foodways*. She is author of *A Tortilla Is Like Life: Food and Culture in the San Luis Valley of Colorado* (2009), *Around the Tuscan Table: Food, Family and Gender in Twentieth Century Florence* (2004), and *The Anthropology of Food and Body: Gender, Meaning, and Power* (1999). She is editor of *Food in the USA* (2002), *Food and Culture: A Reader* (with Penny Van Esterik, 1997, 2008, 2013), *Taking Food Public: Redefining Foodways in a Changing World* (with Psyche Williams-Forson, 2012), and *Food Activism: Agency, Democracy, and Economy* (with Valeria Siniscalchi, Bloomsbury 2014). Counihan has been a visiting professor at Boston University (USA), the University of Gastronomic Sciences (Italy), the University of Cagliari (Italy), the University of Sassari (Italy), the École des Hautes Études en Sciences Sociales (France), and Aarhus University (Denmark). Her current research is on food activism in Italy.

Acknowledgments

Thanks to my Millersville University Sociology-Anthropology Department colleagues, especially Marlene Arnold, with whom I shared responsibility for teaching ethnographic methods for twenty-five good years. Thanks to my Millersville students, especially the anthropology majors and minors, for their intriguing projects and excitement about doing ethnography. Thanks to the stalwart Boston University gastronomy graduate students who took my Food Ethnography class in spring 2011 and fall 2012. Special thanks to Gastronomy Program coordinator and friend Rachel Black for support while I was a visiting professor at Boston University from 2011 to 2013, and for many good ideas about food anthropology. Thanks also to Rebecca Alssid, Dean Jay Halfond, and Dean Tanya Zlateva of Boston University's Metropolitan College.

Appendix 1: Food Ethnography Course Syllabus

Dr. Carole Counihan
Boston University Metropolitan College

Food Ethnography

This course explores what food ethnography is and how food ethnographers work through readings, discussion, and a major semester-long independent research project. The class will involve both practicing ethnography and critiquing it, holding an ongoing discussion of the challenges and contributions of ethnographic research. Students will write a research design for an ethnographic project on some aspect of Boston's multifaceted food system, carry it out, analyze their data, and write up and orally present the results. Students will study several ethnographic methods, learn about research ethics, go through the Boston University IRB, and explore various research dilemmas. They will learn how time-consuming and challenging ethnographic research is. They will examine the process of writing and the pros and cons of different ways ethnographers analyze and write up their data. They will pay particular attention to the ways that studying food culture ethnographically presents unique data and insights.

Course Objectives

1. Students will learn what food ethnography is.
2. Students will learn how to conduct an ethnographic research project from start to finish: construct a research design, secure IRB approval, conduct independent fieldwork, analyze data, and write a research paper and give an oral presentation.
3. Students will understand human subjects guidelines, fieldwork ethics, and the code of ethics of the American Anthropological Association, and they will apply ethical codes to their own research.
4. Students will learn and use several ethnographic methods including participant observation, interview, life history, photography, mapmaking, and informant documentation.
5. Students will gain in-depth expertise about one specific facet of Boston food culture.

Books

Cerwonka, Allaine, and Liisa H. Malkki. 2007. *Improvising Theory: Process and Temporality in Ethnographic Fieldwork.* Chicago: University of Chicago Press.

Coleman, Leo, ed. 2012. *Food: Ethnographic Encounters.* Oxford: Berg.

Fetterman, David. 2009. *Ethnography: Step-by-Step.* 3rd ed. Thousand Oaks, CA: Sage.

Glasser, Irene. 2010 [1988]. *More than Bread: Ethnography of a Soup Kitchen.* Tuscaloosa: University of Alabama Press.

Pink, Sarah. 2009. *Doing Sensory Ethnography.* London: Sage.

Articles

American Anthropological Association. 2012. Statement on Ethics and Principles of Professional Responsibility. http://www.aaanet.org/profdev/ethics/upload/Statement-on-Ethics-Principles-of-Professional-Responsibility.pdf

Counihan, Carole. 2008. Mexicanas' Food Voice and Differential Consciousness in the San Luis Valley of Colorado. In *Food and Culture: A Reader,* ed. Carole Counihan and Penny Van Esterik, 354–368. 2nd ed. New York: Routledge.
Geertz, Clifford. 1966. The Impact of the Concept of Culture on the Concept of Man. *Bulletin of the Atomic Scientists* 22(4): 2–8.
Gugelberger, Georg, and Michael Kearney. 1991. Voices for the Voiceless: Testimonial Literature in Latin America. *Latin American Perspectives* 18(3): 3–14.
Hauck-Lawson, Annie. 1998. When Food is the Voice: A Case Study of a Polish-American Woman. *Journal for the Study of Food and Society* 2(1): 21–28.
Marte, Lidia. 2007. Foodmaps: Tracing Boundaries of 'Home' Through Food Relations. *Food and Foodways* 15(1–2): 261–289.
Salazar, Melissa L. 2012. Visualizing 21st Century Foodscapes: Using Photographs and New Media in Food Studies. In *Taking Food Public: Redefining Foodways in a Changing World,* ed. Psyche Williams-Forson and Carole Counihan. New York: Routledge, pp. 322–342.
Vidal-Ortiz, Salvador. 2004. On Being a White Person of Color: Using Autoethnography to Understand Puerto Ricans' Racialization. *Qualitative Sociology* 27(2): 179–203.
Wall, Sarah. 2008. Easier Said than Done: Writing an Autoethnography. *International Journal of Qualitative Methods* 7(1): 38–53.

Course Requirements

Attendance: This course is a seminar where student discussion is central to learning. Please make every possible effort to attend every class. Students who miss more than three classes will not pass the course.

Class discussion leader (10%): Students in small groups will take a leading role in organizing class discussion of one week's readings. Details will follow.

The following papers related to the research project and the course readings are required:

  *—Paper #1—Initial statement of research project relating it to the week's readings (10%)
  *—Paper #2—Research design with literature review and IRB application (20%)
  *—Paper #3—Data report with paper outline and bibliography (no grade)
  *—Oral presentations (10%)
  *—Paper #4—First Draft Research paper
  *—Paper #5—Final Research paper (50%)

BEWARE!! Ethnographic research is exhilarating, hard, fascinating, scary, time-consuming, and full of glitches. It **always** takes longer than expected. Start early, plan ahead, and build in extra time.

All papers should:
- Be either brought to class (in some cases) or emailed to carole1@bu.edu (in other cases) by the due date and time as directed on the syllabus. Emailed papers should have as file name: **yourlastname-ML642-assignmentname** (e.g. Joplin-ML642-research design)
- Have your name, email address, and date at the top of the first page— please no cover page
- Be word-processed, doubled spaced, in 12 pt font, with page numbers on every page
- Have a descriptive title (not, e.g., "Research Design")
- Use a consistent in-text reference style (e.g. APA) with a "references cited" section at the end containing full and correct bibliographic citations for only and all the works cited in the paper

The project has the following stages:
* **Paper #1—Initial statement of research project (10%), due Sept 12:** a 2–3 page (600–900 word) discussion of the topic and central question of your research project, why you want to study it, what you want to find out, and how you plan to use ethnographic methods, particularly those discussed in the week's reading. **Bring a paper copy to class.**

* **Paper #2—Research design (20%) due Sept 26:** 5–6 pages (1500–1800 words). **Bring paper copy to class.**
- It describes the problem or topic that you are investigating and explains why it is important.
- It discusses what others have written on this topic and the gaps, and cites scholarly sources.
- It describes the place and population you will study.
- It includes a statement of research ethics.
- It includes a sample consent form.
- It contains a complete IRB application.
- It defines your methods in detail, which might include several of the following:

Participant-observation: state who, where, when and what you will be observing
Life histories: whose life history will you gather? List the focus and questions
Interviews: whom will you interview? Include a list of interview questions.
Focus groups: why, with whom, asking what?
Informant documentation: what will you collect and from whom?
Photos, maps, drawings: who, what, where, when, and why?
Web-based research: of what, how, and why?

* **Paper #3—Oral and written data report with paper outline and bibliography (no grade), due Oct 24, Oct 31, or Nov 7:** Prepare a fifteen-minute oral presentation of your paper's overriding focus, the data you have gathered so far, the data you still have to gather, a preliminary outline of your paper, and a bibli-

ography. You should also report on any changes you have made to your project, and any pressing questions, problems, and challenges.

* **Oral presentation (10%) due Dec 5 or Dec 12:** give a 12–15 minute oral presentation of your research accompanied by PowerPoint slides or other visual aids. Details will follow.

* **The research paper (50%)—first draft (ungraded) due in class Nov 28, FINAL PAPER due Dec 12:** This should be 20–30 pages (6000–9000 words), word-processed, double-spaced, with at least 1" margins and page numbers. It should include the following sections:
  – *Abstract*: 100–200-word summary of your paper's focus, methods, data, and findings
  – *Acknowledgments*: thanks to those who were helpful in your project
  – *Introduction*: statement of the research question or problem, placing it in context of the scholarly literature
  – *Methodology*: description of who and what you studied and the methods you used to gather data. (Include interview questions and/or other details in Appendix.)
  – *Findings*: organized description of what you found out—this should be the bulk of your paper
  – *Significance*: discussion of what your findings mean and why your research is important with reference to the scholarly literature
  – *Problems*: discussion of problems you encountered in either conceptualizing or conducting your research and how you would remedy them in the future; what you would do differently if you were to do this project over again
  – *Conclusion*
  – *Appendices* (optional): inclusion of information not in body of paper (e.g., list of informants, list of interview questions, glossary of key terms, list of recipes, etc.)
  – *References cited* listing the scholarly sources cited in your paper

NOTE: To maintain high standards of academic honesty and integrity please abide by the Student Academic Conduct Code of Metropolitan College, Boston University. The code is available at: http://www.bu.edu/met/for-students/met-policies-procedures-resources/academic-conduct-code/

Syllabus

Lectures, Readings, and Assignments are subject to change, and will be announced in class as applicable within a reasonable time frame.

date topic and assignment

9/5 Introduction: food ethnography, ethnographic methods, the course, student projects

READ: Geertz, "The Impact of the Concept of Culture…"
Fetterman, chapters 1–2
Pink, Intro, chapters 1–2

9/12 The ethnographic enterprise and fieldwork: interviews and participant observation. Fieldwork practice, etiquette and equipment.
* **2–3 page description of fieldwork project ideas due—bring copy to class for discussion**
READ: Fetterman, chapters 3–4
Pink, chapters 3–5

9/19 Photography, food-mapping, informant documentation, ethics in anthropology
READ: Fetterman, chapter 7 ** **Group One leads discussion** **
Pink, chapter 6
Marte, "Food Maps"
Salazar, "Visualizing 21st Century Foodscapes"
"American Anthropological Association Code of Ethics"
BU IRB website and application
Improvising Theory, pp. 41–43
Guest Lecture: BU IRB representative

9/26 Food voice, *testimonios*
* **Research design with literature review and IRB application due—bring hard copy to class**
READ: Counihan, "Differential Consciousness"
Hauck-Lawson, "When Food is a Voice"
Gugelberger and Kearney, "Voices for the Voiceless"

10/3 Fieldwork and auto-ethnography ** **Group Two leads discussion** **
READ: *Improvising Theory*, pp. 1–43
Glasser, chapters 1–4
Vidal-Ortiz, "On Being a White Person of Color: Using Autoethnography…"
Wall, " Easier Said than Done: Writing an Autoethnography"

10/10 Challenges of fieldwork: personal, structural, methodological
READ: *Improvising Theory* pp. 44–104 ** **Group Three leads discussion** **
Glasser, chapters 5–7

10/17 Tacking between theory and data, confounding realities, telling truths, making change?

READ: *Improvising Theory*, pp. 105–132 ** **Group Four leads discussion** **
Glasser, chapters 8–11

10/24   Data reports and writing
* **Oral data report for group one due**
READ: *Improvising Theory*, pp. 132–162
Coleman chapters 1–3

10/31   Wrapping up fieldwork, writing the paper, drawing conclusions, assessing significance
* **Oral data report for group two due**
READ: *Improvising Theory*, pp. 162–187
Coleman, chapters 4–6

11/7   Analyzing data, organizing data, writing
* **Oral data report for group three due**
READ: Fetterman, chapter 5
Pink, chapter 7
Coleman, chapters 7–9

11/14   Writing the paper, drawing conclusions, assessing significance
READ: Fetterman, chapter 6
Pink, chapter 8
Coleman, chapters 10–11

11/21—NO CLASS—THANKSGIVING BREAK

11/28   Issues in writing, insights, dilemmas, challenges
* **Bring first draft to class**

12/5   * **Student presentations**

12/12   * **Student presentations**
* **Research paper due**

Appendix 2: Food Ethnographies

The following ethnographies have a major focus on foodways: Becker (1999) on concepts of body and self in Fiji, Bestor (2004) on the renowned Tokyo fish market, Black (2012) on the Torino central food market, Christie (2008) on Mexican food spaces, Coleman (2012) on diverse anthropologists' personalistic accounts of food's role in their fieldwork, Counihan (2004, 2009) on foodways and gender in an Italian extended family in Tuscany and in a Mexicano community in southern Colorado, Flynn (2005) on food and poverty in urban Tanzania, Glasser (2010), Holtzman (2009) on Samburu herders' conceptions of food and memory in Kenya, Kahn (1986) on gender and food in Melanesia, Nichter (2001) on adolescent girls' discourses about food and body in Arizona, Ohnuki-Tierney (1993) on rice and identity in Japan, Paules (1991) on the culture of waitressing in a chain restaurant in New Jersey, Paxson (2012) on craft cheesemakers in the United States, Popenoe (2003) on female fattening practices among Muslims in Niger, Reiter (1996) on fast food workers in Ontario, Sutton (2001) on food and memory in Greece, Weismantel (1988) on gender and poverty in Andean Ecuador, and White (2012) on coffee and coffeehouse culture in Japan.

References

AAA (American Anthropological Association). 2012. Statement on Ethics and Principles of Professional Responsibility. http://www.aaanet.org/profdev/ethics/upload/Statement-on-Ethics-Principles-of-Professional-Responsibility.pdf

Abarca, Meredith. 2006. *Voices in the Kitchen: Views of Food and the World from Mexican and Mexican American Working-Class Women.* College Station: Texas A&M University Press.

Angrosino, Michael. 2006. *Doing Cultural Anthropology: Projects for Ethnographic Data Collection.* Long Grove, IL: Waveland.

Bateson, Gregory, and Margaret Mead. 1942. *Balinese Character: A Photographic Analysis.* New York: Academy of Sciences.

Becker, Anne. 1999. *Body, Self, and Society: The View from Fiji.* Philadelphia: University of Pennsylvania Press.

Bestor, Theodore. 2004. *Tsukiji: The Fish Market at the Center of the World.* Berkeley: University of California Press.

Beverly, John. 1993. *Against Literature.* Minneapolis: University of Minnesota Press.

Black, Rachel. 2012. *Porta Palazzo: The Anthropology of an Italian Market.* Philadelphia: University of Pennsylvania Press.

Cerwonka, Allaine, and Liisa H. Malkki. 2007. *Improvising Theory: Process and Temporality in Ethnographic Fieldwork.* Chicago: University of Chicago Press.

Christie, Maria Elisa. 2008. *Kitchenspace: Women, Fiestas, and Everyday Life in Central Mexico.* Austin: University of Texas Press.

Coleman, Leo, ed. 2012. *Food: Ethnographic Encounters.* Oxford: Berg.

Collier, John, and Malcolm Collier. 1986. *Visual Anthropology: Photography as a Research Method.* Albuquerque: University of New Mexico Press.

Counihan, Carole. 1980. La fotografia come metodo antropologico. *La Ricerca Folklorica* 2: 27–32.

———. 2004. *Around the Tuscan Table: Food, Family, and Gender in Twentieth Century Florence.* New York: Routledge.

———. 2008. Mexicanas' Food Voice and Differential Consciousness in the San Luis Valley of Colorado. In *Food and Culture: A Reader,* ed. Carole Counihan and Penny Van Esterik, 354–368. 2nd ed. New York: Routledge.

———. 2009. *A Tortilla Is Like Life: Food and Culture in the San Luis Valley of Colorado.* Austin: University of Texas Press.
Crane, Julia G., and Michael V. Angrosino. 1992. *Field Projects in Anthropology: A Student Handbook.* 3rd ed. Prospect Heights, IL: Waveland.
Fetterman, David. 2009. *Ethnography: Step-by-Step.* 3rd ed. Thousand Oaks, CA: Sage.
Fitzmaurice, Connor. 2012. Driving Taste: Maneuvering Taste in Boston's Food Truck Economy. Unpublished paper.
Flynn, Karen Coen. 2005. *Food, Culture and Survival in an African City.* New York: Palgrave.
Geertz, Clifford. 1966. The Impact of the Concept of Culture on the Concept of Man. *Bulletin of the Atomic Scientists* 22(4): 2–8.
Glasser, Irene. 2010 [1988]. *More than Bread: Ethnography of a Soup Kitchen.* Tuscaloosa: University of Alabama Press.
Gugelberger, Georg, and Michael Kearney. 1991. Voices for the Voiceless: Testimonial Literature in Latin America. *Latin American Perspectives* 18(3): 3–14.
Hauck-Lawson, Annie. 1998. When Food is the Voice: A Case Study of a Polish-American Woman. *Journal for the Study of Food and Society* 2(1): 21–28.
Hockings, Paul, ed. 2003. *Principles of Visual Anthropology.* 3rd ed. Berlin and New York: Mouton de Gruyter.
Holtzman, Jon. 2009. *Uncertain Tastes: Memory, Ambivalence, and the Politics of Eating in Samburu, Northern Kenya.* Berkeley: University of California Press.
Kahn, Miriam. 1986. *Always Hungry, Never Greedy: Food and the Expression of Gender in a Melanesian Society.* Cambridge: Cambridge University Press.
Katz, Jack. 2006. Ethical Escape Routes for Underground Ethnographers. *American Ethnologist* 33(4): 499–506.
Marte, Lidia. 2007. Foodmaps: Tracing Boundaries of "Home" Through Food Relations. *Food and Foodways* 15(1–2): 261–289.
McCurdy, David, James Spradley, and Dianna Shandy. 2005. *The Cultural Experience: Ethnography in Complex Society.* Long Grove, IL: Waveland.
Murchison, Julian. 2010. *Ethnography Essentials: Designing, Conducting, and Presenting Your Research.* San Francisco: Jossey-Bass.
Nichter, Mimi. 2001. *Fat Talk: What Girls and Their Parents Say about Dieting.* Cambridge, MA: Harvard University Press.
Ohnuki-Tierney, Emiko. 1993. *Rice as Self: Japanese Identities Through Time.* Princeton, NJ: Princeton University Press.
OHRP (Office for Human Research Protections). 2008. *Guidance on Engagement of Institutions in Human Subjects Research.* Washington, DC: Department of Health and Human Services. http://www.hhs.gov/ohrp/policy/engage08.html. Accessed 18 June 2013.
Paules, Greta Foff. 1991. *Power and Resistance among Waitresses in a New Jersey Restaurant.* Philadelphia: Temple University Press.
Paxson, Heather. 2012. *The Life of Cheese: Crafting Food and Value in America.* Berkeley: University of California Press.
Perez, Ramona Lee. 2009. *Tasting Culture: Food, Family and Flavor in Greater Mexico.* Unpublished PhD dissertation, New York University.
Pink, Sarah. 2007. *Doing Visual Anthropology: Images, Media and Representation in Research,* 2nd ed. London: Sage.
———. 2009. *Doing Sensory Ethnography.* London: Sage.

Popenoe, Rebecca. 2003. *Feeding Desire: Fatness, Beauty, and Sexuality among a Saharan People.* London and New York: Routledge.
Reiter, Ester. 1996. *Making Fast Food: From the Frying Pan into the Fryer.* Montreal: McGill-Queen's University Press.
Salazar, Melissa L. 2012. Visualizing 21st Century Foodscapes: Using Photographs and New Media in Food Studies. In *Taking Food Public: Redefining Foodways in a Changing World,* ed. Psyche Williams-Forson and Carole Counihan. New York: Routledge, pp. 322–342.
Salazar, Melissa, Gail Feenstra, and Jeri Ohmart. 2008. Salad Days: Using Visual Methods to Study Children's Food Culture. In *Food and Culture: A Reader,* ed. Carole Counihan and Penny Van Esterik. 2nd ed. New York: Routledge, pp. 423–437.
Spradley, James. 1979. *The Ethnographic Interview.* Belmont, CA: Wadsworth.
Sullivan, Gerald. 1999. *Margaret Mead, Gregory Bateson, and Highland Bali: Fieldwork Photographs of Bayung Gede, 1936–1939.* Chicago: University of Chicago Press.
Sutton, David E. 2001. *Remembrance of Repasts: An Anthropology of Food and Memory.* Oxford: Berg.
Vidal-Ortiz, Salvador. 2004. On Being a White Person of Color: Using Autoethnography to Understand Puerto Ricans' Racialization. *Qualitative Sociology* 27(2): 179–203.
Wall, Sarah. 2006. An Autoethnography on Learning about Ethnography. *International Journal of Qualitative Methods* 5(2): 1–12.
———. 2008. Easier Said than Done: Writing an Autoethnography. *International Journal of Qualitative Methods* 7(1): 38–53.
Weismantel, M. J. 1988. *Food, Gender and Poverty in the Ecuadorian Andes.* Philadelphia: University of Pennsylvania Press.
White, Merry. 2012. *Coffee Life in Japan.* Berkeley: University of California Press.
Wolf, Margery. 1992. *A Thrice Told Tale: Feminism, Postmodernism, and Ethnographic Responsibility.* Stanford, CA: Stanford University Press.

SECTION V

Linguistics and Food Talk

CHAPTER 9

Introduction to Linguistic Anthropology Food Research Methods

Jillian R. Cavanaugh and Kathleen C. Riley

Language and food are intertwined not only through their orality, but also because both are signifying media through which humans negotiate their material and social existence. Many studies of language incidentally include data about growing, sharing, cooking, eating, and advertising food; similarly, many studies of food include linguistic data: words and genres representing food, speech acts organizing its production and consumption, texts detailing its preparation and distribution. And yet the many intrinsic relationships between language and food—between their material production and symbolic comprehension—have only begun to be explicitly theorized or conceptualized. This introductory chapter is intended as a first step toward looking at how extant research has generally analyzed the intersection between foodways (i.e., how humans produce, exchange, consume, and think about food) and discourse (i.e., how humans use language for everyday talk as well as ideological pronouncements). The following four chapters will then flesh this out by investigating how research examines or has the potential to examine (1) food talk, or the social interactions that frame, embody, and embroider the procuring, cooking, and eating of culinary fare, (2) cultural domains and other shared cultural knowledge about food; (3) food texts, including all the communicative forms that take shape in our attempts to represent food, and (4) historical sources relating to food (from cookbooks to blogs).

Methods for teasing out the threads that bind food and talk together can be found in linguistic anthropology, sociolinguistics, linguistic ethnography, discursive psychology, cognitive analysis, discourse analysis, textual analysis, historical anthropology, and semiotic anthropology. As of this writing, there are no extant methods manuals explaining how to research food and language together, and the methods available for studying these relationships have not been otherwise catalogued (though see the brief article on the topic by Cavanaugh et al. 2014). In this chapter we examine the most common approaches to conducting research on food and language. We begin with a brief overview of how the two have been examined together across a range of anthropological research, which leads to a discussion of various theoretical and methodological threads that tie these approaches together. We then focus on the methods used in these studies and conclude by introducing the rest of the chapters in this section. After the text, we list key citations on language and food methods; available qualitative data analysis (QDA) software; and clearinghouse websites and other resources for guidance.

Food and Language: How Are They Connected (for humans and for anthropologists)?

There are old and new hypotheses concerning evolutionary links between cooking, caloric intake, larger brains, smaller jaws, and the development of language; between female food gathering and "motherese" (the language caregivers use with children); and between mealtime sharing and hearthside gossip (Falk 2009; Wrangham 2009; Dunbar 1992). The methods for studying these issues are derived from paleoanthropology, archaeology, biological anthropology, and linguistics as researchers examine the jaws, teeth, spinal tilts, tools, hearths, middens, and other material evidence of how our ancestors were biologically built, what technologies they developed to adapt their biological selves to their environments, and how both biology and technology contributed to their social evolution and their development of language and foodways in particular. Inherent in these methods are deeply grounded understandings about both the material and social sides of food and talk: language is a resource and tool that allows for the production, distribution, and consumption of food; and food is a semiotic vehicle that drives the socialization (i.e., ways in which one learns to be a member of a culture) of the concrete forms of language. Thus, it is no wonder that many other studies touching on food and talk find interwoven connections between the two.

In the work of French theorists, language and food are palpable metaphors in the analysis of culture. For Levi-Strauss in *The Raw and the Cooked* (1983), humans are cooked (read: socialized) through the mediation of fire (read: language). For Barthes in *Empire of Signs* (1983), foodways (sushi and chopsticks) and language (Japanese writing and grammar) provide symbolic reflections of cultural difference. For Bourdieu (1984), food and language are similarly embodied, each pointing to social distinctions and aiding in the reproduction of political-economic and social hierarchies. The research that supports these findings draws on ethnographic, sociological, and textual analytic methods.

This notion of food as a symbolic code operating much like language can also be found in the Anglo-Saxon discipline of sociocultural anthropology (e.g., Douglas 2008). However, far more important to this ethnographic tradition are the notions that foodways are contained by discourse, that discourse is contextualized by foodways, and that such connections need to be unearthed through extended participant observation. For Malinowski (1965), language made sense only when planted squarely in its context of use (e.g., while gardening), and food could only be grown when urged into being by language (i.e., gardening magic). For Frake (1964), knowing how to ask for a drink in Subanun was a matter of communicative competence (the ways people communicate specific to a particular cultural context), the acquisition of which depended (for the anthropologist) on the ethnographic method of analyzing situated speech events in terms of a number of defining features, such as who could say what to whom, and what the overall goals of the interaction were (see Hymes 1964 and Gumperz and Hymes 1972 for discussions of this method, called the ethnography of communication).

Some anthropologists study the way people talk about food, using this as a window onto a wide range of cultural phenomena. Berlin (1972), a pioneer of ethnosemantics (the study of how language expresses the world views of a people through the lexical and grammatical forms in which things, thoughts, and feelings are categorized), turned to studying ethnobotanical terms in order to understand the proclivities and obsessions of a culture (e.g., the proliferation of Tzeltal terms for distinctive types of chili peppers). In a related fashion, American culinary terms such as spaghetti, sushi, and salsa can be analyzed as symbolic ingredients in the formation of immigrant groups in the US (De Fina 2007; Gabaccia 2000). Food terms borrowed from ethnic groups may also take on particular salience when transformed into ethnic metonyms and racial slurs, like the use of the term "beaners" by Anglo managers with Hispanic kitchen staff in Barrett's (2006) analysis of an Anglo-run Mexican restaurant in Texas.

Other anthropologists have treated food interactions as the context for analyzing culturally significant forms of discourse—whether ethnographically noted, or recorded and then transcribed—that in turn shed further light on a range of cultural practices and ideologies. As Gewertz (1984) illustrated, Chambri conflict discourse that accompanied the preparation of a sago soup could only be translated (i.e., understood by the ethnographer) by placing it within the context of the larger language of exchange of foodstuffs in that part of Papua New Guinea. And Silverstein (2006), working from transcribed audio recordings of wine tastings, has explored how words are not only semantic containers for our dietary obsessions (e.g., with wine), but also help to shape our taste for and willingness to buy into a hyper-inflated symbolic marketplace. Other researchers have studied how language is learned through social interactions around food events and how cultural norms are learned and expressed through talk during mealtime speech events from Papua New Guinea to Italy (Ochs, Pontecorvo, and Fasulo 1996; Paugh and Izquierdo 2009; Schieffelin 1990; Tannen 2005). Such studies have focused on how the exchange of both words and food within domestic settings gives shape to everyday social life as well as to social formations on a larger scale.

Generally speaking, we see several theoretical relationships between food and language threading their way through all of these anthropological studies. First, at the macro level, both everyday linguistic practices and foodways are seen to be shaped by political-economic structures and to reflect transformations in those formations. Secondly, discourses *about* food and foodways, ranging from fast-food advertising, school nutrition policies, and food security charity pleas to daily expressions of taste such as "yuck" and "yum," play significant roles in the construction of communities and identities. Third, just as language ideologies—ideas and feelings about the form and the use of language—may be explicitly articulated as well as covertly embedded in patterns of language use, so too are food ideologies found in the food practices of farmers, chefs, and diners, not just in what they say about food. Finally, these food and language ideologies are embedded within particular contexts and come to make sense in particular ways to particular people; that is, linguistic repertoires (the linguistic resources individuals and communities have at their disposal) and language attitudes are socialized in part via food practices, while foodways and food ideologies are socialized via communicative exchanges.

In short, food and words are not merely ingredients simmered together into a uniquely human stew. They are also the plough, the market, the stewpot, the menu, the blog, and the Zagat guide—they are resources that we as humans use and turn to as we make sense of our world. As such, foodways and discourse need to be jointly theorized, and, perhaps even more importantly, methods need to be developed for analyzing their interrelationships within precise ethnographic contexts.

Food and Language Research Methods: A Brief Sketch

In terms of methodology, all of the anthropological approaches mentioned thus far share an interest in identifying the intersection between food-infused ethnographic settings and language use. Paleoanthropological approaches attend to the reconstruction of food-focused interactions based on evidence about environmental settings, biological adaptations, technological innovations, and social organization. Discourse-based approaches (such as discursive psychology and conversation analysis) privilege the methods that best focus on linguistic data (whether spoken or written) while staying attentive to the food-based social contexts of interaction. Sociocultural approaches (such as cultural anthropology or ethnohistory) use methods that collect data about cultural foodways, much of which (both the data and the foodways) are also inevitably linguistic in nature. We now outline some of the methods that, while also underpinning much of anthropological research in general, take specific forms when employed by researchers attentive to language and culture (e.g., linguistic anthropologists, linguistic ethnographers, sociolinguists) whose focus has turned to foodways. Thus, we look here at how participant observation, detailed field notes, photographs, interviews, focus groups, audio recording, and video recording can be used to investigate what people say when engaged in food-related activities, and how food is made meaningful through discourse and interaction. Many of these methods will be discussed in more detail in other chapters, in this and other sections.

Participant observation can and has been used to qualitatively assess how food and language are encountered and experienced by various groups of people. Much has been written about this method (from Malinowski on, as is discussed in many chapters in this volume, but see in particular Geertz's [1973] notion of "thick description"). Here we wish to point out that ongoing, consistent participant observation in food-centered discourse events—from dinner tables to market squares—can reveal striking patterns in terms of the co-occurrence of particular forms of language with particular forms of food consumption, distribution, and production. And however the activities of everyday life are subsequently theorized—whether as evidence of how food operates as a form of language that structures social relationships and identities, as in Jarvenpa (2008), or as showing how people use talk about food to narrate the arc of their lives, as in Counihan (2004)—the method of participant observation, in which the analyst becomes a part of the social landscape (e.g., learning to talk while eating or preparing food [Riley 2009, 2012]), has proven extremely useful.

Less often discussed but no less important is the method of writing detailed field notes in conjunction with participant observation. Whether this is done in real time, as activities are unfolding around the researcher (messy handwritten notes, jottings on a tablet or phone, or quick voice recordings), or later, after the events have ended and the researcher writes from memory what occurred, field notes have long been a major source of data for anthropologists, including those interested in food. Those focused in particular on food and language will record observations on how food is talked about, the names of different foods or food-centered events, or narratives that include or center around food. Researchers differ in their manner of writing field notes and what they include in them (e.g., they may include their personal reflections on and reactions to the events and people they describe, or they may use pseudonyms for informants or their real names). What researchers do with field notes also differs; some feed them into qualitative data analysis software (see examples of these in the resource list below), while others may take a more intuitive, inductive approach to sifting through and seeking to synthesize the contents of their note-taking. Although researchers may include excerpts from their field notes in their published writings (e.g., Fischer 2010), field notes overall are considered private and confidential, and are treated as such.

Interviews and oral histories are another important set of methods for gathering evidence related to language and food. Carefully analyzed interviews (whether semi-structured or formal) conducted with people who produce, prepare, or consume food can illuminate how food is thought about and represented through language. Counihan (2008) provides a clear introduction to how she collects her "food centered life histories" (in this case, those of Mexicanas in Colorado). Jourdan and Poirier (2012) have also used oral histories to examine generational food change in Quebec. Garth (2009) used interviews to map out Cubans' strategies, now and in the past, for procuring ingredients for preparing culturally meaningful meals in a chronically food-insecure setting. And Abarca (2007), through the method she labels the "kitchen chat"—a kind of informal and extended interview contextualized by the food activities of a few key informants—seeks to understand how Mexican and Mexican-American women are empowered by taking their private cooking skills out into the public sphere. Fischer (2010) employed an oral history approach—a series of interviews, sometimes conducted over a number of years, intended to establish an individual's memories of an entire period of social history—to collect and analyze elderly women's accounts of scrounging and hoarding food in both socialist and postsocialist Hungary.

Conducting focus groups is another method for analyzing directed talk by groups of informants who are selected by the researcher because they belong to a certain category of people or are seen to represent specific types of people, such as "housewives" or "stay-at-home dads." Researchers assemble such groups to ask various types of questions (e.g., open-ended or directed), expecting the social interaction among group members to be an additional source of information on how people relate to food through language. For instance, Johansson et al. (2009) gathered groups of children in four Nordic cities to define their notions of "good/healthy" versus "special/treat" foods based on photographs they had taken of the food around them.

Visual and/or audio recording devices are also commonly used to investigate how food and language co-occur. Photographs of food-related events document the various types of sociality that occur within them, depicting participants talking, singing, or otherwise linguistically engaged. These may also include photographs of food in the process of being produced, processed, prepared, distributed, and consumed, as in the work of Salazar, Feenstra, and Ohmart (2008), who took photographs of the salads schoolchildren composed at school and elicited their comments about them, or Strangelman (2010), who used photographs of a Guinness brewery to jog the brewers' memories of food, drink, and sociality at work in former days.

Audio recording is a common tool for those who are interested in preserving both how people use language and what exactly they say. Ironically, the very presence of food and food-related activities may pose challenges for audio recordings, as, for example, the sounds produced by the activities surrounding eating (utensils on plates, requests for another helping, chewing, etc.) will play an active role in the acoustic landscape that is captured in an audio recording. Nonetheless, audio recordings may also provide invaluable evidence of the language that people use around and about food. For instance, Krögel (2009) would take notes on her Quechua-speaking informants' naturally occurring oral narratives, which inevitably made reference to the power (social and supernatural) of food, and then ask later on, for the sake of her tape recorder, for retellings of these locally popular tales.

Video recording, another useful tool for recording human interaction around and about food, captures both visual and audio evidence of such interactions in an integrated format. That is, video recording allows us to analyze not only what people are doing as they talk about food, but also how they interact around food. Much recent mealtime discourse research (e.g., Ochs and Taylor 1995; Paugh and Izquierdo 2009; Karrebæk 2012) makes use of such video data with the aim of analyzing not only the verbal but also the nonverbal forms of communication in the negotiation and socialization of food-and-language practices, and of other cultural beliefs and practices, in the presence of food.

However, both audio and video recording (whether of natural talk or of interviews and focus groups) requires an additional commitment: transcription of what is recorded. Scholars writing about transcription have noted that it necessarily involves processes of selection—that is, decisions to include or exclude various forms of material. Should one transcribe every clearing of the throat or act of lip-smacking? Every "er," "um" and "ahhh"? Is it necessary to represent non-standard speech varieties and other co-occurring actions or events? Such choices drive how "rich" or elaborated the transcript will ultimately be, that is, whether it includes every representational feature possible, down to the phonetic shape of every utterance, participants' eye gazes and gestures, and tones/pitches/volumes of utterances. Such choices inevitably involve trade-offs in terms of the clarity of the resulting transcript: the more elaborated it is, the more difficult it can be to read. As such, transcription necessarily involves choices that many (Sacks, Schegloff, and Jefferson 1974; Ochs 1979; Vigouroux 2009, among others) have argued should be driven by and support the scholar's research goals. Such choices should also be explicitly discussed as part of the methods used to arrive at the particular analysis. Whether simply described in field notes or also audio- and/or videotaped and transcribed, contextualized discourse approaches such as these will be discussed more thoroughly in our chapter on Food Talk.

Another research method that may be used to investigate food and language together, at times alongside other methods described above, is the collection and analysis of food-related documents such as cookbooks, menus, diaries, letters, blogs, and brochures. Appadurai (1988), for instance, demonstrated how the emergence of cookbooks in India was part of constructing the modern nation-state. Such written materials may be historical or contemporary, easily accessible or hard to find, and may also include compiled media-related materials like blogs, food journalism, and other food writing. For example, Albala, in his chapter in this section, writes about primary source materials as rich sources of food data that anthropologists can share with historians. Documents about food might take perspectives as different as an economic history of farming and an account of what kitchen inventories tell us about how home cooks approach constructing family meals. Food and language are brought together when documents discuss food—how people produce, circulate, and consume it—as in the work of Owens (2011) and Kashay (2009), who have investigated missionary letters and official colonial accounts of food practices.

Cultural domain analysis and related methods, described in Zycherman's chapter in this section, are geared to reveal cognitive categories concerning food. Researchers work with informants to reveal how food is categorized in various ways: into food groups, around food-centered activities, by production practices, etc. Such categories or domains are revealed through verbal interaction centered on the production of lists of items and/or the sorting of such items into salient categories. Language, then, takes the form of food-related terms and descriptions of these terms and their usage, which the researcher records via note-taking or audio-recording.

In her chapter in this section, Riley discusses various methods of text(ual) analysis, identifying the diverse forms of food texts that are collected and produced by researchers and the many ways of examining and representing them. For instance, food texts can include verbal and non-verbal communicative forms ranging from the Bible to a TV food show and can be analyzed using a host of more or less old-fashioned methods—from literary criticism to computer search engines. This chapter itself could be considered a text worthy of such analysis and could be studied not only for what it says, but also how and why.

Concluding Thoughts

It seems a truism to note that humans talk about food, or that they talk around food—while they consume it, prepare it, distribute it, and produce it—and that this is both humanly universal while also culturally specific across groups. At the same time, food itself can be seen to resemble language, as a symbolic code or vehicle for making meaning. We have sought to sketch out here some of the ways in which scholars have studied language and food simultaneously. The following chapters will delve more deeply into the specific methods scholars are developing for probing the connections between foodways and discourse. The short lists of resources we offer here for researching these connections are not meant to be exhaustive by any means but simply suggestive, offering students and other researchers a way in and a way to begin.

Jillian R. Cavanaugh is Associate Professor in the Department of Anthropology and Archaeology at Brooklyn College CUNY and the Anthropology Program at the Graduate Center CUNY. She is a linguistic anthropologist whose research has considered language shift and social transformation, language ideologies, language and materiality, language and gender, and the value of heritage food. Her work has appeared in *American Anthropologist,* the *Journal of Linguistic Anthropology,* and *Ethnos,* among others, and she is presently co-editing (with Kathleen C. Riley) a special issue of *Semiotics Review* on food and language.. Her current research is with food producers in northern Italy. She received her PhD in anthropology at New York University.

Kathleen C. Riley has taught linguistic and cultural anthropology at Concordia University, City College, Queens College, Fordham University, Barnard College, and Rutgers University. She has conducted fieldwork on food change, language socialization, and cultural identity in the Marquesas, Vermont, France, Montreal, and New York City, and has published articles in the *Journal of Linguistic Anthropology* and *Language and Communication,* as well as in several edited collections. She has co-edited (with Christine Jourdan) a special issue of *Anthropologie et Sociétés* on food glocalization and is presently co-editing (with Jillian Cavanaugh) a special issue of *Semiotics Review* on food and language.

Key Texts on Language and Food Methods
(also found below in reference list)

On Oral History and Food Voice
Counihan, Carole. 2008. *Mexicanas*' Food Voice and Differential Consciousness in the San Luis Valley of Colorado. In *Food and Culture: A Reader,* ed. Carole Counihan and Penny Van Esterik, 354–368. New York: Routledge.

On the Ethnography of Speaking
Gumperz, John, and Dell Hymes, eds. 1972. *Directions in Sociolinguistics: The Ethnography of Communication.* New York and London: Holt, Rinehart and Winston.
Hymes, Dell. 1964. Introduction: Toward Ethnographies of Communication. *American Anthropologist* 66(6–2): 1–34.

On Ethnographic Participant Observation
Geertz, Clifford. 1973. Thick Description: Toward an Interpretive Theory of Culture. In *The Interpretation of Cultures: Selected Essays,* 3–30. New York: Basic Books.

Malinowski, Bronislaw. 1965. *Coral Gardens and Their Magic: A Study of the Methods of Tilling the Soil and in Agricultural Rites in the Trobriand Islands.* Bloomington: Indiana University Press.

On the Practice of Transcription

Ochs, Elinor. 1979. Transcription as Theory. In *Developmental Pragmatic,* ed. Elinor Ochs and Bambi B. Schieffelin, 43–72. New York: Academic Press.

Sacks, Harvey, Emanuel A. Schegloff, and Gail Jefferson. 1974. A Simplest Systematics for the Organization of Turn-Taking for Conversation. *Language* 50: 696–735.

Clearinghouse Sites/Resources for Guidance
SLA website http://kit.linguisticanthropology.org/
Max Planck Field Manuals website http://fieldmanuals.mpi.nl/

Qualitative Data Analysis Programs
Atlas.ti (http://www.atlasti.com/index.html)
Dedoose (http://www.dedoose.com)
Nvivo (http://www.qsrinternational.com/products_nvivo.aspx)

References

Abarca, Meredith. 2007. *Charlas Culinarias*: Mexican Women Speak from Their Public Kitchens. *Food and Foodways: Explorations in the History and Culture of Human Nourishment* 15(3–4): 183–212.

Appadurai, Arjun. 1988. How to Make a National Cuisine: Cookbooks in Contemporary India. *Comparative Studies in Society and History* 30(1): 3–24.

Barrett, Rusty. 2006. Language Ideology and Racial Inequality: Competing Functions of Spanish in an Anglo-Owned Mexican Restaurant. *Language in Society* 35: 163–204.

Barthes, Roland. 1983. *Empire of Signs.* New York: Hill and Wang.

Berlin, Brent. 1972. Speculations on the Growth of Ethnobotanical Nomenclature. *Language and Society* 1(1): 51–86.

Bourdieu, Pierre. 1984. *Distinction: A Social Critique of the Judgment of Taste.* Cambridge, MA: Harvard University Press.

Cavanaugh, Jillian R., Kathleen C. Riley, Alexandra Jaffe, Christine Jourdan, Martha Karrebæk, and Amy Paugh. 2014. What Words Bring to the Table: The Linguistic Anthropological Toolkit as Applied to the Study of Food. *Journal of Linguistic Anthropology* 24(1): 84–97.

Counihan, Carole. 2004. *Around the Tuscan Table: Food Family, and Gender in Twentieth Century Florence.* New York: Routledge.

———. 2008 *Mexicanas*' Food Voice and Differential Consciousness in the San Luis Valley of Colorado. In *Food and Culture: A Reader,* ed. Carole Counihan and Penny Van Esterik, 354–368. 2nd ed. New York: Routledge.

De Fina, Anna. 2007. Code-Switching and the Construction of Ethnic Identity in a Community of Practice. *Language in Society* 36: 371–392.

Douglas, Mary. 2008. Deciphering a Meal. In *Food and Culture: A Reader*, ed. Carole Counihan and Penny Van Esternik, 36–54. 2nd ed. New York: Routledge.

Dunbar, Robin. 1992. Why Gossip Is Good For You. *New Scientist* 136(1848): 28–31.

Falk, Dean. 2009. *Finding Our Tongues: Mothers, Infants and the Origins of Language*. New York: Perseus/Basic Books.

Fischer, Lisa Pope. 2010. Turkey Backbones and Chicken Gizzards: Women's Food Roles in Post-socialist Hungary. *Food and Foodways* 18: 233–260.

Frake, Charles O. 1964. How to Ask for a Drink in Subanun. *American Anthropologist* 66: 127–132.

Gabaccia, Donna R. 2000. *We Are What We Eat: Ethnic Food and the Making of Americans*. Cambridge: Harvard University Press.

Garth, Hannah. 2009. Things Became Scarce: Food Availability and Accessibility in Santiago de Cuba Then and Now. *Napa Bulletin* 32: 178–192.

Geertz, Clifford. 1973. Thick Description: Toward an Interpretive Theory of Culture. In *The Interpretation of Cultures: Selected Essays*, 3–30. New York: Basic Books.

Gewertz, Deborah. 1984. Of Symbolic Anchors and Sago Soup: The Rhetoric of Exchange among the Chambri of Papua New Guinea. In *Dangerous Words: Language and Politics in the Pacific*, ed. Donald L. Brenneis and Fred R. Myers, 192–213. New York: New York University Press.

Gumperz, John, and Dell Hymes, eds. 1972. *Directions in Sociolinguistics: The Ethnography of Communication*. New York and London: Holt, Rinehart and Winston.

Hymes, Dell. 1964. Introduction: Toward Ethnographies of Communication. *American Anthropologist* 66(6–2): 1–34.

Jarvenpa, Robert. 2008. Diets of Experience: Food Culture and Political Ecology in Northern Canada and Northern Finland. *Food and Foodways* 16: 1–32.

Johansson, Barbara, Joanna Mäkelä, Gun Roos, Sandra Hillén, Gitte Laub Hansen, Tine Mark Jensen, and Anna Huotilainen. 2009. Nordic Children's Foodscapes: Images and Reflections. *Food, Culture, and Society* 12(1): 25–51.

Jourdan, Christine, and Sylvain Poirier. 2012. Le Goût en Héritage : Exploration des Transformations Alimentaires dans quelques Familles Montréalaises. *Anthropologica* 54(2): 281–292.

Kashay, Jennifer Fish. 2009. Missionaries and Foodways in Early 19th-Century Hawai'i. *Food and Foodways* 17: 159–180.

Karrebæk, Martha Sif. 2012. "What's in Your Lunch-Box Today?" Health, Ethnicity and Respectability in the Primary Classroom. *Journal of Linguistic Anthropology* 22(1): 1–22.

Krögel, Alison. 2009. Dangerous Repasts: Food and the Supernatural in the Quechua Oral Tradition. *Food and Foodways* 17: 104–132.

Levi-Strauss, Claude. 1983. *The Raw and the Cooked: Mythologiques*, vol. 1. Chicago: University of Chicago Press.

Malinowski, Bronislaw. 1965. *Coral Gardens and Their Magic: A Study of the Methods of Tilling the Soil and in Agricultural Rites in the Trobriand Islands*. Bloomington: Indiana University Press.

Ochs, Elinor. 1979. Transcription as Theory. In *Developmental Pragmatics*, ed. Elinor Ochs and Bambi B. Schieffelin, 43–72. New York: Academic Press.

Ochs, Elinor, Clotilde Pontecorvo, and Alessandra Fasulo. 1996. Socializing Taste. *Ethnos* 61(1–2): 7–46.

Ochs, Elinor, and Carolyn Taylor. 1995. The "Father Knows Best" Dynamic in Dinnertime Narratives. In *Gender Articulated: Language and the Socially Constructed Self*, ed. Kira Hall and Mary Bucholtz, 97–120. New York: Routledge.

Owens, Sarah E. 2011. Food, Fasting, and Itinerant Nuns. *Food and Foodways* 19: 274–293.

Paugh, Amy, and Carolina Izquierdo. 2009. Why Is This a Battle Every Night? Negotiating Food and Eating in American Dinnertime Interaction. *Journal of Linguistic Anthropology* 19(2): 185–204.

Riley, Kathleen C. 2009. Who Made the Soup? Socializing the Researcher and Cooking Her Data. *Language and Communication* 29(3): 254–270.

———. 2012. Learning to Exchange Words for Food in the Marquesas. In *Food: Ethnographic Encounters*, ed. Leo Coleman, 111–126. Oxford: Berg Publishers.

Sacks, Harvey, Emanuel A. Schegloff, and Gail Jefferson. 1974. A Simplest Systematics for the Organization of Turn-Taking for Conversation. *Language* 50: 696–735.

Salazar, Melissa, Gail Feenstra, and Jeri Ohmart. 2008 Salad Days: A visual Study of Children's Food Culture. In *Food and Culture,* ed. Carole Counihan and Penny Van Esterik, 423–437. 2nd ed. New York: Routledge.

Schieffelin, Bambi B. 1990. *The Give and Take of Everyday Language.* Cambridge: Cambridge University Press.

Silverstein, Michael. 2006. Old Wine, New Ethnographic Lexicography. *Annual Review of Anthropology* 35: 481–496.

Strangleman, Tim. 2010. Food, Drink and the Cultures of Work: Consumption in the Life and Death of an English Factory. *Food, Culture and Society* 13(2): 257–278.

Tannen, Deborah. 2005. *Conversational Style: Analyzing Talk among Friends.* 2nd ed. New York: Oxford University Press.

Vigouroux, Cecile. 2009. The Making of a Scription: A Case Study on Authority and Authorship. *Text & Talk* 29(5): 615–637.

Wrangham, Richard. 2009. *Catching Fire: How Cooking Made Us Human.* New York: Basic Books.

CHAPTER 10

Food Talk
Studying Foodways and Language in Use Together

Kathleen C. Riley and Jillian R. Cavanaugh

Introduction

Anthropologists have been investigating relationships between food and talk for decades, whether they were aware of it or not. Early studies of food production, preservation, distribution, preparation, and consumption also included evidence of language in use: lists of native terms for foods and dishes, ritual phrases to be said when hunting game or growing yams, and rules for talking while taking food or drink. Our primary focus here, however, is the work of linguistic anthropologists who explicitly look at how language and food meaningfully co-occur within specific sociocultural contexts. The methods used in such endeavors share much with other linguistic anthropological studies: ethnographic participant observation, contextualized interviews and focus groups, and analysis of language in use. The latter includes audio and/or video recordings of naturally occurring speech activities, followed by transcription and analysis of these recordings, sometimes with the assistance of participants themselves. In this overview, we offer the first systematic review of methods useful for looking at how our interactions with food are connected to how we interact using language (but see also the introduction to the topic in Cavanaugh et al. 2014).

In what follows, we review past and contemporary work, at times referring to as-yet unpublished research. We categorize this work by types of methods employed: (1) researcher-elicited talk about and around food, (2) audio- or video-recorded naturally occurring food-and-talk events, and (3) various types of mediated engagement with food involving language. Researchers use these methods to answer a range of research questions, looking at food talk in terms of its content (what is said), form (how it is said), and/or function (the effects it has on the world). Here we specify methods while also indicating the kinds of research questions that can be answered by analyzing food talk. We conclude by mentioning some studies that intermingle these methodologies in exciting ways. After the text, we list some online resources that have been of special relevance to these studies and offer some key texts.

Researcher-Elicited Talk about and around Food: Interviews and Focus Groups

Researchers have employed various methods—interviews, focus groups, photo elicitation, and food journals—to elicit talk about food, frequently in the presence of food, in order to collect food-focused narratives, jokes, opinions, and other types of linguistic data. Analyses of food talk collected in these ways tend to emphasize *what* has been said—the content of language—identifying key words and phrases or whole stories, and presenting these to readers in the form of short or long quotes or statistics about how often certain terms were used (see also the chapter in this volume by Zycherman). This type of food talk is frequently examined as a mode of self-expression, just as preparing and consuming food may be a form of personal expression, in interaction with both sociocultural norms and institutions. For instance, Counihan has used food-focused interviews in Tuscany (2004) and Colorado (2008), eliciting and recording individuals' personal and social histories by asking them to describe their most significant food memories. By lightly editing, rearranging, and publishing these transcribed narratives as "food-centered life histories," she aims "to give voice to the traditionally muted" (2004: 2), in particular female, working-class, and ethnically marginalized subjects; she uses the term "food voice," which has political as well as linguistic meaning (Counihan 2008: 354). Abarca (2006) takes a similar approach, collecting what she refers to as *charlas culinarias* (culinary chats) with working-class Mexican and Mexican-American women. She explains how as a researcher she learned to drop her academese and speak *with* rather than *to* her subjects in order to engage in the "kitchen talk" that allows her subjects to express the real *sazón* of their lives. In their study of Swedish parents' approach to food socialization (teaching their children how and what to eat), Anving and Sellergerg (2010) used an open-ended interviewing technique to elicit conversations around a set of themes, which they then analyzed qualitatively as evidence of "the subtle codes and rules that surround everyday food practices" (ibid.: 204). They found that middle-class Swedish parents appeared to socialize their children to eat like "we" do on the one hand, and stay open to trying the food of others on the other.

Researchers also use photo elicitation as an interview method, snapping photos of people engaged with food or enlisting their subjects' participation as fellow researchers, providing them with cameras, and asking them later to discuss the food images they constructed. Salazar, Feenstra, and Ohmart (2008), for instance, elicited schoolchildren's thoughts about the "salads" they had created at the school salad bar. This method allows for a comparison of how people use words versus images to represent their foodways and their sense of identity as transmitted by food, which may reveal interesting discontinuities between what individuals photograph and what they say about themselves (see also Sharma and Chapman 2011).

Another useful technique for eliciting food talk is the tasting event. Riley (2012b) used this method with schoolchildren in NYC to find out their thoughts about how food is grown, preserved, transported, cooked, and eaten as well as their feelings about what makes it healthy and/or tasty. Bassene and Szatrowski (2014) used taster lunches in Senegal to elicit language use that would allow them to study how both food and language are used to index identity. Participants switched among languages as well as foods in meaningful ways.

The focus group, in which researchers gather a group of people for directed discussion of particular topics, is another productive avenue for instigating talk about food. Bildtgård (2010) used focus groups and open-ended survey questions to elicit talk about food values in France and Sweden, and then used QDA miner software (see the introduction to this section as well as Riley's chapter for more about this sort of software) to pick out recurring words, which he interpreted as central to what French versus Swedish respondents believe about what it means to "eat well." Several notions were shared by the two cultures—e.g., the importance of a balanced diet and the pleasure of taste—but two notions were not shared: the French valued conviviality whereas the Swedish emphasized the need for regular mealtimes.

Some focus group studies have the explicit aim of improving the way families and youth prepare, consume, and communicate about food. For instance, one study among seniors at a high school in New Mexico was organized to find out what factors affected these teenagers' more or less "healthy" food choices (Walters 2011). Many students mentioned family, culture, school, and peers. Interestingly, they tended to be critical of mass media influences and aware that environmental constraints (money and convenience) affect access to healthy foods. Another study based on focus group discussions among Mexican Americans in Texas (Cosgriff-Hernández et al. 2011) explored how discussions of the risks and benefits of traditional and new food habits (the lard in Mexican cooking, the fast pace of an American lifestyle, etc.) may help communities move toward healthier foodways. In one more such study (Kaplan et al. 2011), the researchers conducted multigenerational focus groups among low-income families in Pennsylvania in order to discuss who was involved in family food decisions. This method showed that children who were included in the food talk had healthier foodways while the study itself provided an excellent model for how to actively encourage intergenerational talk about food.

Some researchers enlist research participants to track their daily foodways in food journals. Jourdan (2010) used this method for many years in the Solomon Islands, while Riley (2012b) mixed this method with photo elicitation in her research on school food change in NYC, asking students to provide photos from their family food journals for a group discussion with other students. Similarly, Johansson et al. (2009) gave children in four Nordic cities cameras and instructed them to photograph healthy and unhealthy foods, preferred and dispreferred foods, everyday and special meals, and school and home meals. The children were then brought together for small group discussions of their photographs and how they attempt to resolve some of the contradictory messages they receive about healthy everyday foods versus special treat foods. Salazar (2012) combined several of these methods, asking immigrant youth in her study to photograph and discuss the foods they ate, and to map their food practices using a variety of digital technologies (e.g., Google Maps and Flickr) to track and comment on when and where they were eating what.

These studies focus primarily on the content of the talk—what participants explicitly say about food—while exploring food's place in speakers' social lives and its cultural and emotional meanings. However, these methods do not necessarily lend themselves to the analysis of *how* food narrators speak and interact with one another in non-elicited—that is, naturally occurring—ways. The next section turns to researchers who consider food talk in naturally occurring contexts, looking at the forms and functions of language as well as its content.

Ethnography of Naturally Occurring Food-and-Talk Events

Researchers have explored how food is linked to naturally occurring talk across a range of contexts by engaging in first-hand participant observation, recording and transcribing some food talk interactions, and analyzing the symbolic and social effects of specific food talk activities. Close attention to and detailed recording and analysis of a particular social event corresponds to the analytic assumption that the co-occurrence of specific cultural practices, including what is said and how it is said with what is consumed and how it is consumed, will be intimately connected with the function or effects of the overall event in question. For example, Malinowski (1965) studied how magic must be spoken to make yams grow in the garden, while Gewertz (1984) looked at how soup made from sago (a starchy plant) could be successfully exchanged only if certain words were spoken and social rules followed. In these activities, specific forms of food and talk are equally essential for the activity to be successful, and must be studied together.

A key method underlying much research on naturally occurring food talk is the ethnography of communication, designed to document and demonstrate language use as central to social life across cultures, as well as to show how patterns of language use differ cross-culturally (Bauman and Sherzer [1974] and Gumperz and Hymes [1972] offer seminal examples of these sorts of studies). Ethnographers of communication produce detailed ethnographic descriptions of speech events that may be audio- or video-recorded or recorded in detailed ethnographic field notes, and include what else is happening during the focal event—such as food activities. Hymes (1964) suggested breaking speech events into their constitutive components for analysis and proposed the use of SPEAKING as a heuristic mnemonic to remind researchers of the focal elements: *S*ettings (when and where an event happens), *P*articipants (who is involved), *E*nds (goals), speech *A*cts (what smaller parts make up the event—e.g., questions and answers), *K*eys (moods), *I*nstrumentalities (channels and codes), *N*orms (rules governing the event), and *G*enres (what type of event it is—e.g., a sermon, oratory, or gossip session). Building on this paradigm, Riley has recently formulated (and launched for use in a student research project entitled the "Mealtime Discourse Project") another ethnographic note-taking mnemonic, EATING, to be used alongside SPEAKING for the purposeful study of food-and-talk events: *E*tiquette (cultural norms governing the food event), *A*ctions (specific actions involved in procuring, preparing, serving, and eating food), *T*ools (equipment used for the food event, such as cooking utensils or serving dishes), *I*ngredients (raw and processed foods prepared for consumption), *N*otions (ideas and beliefs about food expressed or demonstrated), *G*ender (rights and/or obligations of participants based on socially constructed identities and roles—consider age, ethnicity, class, and sexuality as well as gender). Used together, the SPEAKING and EATING heuristics help researchers record and shed light on how food and talk are used together in particular settings in meaningful ways.

While not using these exact heuristics, a number of studies have otherwise employed ethnographic observation to record multimodal and multisensual interactions around the production, preparation, and distribution of food. These include studies of community gardens (Seegert 2012), farmers markets (Eckstein and Conley 2012; McCullen 2011), and food banks (Schuwerk 2011). In these cases, the researchers examined not only the spoken exchanges, but also the body language and written signage, as well as the visuals, sounds, smells, tastes, and textures that played a communicative role at their field sites.

Perhaps the most studied food-and-talk event is the family or community meal. Beeman (2014) employed Hymes' ethnography of SPEAKING model to analyze how humans use language and other nonverbal communicative resources (including food) to organize meal events into ritual stages through comparison of meals across four cultures (U.S., German, Japanese, and Middle Eastern). Koike (2014) recorded and analyzed mealtime interactions among Japanese youth as they used talk about food to index culturally significant categories (seasons, Japanese regions, Japanese nationality, etc.) as well as to repair gaps in knowledge about food. Di Giovine (2010) studied his own immigrant family's celebration of the Italian-American Christmas Eve feast (the *Vigilia*) to demonstrate how specific foods and the use of Italian and English mean different things across the generations. In a contrastive study of two sub-Arctic peoples, Jarvenpa (2008) used participant observation at various eating events (meal breaks during food production, home meals, and feasts in modernized settings) to understand how indigenous and modern ingredients, preparations, and talk about the food played different roles depending on the eating venue. Hellman (2008) investigated a community in West Java where table etiquette based on local readings of Islamic law demands silence while eating. To understand how the exchange of food during ritual ceremonies creates community ties while the exchange of words during everyday meals would disrupt them, Hellman used participant observation during mealtimes, interviews about the meaning of fasting and breaking the fast during Ramadan, and fine-grained readings of passages from the Koran.

Researchers increasingly focus on naturally occurring speech acts and genres that occur in food-consumption settings, like storytelling, speech-making, praying, joking, gossiping, insulting, and ordering. In such food talk events, speakers are sometimes highly conscious of the important relationship between food and language in their linguistic performances, while other times they are not. For instance, in Kuroshima's (2014) study of how sushi is ordered in Japanese restaurants, the openings, commands, and closings are clearly ritualized but do not appear to involve any culturally significant messaging about the foods. By contrast, Krögel (2009) uncovered a great weight of culturally loaded food messages in traditional tales of witches and other supernatural forces that she recorded while the participating tellers were involved in everyday domestic chores. She found that Quechua-speaking storytellers and their audiences believe in the power of food to curse and cure people as well as to forge family ties and establish insider/outsider identities (e.g., indigenous peasant vs. urban mestizo). Barrett (2006), in his ethnographic research among Mexican and Anglo workers in a Mexican restaurant in Texas, recorded on his server's notepad a range of speech acts—e,g., the use of insulting epithets such as "beaners" by Anglos or the use of Spanish by Mexican staff to spread word of special meals being cooked for kitchen staff only.

Finally, one very productive area of food-and-language study has employed methods formulated within the language socialization paradigm, which has two basic tenets: learning language is central to how individuals are socialized into their particular cultural groups, and such socialization processes differ across cultural groups (for an overview and collection of language socialization studies, see Duranti, Ochs, and Schieffelin 2012). Language socialization methodology includes longitudinal (long-term) ethnographic participant observation and regularly repeated audio or video recording of naturally occurring interaction among children and caregivers, which is then transcribed and analyzed (frequently with the assistance of the caregivers) as culturally situated and shaped talk (see Garrett 2007 for details about language socialization methods). When language socialization occurs within food-focused family contexts, children learn about food through interaction and learn about social interaction through food (Riley 2012a; Schieffelin 1990).

Large collections of mealtime talk have been collected and analyzed using language socialization methods in several Western societies (see Ochs and Shohet 2006 and Blum-Kulka 2008 for overviews). UCLA's Center on the Everyday Lives of Families study (http://www.celf.ucla.edu/) involved repeated videotaping and transcribing of middle-class dinners over several years in the late 1980s, while research conducted with middle-class families in Sweden, Italy, and Israel used similar methods: videotaping family interactions intensively throughout the day, especially around mealtimes, for several days and then transcribing the recordings, highlighting and analyzing various types of speech events. Some of these researchers look at how foodways are organized through linguistic interaction; others focus on how forms of language, cultural values, and social roles are acquired through interactions around food (e.g., Aronsson and Gottzén 2011; Aukrust and Snow 1998; Blum-Kulka 1997; Ochs and Taylor 1995; Ochs, Pontecorvo, and Fasulo 1996; Paugh 2005; Paugh and Izquierdo 2009; Riley 2009, 2012a). In all of these studies, researchers audio- or video-recorded and analyzed naturally occurring talk in food-related contexts in order to understand not only how food and talk are interrelated, but also how such connections contribute to broader social and cultural meanings and values. Part of the strength of this approach is that scholars have begun to think carefully about how to effectively collect the necessary audio and video data (see Ochs et al. 2004) as well as how to represent these data on the page for deeper analysis.

As discussed in the introductory chapter to this section, transcribing involves the principled selection of what to include and what to leave out. Because writing on the flat, printed page cannot possibly represent every interactional feature manifested in a given recorded speech interaction, researchers face choices about what to write down and how to write it. Should they, for example, write down the exact phonetic form of every utterance or use eye-dialect (common conventions for representing how speech sounds, such as, "I'm gonna go"); record the shape and direction of every gaze and gesture or generalize; indicate the form and duration of every pause and interruption with a precise measurement (e.g., [0.3] for seconds) or approximate short pauses with a three-dot ellipses)? Choices such as these affect how complex the transcript will be to print and interpret, but they also shape the final analysis because in the process of transcribing, the analyst is actually also shaping the data. Thus, the analytical intentions underlying these choices must be accounted for prior to presenting the final analysis. Scholars have subjected the intricacies and implications of transcription to intense scrutiny (see Sacks, Schegloff, and Jefferson 1974; Ochs 1979; Vigouroux 2009; Philips 2013).

So far we have been considering how humans use verbal and nonverbal modes to interact in and around food. However, face-to-face interactions are not the only ways in which people use language to express their food thoughts, tastes, and feelings. We turn now to how researchers have included other media in their considerations of the connections between food and language.

Mediated Food Interactions

Researchers interested in food talk have been exploring methods for collecting and analyzing how interactions mediated by technologies (such as writing, telephone, and computer) around and about food show up alongside or interwoven with the face-to-face food talk individuals engage in every day (this interwoven quality is sometimes referred to as "intertextuality"; see, for instance, Bauman 2004). The chapters by Riley and Albala in this volume discuss some of the many ways of studying mediated texts related to food. In this section, however, we focus on textual forms that operate somewhat like talk in that the mediated communications are presumed (by both the communicators and the researchers) to be interactive. That is, the writers anticipate responses from their readers, and the readers expect to have some chance to respond, despite the fact that some type of technology (from the printing press to a smartphone) is intervening in the communication. In this case, researchers look at how a range of technologically mediated forms of interaction—op-eds, advertisements, blogs, social media sites, and so on—are embedded within social interaction, and analyze not just *what* is said but also *how* it is said, as well as its intended and realized impact.

One useful method includes collection and analysis of advertising (in print, radio, TV, or Web format) and consumers' interactions around particular advertisements (either spontaneously or in response to researchers' directed questioning). Jourdan (2010) examined how mottos and jingles from rice advertisements were recycled in everyday talk in the Solomon Islands over a twenty-year span, during which time idioms and discussions of rice used the term sometimes as a valued indicator of modernity and urbanity and sometimes as an imposition of foreign exploiters (i.e., the Chinese). Similarly, Manning (2012) documented advertisements and everyday talk about a local soda versus the interloper Coca-Cola in socialist and postsocialist Georgia in order to track a shift from idealizing the latter to nostalgia for the former.

Some research looks at connections between everyday talk and media discourse. For example, Manning (ibid.) conducted an intertextual analysis of local practices and meanings of wine and feasting in socialist and postsocialist Georgia by comparing cartoons representing various food-and-talk events—such as toasts at feasts—to the talk he participated in at such events. Manning (2008) also collected website rants by Starbucks employees representing interactions with "stupid customers" and compared them with official "advice" found on the Starbucks website about how not to feel stupid when ordering at a Starbucks amidst the proliferation of Starbucks lingo. In these studies, similarities and contrasts between spoken and mediated language provide evidence of how cultural meanings and values about food-related activities circulate and are taken up.

Some researchers have focused specifically on the talk-like nature of mediated interactions, looking at how food discussions on social media are embedded within broader sociocultural debates and events. Jourdan and Hobbis (2013) used critical analysis of online media such as blogs to examine the distribution and negotiation of responsibility in a 2011 European food scare involving organic cucumbers. Cavanaugh (2013) used ongoing participant observation alongside attention to linguistic form to discuss a debate on Facebook about a kebab stand, showing how affinity and alignment are created and boundaries between insiders and outsiders are constructed through linguistic means. Cavanaugh et al. (2014) reviewed the work of several other researchers who have looked at texts and talk together.

Current and Future Possibilities for the Study of Food Talk

This chapter has briefly reviewed methods designed and employed to capture evidence of how humans interact using food and language simultaneously. In conclusion, we focus on two avenues of study that incorporate several methods to address how everyday contexts involving food and language are connected to large-scale political, economic, social, and cultural processes and structures.

The first approach involves ethnographic participation in contexts of food production and circulation, in conjunction with analysis of documents and media related to food production and circulation. One such project currently being undertaken by Jillian Cavanaugh in northern Italy (2005, 2007; Cavanaugh and Shankar 2014; also see Cavanaugh et al. 2014 for details on similar work being conducted in Corsica by Alexandra Jaffe) focuses on the economics and politics of food production. Data collection strategies include ethnographic participant observation with food producers and allies like food activists, often in conjunction with photographing their activities; audio recording of various types of naturally occurring verbal interactions like food tastings and market interactions; transcription of these recordings, often with native-speaker consultants; extensive collection of documents pertaining to food production and circulation; and monitoring of various media forms that address food production. The research also focuses on food certification processes such as EU origin designation certification schemes, which consist almost entirely of language and thus represent a particularly ripe opportunity for the application of linguistic anthropological methods and analysis (see below for a list of online resources on these certification processes). These methods were chosen in order to capture as many facets of food production and the labor that goes into it as possible, so as to explore not just the material processes that produce food, but also how food producers increasingly must be able to talk to clients, inspectors, and various types of bureaucrats, as well as engage with a number of documents, as part of their work. Looking across the data that these methods produce (transcripts, field notes, photographs, documents, newspaper articles) has revealed, for instance, that notions such as "food safety" rely as much on linguistic as material labor. That is, producers must not only physically make a safe product, but also be able to successfully represent it as safe—for instance, in inspection documents and labels, and conversations with customers.

The second approach involves an expansion of the language socialization paradigm with the goal of linking everyday interactions captured in audio and video recordings with broader cultural food discourses and the circulation of ideas about food, children, health, and education. Riley's (2012b) study of language socialization and the school-food change movement at an elementary school in New York City examines global discourses about nutrition and sustainability and their impact on attempts at the school to transform the food eaten and the food knowledge acquired by students. To examine the ways in which children digested the food and food knowledge being served at the school, Riley used a mix of methods to collect and analyze data: ethnographic SPEAKING-and-EATING field notes, interviews, family foodways journals, recordings and subsequent transcriptions of adult focus groups and student food chats (in which food and photographs are used to elicit talk among children), and public media discourses that project participants were responding to. Riley has applied similar methods in the Marquesas, French Polynesia, contextualizing her food-and-language socialization research there by recording and transcribing naturally-occurring food talk (Riley 2012a) against a critical reading of ethno-historical textual data as well as present-day public discourse about food production, distribution, production, and consumption (Riley 2013). In both these studies (in very different cultural settings), Riley sought first to identify the intertextual connections between the macro and micro discourses about food produced and consumed in public contexts such as schools and media (see the online resources below for examples of the mediated discourses being examined); and second to analyze the socializing food talk that children and adults produced and digested, thereby reproducing and transforming the foodways knowledge and practices for the next generation (for similar work, see Karrebæk's [2012, 2014] research with immigrant children in Danish schools).

The multifaceted methods involved in these current projects seek to encompass numerous points of view and scales of interaction between people about, around, and through food. It is certain that new methods of collecting food-talk data and new ways of analyzing data collected using conventional methods are proliferating as we write. Thus, we see this chapter as just an initial survey of possible approaches to studying how humans use food and language to interact and understand ourselves and our world.

Jillian R. Cavanaugh is Associate Professor in the Department of Anthropology and Archaeology at Brooklyn College CUNY and the Anthropology Program at the Graduate Center CUNY. She is a linguistic anthropologist whose research has considered language shift and social transformation, language ideologies, language and materiality, language and gender, and the value of heritage food. Her work has appeared in *American Anthropologist,* the *Journal of Linguistic Anthropology,* and *Ethnos,* among others, and she is presently co-editing (with Kathleen C. Riley) a special issue of *Semiotics Review* on food and language. Her current research is with food producers in northern Italy. She received her PhD in anthropology at New York University.

Kathleen C. Riley has taught linguistic and cultural anthropology at Concordia University, City College, Queens College, Fordham University, Barnard College, and Rutgers University. She has conducted fieldwork on food change, language socialization, and cultural identity in the Marquesas, Vermont, France, Montreal, and New York City, and has published articles in the *Journal of Linguistic Anthropology* and *Language and Communication,* as well as in several edited collections. She has co-edited (with Christine Jourdan) a special issue of *Anthropologie et Sociétés* on food glocalization and is presently co-editing (with Jillian Cavanaugh) a special issue of *Semiotics Review* on food and language.

Online Resources

The Internet is now filled with food-related websites that provide both information (gray literature) and opportunities for dialogue about how food is produced, distributed, prepared, and consumed. Websites are launched by regional and national governments, corporations, and NGOs, many of whom are voicing concerns about an array of issues, from famine and obesity to fair trade and sustainable farming. Online documents range from policy papers and grant applications to fact sheets and surveys addressing food safety, food certification, agricultural subsidies, school food, etc. These sites may be largely designed for internal review or for public outreach, to educate or to advertise. In other words, researchers interested in food need to learn to apply food-and-language techniques to reading this material with an analytic eye. We list here just a few of the websites related to food research and governance in the United States and Europe that have been relevant to our own work in Italy, France (and French Polynesia), and the United States.

United States Department of Agriculture (USDA)—Food Safety and Inspection Services http://www.fsis.usda.gov/wps/portal/informational/aboutfsis
United States Food and Drug Administration http://www.fda.gov/
National Farm to School Network http://www.farmtoschool.org/
Food Day Organization http://www.foodday.org/

European Commission (EC) Agricultural and Rural Development—Quality policy http://ec.europa.eu/agriculture/quality/index_en.htm

European Commission Agricultural and Rural Development—DOOR (Database of Origins and Registration) http://ec.europa.eu/agriculture/quality/door/list.html;jsessionid=pL0hLqqLXhNmFQyFl1b24mY3t9dJQPflg3xbL2YphGT4k6zdWn34!-370879141

European Commission Agricultural and Rural Development—Food quality certification schemes http://ec.europa.eu/agriculture/quality/certification/index_en.htm

European Commission Agricultural and Rural Development—Local farming and direct sales commission report http://ec.europa.eu/agriculture/quality/local-farming-direct-sales/index_en.htm

Ministere de l'Agriculture, de l'Agroalimentaire, et de la Foret http://alimentation.gouv.fr/

Observatoire Cniel des Habitudes Alimentaires http://www.lemangeur-ocha.com/

Du champ a la table (CNRS Institute) http://duchampalatable.inist.fr/

Key Texts on Food Talk Methods

Overview

Cavanaugh, Jillian R., Kathleen C. Riley, Alexandra Jaffe, Christine Jourdan, Martha Karrebæk, and Amy Paugh. 2014. What Words Bring to the Table: The Linguistic Anthropological Toolkit as Applied to the Study of Food. *Journal of Linguistic Anthropology* 24(1): 84–97.

Researcher-Elicited Talk: Interviews and Focus Groups

Bildtgård, Torbjörn. 2010. What It Means to "Eat Well" in France and Sweden. *Food and Foodways* 18: 209–232.

Counihan, Carole. 2008. Mexicanas' Food Voice and Differential Consciousness in the San Luis Valley of Colorado. In *Food and Culture: A Reader*, ed. C. Counihan and P. Van Esterik, 354–368. 2nd ed. New York: Routledge.

Salazar, Melissa, Gail Feenstra, and Jeri Ohmart. 2008. Salad Days: A Visual Study of Children's Food Culture. In *Food and Culture*, ed. Carole Counihan and Penny Van Esterik, 423–437. 2nd ed. New York: Routledge.

Ethnography of Food-and-Talk Events: SPEAKING-EATING and Transcription

Garrett, Paul. 2007. Researching Language Socialization. In *Encyclopedia of Language and Education*, 2nd ed., vol. 10, ed. Nancy H. Hornberger, 189–201. Heidelberg: Springer.

Hymes, Dell. 1964. Introduction: Toward Ethnographies of Communication. *American Anthropologist* 66(6–2): 1–34.

Philips, Susan. 2013. Method in Anthropological Discourse Analysis: The Comparison of Units of Interaction. *Journal of Linguistic Anthropology* 23(1): 82–95.

Sacks, Harvey, Emanuel A. Schegloff, and Gail Jefferson. 1974. A Simplest Systematics for the Organization of Turn-Taking for Conversation. *Language* 50: 696–735.

Mediated food interactions: intertextual approaches

Manning, Paul. 2012. *Semiotics of Drink and Drinking*. London: Continuum.

Jourdan, Christine, and Stephanie Hobbis. 2013. Tensions internationales autour d'un concombre tueur : confiance et glocalisation alimentaire. *Anthropologie et Sociétés* 37(2): 173–192.

Cavanaugh, Jillian. 2013. Il y a kébab et kébab: Conflit local et alimentation globale en Italie du nord. *Anthropologie et Sociétés* 37(2): 193–212.

References

Abarca, Meredith E. 2006. *Voices in the Kitchen: Views of Food and the World from Working-Class Mexican and Mexican-American Women*. College Station: Texas A&M University Press.

Anving, Terese, and Ann-Mari Sellerberg. 2010. Family Meals and Parents' Challenges. *Food, Culture and Society* 13(2): 200–214.

Aronsson, Karin, and Lucas Gottzén. 2011. Generational Positions at a Family Dinner: Food Morality and Social Order. *Language in Society* 40: 405–426.

Aukrust, Vibeke G., and Catherine E. Snow. 1998. Narratives and Explanations during Mealtime Conversations in Norway and the US. *Language in Society* 27: 221–246.

Bassene, Mamadou, and Polly Szatrowski. 2014. Food and Identity in Wolof and Eegimaa: We Eat What We Are. In *Language and Food: Verbal and Nonverbal Experiences,* ed. Polly E. Szatrowski, 103–130. Amsterdam: John Benjamins.

Barrett, Rusty. 2006. Language Ideology and Racial Inequality: Competing Functions of Spanish in an Anglo-Owned Mexican Restaurant. *Language in Society* 35: 163–204.

Bauman, Richard. 2004. *A World of Others' Words: Cross-Cultural Perspectives on Intertextuality.* Malden, MA: Blackwell.

Bauman, Richard, and Joel Sherzer, eds. 1974. *Explorations in the Ethnography of Speaking.* Cambridge: Cambridge University Press.

Beeman, William O. 2014. Negotiating a Passage to the Meal in Four Cultures. In *Language and Food: Verbal and Nonverbal Experiences,* ed. Polly E. Szatrowski, 31–52. Amsterdam: John Benjamins.

Bildtgård, Torbjörn. 2010. What It Means to "Eat Well" in France and Sweden. *Food and Foodways* 18: 209–232.

Blum-Kulka, Shoshana. 1997. *Dinner Talk: Cultural Patterns of Sociability and Socialization in Family Discourse.* Mahwah, NJ: Lawrence Erlbaum Associates.

———. 2008 Language Socialization and Family Dinnertime Discourse. In *Encyclopedia of Language and Education,* 2nd ed., vol. 8, *Language Socialization,* ed. P. A. Duff and N. H. Hornberger, 87–99. New York: Springer.

Cavanaugh, Jillian R. 2005. Lard. In *Fat: The Anthropology of an Obsession,* ed. Don Kulick and Anne Meneley, 139–151. New York: Tarcher/Penguin USA.

———. 2007. Making Salami, Producing Bergamo: The Transformation of Value. *Ethnos* 72(2): 149–172.

———. 2013. Il y a kébab et kébab: Conflit local et alimentation globale en Italie du nord. *Anthropologie et Sociétés* 37(2): 193–212.

Cavanaugh, Jillian R., Kathleen C. Riley, Alexandra Jaffe, Christine Jourdan, Martha Karrebæk, and Amy Paugh. 2014. What Words Bring to the Table: The Linguistic Anthropological Toolkit as Applied to the Study of Food. *Journal of Linguistic Anthropology* 24(1): 84–97.

Cavanaugh, Jillian R., and Shalini Shankar. 2014. Producing Authenticity in Global Capitalism: Language, Materiality, and Value. *American Anthropologist* 166(1): 51–64.

Cosgriff-Hernández, Kevin-Khristián, Amanda R. Martinez, Barbara F. Sharf, and Joseph R. Sharkey. 2011. "We Still Had to Have Tortillas": Negotiating Health, Culture, and Change in the Mexican American Diet. In *Food as Communication: Communication as Food,* ed. Janet M. Cramer, Carlnita P. Greene, and Lynn M. Walters, 115–135. New York: Peter Lang.

Counihan, Carole. 2004. *Around the Tuscan Table: Food Family, and Gender in Twentieth Century Florence.* New York: Routledge.

———. 2008. *Mexicanas'* Food Voice and Differential Consciousness in the San Luis Valley of Colorado. In *Food and Culture: A Reader,* ed. C. Counihan and P. Van Esterik, 354–368. 2nd ed. New York: Routledge.

Di Giovine, Michael A. 2010. *La Vigilia Italo-Americana*: Revitalizing the Italian-American Family through the Christmas Eve "Feast of the Seven Fishes." *Food and Foodways* 18: 181–208.

Duranti, Alessandro, Elinor Ochs, and Bambi B. Schieffelin, eds. 2012. *The Handbook of Language Socialization.* Malden, MA: Wiley-Blackwell.

Eckstein, Justin, and Donovan Conley. 2012. Spatial Affects and Rhetorical Relations: At the Cherry Creek Farmers' Market. In *The Rhetoric of Food: Discourse, Materiality, and Power,* ed. Joshua J. Frye and Michael S. Bruner, 171–189. New York: Routledge.

Garrett, Paul. 2007. Researching Language Socialization. In *Encyclopedia of Language and Education,* 2nd ed., vol 10, ed. Nancy H. Hornberger, 189–201. Heidelberg: Springer.

Gewertz, Deborah. 1984. Of Symbolic Anchors and Sago Soup: The Rhetoric of Exchange among the Chambri of Papua New Guinea. In *Dangerous Words: Language and Politics in the Pacific,* ed. Donald L. Brenneis and Fred R. Myers, 192–213. New York: New York University Press.

Gumperz, John, and Dell Hymes, eds. 1972. *Directions in Sociolinguistics: The Ethnography of Communication.* New York and London: Holt, Rinehart and Winston.

Hellman, Jörgen. 2008. The Significance of Eating during Ramadan: Consumption and Exchange of Food in a Village in West Java. *Food and Foodways* 16: 201–226.

Hymes, Dell. 1964. Introduction: Toward Ethnographies of Communication. *American Anthropologist* 66(6–2): 1–34.

Jarvenpa, Robert. 2008. Diets of Experience: Food Culture and Political Ecology in Northern Canada and Northern Finland. *Food and Foodways* 16: 1–32.

Johansson, Barbro, Johanna Mäkelä, Gun Roos, Sandra Hillén, Gitte Laub Hansen, Tine Mark Jensen, Anna Huotilainen. 2009. Nordic Children's Foodscapes: Images and Reflections. *Food, Culture, and Society* 12(1): 25–51.

Jourdan, Christine. 2010. The Cultural Localization of Rice in Solomon Islands. *Ethnology* 49(4): 263–282.

Jourdan, Christine, and Stephanie Hobbis. 2013. Tensions internationales autour d'un concombre tueur : confiance et glocalisation alimentaire. *Anthropologie et Sociétés* 37(2): 173–192.

Kaplan, Matthew, Lynn James, Frances Alloway, and Nancy Ellen Kiernan. 2011. Youth Empowerment in Family Conversations and Decision-Making about Food. In *Food as Communication: Communication as Food,* ed. Janet M. Cramer, Carlnita P. Greene, and Lynn M. Walters, 337–358. New York: Peter Lang.

Karrebæk, Martha Sif. 2012. "What's in Your Lunch-Box Today?" Health, Ethnicity and Respectability in the Primary Classroom. *Journal of Linguistic Anthropology* 22(1): 1–22.

———. 2014. Healthy Beverages? The Interactional Use of Milk, Juice and Water in an Ethnically Diverse Kindergarten Class in Denmark. In *Language and Food: Verbal and Nonverbal Experiences,* ed. Polly E. Szatrowski, 279–299. Amsterdam: John Benjamins.

Koike, Chisato. 2014. Food Experiences and Categorization in Japanese Talk-in-Interaction. In *Language and Food: Verbal and Nonverbal Experiences,* ed. Polly E. Szatrowski, 159–183. Amsterdam: John Benjamins.

Krögel, Alison. 2009. Dangerous Repasts: Food and the Supernatural in the Quechua Oral Tradition. *Food and Foodways* 17: 104–132.

Kuroshima, Satomi. 2014. The Structural Organization of Ordering and Serving Sushi. In *Language and Food: Verbal and Nonverbal Experiences,* ed. Polly E. Szatrowski, 53–75. Amsterdam: John Benjamins.

Malinowski, Bronislaw. 1965. *Coral Gardens and Their Magic: A Study of the Methods of Tilling the Soil and in Agricultural Rites in the Trobriand Islands.* Bloomington: Indiana University Press.

Manning, Paul. 2008. Barista Rants about Stupid Customers at Starbucks: What Imaginary Conversations Can Tell Us about Real Ones. *Language and Communication* 28(2): 101–126.

———. 2012. *Semiotics of Drink and Drinking.* London: Continuum.

McCullen, Christie. 2011. The White Farm Imaginary: How One Farmers Market Refetishizes the Production of Food and Limits Food Politics. In *Food as Communication: Communication as Food,* ed. Janet M. Cramer, Carlnita P. Greene, and Lynn M. Walters, 217–234. New York: Peter Lang.

Ochs, Elinor, Anthony P. Graesch, Angela Mittman, Thomas Bradbury, and Rena Repetti. 2004. Video Ethnography and Ethnoarchaeological Tracking. In *The Work and Family Handbook: Multi-Disciplinary Perspectives, Methods, and Approaches,* ed. Marcie Pitts-Catsouphes, Ellen Ernst Kossek, and Stephen Sweet, 387–409. Mahwah, NJ: Lawrence Erlbaum Associates.

Ochs, Elinor, Clotilde Pontecorvo, and Alessandra Fasulo. 1996. Socializing Taste. *Ethnos* 61(1–2): 7–46.

Ochs, Elinor, and Merav Shohet. 2006. The Cultural Structuring of Mealtime Socialization. In *New Directions in Child and Adolescent Development Series #11: Family Mealtime as a Context of Development and Socialization,* ed. R. Larson, A. Wiley, and K. Branscomb, 35–50. San Francisco: Jossey-Bass.

Ochs, Elinor, and Carolyn Taylor. 1995. The "Father Knows Best" Dynamic in Dinnertime Narratives. In *Gender Articulated: Language and the Socially Constructed Self,* ed. Kira Hall and Mary Bucholtz, 97–120. New York: Routledge.

Paugh, Amy. 2005. Learning about Work at Dinnertime: Language Socialization in Dual-Earner American Families. *Discourse & Society* 16(1): 55–78.

Paugh, Amy, and Carolina Izquierdo. 2009. Why Is This a Battle Every Night? Negotiating Food and Eating in American Dinnertime Interaction. *Journal of Linguistic Anthropology* 19(2): 185–204.

Philips, Susan. 2013. Method in Anthropological Discourse Analysis: The Comparison of Units of Interaction. *Journal of Linguistic Anthropology* 23(1): 82–95.

Riley, Kathleen C. 2009. Who Made the Soup? Socializing the Researcher and Cooking Her Data. *Language and Communication* 29(3): 254–270.

———. 2012a. Learning to Exchange Words for Food in the Marquesas. In *Food: Ethnographic Encounters*, ed. Leo Coleman, 111–126. Oxford: Berg.

———. 2012b. *"Don't Yuck My Yum": Negotiating Physical Health and Moral Goodness via Food*. Nanterre, France: European Association of Social Anthropology.

———. 2013. Fêtes traditionnelles et festivals glocalisés aux Marquises: Utilisation des systèmes alimentaires syncrétiques pour forger des identités hybrides. *Anthropologie et Sociétés* 37(2): 91–111.

Sacks, Harvey, Emanuel A. Schegloff, and Gail Jefferson. 1974. A Simplest Systematics for the Organization of Turn-Taking for Conversation. *Language* 50: 696–735.

Salazar, Melissa L. 2012. Visualizing 21st Century Foodscapes: Using Photographs and New Media in Food Studies. In *Taking Food Public: Redefining Foodways in a Changing World*, ed. Psyche Williams-Forson and Carole Counihan, 322–339. New York: Routledge.

Salazar, Melissa, Gail Feenstra, and Jeri Ohmart. 2008. Salad Days: A Visual Study of Children's Food Culture. In *Food and Culture*, ed. Carole Counihan and Penny Van Esterik, 423–437. 2nd ed. New York: Routledge.

Schieffelin, Bambi B. 1990. *The Give and Take of Everyday Language*. Cambridge: Cambridge University Press.

Schuwerk, Tara J. 2011. Food Bank Culture: Food and Nutrition Communication in a Hunger-Relief Organization. In *Food as Communication: Communication as Food*, ed. Janet M. Cramer, Carlnita P. Greene, and Lynn M. Walters, 381–403. New York: Peter Lang.

Seegert, Natasha. 2012. Resignified Urban Landscapes: From Abject to Agricultural. In *The Rhetoric of Food: Discourse, Materiality, and Power*, ed. Joshua J. Frye and Michael S. Bruner, 121–138. New York: Routledge.

Sharma, Sonya, and Gwen Chapman. 2011. Food, Photographs, and Frames: Photo Elicitation in a Canadian Qualitative Food Study. *Cuizine: The Journal of Canadian Food Cultures / Cuizine : revue des cultures culinaires au Canada* 3(1). DOI 10.7202/1004726ar http://www.erudit.org/revue/cuizine/2011/v3/n1/1004726ar.html

Vigouroux, Cecile. 2009. The Making of a Scription: A Case Study on Authority and Authorship. *Text & Talk* 29(5): 615–637.

Walters, Lynn M. 2011. High School Students' Perceptions of Environmental and Communicative Influences on Eating Behavior. In *Food as Communication: Communication as Food*, ed. Janet M. Cramer, Carlnita P. Greene, and Lynn M. Walters, 429–444. New York: Peter Lang.

CHAPTER 11

An Introduction to Cultural Domain Analysis in Food Research
Free Lists and Pile Sorts

Ariela Zycherman

Introduction to Cultural Domains

Cultural domain analysis (CDA) is a methodology of cognitive anthropology, an area of anthropological inquiry stemming from ethnoscience, which studies the ways people conceive and experience events and objects in their worlds (Casson 1994; D'Andrade 1995). A cultural domain is "an organized set of words, concepts, or sentences, all on the same level of contrast, that jointly refer to a single conceptual sphere" (Weller and Romney 1988: 9) In other words, a domain is a set of terms, ideas, or items that all belong to the same category, for example, "food." CDA therefore examines the components of a given domain. A domain can be a list of observable things like fruits, plants, or desserts; or it can be concepts like words on menus, fattening foods, or occupations related to food. All the items included in a domain are alike in some way. One of the unique characteristics of cultural domains is that the components of the domain are determined by consensus: the domain is an example of shared knowledge between members of the group. Components of the domain are not determined by an individual informant's preferences but rather reflect an informant's perceptions that an item has a place in that domain (Borgatti and Halgin 2013). So the question about the contents of a fruit domain is not "What are all the fruits you like?" but "What are all the fruits you know?"

CDA has an emic perspective, meaning that the terms being used are those of the group being studied and not those of the researcher or other external categories (Borgatti 1994). Identifying the group you are researching sets the initial limitations of the study: is it all Americans? Is it East Asian immigrants in New York City? Is it preschool-age children? Or is it the Kayapo? Identifying the group is important because of the assumption that its members possess a knowledge shared between them. The key to beginning CDA is to distinguish what is actually a domain in the terms used by the group you are studying. By encouraging the informants to define the domain in their own terms, you avoid the imposition of your own biases and categorizations on the outcome. If for example, you are not sure what domain a tomato is in, you might ask, "What other things are like a tomato?" A group of grocers might say carrots, lettuce, and radishes, and refer to the group of items as "produce." Alternatively, a group of chefs asked the same question might list the same items but refer to them as "vegetables," while a scientist might mention grapefruits, blueberries, and apples and tell you these things are all fruits. Muller and Almedon (2008), for example, used CDA to identify the components of "famine foods" and "traditional vegetables" in Niger to better understand how the terms were being used. You might find overlapping domains related to food and eating. For example, a potato might fit into the domain of vegetable but it also might fit into the domain of tuber or carbohydrate. And lastly, multiple subdomains might contribute to a larger domain, as Tapper and Tapper (1986) showed in their research among the Durrani Pashtuns, where they identified four subdomains as part of a broader food system.

CDA can produce diverse types of data: the vocabulary for items in a domain, the attributes of items in a domain, the relationships between items in a domain, comparisons between items in a domain, how much an individual knows of a domain, and differences between various people's knowledge of the domain. The type of data yielded is related to the question you ask (see Bernard and Ryan 2010: chap. 8 for an in-depth "how to" of cultural domain data collection and analysis, in which many of their examples are related to their own food research). An expansive example of the types of information you can generate from CDA and the ways it works congruently with other forms of data collection is Szurek's (2011) research on how cultural knowledge, eating, and social relationships are related to health among Mexican immigrants in Alabama.

In addition to inquiry-focused research, CDA is often used in applied settings related to health promotion, nutrition initiatives, education programs, and the food industry. Kuhnlein et al. (2006) and The Centre for Indigenous Peoples' Nutrition and Environment at McGill University include many techniques of CDA in their methodological guidelines for documenting traditional food systems of indigenous peoples. This protocol is put to use in many of the case studies offered in the Food and Agriculture Organization of the United Nations' publication "Indigenous Peoples' Food Systems: the Many Dimensions of Culture, Diversity and Environment for Nutrition and Health" (Kuhnlein, Erasmus, and Spigelski 2009). Similarly, Blum et al. (1997) created a protocol for community assessments of natural food sources of vitamin A, which draws heavily on the methodologies of CDA. These protocols are often put into practice to create more culturally sensitive solutions to social and or practical issues. In the context of nutritional development programs, Monárrez-Espino, Greiner, and Martínez (2004) used free listing and paired comparisons—methodologies typically associated with CDA—to identify foods to be removed and added to the government-issued food-aid basket in order to improve the nutritional health of the Tarahumaras of Mexico. Dongre, Deshmukh, and Garg (2008) used these methodologies to reappraise the effectiveness of the Integrated Child Development Service Scheme in India, a supplementary nutrition program, to fulfill the Millennium Development Goal One aim of halving hunger by 2015. Additionally, Hough and Ferraris (2010) recommend these methods for studying the domain of food for market research. Ares and Deliza (2010) put these methods into practice to identify aspects of labeling and packaging for milk dessert products in Uruguay that might be useful for designing labels and packages that meet consumers' needs and expectations.

Free Lists

Two questions are crucial for understanding a domain. The first is, what is in the domain? And the second is, how is the domain structured? To uncover the terms or items included in a domain, free lists are a good place to start. In a free list, informants are asked to list all the items that are part of that domain or the attributes of that domain (once it is identified). For example you might say, "Tell me all the types of apples you know." By doing so, the free list provides not only an inventory of the domain, but also its boundaries (Quinlan 2005). To do the free list, you can either ask the informant to list the items while you, the researcher, record them, or you can let the informants write down the information on their own. To adequately generate the terms of a domain, Weller and Romney (1988) recommend between twenty and thirty informants. Free lists are an easy and quick way to generate a large amount of data. Not only can they be useful as a preliminary technique to understand how people think about a topic you are interested in; but free lists can also be a very powerful technique for generating information about the values and structures inherent to the group you are studying. In my own research among the Tsimane' Indians of the Bolivian Amazon, I examine the ways broad regional development is experienced through food. I use free listing as a method to generate data on the items Tsimane' regard as foods they eat as well as to understand how market commodities, agricultural products, and wild forest food items are related to each other within the domain of food. Traphagan and Brown (2002) took this same approach in their study of Japanese fast food restaurants, demonstrating how free lists can unearth changing approaches to food and reveal how new styles of eating can express long-standing cultural practices, particularly those concerning social relationships.

The domain of "food" is broad and might not be appropriate for all studies. Most examples look at subdomains or focused categories within the domain of food, like "junk foods" or "fish of the Northwest Coast." Libertinoa et al. (2012), for example, used free lists to elicit knowledge about the domain of menu items (or dishes) that people knew. Others, like Lucen, Barg, and Long (2010) used free lists to identify incentives and hurdles to fruit, vegetable and fast food consumption among low-income African Americans. Free listing is particularly prominent in ethno-botanical studies, where it is used to uncover expertise in ecological diversity and traditional ecological knowledge, specifically, of wild edibles (see Ghorbani, Langenberger, and Sauerbor 2012; Goland and Bauer 2004; Mengistu and Hager 2008; Rivera et al. 2007; Setalaphruk and Price 2007; Watkins 2010). For example in Italy, Pieroni at al. (2005) used free lists to elicit names of noncultivated food plants that were still in regular use, as well as those that were used in the past. Free listing is increasingly popular in food industry research looking at customer behavior and knowledge. For example Antmann et al. (2011) used the free listing technique to compare how three different Spanish-speaking countries—Argentina, Spain, and Uruguay—described the domain of food texture, and then used this information to eliminate discrepancies in the marketing of the product between countries. Varela and Fiszman (2013) used free listing techniques to identify consumers' knowledge of additives, thickeners, and the foods containing them in order to understand how educated consumers were about hydrocolloids and how this influenced consumer decision-making.

Three major assumptions in free listing are important when thinking about analysis. First, people tend to list items in order of familiarity. Second, individuals who know more on the subject list more items or terms than people who know less. And third, terms mentioned by most respondents indicate locally prominent items (Quinlan 2005). In a typical analysis, what the domain consists of is determined by two different measures of items: frequency and saliency. Frequency, which refers to the number of times each item is mentioned, gives you a sense of which items are the most important members of the domain. Most commonly you will find that many people list a core group of items, and that many other items are listed only once by a single informant. This is referred to as a core-periphery structure (Borgatti and Halgin 2013). When defining the terms of the domain, you include those items listed by multiple informants and ignore those listed by only a few informants (but do not throw that information away, as it can be interesting for other reasons). This concentration on items mentioned by most informants speaks to the concept inherent to the domain: that it is a shared knowledge held by members of a group, and there is consensus about the items included in the domain. However, whereas frequency is an important measure, it is the measure of saliency, sometimes measured by Smith's S index (Smith 1993), that allows you to analyze the lists not only by the frequency of items mentioned, but also by the position or order in which items are mentioned. If, for example, you were looking at ice cream flavors and vanilla, strawberry, and chocolate were the most frequently mentioned but every time pistachio was mentioned it was mentioned first, you would want to know why. This is an important measure because it raises the question of why some items are more salient than others.

Pile Sorts

While free lists are used to unearth the components of a domain, pile sorts are used to elicit similarities or differences among items (Borgatti and Halgin 2013). As the name implies, this method asks informants to sort items into piles. Items used for a pile sort can come from the results of the free lists but can also be generated separately as predetermined items. Pile sorts can be conducted in a number of ways. Most frequently cards with the names of the items are used. Occasionally the actual item is used, as when Wilson and Dufour (2006) used manioc leaves in their study of manioc cultivar selection. In my own research, I found that putting the names of the food on the cards was not a possibility because many Tsimane' cannot read easily. Instead, I used cards with pictures of the food items pasted on them. Whereas some studies ask informants to sort items into pre-labeled piles (Jenike et al. 2011; Roos 2002), I used a "free pile-sort" technique (Bernard 2011; Weller and Rommey 1988) in which I allowed informants to dictate the terms of the pile sort. Sometimes informants will ask to put a card in more than one pile. Although the easy answer is no, allowing informants the freedom to place a card in more than one pile yields richer data (Bernard 2011).

Pile sorts have proved invaluable in nutritional and health studies related to food choices, food allocation, and food conceptions (See Chotiboriboon et al. 2009; Cortes et al. 2001; Gittelsohn et al. 1996; Gittelsohn et al. 2000; Gittelsohn and Mookjherji 1997; Jenike 2011; Michaela and Contento 1986; Roos 1998, 2002; Thompson et al. 2011). For example, Quintiliani et al. (2008) used a modified free list exercise and pile sorts to identify characteristics of a healthy lifestyle related to nutrition and exercise. The research team then used the results to make suggestions for designing population-specific interventions. Pile sorts have also been used extensively in studies of indigenous and regional food systems to group how people think about food, environment, production, and distribution (see Creed-Kanashiro et al. 2009; Newkirk, Oths, and Dressler 2009; Nolan 2002; Price and Gurung 2006; Wilson 2003).

Pile sorts are analyzed to highlight similarities, dissimilarities, and particular attributes of items within piles. Most often this analysis utilizes multidimensional scaling (MDS). MDS is a visualization method that translates numerical data into graphic depictions to demonstrate how items are related to each other or not (see Bernard 2011 for a good tutorial). These data can also lead to folk taxonomies, as Perchonock and Werner (1969) demonstrated in their early study of Navajo foods.

Other Methods and Analysis

Free lists and pile sorts are the methods most frequently used for CDA because of their ease of execution and the wealth of data they produce. But there are other techniques that can also be useful in studying the cognitive dimensions of food. Triads are an alternate way to measure similarities between items. In a triad exercise, three items from the domain are presented to the respondent, who must pick out the one that is the most different of the three. Triads can be useful for sparking discussion about the attributes that make items similar or different in a domain (Borgatti and Halgin 2013). Other useful methods include rankings, where informants are asked to place items from the domain on a scale—for example, "From 1 to 5, how much do you like Brussels sprouts?"—and paired comparisons, where you ask people to judge or explain the differences between two domain items, for example, "Which of these two foods is the sweetest?" Finally, true/false questions allow informants to respond to attributes of domain items. For example, "True or False? Pasta is an ingredient in Japanese food."

Besides providing information on the items that are part of the domain, these methods reveal information about the people who list them. This can mean knowledge about the domain as it relates to subgroups (age, gender, ethnicity, socioeconomic status, etc.) or how much knowledge an individual possesses of the domain and how it compares to others' knowledge (Furlow 2003; Quinlan 2005; Weller and Romney 1988). The approach known as cultural consensus modeling aggregates the answers in CDA—generating culturally correct responses—and then compares individual knowledge with the consensus (Romney et al. 1986; Weller 2007).

Results from free lists and pile sorts should be imputed and organized in a data matrix for ease of analysis (See Borgatti and Halgin 2013); Microsoft Excel is good for this. A software program called ANTHROPAC can be used to to aid in the management and the analysis of free lists, pile sorts, triads, and other methods central to CDA (see Borgatti 1996). It will also generate lists of triads or paired comparisons, freeing the researcher from having to do it by hand. ANTHROPAC can generate cultural consensus analysis, multivariate analysis, multidimensional scaling, and correspondence analysis. The program runs on DOS and Windows and can be downloaded at http://www.analytictech.com/. UCINET software is also good for this type of work. Meanwhile, many researchers have turned to other programs, like R statistical software, to generate more compelling graphics from the data.

Including Cultural Domain Analysis in Your Research

Deciding whether to include CDA in your research methodology depends on the kinds of question you wish to answer and your research goal. To review, CDA generates information on the knowledge a group has of items included in a domain. It can generate data on the relationships (i.e., similarities or differences) between items in the domain, and it can generate attributes of items or domains. On the one hand, singular methods of CDA or use of multiple CDA methods together might generate enough knowledge for an entire project. If you were interested in how much ecological knowledge urban Swedes have of wild edibles, you could collect free lists on wild edibles from people in two or three cities and use them to generate a list of domain items. Then you could compare compiled lists by gender, age, location, socioeconomic status, frequency of foraging activities, and so on. You could also conduct a pile sort to see how these items are grouped. Are they found in urban spaces or in the countryside? Which are theoretically known and which are actually available? And how are these categories decided? This could be an entire project in and of itself.

Alternatively, you might want to use CDA in conjunction with other methodologies as part of a broader set of questions. For example, my larger research project among the Tsimane', historically a subsistence population, looks at the way increased market activity relates to alimentary processes. Understanding the domain of food can connect food items to larger questions of environmental use, labor and work, and consumption practices. I used CDA along with other methods like participant observation, direct observation, interviews, and 24-hour dietary recalls to paint a more compressive picture. To begin I used free lists to generate knowledge of food items eaten by the Tsimane'. The Tsimane' listed over 270 food items, pointing to a vast knowledge of edible forest-based foods, prepared dishes, and market commodities. However, comparison to the 24-hour dietary recalls revealed that despite this diverse knowledge of things Tsimane' *can* eat, their everyday diet is restrictive and fairly limited in diversity. From the analysis I also learned that forest-produced foods, particularly animals and fish, have higher saliency than items purchased in the market place. This brought up questions about the importance of the forest and subsistence activities even when forest foods are not readily available. I used a pile sort activity to see how Tsimane' understood similarities and differences between some of the items in their diet. I picked forty-two items mentioned in the free lists that were either talked about often and/or consumed with some regularity. The analysis resulted in four piles. For three of them, informants demonstrated a high level of agreement that the items in the piles (animals, fish, and fruit) were similar. The fourth was less certain; it contained agricultural items eaten frequently and sold, in addition to market commodities. Along with interviews conducted during the pile sort and at other points in time, these results offered clarity regarding both forest-based foods and the types of uncertainty, tension, and negotiation Tsimane' are experiencing as they engage with cash cropping, subsistence agriculture, and other forms of cash-generating activities.

Conclusion

In this chapter I have introduced CDA as a methodology to explore what people know about food, highlighting two approaches to uncovering their knowledge: free lists and pile sorts. Most studies that utilize CDA related to food concentrate in ethnobotany, nutrition, and health, but it is also increasingly popular in the food industry as a method of learning about consumer behavior and knowledge. However, most social groups have food rules and ideas, so there is potential to apply cultural domain analysis to a broader host of food-related questions.

Ariela Zycherman, PhD, is an American Association for the Advancement of Science (AAAS) Science and Technology Policy Fellow at the National Science Foundation. Prior to this she was a Food Studies Postdoctoral Fellow at the Institute for Humanities at the University of Illinois, Chicago where this chapter was drafted. Her research looks at alimentary changes in relation to shifting economic and environmental conditions. In addition to Bolivia, she has conducted research in Argentina, New York City, Mexico, and Texas.

References

Antmann, Gabriela, Gastón Ares, Paula Varela, Ana Salvador, Beatriz Coste, and Susana Fiszman. 2011. Consumers' Texture Vocabulary: Results from a Free Listing Study in Three Spanish-Speaking Countries. *Food Quality and Preference* 22: 165–172.

Ares, Gastón, and Rosires Deliza. 2010. Identifying Important Package Features of Milk Desserts Using Free Listing and Word Association. *Food Quality and Preference* 21(6): 621–628.

Bernard, H. Russell. 2011. *Research Methods in Anthropology.* 5th ed. Blue Ridge Summit, PA: AltaMira.

Bernard, H. Russell, and G. W. Ryan. 2010. *Analyzing Qualitative Data: Systematic Approaches.* Thousand Oaks, CA: Sage.

Blum, Lauren, Pertti J. Pelto, Gretel H. Pelto, and Harriet V. Kuhnlein. 1997. *Community Assessment of Natural Food Sources of Vitamin A Guidelines for an Ethnographic Protocol.* Ebook. Bellevue, Quebec: Center for Nutrition and the Environment of Indigenous Peoples. http://www.idrc.ca/EN/Resources/Publications/Pages/IDRCBookDetails.aspx?PublicationID=294. Accessed 10 September 2016.

Borgatti, Stephen. 1994. Cultural Domain Analysis. *Journal of Quantitative Anthropology* 4: 261–278.

———. 1996. *ANTHROPAC 4.0 Methods Guide*. Natick, MA: Analytic Technologies.
Borgatti, Stephen, and Daniel S. Halgin. 2013. Elicitation Techniques for Cultural Domain Analysis. In *Specialized Ethnographic Methods: A Mixed Methods Approach*, ed. Jean J. Schensul and Margaret D. LeCopmte, 80–116. Walnut Creek, CA: AltaMira.
Casson, Ronald. 1994. Cognitive Anthropology. In *Handbook of Psychological Anthropology*, ed. Philip. K. Bock, 61–96 Westport, CT: Greenwood Press.
Chotiboriboon, Sinee, Sopa Tamachotipong, Solot Sirisai, Sakorn Dhanamitta, Suttilak Smitasiri, Charana Sappasuwan, Praiwan Tantivatanasathien, and Pasami Eg-Kantrong. 2009. Thailand: Food System and Nutritional Status of Indigenous Children in a Karen Community. In *Indigenous Peoples' Food Systems: The Many Dimensions of Culture, Diversity and Environment for Nutrition and Health*, ed. Harriet Kuhnlein, Bill Erasmus, and Dina Spigelski, 159–184. Rome: Food and Agriculture Organization of the United Nations and the Centre for Indigenous Peoples' Nutrition and Environment.
Cortes, Leslie, Joel Gittelsohn, Julia Alfred, and Neal Palafox. 2001. Formative Research to Inform Intervention Development for Diabetes Prevention in the Republic of the Marshall Islands. *Health Education Behavior* 28: 696–715.
Creed-Kanashiro, Hilary, Marion Roche, Irma Testa Cerron, and Harriet Kuhnlein. 2009. Traditional Food System of an Awajun Community in Peru. In *Indigenous Peoples' Food Systems: The Many Dimensions of Culture, Diversity and Environment for Nutrition and Health*, ed. Harriet Kuhnlein, Bill Erasmus, and Dina Spigelski, 59–81. Rome: Food and Agriculture Organization of the United Nations and the Centre for Indigenous Peoples' Nutrition and Environment.
D'Andrade, Roy. 1995. *The Development of Cognitive Anthropology*. Cambridge: Cambridge University Press.
Dongre, A. R., P. R. Deshmukh, and B. S. Garg. 2008. Eliminating Childhood Malnutrition: Discussions with Mothers and Anganwadi Workers. *Journal of Health Studies* 1(2–3): 48–52.
Furlow, Christopher. A. 2003. Comparing Indicators of Knowledge within and between Cultural Domains. *Field Methods* 15(1): 51–62.
Ghorbani, Abdolbaset, Gerhard Langenberger, and Joachim Sauerbor. 2012. A Comparison of the Wild Food Plant Use Knowledge of Ethnic Minorities in Naban River Watershed National Nature Reserve, Yunnan, SW China. *Journal of Ethnobiology and Ethnomedicine* 8(17): 1–9.
Gittelsohn, Joel, Stewart B. Harris, Krista L. Burris, Louisa Kakegamic, Laura T. Landman, Anjali Sharma, Thomas M. S. Wolever, Alexander Logan, Annette Barnie, and Bernard Zinman. 1996. Use of Ethnographic Methods for Applied Research on Diabetes among the Ojibway-Cree in Northern Ontario. *Health Education Quarterly* 23: 235–382.
Gittelsohn, Joel, and Sangeeta Mookjherji. 1997. The Application of Anthropological Methods to the Study of Intrahousehold Resource Allocation. In *Intrahousehold Resource Allocation in Developing Countries: Models, Methods, and Policy*, ed. Lawrence Hadad, John Hoddinott, and Harold Alderman, 165–178. Baltimore, MD: International Food Policy Research Institute (IFPRI) by Johns Hopkins University Press.
Gittelsohn, Joel, Elanah Toporoff, Mary Story, Marguerite Evans, Jean Anliker, Sally Davis, Anjali Sharma, and Jean White. 2000. Food Perceptions and Dietary Behavior of American-Indian Children, Their Caregivers, and Educators: Formative Assessment Findings from Pathways. *Journal of Nutrition Education* 32(1): 2–13.

Goland, Carol, and Sarah Bauer. 2004. When the Apple Falls Close to the Tree: Local Food Systems and the Preservation of Diversity. *Renewable Agriculture and Food Systems* 19(4): 228–236.

Hough, Guillermo and Daniela Ferraris. 2010. Free Listing: A Method to Gain Initial Insight of a Food Category. *Food Quality and Preference* 21(3): 295–301.

Jenike, Mark, Kelsey Lutz, Céline Vaaler, Sarah Szabo, and John E. Mielke. 2011. Thinking about Food, Drink, and Nutrition among Ninth Graders in the United States Midwest: A Case Study of Local Partnership Research. *Human Organization* 70(2): 139–152.

Kuhnlein, Harriet, Bill Erasmus, and Dina Spigelski, eds. 2009. *Indigenous Peoples' Food Systems: The Many Dimensions of Culture, Diversity and Environment for Nutrition and Health.* Rome: Food and Agriculture Organization of the United Nations and the Centre for Indigenous Peoples' Nutrition and Environment.

Kuhnlein, Harriet, Suttilak Smitasiri, Salome Yesudas, Lalita Bhattacharjee, Li Dan, and Salek Ahmed. 2006. *Documenting Traditional Food Systems of Indigenous Peoples: International Case Studies. Guidelines for Procedures.* Ste-Anne-de-Bellevue: Centre for Indigenous Peoples' Nutrition and Environment. https://www.mcgill.ca/cine/files/cine/manual.pdf Accessed 10 September 2016.

Libertinoa, Luciano, Daniela Ferrais, Maria de las Mercedes Lopez Osornio, and Guillermo Hough. 2012. Analysis of Data From a Free-Listing Study of Menus by Different Income-Level Populations. *Food Quality and Preference* 24(2): 269–275.

Lucen, Sean, Frances K. Barg, and Judith A. Long. 2010. Promoters and Barriers to Fruit, Vegetable, and Fast-Food Consumption among Urban, Low-Income African Americans: A Qualitative Approach. *American Journal of Public Health* 100(4): 631–625.

Mengistu, Fentahun, and Herbert Hager. 2008. Wild Edible Fruit Species Cultural Domain: Informant Species Competence and Preference in Three Districts of Amhara Region, Ethiopia. *Ethnobotany Research and Applications* 6: 487–502.

Michaela, John, and Isobel Contento. 1986. Cognitive, Motivational, Social, and Environmental Influences on Children's Food Choices. *Health Psychology* 5(3): 209–230.

Monárrez-Espino, Joel, Ted Greiner, and Homero Martínez. 2004. Rapid Qualitative Assessment to Design a Food Basket for Young Tarahumara Children in Mexico. *Scandanavian Journal of Nutrition* 48(1): 4–12.

Muller, Jocelyn, and Astir M. Almedom. 2008. What Is "Famine Food"? Distinguishing Between Traditional Vegetables and Special Foods for Times of Hunger/Scarcity (Boumba, Niger). *Human Ecology* 36: 599–607.

Newkirk, Christine, Kathryn S. Oths, and William W. Dressler. 2009. Intracultural Diversity in Food Knowledge in Southern Brazil. *Ecology of Food and Nutrition* 48(4): 285–302.

Nolan, Justin. 2002. Wild Plant Classification in Little Dixie: Variation in a Regional Culture. *Journal of Ecological Anthropology* 6: 69–81.

Perchonock, Norma, and Oswald Werner. 1969. Navajo Systems of Classification: Some Implications for Ethnoscience. *Ethnology* 8(3): 299–342.

Pieroni, Andrea, Sabine Nebel, Rocco Franco Santoro, and Michael Heinrich. 2005. Food for Two Seasons: Culinary Uses of Non-cultivated Local Vegetables and Mushrooms in a South Italian Village. *International Journal of Food Sciences and Nutrition* 56(4): 245–272.

Price, Lisa L., and Astrid B. Gurung. 2006. Describing and Measuring Ethno-entomological Knowledge of Rice Pests: Tradition and Change among Asian Rice Farmers. *Environment, Development and Sustainability* 8(4): 507–517.

Quinlan, Marsha. 2005. Considerations for Collecting Freelists in the Field: Examples from Ethobotany. *Field Methods* 17(3): 1–16.

Quintiliani, Lisa, Marci Campbell, Pamela Haines, and Kelly Webber. 2008. The Use of the Pile Sort Method in Identifying Groups of Healthful Lifestyle Behavior among Female Community College Students. *Journal of American Dietetic Association* 108: 1503–1507.

Rivera, Diego, Concepcion Obon, Cristina Inocencio, Michael Heinrich, Alonso Verde, Jose Fajardo, and Jose Antonio Palazon. 2007. Gathered Food Plants in the Mountains of Castilla-La Mancha (Spain): Ethnobotany and Multivariate Analysis. *Economic Botany* 61(3): 269–289.

Romney, A. Kimball, Susan Weller, and William H. Batchelder. 1986. Culture and Consensus: A Theory of Culture and Informant Accuracy. *American Anthropologist* 88(2): 313–338.

Roos, Gun. 1998. Pile Sorting: "Kids Like Candy." In *Using Methods in the Field: A Practical Introduction and Casebook,* ed. Victor C. De Munck and Elisa Janine Sob, 97–110. Walnut Creek, CA: AltaMira.

———. 2002. Our Bodies Are Made of Pizza: Food and Embodiment Among Children in Kentucky. *Ecology of Food and Nutrition* 41(1): 2002.

Setalaphruk, Chantita, and Lisa Price. 2007. Children's Traditional Ecological Knowledge of Wild Food Resources: A Case Study in a Rural Village in Northeast Thailand. *Journal of Ethnobiology and Ethnomedicine* 3(33): 1–11.

Smith, J. Jerome 1993. Using ANTHROPAC 3.5 and a Spreadsheet to Compute a Freelist Salience Index. *Cultural Anthropology Methods Newsletter* 5(3): 1–3.

Szurek, Sarah. 2011. Cultural Models of Food and Social Networks Among Mexican Immigrants in the Southeast United States. Dissertation Thesis. University of Alabama.

Tapper, Richard, and Nancy Tapper. 1986. "Eat This, It'll Do You a Power of Good": Food and Commensality among Durrani Pashtuns. *American Ethnologist* (13)1: 62–79.

Thompson, Kirrilly, Sarah Blunden, Emily Brindal, and Gilly Hendrie. 2011. When Food Is Neither Good Nor Bad: Children's Evaluations of Transformed and Combined Food Products. *Journal of Child Health Care* 15(4): 261–271.

Traphagan John W., and L. Keith Brown. 2002. Fast Food and Intergenerational Commensality in Japan: New Styles and Old Patterns. *Ethnology* (41)2: 119–134.

Varela, Paula, and Susana. M. Fiszman. 2013. Exploring Consumers' Knowledge and Perceptions of Hydrocolloids Used as Food Additives and Ingredients. *Food Hydrocolloids* 30: 477–484.

Watkins, Tammy. 2010. The Prevalence of Wild Food Knowledge among Nomadic Turkana of Northern Kenya. *Journal of Ethnobiology* 30(1): 137–152.

Weller, Susan. 2007. Cultural Consensus Theory: Applications and Frequently Asked Questions. *Field Methods* 19: 339.

Weller, Susan, and A. Kimball. Romney. 1988. *Systematic Data Collection.* Newbury Park, CA: Sage.

Wilson, Warren M. 2003. Cassava (Manihot esculenta Crantz), Cyanogenic Potential, and Predation in Northwestern Amazonia: The Tukanoan Perspective. *Human Ecology* 31(3): 403–416.

Wilson, Warren, M and Darna L. Dufour. 2006. Ethnobotanical Evidence for Cultivar Selection among the Tukanoans: Manioc (Manihot esculenta Crantz) in the Northwest Amazon. *Culture & Agriculture* 28(2): 122–130.

CHAPTER 12

Food and Text(ual) Analysis
Kathleen C. Riley

> My thoughts on the limits of eating follow in their entirety the same schema as my theories on the indeterminate or untranslatable in a text. There is always a remainder that cannot be read, that must remain alien.
> —Jacques Derrida in "An Interview with Jacques Derrida on the Limits of Digestion"

Texts have been analyzed for millennia by spiritual leaders, philosophers, and literary critics. Written texts in particular, from the Upanishads and Torah to belles lettres and novels, have been "read" by readers who perform exegeses, extracting "meaning" (God's, a human author's, the readers') and focusing more or less on the texts' forms, functions, and contexts. However, in the last several decades, the term "text" has been radically expanded to cover not only written documents but also a range of multisensory (audio, visual, tactile, gustatory, etc.) communications, many of which were not originally produced or framed as spiritual or literary forms to be consciously analyzed and consumed. Additionally, the "readers" now include not only fundamentalist preachers and poetry professors but also political pundits and social activists, many of whom rely increasingly on technological mediation for their readings; and many of these analyses have become themselves metatexts to be read by researchers.

This history of reading texts is replete with evidence of the human interest in food, from biblical directives about what to produce, prepare, and eat, and how (e.g., Leviticus 11 and Deuteronomy 14), to cartoons, films, and advertisements laced with food images that both reflect and shape our sociocultural beliefs about who we and others are (see Thursby 2008 for a good set of food text bibliographies). In other words, food texts have always been rampant, but now their metatextual analyses have gone viral. This chapter is a brief introduction to the methods for examining this cornucopia of material. Its focus extends to the meaningful content of texts and beyond, discussing how those meanings are semiotically constructed, deconstructed, and disseminated.

Food (Meta)texts: Forms and Contexts, Meanings and Functions

Since food texts abound, let us begin by textually labeling a few of their many forms, mentioning some of the contextual places (print and virtual) where they can be found, and touching on a few of their meanings and functions. First, one finds compilations of words and their etymologies (Ayto 2012), idioms and their definitions (http://www.idiomconnection.com/food.html)—especially useful for language-learners, quotes (http://www.quotationspage.com/subjects/food/) and aphorisms (Brillat-Savarin 1971) (why do people love these so?), as well as cooking shows (http://www.cookingchanneltv.com/shows/a-z.html), food activist films (http://grist.org/food/26-films-every-food-activist-must-watch/), and food ads for industry professionals (http://adsoftheworld.com/taxonomy/industry/food). There are collections of poems (Young 2012) and cartoons (Ziegler 2004), etiquette manuals on how to eat properly (Post et al. 2014), and guides on how not to overeat (J. Simon 2012). One can find Platonic dialogues about how the bowels were constructed to save humans and civilization from gluttony (Archer-Hind 1888: 271), paleo-diet cookbooks for learning how to eat like our pre-agricultural ancestors (Cordain 2011), recipes to reproduce meals from famous fictional scenes (Shapiro 1996), dummies' guides for urban gardening (P. Simon 2013), editions of the forgotten texts of the failed WPA program "America Eats" (Kurlansky 2009), and agriculture bills on their way through Congress (http://agriculture.house.gov/issues/issue/?IssueID=14896). There are also websites devoted to fighting the obesity pandemic (http://www.cdc.gov/obesity/), providing global famine relief (http://www.wfp.org/), supporting breastfeeding (http://www.llli.org/), and protecting whales and dolphins from predatory fishermen (http://www.internationalwhaleprotection.org/). And these are just a drop in the deluge of books, blogs, and TV programs about food that discuss how and why we (ought to) produce, distribute, prepare, consume, and digest food as we do (see Korsmeyer 2005 for a great selection of classic food texts from Hume and Proust to Suzuki and Mintz).

Then there are the texts about food texts—what I am calling here food "metatexts." These range from cultural analyses of food expressions, myths, legends, and folklore from around the world (Andrews 2000; Jurafsky 2014; Levi-Strauss 1983) to newspaper blogs about how healthy food labels are used as lucrative corporate strategies http://www.washingtonpost.com/blogs/wonkblog/wp/2014/06/24/the-word-natural-helps-sell-40-billion-worth-of-food-in-the-u-s-every-year-and-the-label-means-nothing/. Some deconstruct the health contradictions created by food industry texts (Nestle 2002) while others examine historical records for clues to understanding how Europeans talked at table during the Renaissance (Jeanneret 1991). Essays analyzing cookbooks, recipes, and menus abound (Appadurai 2008; Goody 2008) as food scholars study how humans use taste to construct social categories of identity based on age, gender, class, ethnicity, and nationality. Literary critics once considered taste to be a lowly sense—too immediate and practical to contribute meaning to high culture—but in a recent volume Delville (2008) seeks instead to valorize "gastroaesthetics" for the analysis of food poetry. In the world of food politics, scholars analyze the food-related policies and white papers produced by governments, NGOs, and corporations, asking how hunger, health, agriculture, and profit are regulated (Imhoff 2012; Mudry 2011; Schuwerk 2011; Singer 2011). And these are only the texts about *written* food texts.

Also numerous are the metatexts about audio and visual food texts, such as the volume produced in conjunction with a special exhibit at the Art Institute of Chicago in which American paintings about food are "read" for their cultural significance (Barter 2013; see also Nygard 2013 for an overview of food art analyses). One of the most popular forms of food scholarship analyzes the semiotic sense-making and political-economic impact of mediatized food: food advertising (e.g., Belasco and Scranton 2002; Parkin 2006), food magazines (e.g., Warde 1997; Parasecoli 2008), food television (e.g., Holden 2008; Murray 2013), and food films (Lindenfeld 2011; Bower and Piontek 2013). Much of this is an outgrowth of the now well-established practice within the structural, poststructural, and semiotic branches of sociology and anthropology of treating and studying food and foodways as in and of themselves a form of textual material in need of interpretation (e.g., Levi-Strauss 1990; Douglas 1973; Barthes 2008; Bourdieu 1984).

In this critical reading tradition, two models for analyzing food as text are "foodscapes" (e.g., Johnston and Baumann 2010) and "food as performance" (see, e.g., two special issues on food and performance: an issue of *Text and Performance Quarterly* introduced by Lindenfeld and Langellier in 2009 and an issue of *Performance Research* beginning with Kirshenblatt-Gimblett 1999). A number of texts and collections of texts now take an interdisciplinary approach to exploring a wide array of food texts such as pop lyrics, dinner talk, chef interviews, toasts, etiquette manuals, art, folktales, festivals, films, journalism, and cartoons (Albala 2013; Ferguson 2014; Manning 2012; Thursby 2008; Cramer, Greene, and Walters 2011; Gerhardt, Frobenius, and Hucklenbroich-Ley 2013; Hosking 2010; Lavric and Konzett 2009, Szatrowski 2014; Williams-Forson and Counihan 2012).

Having touched here, if ever so briefly, on the plethora of possible forms, meanings, contexts, and functions of both food texts and metatexts, I turn now to examining some of the methods that have been applied (and illustrated in many of the metatexts referenced above) in the collection and analysis of food textual data. As will become apparent, additional food texts are created every time anthropologists set out to study foodways. For instance, anthropologists write field notes about what they observe, extract and represent quotes from interviews they conduct, and construct and offer transcripts of the food talk that they record. These too must be included now in the near-to-bursting granary of food texts for which we need methodological tools of analysis.

Methods for Analyzing Food (Meta)texts

In one way or another, all the chapters in this section examine methods for the study of food texts. Zycherman's chapter looks at how anthropologists may elicit word lists (i.e., a form of text) and then analyze them as evidence of the speakers' classificatory schemas and associations. In this case, the focus of the studies is almost entirely on the content of the lists and how words reference semantico-cognitive categories. Albala's chapter discusses methods for finding and analyzing primary historical sources (usually written, but also visual) with an anthropological lens. This form of textual analysis focuses primarily on the extraction of referential information about who was producing, exchanging, preparing, and consuming food when, where, and how. However, when it comes to historical readings, the analyst understands that the information represented in such texts was shaped by whoever produced and presented them when, where, and how. This is related to the methods discussed in Riley and Cavanaugh's chapter on the collection and analysis of food talk (whether elicited, natural, or mediated), in which there is an explicit focus on interpreting the forms and goals of the discursive texts in their contexts of production and reproduction.

In this section, I will extract a few key methods for reading food (meta)texts, whatever their modality (e.g., spoken, written, visual, or otherwise sensory). However, I wish first to announce my bias: at this point in history, textual analysis precludes any attempt to arrive at a single all-purpose meaning, acknowledging instead the multiplicity of possible readings. That is, analysts necessarily go after not only the intentional goal of the author, but also the fluctuating impact on a given audience in various contexts. In other words, the goal of textual analysis is to interpret the ways in which texts are understood by and influence those who are exposed to them. To do this, linguistic anthropologists study how texts are entextualized—how they are decontextualized from their original contexts and recontextualized in new contexts, which are then intertextually circulated in ways that produce new readings (see Urban and Silverstein 1996 for a set of articles that explore the causes and consequences of entextualization). In the remaining few paragraphs, I will look briefly at how food texts are formed and transformed by both participants and researchers, and how their multiply indeterminate readings can affect those who produce and read them as well as those about whom they are produced.

Collecting and Constructing Food (Meta)texts

As mentioned above and in several of the chapters (especially Cavanaugh and Riley's introduction to this section and Riley and Cavanaugh's chapter "Food Talk"), linguistic anthropologists produce food texts while also collecting them. For instance, each time we write field notes based on our ethnographic observations of people engaging in food practices, we are noting what and how they communicate about the food (one food text) as well as how the food is used to communicate (a second food text). Each time we transform food talk (whether an interview or an everyday interaction in a natural context) into a transcript, we are creating a metatext that is then available for further analysis. And each time we read a handwritten document or surf the Internet, extracting passages or noting websites as instances of food discourse for later analysis, we are similarly decontextualizing and recontextualizing this textual material—constructing it as we collect it—and thus adding another level of abstraction to our analytic work. This factor has an impact on our final analyses, and thus must be acknowledged and theoretically accounted for (see Bateson 1972 for a discussion of metacommunication, levels of abstraction, and their analytic impact).

Traditionally scholars refer to these forms of textual data as qualitative data. That is, analysis of data like these is presumed to be limited by the small scale of the collection site and the slow pace of the collection process. The data cannot be reduced to high-volume, standardized, regularized bits of information (i.e., quantitative data) that can be analyzed statistically to produce large-scale generalities. The benefit of these methods lies instead in our gradual, subjective processes of data-gathering, in which we discover factors that could not have been anticipated by a researcher who approaches the setting with presumptive hypotheses about what s/he will find. This inductive approach is frequently referred to as "grounded theory"—i.e., the notion that our interpretation of what is going on in a particular context, and therefore our theories about what is happening in general in settings such as this, must be based on feedback between the models of the world that we bring to the field of study when we arrive and the understandings that dawn on us as we immerse ourselves in that new world. According to this logic, it is impossible to go to the field with fully predetermined methods for collecting our data and already prepared containers for bringing our data home in. In other words, linguistic anthropologists frequently return from the field with very messy data. However, this does not mean there is no hope of making sense of them. Indeed, much of the process of analysis (i.e., taking apart in order to recombine with new insight) takes the form of sifting through and finding the containers (e.g., semantico-cognitive categories) we were not even aware we were using as we collected our data in the field. Thus, our research findings prove to be literally that: findings.

Several of the key texts on working with qualitative data listed below (Bernard and Ryan 2010; Gibson and Brown 2009; Hesse-Biber and Leavey 2011) provide good introductions to the construction of textual data via ethnographic observation, interviewing, and discourse recording and transcription. Useful discussions of the cross-disciplinary methods applied in the gathering and construction of textual data about foodways in particular can be found in Cavanaugh et al. (2014) and in several essays in Albala 2013 (especially Lizie 2013 and Buccini

2013) as well as in the introductions to a couple of the recent volumes that take on the intersection of food and language (Cramer, Greene, and Walters 2011; Gerhardt et al. 2013; Szatrowski 2014).

Coding and Reading Food-Focused (Meta)texts

Traditionally, researchers who collect qualitative data have developed assorted idiosyncratic means of sifting through the data they collect in the field. We type and rethink field notes, type and revise transcripts, re-read and reconsider the research documents we collected before we left. This goes on in the field, affecting our data-collection process in the grounded way discussed above, and continues after we return from the field, affecting our analyses and the conclusions we reach. In this process, we are constructing categories to think with. For example, in the case of food we classify the food expressions our participants use, categorize the food practices they socialize their children to engage in, and code the speech genres they use while growing, cooking, buying, and eating food. And we check all of this against both what previous researchers said they were doing, and what the fact sheets and policy papers put out by administrators, educators, and health workers report they are or ought to be doing. In other words, our findings are forged out of the process of looking.

For a good introduction to the questions, researchers ask themselves about texts and the methods they use to address these questions (see Frey, Botan, and Kreps 1999). These authors make clear that analysis can take several directions depending both on the kinds of data and the kinds of questions being asked. Although they relegate "textual analysis" to what I would call the analysis of publicly disseminated texts and treat the rest of what I include in "textual analysis" (interviews, ethnographic observations, and everyday discourse) as "naturalistic inquiry," they nonetheless make an interesting analytical distinction between the rhetorical force of a text and its content or messages. Denzin and Lincoln's (2005) handbook includes many fascinating essays on doing qualitative research, but one author in particular, Silverman (2005), offers some excellent words of wisdom about engaging in the textual analysis of interview narratives, public texts, and transcribed discourse. He argues effectively that the strength of qualitative analysis is its ability to probe deeply into not only the apparent but also the subtler messages of texts, constructing new theories based on what is found rather than imposing presumptive categories on the participants' words. Finally, McKee (2003) offers a very readable introduction to the post-structuralist uncertainties of doing textual analysis, that is, of interpreting texts from the multiple perspectives of the sense-making communities who produce and consume them, thus undermining the possibility of producing "scientific" and "reproducible" readings of texts.

In the olden days, a lot of the sorting and linking, looking and thinking involved in making sense out of texts included methodological tools such as scissors, tape, index cards, highlighter pens, and one's subjective sensibilities, used to identify and interpret recurring lexicalized themes, rhetorical figures, pragmatic strategies, semiotic effects, and so forth. In the last two decades, however, qualitative research methods have become increasingly codified as more and more researchers use computer-mediated means of data mining, coding, sorting, comparing, modeling, and networking. The qualitative research manuals listed in the key texts below offer great overviews of how to approach a corpus of gathered textual data (e.g., Bernard and Ryan 2010; Gibbs 2007; Gibson and Brown 2009; Hesse-Biber and Leavy 2011). They also provide instructive summaries on using computer software to assist in the analysis of texts, but for an in-depth and up-to-date look at this very hot topic, see Silver and Lewins (2014) as well as the list of online resources about computer-assisted qualitative data analysis software (CAQDAS) at the end of this chapter.

After collecting/constructing and coding/reading food (meta)texts, a couple of questions remain concerning our attempts as researchers to make meaning out of food texts and metatexts: first, how do we deal with the ethical contingencies involved in conducting and publishing this sort of research; and second, should we—and if so how can we—apply what we learn from this research to bring about good and significant change in the world? I will conclude by briefly addressing these questions.

Making Meaning out of Food (Meta)texts, Keeping Ethics and Activism in Mind

As explored in this chapter, humans make meaning out of an array of food-focused textual materials, from gardening spells and cooking shows to supermarket circulars and etiquette manuals. Food researchers treat all of these texts (and the metatexts we create ourselves) as needing not only investigation and interpretation, but also ethical safeguards on the one hand and activist intervention on the other. So by way of conclusion and as part of the larger project of discovering methods for making meaning out of food (meta)texts, I reflect here on a couple of methodological approaches to these two interrelated topics: first, how ethics are implicated in the collection, analysis, and publication of food textual data; and second, how food text researchers sometimes seek not just to understand but also to transform the meaning-making practices of humans for the good of future generations. I will take them in reverse order, starting from the desired benefits and working backwards to the unintended risks.

Some of the food topics that lend themselves to activist research include school food (Poppendieck 2010), agribusiness and the environment (Kimbrell 2002), and food justice (Gottlieb and Joshi 2010). All these areas of research rely on the analysis of food texts and metatexts (from ethnographic observations to census documents). However, the goal for each of these researchers is to turn research into activism—that is, strategies for making a real difference. Sometimes the mere act of doing the research raises consciousness in the settings (from schools to NGOs) where interviews and focus groups are conducted (e.g., Vanegas and Riley 2013). Publication of the research sometimes has a positive impact when the published text is widely circulated (e.g., Menzel and D'Aluisio 2005). And sometimes researchers end up being hired as consultants, webmasters, organizers, or teachers by the very organizations we are studying because we have become so knowledgeable about the impediments and best practices involved in doing what the organization is attempting to do.

However, in the process of arriving at these desired effects, researchers also need to worry about the unintended but undesirable impacts we may have on the humans and communities we are studying. All researchers who study human subjects in any direct way (that is, not through publicly accessible texts, but by way of almost any other form of research) must learn to conduct research in a sensitive, respectful manner. Part of this learning process now includes applying for permission from Institutional Review Boards (IRB) to conduct our research. In other words, in the process of thinking through the settings, populations, goals, and methods of a study, we must also think about how to safeguard the well-being of those whom we subject to scrutiny. We must consider whether our observing presence, interview questions, recording techniques, data storage, or publication of the findings will invade their privacy or endanger them physically or psychologically. Put another way, the power of words means that all the food metatexts that research constructs have the potential to hurt our subjects in unexpected ways (leaking secrets, misrepresenting, insulting or embarrassing, etc.). So before we begin our research, we must find ways to explain to our subjects both the benefits we hope for and the possible risks of our research, and so acquire their informed consent before proceeding (see Hesse-Biber and Leavey 2011 for more details about ethical research procedures).

Still, even with these IRB protocols in place, we frequently encounter unanticipated ethical dilemmas in the field. Ideally, we keep in touch with our IRB throughout the research process and in this way seek advice from objective outsiders. In practice, though, anthropologists conducting research far from home need to be prepared to think through such difficulties without guidance. And this is only about the collection and storage of firsthand textual data. All researchers (even those dealing with publicly accessible data) confront ethical issues with respect to how they analyze and publish their data and findings. There are no foolproof measures for working through the ethical quagmires involved in a given study, but a growing number of research organizations attempt to offer policy statements and guidelines for how to anticipate some of the difficulties that may arise (e.g., see AAA's code of ethics http://www.aaanet.org/issues/policy-advocacy/code-of-ethics.cfm).

I have briefly discussed these two questions of ethical research and research activism here at the end in order to emphasize that any attempt to analyze food (meta)texts (whether widely circulated tweets or privately whispered narratives) may lead us into ethical dilemmas—on the one hand because we want our meaning-making to provide purposeful, positive benefits, and on the other because we need to avoid unintended, negative consequences. Unfortunately, the desire to do good can sometimes compromise our principles to do no harm. Nonetheless, the very personal, sensitive, and ubiquitous nature of food makes this research topic not only vulnerable to trespass but also rife with hopeful outcomes. Thus, my final word of methodological advice is to walk softly and carry a generous spoon.

Kathleen C. Riley has taught linguistic and cultural anthropology at Concordia University, City College, Queens College, Fordham University, Barnard College, and Rutgers University. She has conducted fieldwork on food change, language socialization, and cultural identity in the Marquesas, Vermont, France, Montreal, and New York City, and has published articles in the *Journal of Linguistic Anthropology* and *Language and Communication,* as well as in several edited collections. She has co-edited (with Christine Jourdan) a special issue of *Anthropologie et Sociétés* on food glocalization and is presently co-editing (with Jillian Cavanaugh) a special issue of *Semiotics Review* on food and language.

Online Resources

Overviews

Text analysis: http://textanalysis.info/
Content analysis: http://www.content-analysis.de/
Computer Assisted Qualitative Data Analysis Software (CAQDAS): http://www.surrey.ac.uk/sociology/research/researchcentres/caqdas/
Research ethics: http://www.aaanet.org/issues/policy-advocacy/code-of-ethics.cfm

Qualitative Data Analysis Software

ANTHROPAC http://www.analytictech.com/anthropac/apacdesc.htm
Atlas.ti http://www.atlasti.com/index.html
Dedoose http://www.dedoose.com/
HyperRESEARCH http://www.researchware.com/products/hyperresearch/hr-nutshell.html
MAXqda http://www.maxqda.com/
Nvivo http://www.qsrinternational.com/products_nvivo.aspx
QDA Miner http://provalisresearch.com/products/qualitative-data-analysis-software/
UCINET https://sites.google.com/site/ucinetsoftware/home
WORDij http://www.content-analysis.de/2010/09/24/wordij.html

Transcription Software

CHAT and CLAN (links transcripts with audio files) http://childes.psy.cmu.edu/
HyperTRANSCRIBE http://www.researchware.com/products/hypertranscribe.html

Key Texts for the Analysis of Food Texts

Albala, Ken, ed. 2013. *Routledge International Handbook of Food Studies.* New York: Routledge.
Bernard, H. Russell, and Gery W. Ryan. 2010. *Analyzing Qualitative Data: Systematic Approaches.* Los Angeles: Sage.
Cavanaugh, Jillian R., Kathleen C. Riley, Alexandra Jaffe, Christine Jourdan, Martha Karrebæk, and Amy Paugh. 2014. What Words Bring to the Table: The Linguistic Anthropological Toolkit as Applied to the Study of Food. *Journal of Linguistic Anthropology* 24(1): 84–97.
Cramer, Janet M., Carlnita P. Greene, and Lynn M. Walters, eds. 2011. *Food as Communication, Communication as Food.* New York: Peter Lang.
Gerhardt, Cornelia, Maximiliane Frobenius, and Susanne Hucklenbroich-Ley, eds. 2013. *Culinary Linguistics: The Chef's Special.* Amsterdam: John Benjamins.
Gibbs, Graham. 2007. *Analyzing Qualitative Data.* Los Angeles: Sage.
Gibson, William J., and Andrew Brown. 2009. *Working with Qualitative Data.* Los Angeles: Sage.
Hesse-Biber, Sharlene Nagy, and Patricia Leavy. 2011. *The Practice of Qualitative Research.* 2nd ed. Los Angeles: Sage.
Szatrowski, Polly E., ed. 2014. *Language and Food: Verbal and Nonverbal Experiences.* Amsterdam: John Benjamins.

References

Albala, Ken, ed. 2013. *Routledge International Handbook of Food Studies.* New York: Routledge.
Andrews, Tamra. 2000. *Nectar and Ambrosia: An Encyclopedia of Food in World Mythology.* Santa Barbara, CA: ABC-CLIO.
Appadurai, Arjun. 2008. How to Make a National Cuisine: Cookbooks in Contemporary India. In *Food and Culture: A Reader,* ed. Carole Counihan and Penny Van Esterik, 289–307. 2nd ed. New York: Routledge.
Archer-Hind, R. D., ed. 1888. *The Timaeus of Plato.* London: Macmillan. Accessed 3 September 2016 at https://archive.org/details/timaeusofplato00platiala.
Ayto, John. 2012. *The Diner's Dictionary: Word Origins of Food and Drink.* Oxford: Oxford University Press.
Barter, Judith A., ed. 2013. *Art and Appetite: American Painting, Culture, and Cuisine.* Chicago: The Art Institute of Chicago.
Barthes, Roland. 2008. Toward a Psychosociology of Contemporary Food Consumption. In *Food and Culture: A Reader,* ed. Carole Counihan and Penny Van Esterik, 28–35. 2nd ed. New York: Routledge.
Bateson, Gregory. 1972. *Steps to an Ecology of Mind: Collected Essays in Anthropology, Psychiatry, Evolution, and Epistemology.* Chicago: University of Chicago Press.

Belasco, Warren, and Philip Scranton, eds. 2002. *Food Nations: Selling Taste in Consumer Societies.* New York: Routledge.
Bernard, H. Russell, and Gery W. Ryan. 2010. *Analyzing Qualitative Data: Systematic Approaches.* Los Angeles: Sage.
Bourdieu, Pierre. 1984. *Distinction: A Social Critique of the Judgement of Taste,* trans. Richard Nice. Cambridge, MA: Harvard University Press.
Bower, Anne, and Thomas Piontek. 2013. Food in Film. In *Routledge International Handbook of Food Studies,* ed. Ken Albala, 177–186. New York: Routledge.
Brillat-Savarin, Jean Anthelme. 1971 [1825]. *The Physiology of Taste, or Meditations on Transcendental Gastronomy,* trans. M. F. K. Fisher. New York: Alfred Knopf.
Buccini, Anthony F. 2013. Linguistics and Food Studies: Structural and Historical Connections. In *Routledge International Handbook of Food Studies,* ed. Ken Albala, 146–158. New York: Routledge.
Cavanaugh, Jillian R., Kathleen C. Riley, Alexandra Jaffe, Christine Jourdan, Martha Karrebæk, and Amy Paugh. 2014. What Words Bring to the Table: The Linguistic Anthropological Toolkit as Applied to the Study of Food. *Journal of Linguistic Anthropology* 24(1): 84–97.
Cordain, Loren. 2011. *The Paleo Diet: Lose Weight and Get Healthy by Eating the Foods You Were Designed to Eat.* Hoboken, NJ:Wiley.
Cramer, Janet M., Carlnita P. Greene, and Lynn M. Walters, eds. 2011. *Food as Communication, Communication as Food.* New York: Peter Lang.
Delville, Michel, ed. 2008. *Food, Poetry, and the Aesthetics of Consumption: Eating the Avant-Garde.* New York: Routledge.
Denzin, Norman K., and Yvonna S. Lincoln, eds. 2005. *The Sage Handbook of Qualitative Research.* 3rd ed. Thousand Oaks, CA: Sage.
Douglas, Mary, ed. 1973. *Food in the Social Order.* London: Routledge.
Ferguson, Priscilla Parkhurst. 2014. *Word of Mouth: What We Talk about When We Talk about Food.* Oakland: University of California Press.
Frey, Lawrence R., Carl H. Botan, and Gary L. Kreps. 1999. *Investigating Communication: An Introduction to Research Methods.* 2nd ed. Boston: Allyn & Bacon.
Gerhardt, Cornelia, Maximiliane Frobenius, and Susanne Hucklenbroich-Ley, eds. 2013. *Culinary Linguistics: The Chef's Special.* Amsterdam: John Benjamins.
Gibbs, Graham. 2007. *Analyzing Qualitative Data.* Los Angeles: Sage.
Gibson, William J., and Andrew Brown. 2009. *Working with Qualitative Data.* Los Angeles: Sage.
Goody, Jack. 2008. The Recipe, the Prescription, and the Experiment. In *Food and Culture: A Reader,* ed. Carole Counihan and Penny Van Esterik, 78–90. 2nd ed. New York: Routledge.
Gottlieb, Robert, and Anupama Joshi. 2010. *Food Justice.* Cambridge, MA: MIT Press.
Hesse-Biber, Sharlene Nagy, and Patricia Leavy. 2011. *The Practice of Qualitative Research.* 2nd ed. Los Angeles: Sage.
Holden, T. J. M. 2008. The Overcooked and Underdone: Masculinities in Japanese Food Programming. In *Food and Culture: A Reader,* ed. Carole Counihan and Penny Van Esterik, 202–220. 2nd ed. New York: Routledge.
Hosking, Richard, ed. 2010. Food and Language (Oxford Symposium on Food and Cookery). Devon: Prospect Books.

Imhoff, Daniel. 2012. *Food Fight: The Citizen's Guide to the Next Food and Farm Bill.* Healdsburg, CA: Watershed Media.
Jeanneret, Michel. 1991. *A Feast of Words: Banquets and Table Talk in the Renaissance,* trans. Jermy Whiteley and Emma Hughes. Cambridge: Polity Press.
Johnston, Josée, and Shyon Baumann. 2010. *Foodies: Democracy and Distinction in the Gourmet Foodscape.* New York: Routledge.
Jurafsky, Dan. 2014. *The Language of Food: A Linguist Reads the Menu.* New York: W. W. Norton & Company.
Kimbrell, Andrew, ed. 2002. *Fatal Harest: The Tragedy of Industrial Agriculture.* Washington, DC: Island Press.
Kirshenblatt-Gimblett, Barbara. 1999. Playing to the Senses: Food as a Performance Medium. *Performance Research* 4(1): 1–30.
Korsmeyer, Carolyn. 2005. *The Taste Culture Reader: Experiencing Food and Drink.* Oxford: Berg.
Kurlansky, Mark, ed. 2009. *The Food of a Younger Land.* New York: Riverhead Books.
Lavric, Eva, and Carmen Konzett, eds. 2009. *Food and Language, Sprache und Essen.* Frankfurt: Peter Lang.
Levi-Strauss, Claude. 1983. *From Honey to Ashes: Introduction to a Science of Mythology,* vol. 2, trans. John and Doreen Weightman. Chicago: University of Chicago Press.
———. 1990. *The Origin of Table Manners: Mythologiques,* vol. 3, trans. John and Doreen Weightman. Chicago: University of Chicago Press.
Lindenfeld, Laura A. 2011. Feasts for Our Eyes: Viewing Films on Food through New Lenses. In *Food as Communication, Communication as Food,* ed. Janet M. Cramer, Carlnita P. Greene, and Lynn M. Walters, 3–21. New York: Peter Lang.
Lindenfeld, Laura, and Kristin Langellier. 2009. Introduction. *Text and Performance Quarterly* 29(1): 104.
Lizie, Arthur. 2013. Food and Communication. In *Routledge International Handbook of Food Studies,* ed. Ken Albala, 27–38. New York: Routledge.
Manning, Paul. 2012. *The Semiotics of Drink and Drinking.* New York: Continuum.
McKee, Alan. 2003. *Textual Analysis: A Beginner's Guide.* London: Sage.
Menzel, Peter, and Faith D'Aluisio. 2005. *Hungry Planet: What the World Eats.* Napa, CA: Material World Press.
Mudry, Jessica. 2011. Quantifying the American Eater: USDA Nutrition Guidance and a Language of Numbers. In *Food as Communication, Communication as Food,* ed. Janet M. Cramer, Carlnita P. Greene, and Lynn M. Walters, 235–254. New York: Peter Lang.
Murray, Sarah. 2013. Food in Television. In *Routledge International Handbook of Food Studies,* ed. Ken Albala, 187–197. New York: Routledge.
Nestle, Marion. 2002. *Food Politics: How the Food Industry Influences Nutrition and Health.* Berkeley: University of California Press.
Nygard, Travis. 2013. Food and Art. In *Routledge International Handbook of Food Studies,* ed. Ken Albala, 169–176. New York: Routledge.
Parasecoli, Fabio. 2008. Feeding Hard Bodies: Food and Masculinities in Men's Fitness Magazines. In *Food and Culture: A Reader,* ed. Carole Counihan and Penny Van Esterik, 187–201. 2nd ed. New York: Routledge.
Parkin, Katherine J. 2006. *Food Is Love: Food Advertising and Gender Roles in Modern America.* Philadelphia: University of Pennsylvania Press.

Poppendieck, Janet. 2010. *Free for All: Fixing School Food in America*. Berkeley, CA: University of California Press.
Post, Peggy, Daniel Post Senning, Lizzie Post, and Anna Post. 2014. *Emily Post's Etiquette*. 18th ed. New York: Morrow.
Schuwerk, Tara J. 2011. Food Bank Culture: Food and Nutrition Communication a Hunger-Relief Organization. In *Food as Communication, Communication as Food*, ed. Janet M. Cramer, Carlnita P. Greene, and Lynn M. Walters, 381–403. New York: Peter Lang.
Shapiro, Anna. 1996. *A Feast of Words: For Lovers of Food and Fiction*. New York: W.W. Norton.
Silver, Christina, and Ann Lewins. 2014. *Using Software in Qualitative Research: A Step-by-Step Guide*. 2nd ed. Los Angeles and London: Sage.
Silverman, David. 2005. Analyzing Talk and Text. In *Handbook of Qualitative Research*, ed. Norman K. Denzin and Yvonna S. Lincoln, 821–834. 2nd ed. Thousand Oaks, CA: Sage.
Simon, Julie M. 2012. *The Emotional Eater's Repair Manual: A Practical Mind-Body-Spirit Guide for Putting an End to Overeating and Dieting*. Novato, CA: New World Library.
Simon, Paul. 2013. *Urban Gardening for Dummies*. Hoboken, NJ: Wiley.
Singer, Ross. 2011. The Corporate Colonization of Communication about Global Hunger: Development, Biotechnology, and Discursive Closure in the Monsanto Pledge. In *Food as Communication, Communication as Food*, ed. Janet M. Cramer, Carlnita P. Greene, and Lynn M. Walters, 405–427. New York: Peter Lang.
Szatrowski, Polly E., ed. 2014. *Language and Food: Verbal and Nonverbal Experiences*. Amsterdam: John Benjamins.
Thursby, Jacqueline S. 2008. *Foodways and Folklore: A Handbook*. Westport, CT: Greenwood Press.
Urban, Greg, and Michael Silverstein. 1996. *Natural Histories of Discourse*. Chicago: University of Chicago Press.
Vanegas, Yexenia, and Kathleen C. Riley. 2013. *School Food Fights and Discourse-Based Activist Anthropology: Effecting Change in Howe the Next Generation Eats, Thinks, and Talks about Food*. Chicago, IL: AAA.
Warde, Alan. 1997. *Consumption, Food and Taste*. London: Sage.
Williams-Forson, Psyche, and Carole Counihan, eds. 2012. *Taking Food Public: Redefining Foodways in a Changing World*. New York: Routledge.
Young, Kevin. 2012. *The Hungry Ear: Poems of Food and Drink*. New York: Bloomsbury.
Ziegler, Jack. 2004. *How's the Squid? A Book of Food Cartoons*. New York: H.N. Abrams.

CHAPTER 13

Analysis of Historic Primary Sources

Ken Albala

The disciplines of anthropology and history overlap in many significant ways, particularly on the topic of food. Thus a description of the resources and research methods used by historians will be especially useful for anthropologists. In fact, food historians use the work of anthropologists, sometimes scarcely recognizing a distinction between the fields, while the work of leading food anthropologists such as Sidney Mintz or Margaret Visser could justifiably be considered history since it deals primarily with the past.

Numerous types of source material can serve as primary documents in historical food research. The term primary denotes texts that were written by participants or observers in the past rather than works by historians commenting on the past, which are considered secondary sources. The lines between these types of writing are not always so hard and fast, though. If one is writing about a historian, then that person's work becomes a primary document. Equally, the age of the text is not necessarily an indication of status as primary document; one could analyze a blog entry written last month as such. Despite these ambiguities, a useful way to differentiate types of sources is to consider primary anything that is the subject of research, secondary anything that comments upon these and tertiary anything drawn from secondary scholarship, such as an encyclopedia entry, book review, or historiographical essay. A cookbook published in 1470 would thus be a primary source, a historian commenting on it in 2007 would be secondary, and the words you are reading now are tertiary. Historians depend on primary documents for research in order to generate new insights based on the historical record, rather than rehash material taken from other historians. A single document may be used by many researchers, each interpreting it differently depending on the research question, theoretical background, or methodology. That is, history is always a matter of interpretation rather than a mere assemblage of facts.

The term document might seem to suggest that the source must be a piece of paper or something written. While this is often the case, historians also make use of other kinds of evidence and consider them documents of the past on equal footing with written materials, though often interpreted in rather different ways. Thus a painting, perhaps showing a kitchen, can be an invaluable source for a historian, as can an advertisement or photograph. An object such as a whisk or refrigerator or the kitchen itself can reveal as much as a will or tax inventory listing such artifacts of material culture. Here history intersects with archaeology as well, and not only when referring to prehistoric peoples. A modern trash heap can be an excellent resource for investigating foodways. Music is also a perfectly viable medium for food research; songs about food proliferate in most societies. Likewise, films, radio broadcasts, websites, and virtually anything that can be analyzed is a legitimate primary source. For example, if one were researching breakfast cereal in the early twentieth century, an advertisement or government-sponsored promotion, a jingle, a bowl with the company logo, or even the cereal box itself might be just as valuable as the company records or other written materials.

As might be expected, written documents provide the most abundant information for food and nutrition research. Over the past century, the focus of historical research on food has shifted dramatically depending on the preoccupations of each generation of scholars, so naturally the types of documents studied have also changed. The study of food history goes back to classical times if we consider the *Deipnosophists* of Athenaeus (2001), a recounting of every literary reference to food and dining in the ancient world. In more recent times there have been antiquarian editions of historic cookbooks such as *Apicius* (2006) or the *Forme Of Cury* or popular titles like the great chef Alexis Soyer's *Pantropheon* (1853). Food history is not new, but in general food has only quite recently been considered a topic worthy of serious study by professional historians. Fundamental historical research methods nonetheless apply to the study of food, as they do any topic.

A century ago, when food began to be considered an integral part of economic history, prices of basic staples such as wheat were analyzed in detail in order to chart standards of living. By comparing average wages, inflation, and prices, historians could determine the percentage of household income spent on ordinary food as compared to luxuries. Treating historical data quantitatively and approaching it scientifically was believed to give the topic status, depicting objective truth in a way that biased national histories and positivist approaches seeking to trace progress in historical sources could not. This scientific methodology gave even food a certain legitimacy because it was really larger historical forces being discussed, rather than the menial minutiae of feeding.

Food was also studied insofar as it played a role in larger political events such as rebellions and revolution. The riots over bread that triggered the French Revolution were studied, but rarely did research inquire about the type of bread eaten, who made it, or how it was baked. Likewise, when the subject of provisioning a great overseas voyage or an expedition to the Antarctic was analyzed using surviving records, they were only examined insofar as they inevitably influenced the outcome of these events, not as food topics in themselves.

On the other hand, farming, as the primary occupation of the majority of people in the premodern world, has been of direct interest to historians. Their focus has been mostly on systems of land tenure, agricultural technologies, and social relations between peasants and the aristocracy, and only peripherally on what was actually grown and consumed. For this kind of research, estate records and legal documents prove very valuable, especially when individuals were brought to court and left testimony. Wills and probate records, tax declarations, and especially documents relating to market regulations or foodstuffs traded long-distance are particularly important for this kind research. So too are ships' logs, records of imposts and duties, and any document recording the growing, processing, and distribution of foodstuffs. Many such documents have been collected and published, but the vast majority remain in manuscript form in government archives and small specialized repositories.

Agriculture itself has always been considered a serious topic, and agronomists have been important sources of information about farming practices ranging from ancient times right down to the present. Because many of these works also deal with broader management of the farm household, they also sometimes discuss food processing and preservation—perhaps curing olives or making wine—and sometimes even include recipes, as in the guide written by Cato the Elder in ancient Rome. There also exist farming diaries written by landowners to track the success of their enterprise. Most of these survive only in manuscript form, but those of more famous figures such as George Washington and Thomas Jefferson have been published. A related genre, the botanical, also yields invaluable information about, say, when the tomato first reached Europe from America, or how a particular plant was first cultivated or used medicinally.

Household management books may also reveal much about foodways of the past. At first written for males, these offered directions for governing servants, stocking larders, and displaying hospitality to guests. Increasingly these roles were delegated to women, especially in less extravagant households, which were increasingly literate in the early modern era. The medieval *Menagier de Paris* is an excellent early example of this genre: it was written by an elderly man for his young bride, in the expectation that after he died she would need various skills to attract a new husband, one being knowing how to cook.

A shift toward social history occurred in the mid-twentieth century, and an increased interest in nutrition among historians of the Annales School in France and English writers such as Jack Drummond pushed historians to take a closer look at exactly what was consumed in the past (Drummond and Wilbraham 1939). This research focused largely on calories, vitamins, and nutrients as well as subsistence crises and nutritional deficiencies such as rickets and scurvy. There was, consequently, closer attention to what constituted the diet of an average person and to some extent how food was cooked and who cooked it. These historians were interested in long-term patterns in history so they still examined official records, but increasingly the microhistorical unit of analysis and an interest in household dynamics, gender roles, and attitudes toward food led this generation of scholars to diaries, autobiographies, and documents that might shed light on the inner workings of the kitchen. Interest in long-term trends and patterns in history drove research in the opposite direction to find quantifiable data that could be compared across centuries. For example, the percentage of meat in the diet, which rose dramatically in the demographic slump following the bubonic plague in the fourteenth and fifteenth centuries, reversed in the sixteenth century when the population grew again, a process described as depecoration. One might even argue that the proliferation of recipes for meat in cookbooks of the late Middle Ages is a direct reflection of these long-term demographic changes.

Cookbooks

Cookbooks remain the best historical source for the study of food, though they must be used with caution because they rarely describe what people actually ate. Reading them from a gastronomic vantage point opened up the entirely new subdiscipline of culinary history, which examines the aesthetic approaches to food in the past as well as what the ingredients were, how they were processed, and why. For many scholars and popular food writers, cooking and tasting recipes from the past became a form of research in itself. The earliest written culinary texts are a series of cuneiform tablets from Mesopotamia about 3,500 years old. From the classical era there are fragments of a cookbook by Archestratus, mostly about fish, and the cookbook attributed to the first-century gourmand Apicius, though compiled several centuries later. There are comparable texts in the Chinese tradition, mostly untranslated. These naturally reveal ingredients, cooking methods, and dining customs, but they also inform us about attitudes toward food. For example, Archestratus tells us where the best fish of a specific species comes from, and that it should be prepared simply without too much fuss or excess seasoning. In other words, the book is about connoisseurship of a kind that could only be cultivated by a man of leisure with wealth and time for travel to seek out the finest ingredients.

The medieval era produced an abundance of cookbooks, mostly written for noble or royal households and thus intentionally displaying the wealth and sophistication of the featured chef and his patron, an aesthetic approach to food that placed high value on rare and exotic imported spices, elaboration of recipes using complex cooking techniques, and subtle surprises. The *Viandier* attributed to Taillevent (1988), written for the French court of Charles V, and the *Forme of Cury* written for Richard II of England are excellent examples of this era.

With the advent of printing and the *De honesta voluptate* written by Platina and Martino of Como, who supplied the recipes, cookbooks began to reach a broader audience and address simpler tastes and increasingly ordinary households, especially when we get to sixteenth-century Germany and England, where cookbooks were first identified has having women authors. By carefully considering the projected audience of cookbooks, one can conduct a kind of social history by asking questions such as who is doing the cooking—a male professional or a housewife? What kind of equipment is called for, and does this reflect the wealth and social status of the household? What ingredients are called, and are they expensive markers of social status?

Indeed, cookbooks leave behind clues about much more than teaching people to cook. For example, the very first indigenous cookbook published in Canada, the *Cuisinière Canadienne* of 1840, contains recipes that are essentially unchanged from several centuries earlier, using spices and sugar in savory dishes that would not have been considered odd to someone in the sixteenth century. The cookbook is not merely backward, it is intentionally traditional in trying to secure a specifically French identity in a place (Montreal) then ruled by the British and witnessing an influx of English-speaking immigrants as well as new, modern foods of the industrial era. Its decidedly antiquated recipes are a means to establish identity in a changing world.

Old cookbooks are also increasingly easy to find online, especially those out of copyright. For those with mastery of foreign languages there are hundreds of sources available on Google Books, the Internet Archive and Gutenberg Project, Gallica at the Bibliotheque Nationale, and specialized sites like Feeding America, which features early U.S. cookbooks.

An extensive ancillary literature deals with banquet management and catering guides for professionals, and there are also specialized carving manuals. These proliferated especially in Italy in the late sixteenth and seventeenth centuries and later in France as they became the vanguard of fashion. These guides offer detailed advice about kitchen and wait staff, the various departments commissioned to deal with wine, pastries, and maintenance of linens, as well as cooking and serving food. Whereas these only describe the most elite of kitchens, the very fact that they were printed implies that they encouraged imitation, if perhaps on a lesser scale. They are evidence that culinary customs trickle down from elites to social aspirants, which in turn drives chefs and banquet managers to innovate and thus maintain their distinction. Curiously, this sometimes comes in the form of adopting seemingly simple rustic foodways, which means that the influence upon fashions is indeed multidirectional. Periodically through history, tastes shift from the sumptuous and extravagant to the simple and unaffected, generally in tandem with shifts in art, music, and fashion. These are as easily traced in the gastronomic literature as they can be in books on manners, which are another excellent source for historical and anthropological research.

Although every period has its own criteria for polite table manners, the flourishing of these is linked to the rise of nation-states, the monopolization of violence, and the advent of professional courtiers (Elias, 2000). The Renaissance witnessed numerous guides on manners, starting with Erasmus' book for boys, *De civilitate morum puerilium* (Erasmus 2008). This literature continues unabated down to the present, and its perennial popularity suggests that there are always people not "to the manner born" who want to fit in socially by exhibiting proper use of cutlery, correct table service, and so forth. A countervailing trend is the casualization of formal manners, which, like changes in fashion mentioned above, seems to follow distinct socioeconomic patterns.

These trends can also be easily discerned in menus. Many repositories around the world hold collections of historical menus. With a complete set, trends in taste preferences, the ways dishes wax and wane in popularity, the changing structure of courses within a meal, and even prices can be gauged over time. Menus will obviously reveal the availability of certain ingredients: for example, the disappearance of terrapins can be easily traced, as can increasing squeamishness as organ meats and recognizable animal parts are gradually stricken from menus. Menus are often published in book form as well, and they were a regular feature in Italian cookbooks of the sixteenth and seventeenth centuries. The menu as we know it—a regular feature in proper restaurants—dates back to the nineteenth century. Menus from famous dining spots, political banquets, and even from the *Titanic* can yield very specific information about a certain time and place.

Gastronomic Literature

Since the early nineteenth century and the writings of Grimod de la Reyniere (1803), there has also been a rich literature of restaurant reviews. Mostly found in periodicals, these—perhaps more than most gastronomic texts—reveal specific preferences and preoccupations tied to very specific times and places. Sometimes they describe the service, the decor, or special items on the menu, details that are rarely forthcoming in any other kind of gastronomic text. Gastronomy itself is a related topic that in the Western tradition is said to begin with Jean Anthelme Brillat-Savarin (2009) in the early nineteenth century, though many earlier texts easily qualify for inclusion, as do countless others in non-Western traditions. For example, Lu Yu's classic ninth-century text on tea is purely gastronomic.

Numerous twentieth-century sources can be consulted, not only newspaper food sections but food magazines such as *Gourmet, Bon Appetit, Saveur,* and *Food and Wine*. Moreover, food writing appears in books written by figures such as

M. F. K. Fisher (2004), Craig Claiborne (1990), and James Beard (1996 [1959]), three luminaries of American food writing. Methodologically, when approaching these texts the researcher should pose exactly the same questions asked of any primary source. Who is writing and why? What is the historical context? Who is the projected audience? What values or ideals are evident in the opinions expressed? Do they reveal anything particular about class, gender, race, or ethnicity? Do they reveal anything else about the general mindset and worldview of this time and place? There are of course many other questions one can pursue, depending on what one wants to discover.

These exact same questions can be applied to various other related works of food literature. Alongside the gastronomic texts, and perhaps to counter them, there has always been an extensive dietary literature. This too stretches back to ancient times; in fact, it would be safe to say that the nutritional literature has always been more extensive than the culinary. Every great physician from Hippocrates (1967) to Galen (2003) devoted works to the properties of foodstuffs and how they interact with the human body and affect health. This is equally true of the Chinese tradition originating with *The Yellow Emperor's Classic of Internal Medicine* and the Hindu tradition of the *Caraka Samhita* (2011), the foundational Ayurvedic text. Similar to cookbooks, these texts are not descriptive but prescriptive. Nonetheless, they reveal rich details about the opinions and attitudes of their authors. For example, in a dietary text from sixteenth-century England (Venner 1620), we are told that partridges are too light and delicate for the powerful stomachs of laborers, so they ought to be reserved for noblemen with delicate constitutions, for whom this is the medicinally proper food. Obviously the elevated status of some ingredients and the stigma toward others reflects the deep class-based biases of this civilization.

Scientific texts about food processing are another invaluable resource, whether it be a treatise on the new pressure cooker invented by Denis Papin (1681) in the seventeenth century, or an eighteenth-century book on cheese making by Josiah Twamley (1784), or even a recent text on how breakfast cereals are engineered. Sometimes such texts are published, but they are also found in the corporate archives of many companies alongside inventories, grocery store records, and account books of manufacturers, shippers, wholesalers, and middlemen, not to mention import and export documents and patents. The very first U.S. patent for pearl ash, a chemical leavener for making quick breads like biscuits and pancakes, is itself a primary source document. There are also the records of legal proceedings for food adulteration, labor disputes, trademark litigation, and countless other food-related documents. These offer assiduous researchers the greatest opportunities for statistical analysis, especially when complete sets survive. Access to corporate archives has become more difficult in recent years given the rapid increase of exposés and scandals, but legal records and government documents are usually accessible to the public.

Advertisements are probably the most readily available and easily used resource for food history in the last few centuries. They key into the public's concerns over food in a way few other media can. For example, an early twentieth-century ad for breakfast cereal frightens mothers by telling them their children will be scrawny and underdeveloped unless they are fed vitamin-fortified cereal. The text and image are as much about the competitive American culture as the importance of physical strength. The ad merely plays into fears in order to sell a particular product. Propaganda is closely related and uses many of the same tactics. When Herbert Hoover directed the Food Administration during World War I, a series of ads tried to convince people to voluntarily forgo meat, sugar, and fats so they could be sent to soldiers at the front. Apart from the irony that we are nowadays told to avoid these foods, the posters offer a succinct snapshot of what people believed was wholesome, nutritious, and a source of energy, and exactly what kind of privation they were asked to suffer to win the war: eating corn, fish, and other less desirable foods. That cereal manufacturers promoted their corn-based products as patriotic only adds further depth to the story.

Dietary patterns have also always been closely tied to religion, so unsurprisingly there is also an enormous body of literature connected to various food restrictions and taboos. These might describe how to keep kosher, why the veneration of the cow is important to devout Hindus, or why Seventh-Day Adventists should avoid meat, stimulants, and alcohol. Anthropologists and historians have rightfully mined devotional texts surrounding food, which are not about taboos alone but are also concerned with animal sacrifice, ritual consumption or ceremonial cannibalism, and festive commensality. Fasting is another major topic in the Christian, Muslim, and Judaic traditions, as well as many other religions around the world. These religiously based foodways offer keys to understanding humans' relationship to God and indeed, their entire cosmology (Douglas, 2002; Harris, 1974). For example, in the early church fasting was seen as a way to mortify the flesh so as to make the spirit stronger. Avoiding meat specifically was thought to cool the body, suppressing the libido and making physical purity easier to bear.

Books concerned with food ethics are a similar resource, whether advocating vegetarianism, a locavore diet, organic food, or sustainability. These are obviously current preoccupations, but comparable ones flourished in the past as well, for example, Sylvester Graham's (1837) early nineteenth-century insistence that people should eat whole grains rather than processed white bread.

Literature and art are another vast resource for the history of food. Such a document might be a poem on wine by Omar Khayyam, an ode to a lemon by Pablo Neruda (2004), a haiku about fish, a film like *Ratatouille,* or a radio broadcast or TV show about the hottest new hawker's stall in Singapore. Eating, being among the most important activities of our species, not surprisingly appears in countless works of fiction, whether done by grotesque ravenous giants in Rabelais' *Gargantua and Pantagruel* (1955), starving foundlings in Charles Dickens's *Oliver Twist*

(2008), or a classic muckraking novel like Upton Sinclair's *The Jungle* (2001). Needless to say, still life paintings put food front and center for analysis.

With the increasing number of new media forms, there is naturally a wealth of new data to examine as well. Websites about food include information ranging from recipe banks to mass reviews of restaurants, short instructional videos, and corporate web pages. There are literally millions of sites worthy of analysis. Even social media sites like Facebook leave behind a record that may eventually constitute a suitable historical topic.

Among the most exciting of new media are food blogs, which have mushroomed at an astounding rate (Bauman and Johnson 2010). Apart from possibilities for quantitative analysis and ample photographs of what people have actually eaten, their sheer number and accessibility makes them one of the richest resources available. Although there is no guarantee that bloggers tell the truth, probably no other medium gets closer to offering a glimpse of actual consumption, albeit a select view of what the authors thought might appeal to readers. Unlike most other gastronomic literature, food blogs also often show failures, reworkings of popular recipes, and other snapshots of everyday life, written by people who are admittedly not experts.

Regardless of the type of primary source, the methodology remains the same. Interrogate your subject, coerce the source to reveal what is hidden or not apparent. Look for contextual clues and unintentional slips. Historical research is exactly like sleuthing, except that the subjects do not talk back.

As an example of how to proceed, imagine a potential research project based on a single primary source, a printed cookbook. Normally a historian would use a series of primary and secondary sources, form a hypothesis at some point in the middle of the research, and then test the hypothesis based on the information in the primary sources. For example, to show the increase in use of spices in the fifteenth century, one could compile a data set of ingredients in all available cookbooks and then map it to see if recipes called for greater quantities, greater frequency or use, or perhaps a wider range of spices from further afield. This could be easily tested. Usually, however, the question would be subtler; it might seek to find out what the source reveals about the author, his or her intended readership, the cooking technology, and so on.

For the sake of examining the research process, a single cookbook will be illustrative. *The Eskimo Cook Book* (1952) was compiled by students of the Shishmaref Day School and published by the Alaska Crippled Children's Association in Anchorage, Alaska, as a fundraiser. The students lived on Sarichef Island, a few miles from the Arctic Circle near the Bering Strait. Although the students did eat modern Western foods, their grandparents and others had informed them of many still living Eskimo traditions. Being also very conscious of the fact that their readers were generally white and unfamiliar with Eskimo food, they made an assumption that many of the dishes might be unpalatable to them. For example, in a recipe for Pick'niek, an indigenous plant, the author or informant says it tastes like sugar and is very good with seal oil, but "Maybe the white men don't like them." In another recipe for soured seal liver, the student Agnes Kiyutelluk writes that "Most of the boys and girls don't like it, except the grown-ups and old people. I don't like it either." Here is fairly solid evidence that either foodways in this group were changing or such dishes were an acquired taste that only developed with age.

As a simple enthnography, the cookbook is rich with details about native flora and fauna. It describes cooking technologies in detail. At revealing moments, a recipe might call for macaroni or a can of vegetables, and a caribou soup recipe even specifies Campbell's soup as an ingredient. There is also a recipe for donuts fried in blubber. One might test many possible theses using this cookbook, but as a snapshot of changing traditions it clearly is absolutely fascinating. Any cookbook can be interrogated in the same way by reading between the lines for information, telltale scraps of evidence, and contextual clues.

Ken Albala is Professor of History at the University of the Pacific. He is the author or editor of twenty-four books on food, including *Eating Right in the Renaissance, Food in Early Modern Europe, Cooking in Europe 1250–1650, The Banquet: Dining in the Great Courts of Late Renaissance Europe, Beans: A History* (winner of the 2008 IACP Jane Grigson Award), and *Pancake*. He has also co-edited *The Business of Food, Human Cuisine,* and *Food and Faith in Christian Culture* and edited *A Cultural History of Food: The Renaissance* and *The Routledge International Handbook of Food Studies*. Albala was also editor of the Food Cultures Around the World series with thirty volumes in print, and of the four-volume *Food Cultures of the World Encyclopedia*. He is now the series editor of Rowman and Littlefield Studies in Food and Gastronomy, for which he has written a textbook entitled *Three World Cuisines: Italian, Chinese, Mexican* (winner of the Gourmand World Cookbook Awards' best foreign cuisine book in the world). Albala was also co-editor of the journal *Food Culture and Society* and is editing a three-volume encyclopedia on *Food Issues*. He has also co-authored two cookbooks: *The Lost Art of Real Cooking* and *The Lost Arts of Hearth and Home*. Recent works include a *Food History Reader: Primary Sources, Nuts: A Global History,* a small book entitled *Grow Food, Cook Food, Share Food,* and a translation of the sixteenth-century cookbook *Livre fort excellent de cuysine*. His latest book is *At the Table: Food and Family Around the World*.

References

Apicius. 2006. Trans. Christopher Grocock and Sally Grainger. Totnes: Prospect Books.
Athenaeus. 2011. *Deipnosophists,* trans. Charles Burton Gulick. Cambridge, MA: Harvard University Press.

Baumann, Shyon, and Josée Johnston. 2010. *Foodies.* New York: Routledge.
Beard, James. 1996 [1959]. *The James Beard Cookbook.* 1st ed. 1959. New York: Marlowe and Company.
Brillat-Savarin, Jean-Anthelme. 2009. *The Physiology of Taste,* trans. M. F. K. Fisher. New York: Knopf.
Caraka Samhita. 2011. Trans. R. K. Sharma and Bhagwan Dash. Varanasi: Chowkhamba.
Claiborne, Craig. 1990. *New York Times Cookbook.* Revised ed. New York: New York Times.
Cuisinière Canadienne. 1840. Montreal: Louis Perrault.
Curye on Inglysch. 1985. Ed. Constance B. Heiatt and Sharon Butler. London: Oxford University Press.
Dickens, Charles. 2008. *Oliver Twist.* New York: Sterling Classics.
Douglas, Mary. 2002. *Purity and Danger.* London: Routledge.
Drummond, J. C., and Anne Wilbraham. 1939. *The Englishman's Food: A History of Five Centuries of English Diet.* London: J. Cape.
Elias, Norbert. 2000. *The Civilizing Process,* trans. Edmund Jephcott. Oxford: Blackwell.
Erasmus, Desiderius. 2008. *A Handbook on Good Manners for Children,* trans. Eleanor Merchant. London: Preface.
Eskimo Cook Book, The. 1952. Prepared by Students of Shishmaref Day School. Anchorage: Alaska Crippled Children's Association.
Fisher, M. F. K. 2004. *The Art of Eating, 50th Anniversary Edition.* New York: Houghton Mifflin.
Galen. 2003. *On the Properties of Foodstuffs,* trans. Owen Powell. Cambridge: Cambridge University Press.
Graham, Sylvester. 1837. *A Treatise on Bread.* Boston: Light and Stearns.
Grimod de la Reynière. 1803. *Almanach des Gourmands.* Paris: Maradin.
Harris, Marvin. 1974. *Cows, Pigs, Wars and Witches.* New York: Vintage.
Hess, Karen, ed. 1995. *Martha Washington's Book of Cookery.* New York: Columbia University Press.
Hippocrates. 1967. *On Regimen,* trans. W. H. S. Jones. Cambridge: Harvard University Press.
Khayyam, Omar. n.d. *Rubaiyat,* trans. Edward Fitzgerald. New York: Avenel.
Menagier de Paris: The Good Wife's Guide. Trans. Greco and Rose.
Neruda, Pablo. 2004. *The Essential Neruda.* San Francisco: City Lights.
Papin, Denis. 1681. *A New Digester or Engine for Softening Bones.* London: Dawson.
Platina (Bartolomeo Sacchi). 1998. *De honesta voluptate,* trans. Mary Ella Milham.
Rabelais, François. 1955. *Gargantua and Pantagruel,* trans. J. M. Cohen. Harmondsworth: Penguin.
Sinclair, Upton. 2001. *The Jungle.* Mineoloa, NY: Dover.
Soyer, Alexis. 1853. *Pantropheon.* London: Simpkin Marshall.
Twamley, Josiah. 1784. *Dairying Exemplified.* Warwick: J. Sharp.
Venner, Tobias. 1620. *Via recta ad vitam longam.* London: Edward Griffen for Richard Moore.
Viandier of Taillevent. 1988. Ed. Terence Scully. Ottawa: University of Ottawa Press.
Yellow Emperor's Classic of Internal Medicine. 2002. Trans. Ilsa Veith. Berkeley: University of California Press.

SECTION VI

Food Studies

CHAPTER 14

Introduction to Food Studies Methods

Amy B. Trubek

In his excellent overview of the important concepts that have framed the emerging field of food studies, historian Warren Belasco (2008: 6) argues that although the field has gained a modicum of academic respectability, "it is also inherently subversive." This is because to study food, scholars need to be capable of being generalists: the issues are too complex and contradictory to use the more traditional laser-like focus of the academic scholar, looking closely only at the head of a single straight pin. Food issues, according to Belasco (2008: 7), "require that we think about matters political, historical, economic, sociocultural, and scientific *all at once*. As generalists, we study food as a *system*." Evidence of the increased engagement in such interdisciplinary studies of food includes the presence of new journals (e.g., *Food, Culture and Society, Journal of Agriculture, Food Systems, and Community Development, Gastronomica*), new undergraduate minors and concentrations (at the University of Oregon, College of the Atlantic, University of Michigan, and others), graduate programs (at New York University, Boston University, Chatham University, University of Vermont,), and book series and monographs from numerous scholarly presses (Oxford University Press, University of California Press, University of Texas Press, Bloomsbury, Routledge, and many more). Opportunities to teach and do research about food using an interdisciplinary lens are offered regularly, some examples being a recent postdoctoral position in the humanities at University of Illinois-Chicago and tenure-track positions in public health (University of Michigan) and anthropology (University of Vermont).

First, some background on the field of food studies/food systems. As a human necessity—a requisite for the survival of individuals, groups, and the human species such an important domain of human existence. However, the very necessity of food makes it analytically very difficult to contain. Contemporary academic scholarship has tended to deal with such analytic breadth and complexity by compartmentalizing food. Food production was contained by agronomy. Food transformation and distribution tended to get owned by engineering and business. Food consumption was brought into the realm of science by the disciplines of nutrition and food science. But the *meaning* of food, in and around the requirements of organizing ways to make food and provide it to individuals and societies, often was ignored or marginalized. It probably comes as no surprise that anthropology, with its long history of holism and focus on everyday life, has generated much of the foundational scholarly literature for this emerging new field. There are many examples, but especially notable are Audrey Richards' early food ethnography *Hunger and Work in a Savage Tribe: A Functional Study of Nutrition among the Southern Bantu* (1932), Sidney Mintz's ethnohistorical monograph *Sweetness and Power: The Place of Sugar in Modern History* (1986) (more on his work below), and Carole Counihan and Penny Van Esterik's very successful *Food and Culture: A Reader* (2012).

Food studies scholarship focuses on the meaning humans bring to food, and its investigations are not defined solely by a certain type of activity (e.g., consumption but not production) or by a certain scope or scale of human organization (thus not small-scale societies over individual behaviors). An approach this broad and heterodox often requires using the theories and methods of multiple disciplines: food studies scholars move easily between history, anthropology, literary studies, political science, development studies, et cetera. At the same time, there is a parallel intervention into a more multidisciplinary approach to examining food from fields closely allied with human and environmental health and well-being. Nutritionists and public health researchers increasingly look to mixed-methods approaches for large research studies and seek to create large multidisciplinary teams in order to better address food issues and behavior change (e.g., see Beagan et al. 2008). Among those committed to understanding the interdependence of the natural and human landscapes, research that integrates ecosystems and production systems is increasingly current (e.g., see Bacon et al. 2008).

There are two very important points to consider when looking at the intersection of food studies and anthropological methods: food studies scholarship tends to focus on "an issue" or "a problem" within the larger system, and therefore the researcher needs to adopt a holistic approach. The discipline of anthropology has always been interested in problems that emerge from the field and also has adopted holism as an axiom. Thus, it comes as no surprise that anthropologists and anthropological methods have been adopted by scholars from fields as diverse as cultural studies, history, agroecology, nutrition, and public health.

Two recently published volumes, Warren Belasco's *Food: The Key Concepts* (2008) and Jeff Miller and Jonathan Deutsch's *Food Studies: An Introduction to Research Methods* (2009), provide excellent introductions to the theory and practice of food studies. In *Food: The Key Concepts,* Belasco clearly outlines important themes, in terms of both what has been considered in contemporary food studies research and what areas still need to be closely considered. In particular, he focuses on identity, globalization and industrialization of the food system, health, and ethics. Although written as an introductory text for undergraduates, his intelligent analysis and thorough bibliography also provide much information and insight for scholars interested in doing interdisciplinary food research. Each of the themed chapters synthesizes important and recent food studies scholarship, and the chapter summaries provide concise highlights. Many of the themes Belasco takes up are classic in the canon of anthropology: cuisine, commensality, memory and identity, gender and labor, and more.

Miller and Deutsch's *Food Studies: An Introduction to Research Methods* is an anchor work for anyone interested in embarking in interdisciplinary food studies research, especially scholars focused on questions of meaning and interpretive analysis. They define the predominant research methods as "historical methods, ethnography and narrative, quantitative methods and using physical objects" (Miller and Deutsch 2009: 9). In the field of food studies, there are projects that stay within the methodological frames of a discipline, like primary source texts for historians or surveys for nutritionists, but the field is dominated by projects using multiple methods. A number of more recent food studies monographs certainly confirm Miller and Deutsch's assertion: Andrea Wiley's work on milk (2011), Carolyn de la Pena's study of artificial sweeteners (2011), David Sutton's ethnography of cooking in modern Greece (2014).

These methods are currently the most widely used, but the list does not represent all possible approaches. Miller and Deutsch also very rightly point out that food itself can operate as a methodological tool. Combining participant-observation with cooking or shopping, or asking research subjects to document food intake or food memories can provide any researcher looking at food with rich and complex data. In fact, combining multiple methods to consider a complex and interdependent issue of the food system can involve numerous points of data collection, as in the case of Janet Poppendieck's recent book *Free For All,* about the modern U.S. school food program. She collected food diaries; participated in preparing school lunches; interviewed administrators, cooks, and students; analyzed legislation; and reviewed historical documents (Poppendieck 2010).

The authors also discuss the methodological tools developed by researchers trained in health and life sciences that can add depth and breadth to the more traditional interpretive strategies used by many anthropologists. For example, increasingly sophisticated tools are being used to collect and monitor individual food intake in order to understand patterns at a population level. Dietary recalls are classic in the field of nutrition, but with new technologies (phone apps, websites, digital video) come new strategies. The field of food science has long been interested in sensory perception and has developed a number of methods for understanding individual and group perception (sensory panels, blind tastings, liking analysis, etc.) that are now both the subject of analysis (see Hennion 2005, 2007; Shapin 2012) and part of new research projects (see Chabrol and Muchnik 2011; Di Monaco et al. 2005). Among scholars interested in food production, as in much of the early work by anthropologists interested in ecology (Rappaport 2000; Paxson 2012), there is a focus on documenting how humans engage with a certain natural environment in order to create livelihoods. The complex and contradictory impulses of this engagement, especially in the context of a system that moves across the whole globe when creating interactions between consumption and production, is being documented using qualitative and quantitative methods (see Bray, Plaza Sanchez, and Contreras Murphy 2008; Gewertz and Errington 2010).

In the field of food studies, many scholars cite anthropologist Sidney Mintz's *Sweetness and Power: The Place of Sugar in Modern History*, first published in 1986 and seminal to the development of food studies in terms of both theory and method. Mintz adopted a view both broad and long in his study of the emergence of global production and consumption practices involving cane sugar. In the big picture, he was interested in how the European desire for sugar in the daily diet fueled much colonial expansion while also supporting the rise of industrial capitalism. To make such a broad argument, he considered, as Warren Belasco (2008: 65) puts it, "two very different types of 'meaning': the few from inside and the view from outside. The inside view entails looking at what a product means to the people who produce and consume it." The fine-grained approach involved integrating meanings of both consumption and production, thus a consideration of European ideas of a proper meal alongside an analysis of plantation sugar production in the Caribbean. The outside view was to make the connections to larger structures and systems.

Despite many pronouncements about the eventual triumph of progress through better living with machine-made and globally sourced food, in reality we still are not quite sure how we should feed ourselves. Tensions remain between aspirations—consistency versus diversity, convenience versus connection—as well as between methods—machine versus hand-made, organic versus chemical inputs, small versus large scale. This makes for fruitful research opportunities, as examining the history of progress, protest, and principles shaping food can lead to larger considerations of meaning in modern life. Adoption of a multi-method, multi-scalar approach to understand the many contemporary attempts to integrate structure, function, and meaning is characteristic of much food studies scholarship since the 1980s. As the authors of the sections discussed below also point out, future food studies scholarship needs to continue this tradition of mixed-methods but go even further, and farther afield.

Review of Sections

Lucy Long's discussion of the scholarly focus on food and meaning in food studies makes an important distinction between "meaning as symbol and reference; and meaning as significance." The ubiquity of food allows for myriad interpretations and functions that go far beyond biological necessity. Long reviews the polysemic qualities of food and explains how humans *make* these many meanings of food, or why food matters. She also provides strategies for framing research on food and meaning, and examples of scholarship reflecting these two approaches to meaning.

Following food and drink commodity chains is an important element of food studies scholarship, as witnessed by the influence Sidney Mintz's *Sweetness and Power* has had among many scholars from numerous disciplines. Catherine Tucker points out that studying commodity chains is crucial to understanding the structure, function, and meaning of the modern food system; however, successfully pulling together such far-reaching study domains poses many challenges. From the methodological point of view, "One of the challenges for commodity chain research is that researchers may need to develop a different set of research instruments to collect data on each node or segment of a commodity chain." Despite the difficulties, she also reiterates that overly narrowly focused studies will never capture the total social reality of food and drink in the modern world.

When it comes to studying any manner of food or drink, the necessary and important interaction between biology and culture is another reason to focus on a single food across scholarly domains. Andrea Wiley and Janet Chrzan point out that when the lens is trained on one food, many aspects of culture and human biology come into focus; the ways in which these vary across human populations then provide additional insight into why local meanings might differ. They remind us that projects looking at single foods might allow the interdisciplinary work of food studies scholars to extend beyond the connections between humanities and social science methods to also incorporate insights and ideas from the life sciences. An in-depth discussion of Wiley's own work on milk and milk consumption provides helpful examples of how to widen the net of possible methodologies for food studies scholarship.

In another move to widen the net when food studies scholars do research, Rachel Black asks the important question of why the senses do not always come into play in designing and conducting research involving food. This is part of a larger call within the discipline of anthropology to consider, as David Howes puts it, "participant sensation." Black points out that the senses need to be brought to the fore in food studies, and in multiple ways. These notably include paying attention to food-related sensory experiences when engaged in the classic anthropological method of participant observation, and designing research with methods from multiple disciplines that consider the sensory domains of human experience, including sensory science and aesthetics.

Finally, the profoundly powerful but ultimately extremely vexed notion of food and place is considered as a powerful topic that requires sophisticated methodologies. Food always comes from someplace, but what is the significance—to the environment, to the food, to the consumer? The association between food and place is often overly romantic, especially in parts of the world where industrialized methods of food production dominate. As William Woys Weaver points out, "the culinary reality is always far more complex, and to achieve a truly balanced view of food and place, many methods of research must be brought together in order to confirm or to dispute all types of evidence on the table." In particular, Weaver thinks looking closely at culinary texts is never enough; an examination of the everyday beliefs and practices of people residing in a place must also be part of any research into questions revolving around food and place.

Dr. Amy Trubek is Associate Professor in the Nutrition and Food Science department at the University of Vermont and Faculty Director for UVM's graduate program in food systems. Trained as a cultural anthropologist and chef, she has carried out research in areas including the history of the culinary profession, globalization of the food supply, the relationship between taste and place, and cooking as a cultural practice. She teaches both undergraduate and graduate courses, including Food and Culture, From Farm to Table: The Contemporary Food System, Qualitative Research Methods and Food Systems, and Society and Policy. She is the author of *Haute Cuisine: How the French Invented the Culinary Profession* (2000) and *The Taste of Place: A Cultural Journey into Terroir* (2008), as well as numerous articles and book chapters. She is involved in interdisciplinary research and outreach on the taste of place and cooking pedagogy and assessment. Amy lives with her family on an heirloom apple orchard, where they make fresh cider, hard cider, and ice cider, and pick lots of fresh apples, pears, and plums.

References

Bacon, Christopher M., V. Ernesto Méndez, Stephen R. Gliessman, David Goodman, and Jonathan A. Fox, eds. 2008. *Confronting the Coffee Crisis*. Cambridge: MIT Press.

Beagan, Brenda, Gwen E. Chapman, Andrea D'Sylva, and B. Raewyn Bassett. 2008. "It's Just Easier for Me to Do It: Rationalizing the Family Division of Foodwork." *Sociology* 42: 653–670.

Belasco, Warren. 2008. *Food: The Key Concepts*. New York: Berg.

Bray, David B., José Luis Plaza Sanchez, and Ellen Contreras Murphy. 2008. Social Dimensions of Organic Coffee Production in Mexico. In *Confronting the Coffee Crisis*, ed. Christopher M. Bacon, V. Ernesto Méndez, Stephen R. Gliessman, David Goodman, and Jonathan A. Fox, 237–259. Cambridge, MA: MIT Press.

Chabrol, Didier, and Jose Muchnik. 2011. Consumer Skills Contribute to Maintaining and Diffusing Heritage Food Products. *Anthropology of Food* 8: https://aof.revues.org/6847.

Counihan, Carol, and Penny Van Esterik. 2012 (3rd Edition). *Food and Culture: A Reader.* New York: Routledge.

De La Pena, Carolyn. 2011. *Empty Pleasures: The Story of Artificial Sweeteners from Saccharine to Splenda.* Raleigh: University of North Carolina Press.

Di Monaco, Rossella, Sabrina Di Marzo, Silvana Cavella, and Paolo Masi. 2005. Valorization of Traditional Foods: The Case of Provolone del Monaco Cheese. *British Food Journal* 107(2): 98–110.

Gewertz, Deborah, and Frederick Errington. 2010. *Cheap Meat: Flap Food Nations in the Pacific Islands.* Berkeley: University of California Press.

Hennion, Antoine. 2005. Pragmatics of Taste. In *The Blackwell Companion to the Sociology of Culture,* ed. Mark D. Jacobs and Nancy Weiss Hanrahan, 131–144. Malden, MA: Blackwell.

———. 2007. Those Things That Hold Us Together: Taste and Sociology. *Cultural Sociology* 1(1): 97–114.

Miller, Jeff, and Jonathan Deutsch. 2009. *Food Studies: An Introduction to Research Methods.* New York: Berg Press.

Mintz, Sidney W. 1985. *Sweetness and Power.* Penguin Books.

Paxson, Heather. 2012. *The Life of Cheese: Crafting Food and Value in America.* Berkeley: University of California Press.

Poppendieck, Janet. 2010. *Free For All: Fixing School Food in America.* Berkeley: University of California Press.

Rappaport, Roy A. 2000. *Pigs for the Ancestors: Ritual in the Ecology of a New Guinea People.* 2nd ed. Long Grove, IL: Waveland Press.

Richards, Audrey I. 1932. *Hunger and Work in a Savage Tribe: A Functional Study of Nutrition among the Southern Bantu.* London: Routledge & Kegan Paul.

Shapin, Steven. 2012. The Sciences of Subjectivity. *Social Studies of Science* 42(2): 170–184.

Sutton, David E. 2014. *Secrets from the Greek Kitchen.* Berkeley: University of California Press.

Wiley, Andrea. 2011. *Re-imagining Milk.* New York: Routledge.

CHAPTER 15

Meaning-Centered Research in Food Studies

Lucy M. Long

Introduction

The meanings of food and eating are one of the central themes of food studies. What does it mean, for us as humans and as cultural and social beings, to eat? What do specific foods, events, or actions mean, and how did those meanings get there? What is "meaning," anyway? How can we study it, and what can we do with that knowledge?

As an interdisciplinary field, food studies includes a variety of approaches to the study of food and meaning. Approaches fall into two broad categories: the qualitative, phenomenological or experience-based disciplines in the humanities, and the more quantitative, empirical disciplines in the social sciences. Humanities scholars see meaning as a central question in scholarship and a fundamental motivation for human activities and productions.[1] They approach meaning as an intangible, subjective quality that cannot be captured quantitatively, so they conduct qualitative research using historical and comparative archival research, personal observation, and both informal and formal ethnographies. They also emphasize frameworks (theories) for interpreting phenomena in order to understand the significance activities and forms have for individuals and groups. Conclusions about meaning cannot be tested objectively, but are evaluated according to the logic of the argument as well as the insights they offer. Social sciences, on the other hand, tend to see meaning as objective and measurable factors shaping and resulting from human actions. Collection and interpretation of this data can be tested according to scientific methods, and conclusions are oftentimes then used to develop new models for behavior or for changing food systems and social institutions.

Anthropological research on food and meaning draws from both the humanities and the social sciences. It usually calls for ethnographic fieldwork in order to explore how individuals actually use food in specific situations and perceive the meanings of that food, but it also uses first-person written accounts, historical and contemporary documents, artifacts, and other forms of expression and practice. Ethnography can range from full immersion in a culture to informal and occasional observation. It may involve learning the skills needed to participate in everyday life or specific practices. Also, some cultural scholars analyze the "meanings" of cultural productions according to their own knowledge of other expressive forms, cultural patterns, and contexts. Research projects and publications on food and meaning range from cultural criticism and philosophical musings to ethnographic reports and interpretations of specific food items or cultures.

What Is "Meaning?"

Meaning in relation to food can refer to the domains of food and eating in general or to specific foods and behaviors around food. The former type of meaning is often an elusive speculation on how humans become social and cultural beings through food, or on food's power to express identity, create community, connect individuals to nature, and so on. Similarly, the meaning of a particular food or food behavior can refer to various things: its significance; the purpose behind preparing or consuming it; the identity or beliefs expressed through it; the associations or emotions attached to it; the thing or idea it refers to; the use of food to demonstrate or create status; and its representation of larger historical, social, and cultural patterns.

It is helpful to place definitions of meaning into two broad categories: meaning as symbol and reference; and meaning as significance. Although they overlap, each definition requires a different set of research methodologies and theoretical frameworks, and each definition can answer different questions. This means that a research project surrounding the meaning of food should begin by determining the specific definitions of meaning to be used and the purpose of the inquiry.

Meaning in Food as Symbol and Reference

Food is often seen as standing for something else—that is, as a symbol. It can represent a variety of things: identity, place, status, power, lifestyle, worldview, values, ideas, relationships. The study of signs and symbols emerged as the field of semiotics in the early 1900s and has contributed significantly to cultural anthropology and other interpretive humanities and social science disciplines. The characteristics of symbols have implications for research conducted on meaning in food, and much of the contemporary work on food in anthropology, sociology, folklore, geography, and cultural studies recognizes and utilizes those characteristics them. For example, Visser (1991) explores the meaning of table manners; Ohnuki-Tierney (1993) discusses how rice represents identity in Japan; White (2012) demonstrates that coffee carries rich symbolism, also in Japan; Pilcher (1998) dissects the political implications and impacts of the construction of a national cuisine; and Neustadt (1992) vividly describes and interprets the symbolic meanings of the New England clambake. Wilson and Gillespie's edited volume (1999), presents excellent essays on the meanings of specific food items central to American food history.

The characteristics of symbols that are significant to meaning-centered research on food include:

1) Meaning is not inherent; it is constructed. Neither food in general nor specific foods intrinsically reference something else—their meanings are given to them through usage and social consent, or sometimes they are created and imposed. Research needs to identify not only the meanings, but also when, how, why, and by whom they were constructed.
2) Meanings therefore can change over time and space. A food item may have had a different meaning in the past or in a different place. Historical and comparative research helps to identify such change.
3) Symbols are polysemic, able to carry more than one meaning. Food generally and particular foods have a variety of meanings. Research needs to explore the diversity of meanings, who holds those meanings, and in what contexts.
4) The meaning intended by the producer of a symbol is not necessarily the same as the meaning interpreted by a consumer. Research can focus on the producer's intent or the consumer's interpretation, but it must acknowledge and in some cases account for differences between the two. Ethnographic research usually documents the various interpretations given by each participant in an interaction.
5) The meanings given to symbols are shaped by external forces (history, environment, economics, structures of power, etc.), so they reflect those forces and must be understood within their contexts. Every food carries within it the history of its surrounding culture and can therefore be used to read that culture and the logic behind its development. Research should therefore attempt to identify those forces and their connections to larger patterns.
6) Symbols are ideological; they express values and beliefs. We make food choices according to our ethos and value system as well as current circumstances, tastes, and immediate needs. This means that we express our worldview (ideology) through our food. Research should therefore identify the worldview of the consumers and culture within which consumption is occurring as well as the possible values and beliefs expressed through a specific food or event.

7) Symbols are political. Their creation, use, and interpretation represent issues of power. Each individual has agency in interpreting the meaning of a food, but for that meaning to be accepted and used in society, other individuals have to agree. Such agreement usually occurs according to hierarchies of status, with higher status groups determining meanings. Also, food symbols can be "invented," often for marketing or political purposes, or can emerge organically through use. Research needs to explore the processes by which a food gains that reference.
8) Symbols have the potential for "affective" power. They can elicit emotions and be experienced subconsciously. They also can be aesthetic, generating in response the satisfaction of a sense of beauty or order regardless of their official, cognitive meanings. Research should therefore recognize the emotional and aesthetic aspects of foods that are used as symbols. This calls for attending to the structural qualities of that food or activity and to the evaluative systems for beauty held by the people using it.

We oftentimes think of symbols as objects, but we also talk about symbolic actions and recurring events, or rituals. Food tends to feature significantly in rituals, both giving meaning to the ritual and acquiring meaning from it. An important point for research is that rituals involve intentional recognition and use of the symbolic meanings of a food and therefore offer an ideal opportunity for a documenting individual as well as group perceptions of meaning.

Meaning in Food as Significance

Meaning can also be understood as significance. If a food is significant, it is "meaningful"—it matters to someone or a group in some way. Perhaps it carries memories of loved ones or of places once inhabited; or it represents a relationship important to an individual; or it is an expression of identity, creativity, or belonging. It might also play an integral role in a ritual or celebration or be a part of a larger whole so that even though it is not considered meaningful in itself, its absence makes a ritual feel incomplete.

In all of these cases, the individual has an emotional attachment to the reference of that food symbol and therefore to the food itself. Those emotions can be positive or negative, but their existence is what makes that food matter to them. Symbolic meanings of food can be understood and used on an intellectual or cognitive level, but those meanings do not necessarily matter to individuals unless they are somehow significant in that individual's life. Significance, after all, is more than just a "warm and fuzzy" feeling. Individuals make decisions and choices based on what is significant to them, so attending to what individuals feel matter to them is key to understanding motivations.

Research into meaning as significance should therefore attempt to discover why a food is meaningful for a particular individual or group and how it came to be so. It should also explore the role of memory in constructing meaningfulness as well as the interplay between factors outside the individuals or groups studied and the resources they have and choices they have made. The emotional aspect of symbols makes the people who find them meaningful care how those symbols are used and presented. Issues arise over who has the power to define the meaning of an object and how it should be properly treated. The presence of debate and emotions surrounding a symbol, then, are clues that the symbol is meaningful and holds significance for the participants.

Folklorists have contributed useful case studies of food's significance to both groups and individuals. The edited collections by Brown and Mussell (1984) and by Long (2004) contain numerous examples of specific foods like lobster, pasties, and tamales, as well as foodways practices like holiday celebrations, butchering, eating in Thai restaurants, eating new foods, and so on. Neustadt (1992), mentioned above, offers an exemplary study of the larger cultural and historical meanings of the New England clambake as context for understanding the significance of a specific clambake tradition for the individuals participating in it. Wilson and Gillespie's edited volume (1999) presents excellent essays on the meanings of specific food items central to American food history. Most of the contributors are either folklorists or are familiar with folklore concepts.

What Is Food?

"What is food?" seems like a silly question, but thinking about the different things and ways in which different cultures eat can prompt the realization that a definition might be needed. Food is matter considered appropriate for ingestion. It is not just "stuff we eat" or "stuff that nourishes our bodies." Young children put all sorts of things in their mouths—leaves, bugs, plastic toys, the tails of pet dogs and cats—that are not considered food by their parents or society. The same items in a different culture or prepared in a different form, however, might be considered food. Food, then, is "constructed" in that different groups consider different things appropriate for ingestion. Different groups also have different ideas about how, when, where, with whom, and why certain things can (and should) be eaten, and different notions of the benefits of ingesting them. "Considered" in the definition is a verb, indicating that concepts of food are dynamic and fluid, and also implying that someone or some group is doing that considering, whereby issues of power, authority, and representativeness come into play in defining food.

Food is constructed on three fundamental levels—cultural, social, and personal. These levels suggest types of meanings and the ways those meanings are attached to food. They also call for different approaches in research. Cultural construction refers to the ways in which a group of people sharing a similar worldview and practices (a culture) define what can or cannot be considered food. Some items are categorically considered edible; others are not. Those categories reflect their view of the order of the universe. Similarly, their food experiences shape that worldview. Research into cultural construction of food tends towards the larger, existential questions of what food means to us as human beings or as belonging to a particular culture. For example, humans are generally considered outside the realm of edibility. They can be eaten, as cannibalism demonstrates, but within the Western worldview, they do not belong in the category of food. Pets, similarly, are usually not considered edible, but specific species (e.g., rabbits in much of the United States) are moved in and out of that definition according to culture, group, historical era, economic circumstances, and so on. Research into meanings of food on this level points us to ways in which different cultures define food and its relationship to their view of the universe and of themselves.

As a social construction, food reflects structures, institutions, and hierarchies of power that define taste, propriety, and order, telling us what is palatable, desirable, and proper to consume according to particular groups of people in particular times and places. Meaning at this level refers to food as a status symbol and as a medium for wielding power and knowledge. Research then focuses on how those foods are used, by whom, and how they acquired those meanings. Methods for answering such questions would involve exploring historical foodways and society, analysis of contemporary products (advertising, menus, literature, film, and other mass media), and, possibly, ethnography in order to document the meanings held by particular groups.

Concepts of what is edible and palatable are also constructed on a personal basis, relating to an individual's experiences, beliefs, identity, and personality. Memories of food carry and evoke emotion, rendering foods inedible or unpalatable to individuals. Similarly, personal tastes affect how individuals will treat food in general and specific foods. It is at this level that we see how individuals personalize the cultural and social constructions of food, making them meaningful to themselves and using them in their own expressions of creativity or for negotiating relationships and connections. Research into food as a personal construction tells us how specific individuals (and groups of individuals) create, utilize, and manipulate the meanings of food. Ethnography, life history interviews, and analysis of personal communications (letters, diaries, photo albums) are used to document the meanings individuals attach to food.

Implications for Research

Research into the meanings of food should be founded on these notions of construction. The character of symbols and the notion of significance also provide guidelines for research and suggest the complexity of identifying and interpreting meaning. Here I examine three ideas that are fundamental to meaning-centered research.

(1) Meaning can be explicit or implicit, that is, articulated or unspoken and not consciously recognized.
Explicit meanings are articulated and consciously understood, whereas implicit meanings involve shared, unspoken assumptions. Explicit meanings of food include references that are publicly understood within a given culture. An example for individuals from the United States might be a cake with candles representing a birthday or a turkey representing American Thanksgiving. These meanings can be observed and studied empirically. Implicit meanings, however, are not only unspoken; they often are not even recognized at a conscious level by the users, and they frequently seem too obvious and self-evidently true to warrant discussion. For example, a restaurant serving "American food" would probably offer beef, which is considered edible and palatable by mainstream society and generally poses no question of suitability as food. Rabbit, on the other hand, would raise questions among some Americans, but not others, while cat or dog would certainly be challenged as belonging to the category of food.

Anthropologist Mary Douglas (1975) points out that assumptions are shared, which means that members of a group can interact within similar frameworks for defining the world. Food rules represent their understanding of the universe, as in her example from New Guinea of the division between animal and humankind through discrimination in eating habits.

Implicit meanings are "teased" out by the researcher through ethnography that identifies patterns, and then by the scholar's interpretations of those patterns. In his foundational volume *The Raw and the Cooked,* Claude Levi-Strauss (1969) suggests that cooking represented the basic structures of human thought and culture. Mary Douglas (1972) expands those ideas, arguing that food could represent social structure of specific cultures. Her "Deciphering a Meal" starts from the real-life quandary of providing her family with a simple but satisfying supper. She observes that soup alone did not fit their concept of a proper British meal because it did not contain the requisite number and ordering of dishes. This meaning was implicit: her family did not consciously define such a meal; they simply did not feel a sense of completeness with only soup. Douglas explores the reasons behind their reaction, asking them for explanations while also observing their behavior and how it compared to other occasions and to the "normal" patterns of meals. She points out that although few of us recognize the deeper meanings of our everyday practices, activities, and forms, these fit into an overall structure that enables us to feel a sense of order—or meaning—in our lives. It is the job of the scholar to identify such implicit meanings.

2) Meaning must be understood within its cultural, social, and historical context as well as within the immediate context of the instance of participating in a foodways activity.

Douglas also differentiates herself from Levi-Strauss's structural approach to meaning when she emphasizes the need to identify and analyze food behaviors at "a particular point in time, in a particular social system, over time" (1972: 249). Research, then, should start with specific instances of food and place those within larger contexts. Also, since food's meaning resides in the people using it rather than in the food itself, researchers should document individuals' interpretations and uses of that food. They also should not assume that meanings are universal or can be transferred from one setting to another, as the same act may mean different things depending on context and on how, where, when, with whom, and why it is performed (Abrahams 1977; Bauman 1975, Ben-Amos and Goldstein 1975; Hymes 1974). Researching meaning, therefore, requires close attention to the texts (food item, menu, meal) that are used and the different contexts in which they appear.

The meanings of food are also "situated," determined by the specific context in which the food appears. Drawing from sociolinguistic theory, Dell Hymes developed an "ethnography of speaking" model that can also be applied to food and eating. According to Hymes's model (1974), every individual draws upon a pool of possibilities or resources in making an utterance. That pool is shaped by the culture, historical conditions, natural resources, and identities of the specific individual. The actual utterance is then selected from that pool of resources according to the immediate context and the desired effect of that utterance. Again, that context includes the larger structures—race, class, ethnicity, gender, religion, age, occupation, and so on—that shape the original pool of resources. Each "speech event," then, is an enactment or a performance of an individual's negotiation of his or her resources, context, and intentions. It is through that enactment that individuals then place their own meanings onto the larger world.

Adapting Hymes's concept to an "ethnography of eating" suggests a way for us to research the meanings food holds for individuals and groups. The cultural and social constructions of food as well as their own particular backgrounds shape the pool available for an individual's conceptualizations of food. When it comes time to make a food choice, an individual draws from that pool but also takes into account the specific context of the choice. The meaning of the choice is determined by both the pool and the context.

For example, a man growing up in Thailand has a repertoire of possibilities for satisfying hunger containing certain ingredients, dishes, cooking styles, and eating customs. Yet these possible repertoires will be very different if he is hungry while traveling in the United States. He may still choose Thai food, but, depending on the context, that choice could hold a variety of meanings—nostalgic longing, a desire for familiarity, curiosity about adaptations of forms, assertion of identity, acknowledgement of hospitality, and so on. The meaning surfaces when we weigh the choices made against the other possible options available to him.

An ethnography of eating thus requires research into the larger historical and cultural context of food events in order to identity the resources available for an individual event. That research should involve readings of both scholarly and popular literature as well as archival materials in order to fully understand those contexts. Immediate contexts should then be examined, preferably through ethnography, in order to identify the choices actually made, the participants making them, and the factors shaping those choices. Participants' explanations of their motivations should also be treated as valid expressions of their perceptions but can be weighed against the immediate and larger contexts.

An ethnography of eating approach helps in identifying the reasons behind people's food choices as they understand them. It illuminates meanings and the ways in which those meanings are personally relevant to individuals. It can also identify how meaning as significance became attached to a particular food.

3) Meaning is found not in the product (text), but in the processes surrounding that product. Every symbol is part of a larger system of meaning.
Another principle of symbols that has significant implications for food research is that symbols belong to larger systems and draw their meanings from them. Food has meaning through its interconnectedness with other activities as well as with the processes behind its construction. One approach, then, is to examine foodways—the total network of activities, practices, and concepts surrounding food and eating. As a methodological framework, foodways includes products (the food item itself, recipes, menus, meals), processes (production, procurement, preservation, preparation, presentation, consumption, disposal), contexts (meal system, immediate contexts), and performances (concepts and beliefs about food, intended meanings).

As a system or network, the foodways components are interconnected. Each part of the network shapes, informs, and influences the other components. Cultural symbolism can be attached to a food anywhere within this framework, as can personal meaning or "meaningfulness." An individual can and may insert his or her inventiveness, artistry, or creativity into any part of the system without noticeably changing the final product. Personal meanings of food are fluid and dynamic, and individuals can express and construct them in subtle and even subversive ways by manipulating their foodways.

The concept of foodways offers a methodological framework that enables researchers to identify where the meaning of a food lies for a given individual and how that meaning became attached to that food. For example, a particular dish may be symbolic on a cultural level, (chocolates represent romance) but actually carry a different meaning because of the way it was procured (bought at a bulk food store). Similarly, food products can carry meaning for an individual because of meaningful associations elsewhere in the foodways system. For example, it could matter that the ground beef in chili con carne comes from home-raised cattle rather than the local supermarket. It is the same item, but the association would be different for different eaters. Similarly, the same soup can be served in a handmade mug or in fine porcelain dishware, two methods of presentation that may represent two different occasions, socioeconomic levels, personalities, or simply moods of the server. The same bowl of rice may be consumed with chopsticks or with a fork; the tool and style of consumption may then reflect the consumer's ethnic identity—or the context in which he is eating, such as a Chinese restaurant as opposed to home.

Research Design

Designing a research project on food and meaning requires flexibility and sensitivity on the part of the researcher as well as a constant rethinking of the questions that can be answered, given the specific individuals and opportunities for research available. Research can be driven by theory or by data, and ideally it allows each to inform the other, as in "grounded theory." Methodologies should align with the types of questions asked as well as the opportunities for research and the desired outcome. Ethical considerations are likewise important, as this type of research frequently requires trust between scholar and "subjects."

An important step is to identify possible questions along with potential theoretical frameworks for answering those questions. Typical questions ask what a particular food or foodways tradition means and how it acquired that meaning; whether there are multiple meanings, and whether they represent unique histories, values, or power relationships; what foods are meaningful or significant to a group of people and why. What level of meaning will be explored, and what will be done with the resulting information? Scholarly articles, educational programs, museum exhibits, and so on all call for thorough and careful research, but each also shapes the selection of levels of meaning and the subjects for documentation.

There are several starting points for conducting ethnographic research into the meanings of food: a cultural group, an individual, a particular food item, event, or practice, or a specific component of foodways. Each of these needs to include an ethnography to identify the choices available as well as the actual choices made, along with research into larger contexts and backgrounds.[2]

1. Cultural Group—Ethnography of the food system and foodways of the given group is needed, with identification of the beliefs and practices surrounding food, and of the ingredients, flavors, cooking techniques and styles that represent or are used in that culture. Research into history and

environment of the culture should illuminate the resources available and the external and internal factors shaping it. (E.g., see Pilcher 1998; Ray and Srinivas 2012; Wilk 2006.) Questions: What foods and food practices are considered meaningful within that culture? What does food in general mean in that culture? In what ways is it significant to the identity of that culture and to other aspects of life within that culture?

2. Group within a culture (also called subculture, community, folk group)—Noting its similarity to a larger culture, we can also ask what food means in terms of drawing boundaries with other groups within the larger culture and its role in maintaining that particular group. Ethnic, religious, and regional groups have been emphasized in food studies research. (E.g., see Abarca 2006; Brown and Mussell 1984; Counihan 1999; Kirlin and Kirlin 1991; Long 2009; Weaver 2013.)

3. Individuals—Food-based life histories can provide significant insights into not only the larger food culture but also help in understanding how food becomes meaningful and how its meanings can be constructed, negotiated, and personalized (Counihan 1999).

4. Individual food items—Food "biographies" trace the history of a particular ingredient, recipe, dish, or meal in order to see how its uses and meanings have developed. Ethnographies of individual items can identify the multiple meanings they might carry as well as explore their place within a group or the ways in which they reflect that cultural identity (see Wilson and Gillespie 1999; Long 2007; Ohnuki-Tierney 1993).

5. Food events—Specific instances, enactments, or performances of participation in foodways, such as shopping for food, visiting a restaurant, or consuming food, are events. These can be recurring events, such as meals, in which the meanings are implicit. Research attempts to identify the meanings of such events. (See Meiselman 2000; Visser 1991; O'Connor 2013.)

6. Food rituals—Recurring symbolic food events, usually intentionally conducted with explicit meanings in mind, are rituals whose meanings are often privately contested and varied, and often reflect issues of power as well as historical conditions shaping the group participating in that ritual (Brown and Mussell 1984).

7. Festive events—These frequently include food and often highlight and celebrate the publicly articulated and explicit meanings attached to food, allowing for observation and discussion with participants. Research attends to both public and private meanings. (See Douglas 1984; Neustadt 1992; Long 2003.)

8. Food practices around the components of foodways (also called food traditions)—These sets or repertoires of behaviors and ways of thinking surrounding food can contain multiple meanings, both explicit and implicit, and oftentimes varying among individual participants. Ethnographic

research identifies and contextualizes those meanings. (E.g., Fine 1996; Heldke 2003; Long 2004; Parasecoli 2008; Rousseau 2012; White 2012.)

The foodways framework can be applied at each of these starting points. Not only does it serve as a guide for collecting and organizing documentation; it also helps researchers identify the options available along with the choices individuals and groups have made. After that they look at the historical and contemporary forces shaping these factors and ask individuals about the interpretations and motivations they assign to their personal choices. This last step is crucial in determining the significance and meanings of those food habits.

Meanwhile, researchers need to be aware of their own cultural and personal perspectives. Questions commonly arise after an ethnography or observation identifies a cultural product, behavior, or pattern that stands out in some way to the researcher. That can then be the focus of research, as in my own study of green bean casserole as a family foodways tradition in the Midwest (2007). It is important to recognize why it stands out and to then explore whether it has significance for the culture or group being studied.

Once the food choices and emic meanings have been identified, various scholarly theories can be used to interpret that data.[3] Theory helps, and not only to shed light on that information—it also links specific bits of data, which might in themselves seem insignificant, to larger patterns, concerns, and questions. Such interpretation moves ethnographic research beyond just descriptive listings of food practices or items to suggesting the range of meanings as well as the meaningfulness attached to those practices and items.

Conclusions

Meaning-centered research has a variety of uses. It sheds light on a group's or individual's choices, explaining why a practice has been maintained or discarded and clarifying changes that have been made to it. It uncovers the significance a food or foodways tradition holds for its participants and its role in larger foodways or cultural systems. It places those practices within their historical contexts, highlighting the connections between food and other aspects of our lives. Ultimately, it illustrates how people construct meaning in their lives through food and foodways.

Lucy M. Long has a PhD in Folklore (University of Pennsylvania) and an MA in Ethnomusicology (University of Maryland Baltimore County), and for twenty years taught folklore, American studies, popular culture, international studies, and tourism at Bowling Green State University, Ohio. In 2011, she founded the non-profit Center for Food and Culture, based in Ohio, which serves as an international networking clearinghouse on all aspects of food in order to promote a deeper understanding of the ways in which food connects us all. She is the author or editor of *Culinary Tourism* (2004), *Regional American Food Culture* (2009), *Food and Folklore Reader* (2015), *Ethnic American Food Today: A Cultural Encyclopedia* (2015), *Ethnic American Cooking: Recipes for Living in a New World* (2016), and numerous articles on foodways. She also has produced award-winning documentary videos, sound recordings, and museum exhibits, and frequently works with educational, community-development, and sustainability projects.

Notes

1. An excellent source for humanities research related to food is the Philosophy of Food Project, sponsored by the Department of Philosophy and Religious Studies at the University of North Texas. The meaning of food is also now of interest to the general public, partly from a humanities perspective, as in the PBS special *The Meaning of Food*, but also in relation to concerns about the impacts of our contemporary food habits and the industrial food system on the environment, economy, and health and well-being of society at large. A good deal of popular literature now addresses the negative impacts, calling for attention and change.
2. Sources of ethnographic data on foodways traditions and practices include folklore archives around the world (frequently connected with museums and folklore or ethnology programs at universities but also with state and local arts councils), the Archive of Folk Culture at the Library of Congress and the Office of Folklife and Cultural Heritage at the Smithsonian Institution, both in Washington, DC, and anthropology archives and databases. Libraries frequently include a section on cookbooks, and these, especially community and family cookbooks, can be an excellent source for data as long as they are accurately contextualized. Websites for ethnic organizations, education, traditional and folk arts, and community groups frequently offer data about foodways practices and customs.
3. The collection by Wilson and Gillespie (1999) is particularly useful in exploring the types of research relevant to studying possible meanings of specific food items and the applications of theories for interpreting that research.

References

Abarca, Meredith E. 2006. *Voices in the Kitchen: Views of Food and the World from Working-Class Mexican and Mexican American Women*. College Station: Texas A&M University Press.

Abrahams, Roger. 1977. Toward an Enactment Theory of Folklore. In *Frontiers of Folklore*, ed. William Russell Bascom, 79–102. Boulder, CO: Westview (for the American Association for the Advancement of Science, Washington, DC).

Bauman, Richard. 1975. Verbal Art as Performance. *American Anthropologist* 77: 290–311.

Ben-Amos, Dan, and Kenneth S. Goldstein, eds. 1975. *Folklore: Performance and Communication*. The Hague: Mouton.

Brown, Linda Keller, and Kay Mussell. 1984. *Ethnic and Regional Foodways in the United States: The Performance of Group Identity*. Knoxville: University of Tennessee Press.

Counihan, Carole. 1999. *The Anthropology of Food and Body: Gender, Meaning, and Power*. New York: Routledge.

Douglas, Mary. 1972. Deciphering a Meal. *Daedalus* (Winter). Reprinted in Mary Douglas. 1975. *Implicit Meanings: Essays in Anthropology,* 249–275. London: Routledge & Paul.

———. 1975. *Implicit Meanings: Essays in Anthropology.* London: Routledge & Paul.

———. 1984. *Food in the Social Order: Food and Festivities in Three American Communities.* New York: Russell Sage Foundation.

Fine, Gary Alan. 1996. *Kitchens: The Culture of Restaurant Work.* Los Angeles: University of California Press.

Heldke, Lisa M. 2003. *Exotic Appetites: Ruminations of a Food Adventurer.* New York: Routledge.

Hymes, Dell. 1974. *Foundations in Sociolinguistics: An Ethnographic Approach.* Philadelphia: University of Pennsylvania.

Kirlin, Katherine S., and Thomas M. Kirlin. 1991. *Smithsonian Folklife Cookbook.* Washington, DC: Smithsonian Institution.

Levi-Strauss, Claude. 1969. *The Raw and the Cooked.* New York: Basic.

Long, Lucy M. 2007. Greenbean Casserole and Midwestern Identity: A Regional Foodways Aesthetic and Ethos. *Midwestern Folklore.* 33/1 (2007): 29–44.

———. 2009. *Regional American Food Culture.* Santa Barbara, CA: Greenwood.

———, ed. 2004. *Culinary Tourism.* Lexington: University of Kentucky.

Meiselman, Herbert L. 2003. Apple Butter in Northwest Ohio: Food Festivals and the Construction of Local Meaning. In *Holidays, Rituals and Festivals: Proceedings from the Conference,* eds. Cristina Sanchez Carretero and Jack Santino (University of Alcala, Spain) : 45–66.

———. 2000. Holiday Meals: Rituals of Family Tradition. In *Dimensions of the Meal: The Science, Culture, Business, and Art of Eating,* ed. Herbert L. Meiselman (Gaithersburg: MD: Aspen): 143–159.

Neustadt, Kathy. 1992. *Clambake: A History and Celebration of an American Tradition.* Amherst: University of Massachusetts.

O'Connor, Kaori. 2013. *The English Breakfast: The Biography of a National Meal, with Recipes.* London: Berg.

Ohnuki-Tierney. 1993. *Rice as Self: Japanese Identities Through Time.* Princeton, NJ: Princeton University Press.

Parasecoli, Fabio. 2008. *Bite Me: Food in Popular Culture.* Oxford: Berg.

Pilcher, Jeffrey M. 1998. *Que Vivan Los Tamales! Food and the Making of Mexican Identity.* Albuquerque: University of New Mexico.

Ray, Krishnendu, and Tulasi Srinivas, eds. 2012. *Curried Cultures: Globalization, Food, and South Asia.* Berkeley: University of California.

Rousseau, Signe. 2012. *Food Media: Celebrity Chefs and the Politics of Everyday Interference.* London: Berg.

Visser, Margaret. 1991. *The Rituals of Dinner: The Origins, Evolution, Eccentricities, and Meaning of Table Manners.* New York: Grove Weidenfeld.

Weaver, William Woys. 2013. *As American as Shoofly Pie: The Foodlore and Fakelore of Pennsylvania Dutch Cuisine.* Philadelphia: University of Pennsylvania.

White, Merry. 2012. *Coffee Life in Japan.* Los Angeles: University of California Press.

Wilk, Richard R. 2006. *Home Cooking in the Global Village: Caribbean Food from Buccaneers to Ecotourists.* Oxford: Berg.

Wilson, David Scofield, and Angus K. Gillespie. 1999. *Rooted in America: Foodlore of Popular Fruits and Vegetables.* Knoxville: University of Tennessee Press.

CHAPTER 16

Food and Place

William Woys Weaver

The relationships between food and place are many and complex, especially since, from a historical perspective, the indigenous food culture of any given geographic location has been shaped by the dynamics of environment and agriculture. Thus there are several methods of approach for attempting to create what is commonly known among food ethnographers as a regional "dietary profile" (Yoder 1971): in short, an in-depth dietary portrait of a local food culture and its relationship to the land or to a particular geography, such as lying at the crossroads of a trade route or conversely situated in an isolated mountain valley.

Geography aside, all localized food cultures evolve over time via inputs from external forces, and sometimes they have few or even tenuous relationships with the agriculture or ecology of the same place, as for example the multitudes of themed chain restaurants that line the major highways ringing Columbus, Ohio. The individuals who eat in these packaged culinary environments are consuming food that for the most part originates somewhere else and may be partially prepared in a distant kitchen, frozen, and then finished on-site. This type of non-indigenous, industrialized food and its presence on the culinary landscape in many places around the world (think of McDonalds) represent the polar opposite of the more traditionalist type of local cuisine discussed in this chapter. More importantly, industrialized food is food without an indigenous cultural identity: as a faceless commodity, this food derives reality or authenticity from the way it is packaged and reduced to an acceptable common denominator, regardless of where it is served or eaten.

Just the same, even industrialized food remains part of a larger discussion concerning the meaning of "place" and whether or not place figures in this less traditional, less agriculturally oriented dietary profile, because of the broader and more compelling question, what do the locals eat, or *where* do they eat? This question serves as the structural premise for *Roadfood* (Stern and Stern 2011), a culinary journey in search of local color, or, as the Sterns describe it, a celebration of "real Americana food."

As a result the concept of food and place assumes certain ambiguities, in that it can represent a traditionalist type of diet defined, for example, by village life in Crete (Psilakis and Psilakis 1995); a fabricated nature-based art cuisine like the purist locavore cookery of Fäviken Magasinet, an elite restaurant situated on a remote farm in northern Sweden (Nilsson 2012); or it can mean something much more ephemeral and of the moment, as in the case of grazing from one chain restaurant to another in Columbus, Ohio: Polynesian, Thai, Chinese, Mexican, Cajun, and so on, each with its own defined theme or sense of place as projected by décor and the contents of the menu. For the consumer visiting any of these sites—the village in Crete, restaurant in Sweden, or freeway food chain—place is defined by the intensity of vicarious experience.

This moves the discussion into another gray area suggested by the Sterns' search for real Americana food: the quest for an authenticity that can only be confirmed by the context of place or what food connoisseurship characterizes as *terroir* (food that derives its peculiar character from the soil of a given place). This quest has been championed by the Slow Food Movement (Petrini and Padovani 2006), which has placed great emphasis on artisanal foods from particular localities, especially those foods that can also claim impeccable historical pedigrees, like the Bar-le-Duc Preserve of Lorraine—a fruit "caviar" that must be made exclusively with the heirloom Versailles white or red currants and delicately hand-seeded by *épepineuses* using goose quills. Bar-le-Duc (the place) is thus an essential element in the authenticity and mystique of this preserve, in contradistinction for example to Philadelphia Cream Cheese, which is not made of cream, is not produced in Philadelphia, and bears little resemblance to the original aged cream cheeses of that place.

Down through history, place has often been employed as a device for branding food, either to prove its authenticity or to suggest a passable facsimile. This sometimes freeform labeling can prove misleading for serious food research. The *wyne Greke* (Greek wine) of western European medieval manuscripts did not necessarily mean wine from Greece; more specifically it referred to old sweet wine from the Kingdom of Cyprus. The pitfalls of matching terminologies with material culture—a particularly useful step in looking for evidence of food in historical archival materials like wills, inventories, and legal documents—were recognized by German scholars in the latter part of the nineteenth century. This gave rise to the publication *Wörter und Sachen* (1909–1944), which attempted to blend linguistics with cultural research. As its title suggests, the journal was mainly focused on words (topical vocabularies) and things (material culture), for example the dialectal terms for butter and cheese molds in Northern Italy. It did not attempt to interpret "place" as a dimension of authenticity or creative moment. That imperative has evolved in more recent times as an outgrowth of a negative reaction to industrialized food and its androgynous character.

In dining establishments like Fäviken Magasinet or Noma in Copenhagen (Redzepi 2010) the culinary identity of a particular region has been reinvented with rustic local ingredients drawn from nature. Two kinds of cultural imperatives come into play: on the one hand the chef and his personal vision of real food—his artistic statement—and on the other, the consumer who chooses to be entertained by this performance. This toys with the basic meaning of authenticity, of real food in a traditional sense, and poses another fundamental question: what is Swedish, or more broadly, what is Nordic? Can these cultural identities be reduced to a powder like the mushroom dust that chef Redzepi scatters over entrées of wild-harvest moss? Food does not define the culture that makes it; it is the people, the human side of the equation, who give food its cultural meaning and inherent culinary persona.

Evaluating Sources

The most valuable and unbiased food research is based on knowing the right questions to ask and where to look for the most elusive answers. Too often the quest for cultural identity via place or via best approximation of place devolves into food tourism or food as travelogue, as in the case of the Cretan cookery book (Psilakis and Psilakis 1995) mentioned earlier, which has been published in several languages expressly for tourists visiting the island and is thus a highly filtered view with many inherent biases. Food as travelogue is perhaps best exemplified for American readers by the exploration of local or regional authenticities in articles published by the magazine *Saveur*. That type of imaginative and colorful writing satisfies the expectations of its core readership (well-off consumers who may or may not have the time to travel), but similar explorations have also been expanded into cookbooks, for example *Mugaritz: A Natural Science of Cooking* (Aduriz 2012), featuring a highly refined regional Spanish cuisine. In the course of researching these connections between food and place in this type of literature, a subliminal imperative urges a search for the authentic: that which is special or, in baldest terms, that which is most photogenic.

Food photography drives the food publishing industry because it appeals to the old adage that *the eye eats first*. This self-editing premise both shaped and colored the work of culinary historians in the past because it cherry-picks some preferred authenticies at the expense of others. Food journalism, regional cookbooks, and local color fiction are therefore three places to start in the quest for a definition of food and place, though it must be understood that travelogues and local cookbooks represent a type of fiction or quasi-fiction and thus must be used with caution—mainly for what they do not say, not to mention what they may reveal between the lines about their authors' perceptions.

The culinary reality is always far more complex. To achieve a truly balanced view of food and place, many methods of research must be brought together in order to confirm or dispute all types of evidence on the table. Thus we could suggest that the culinary reality for Columbus, Ohio, suburbanites is not necessarily what they may consume along the freeway while partying on Friday night, or on Sunday when friends and family gather in a different restaurant after church, but rather, and more importantly, what they eat at home on a day-to-day basis. That criterion can apply to any period of history. Amish cookery in Lancaster County, Pennsylvania, is therefore not what Amish cookbook editors want us to know about red velvet cake and Christian epiphanies (Good and Pellman 1984)—on the contrary, their discussion omits what all the Amish in their sum total eat every day, even if it is only take-out pizza.

Countering these built-in mythologies with didactic yet revealing facts requires fieldwork; archival research in old newspapers, diaries, and estate documents; field interviews; and full recognition that in the end, the big picture may not be as visually appealing as cookbook photography. One of the most useful places to begin this quest is in local farm markets, where a cursory picture takes shape regarding what people choose to purchase and who supplies it. It is also here that networks can be established for contacting local individuals and persuading them to engage in an interview. These interviews must include personal narratives, not just from the middle class and its Friday-night culinary aspirations, but also from the poor, who may not own cars (so how and where do they eat out?); the super-rich who can fly off to the Greek islands for a culinary adventure; chefs with their ideas about food and how they relate to it; restaurant employees and what they would rather eat if they earned more money; and even the shut-in elderly, who may remember food from a different era, when things were simple and culinary life was defined by different contingencies. There should be enough representatives from all walks of life that their food memories eventually overlap and create a common consensus about the food culture of that place.

How Do We Establish A Credible Research Model?

To date, studies of food and regional cuisine have been driven by culinary historians with a textualist bent to their scholarship, that is, they have been assembled in patchwork fashion from the "narratives" extrapolated from local cookery books. In the United States this type of approach is exemplified by the work of the late Karen Hess, for example in her edition of *The Carolina Rice Kitchen* (Hess 1992) or more broadly in *The Taste of America* (Hess and Hess 1977). In both of these works, conclusions about the culinary identity of a particular food culture were mostly derived from recipe collections without giving equal weight to what might be learned from agricultural sources, archeology, horticulture, or first-person accounts.

Another example but from a different part of the world would be Phia Sing's *Traditional Recipes from Laos* (Sing 1981), which attempts to define what is Laotian about the food of that Southeast Asian country. Unfortunately, Laos's political borders do not neatly coincide with its cultural and linguistic borders because it has several cultures living side by side, some of which straddle the artificially drawn political boundaries. Thus, to understand and clarify the full meaning of place in Laotian terms, it is also necessary to explore the foods and agricultural profiles of neighboring cultures and states and, by process of elimination, ascertain the core determinants of Laotian culinary identity.

Textualist approaches to food studies are largely an outgrowth of the work of Victorian medievalists, who analyzed old texts as a branch of medieval literature to ascertain possible connections and structural genealogies, frequently producing a questionable diffusionist view of history. This is the case in *A Soup for the Quan* (Buell and Anderson 2000), which attempts to create a dietary profile of the Mongol Empire by analyzing the *Yin-Shan Cheng-Yao*, a medieval Chinese text. This type of work does not draw upon an intimate understanding of medieval hearth cookery, material culture, archaeology, or even upon the horticulture of the times, and though it may prove that ideas, like people, moved around, it does not deal with the culinary reality of anyone except those who were able to read and write. It does not even call into question the role of medieval culinary texts in daily household life.

A seminal but still little known work that largely overturned this medievalist methodology and its strict marriage to literary analysis was the exploration of medieval Polish diets by the late Maria Dembińska (1999), which originated as a published doctoral dissertation in 1963. Rather than rely on recipes that did not survive, Dembińska undertook to sleuth archives, royal billing accounts, and especially meticulous archeology to determine the dietary profile of her medieval society. She found that medieval Poles relied heavily on millet as their primary food crop, and that dishes popular today, like *pirogi* and *bigos,* did not enter the Polish diet until the Renaissance—most likely from Italy via court cuisine. Dembińska's methodology is known in Europe as historical ethnography because it analyzes food culture in terms of change and continuity as informed by folk customs or historical observations of them.

Historical ethnography was championed in the New World by Brazil's Luis da Camara Cascudo, whose *História da Alimentação no Brasil* (1983) established the meaning of Brazilian as interpreted by the composite food cultures that make up that country. His two-volume classic, which should be viewed as a model study for any culture and its food identities, explores the indigenous, African, and European strands that came together uniquely to shape what we now know as Brazilian identity. The bibliography at the end of the survey is itself an open door into Brazil's multitudinous subregionalisms.

This type of approach—viewing the food culture of a particular place through the eyes of the common people who live there—has been taken up by many subsequent scholars, for example in the English work *Traditional Food in Yorkshire* (Brears 1987). The groundwork for this type of perspective was initiated in the United States by Henry Glassie's (1968) *Pattern in the Material Folk Culture of the Eastern United States*. Glassie did not tackle the subject of food or foodways, but rather explored the so-called "culture hearths" that emerged along the Atlantic Seaboard and then gave rise to several distinctive regional American cultures: New England, Middle Atlantic, Chesapeake, Coastal South, and so forth. Traditional objects produced in these different regions reflected distinct localisms, so by studying, say, locally made earthenware cook pots, it is possible to detect different regional ways of preparing similar foods, such as varieties of corn.

Meanwhile, historical agriculture throughout all of these regions was highly diverse for a number of reasons, so any connection to food or their implements of preparation must be confirmed with agricultural data. Regarding the Middle Atlantic region, *The Best Poor Man's Country* (Lemon 1972) explained in detail the farming patterns of wheat, corn, buckwheat, oats, and other grains planted as cash crops and for household consumption. Lemon's conclusions were more or less validated by Elizabeth Ellicott Lea's *Domestic Cookery* (Weaver 2004), since the thrust of her recipes was to provide inexperienced brides with all they needed to know about running a farmhouse kitchen. In terms of place, her book encapsulated daily life in rural Maryland during the 1840s.

Thus, in the new edition of this once popular Quaker cookbook, the editor also made a case for its ethnographic representation of Middle Atlantic food culture from the standpoint of the type of recipes Lea chose for her text as well as what she actually wrote about certain dishes. What emerged was a mélange of influences moving horizontally across geographical and cultural boundaries and vertically across class and economic boundaries. This convergence of influences is never static, but it can be "periodized" to represent the food culture of a particular place in a series of narrative snapshots.

One recent study that deals with food and place in this manner is *La Table du Sud-Ouest et l'emergence des cuisines régionales* (Meyzie 2007). Written as a doctoral dissertation, it contains a number of literary shortcomings (especially an overreliance on estate inventories), yet the overall intellectual content is extremely valuable in that Meyzie defines what the regional cuisine of southwest France *means*. He does this by showing that it evolved its identity between 1700 and 1850 as a blend of influences from elite culture, nostalgic poverty dishes, and even regional agricultural movements. In short, this was a cuisine in constant flux that over time underwent the winnowing modifications of cookbooks and the literary observations of food tourism so that a few special dishes, like confit of goose, assumed the nationalistic character of Frenchness. Local foods were thus transformed into icons.

In truth, France is not the only place in Europe where goose or other fowl are preserved in similar fashion—French writers have simply more successfully refined and marketed their particular brand of this confit. Furthermore, Meyzie is the first to admit that place and cultural identity are complex and not easily defined by dishes singled out by travel journalists. In so many words he posits the question, what makes a confit of goose *taste* French? The confit of southwest France owed its unique features not to any particular recipe, but like the Bar-le-Duc Preserves of Lorraine, it represented a complex and deep-rooted association with place. It became an extension of local identity.

Only a few books in the United States assess food culture in this ethnographic manner. *Cajun Foodways* (Gutierrez 1992) rightly took on the New Orleans packaged food experience as something alien to real Cajun food culture—blackened fish created by Chef Paul Proudhomme, for example. Following a line of research similar to Meyzie's, *As American As Shoofly Pie: The Foodlore and Fakelore of Pennsylvania Dutch Cuisine* (Weaver 2013) was written as a textbook study of food and place and what that means to the people who live there. It consists of a series of essays tackling various types of tensions within the culture, especially how food tourism created the mythic Amish Table and how Amish culture has been incorrectly conflated with the term Pennsylvania Dutch even though the foodways of the Amish minority are mostly derivative from the larger and highly regionalized cookery of the Pennsylvania Dutch majority.

By employing extensive fieldwork based on first-person interviews, the author discovered that although the spoken dialect may be dying out or is at best on hold, cultural identity via diet is widely maintained where sauerkraut is eaten often. This is not an observation that can be deduced from cookbooks; indeed, more than 1,600 dishes were documented in the course of this fieldwork, very few of which can be found in restaurants or in cookbooks. Pennsylvania Dutch food culture is thus extremely private and home-oriented. All the same, though, sauerkraut offers an entry point for a phalanx of traditional foods that would otherwise drop out of the diet. Thus this one dish becomes the cultural link that binds together the many diverse and sometimes highly compartmentalized segments of Pennsylvania Dutch society.

Whereas religion may create real social barriers, sauerkraut is nondenominational and therefore provides a neutral "place" where differences are less important. Thus place cannot only be a particular county in Pennsylvania and its distinctive foodways (e.g., Schuylkill County), it can also be a fire hall supper anywhere in the Dutch Country where sauerkraut brings many divergent social groups together. Pertinent to the overall theme of this chapter, the author explored the various meanings of "local food" in terms of its subregional diversity as well as dietary boundaries defined by class and economics. Thus food and place are actually multidimensional because place in a cultural sense is not a level field.

Place-Based Research Step By Step

Place-based research is most effective when a clearly defined method of approach is developed prior to fieldwork. Creating a template will supply a practical framework for the research project as well as define overall objectives.

1. Ask the Question: Choose a topic that will not pose a linguistic problem, but if you want to explore non-Anglo cultures such as the foods of South America, then you should be prepared to learn Spanish (or Portuguese in the case of Brazil) and to consult dictionaries of South American dialects since they turn up in food contexts regularly—on menus, for example.
2. Survey Archives and Libraries: If your interest lies in Andean South America, explore what has been written about the country or countries of your choice, and mine published bibliographies for books that may take you deeper into the subject, such as surveys of micro-climates and regional botanies, which are the factors that shape food consumption.
3. Use Maximally Diverse Sources: Look for books or scholarly articles (some are available online) that provide insights into the local popular culture or even into local agriculture, as in the case of the FAO publications of the International Plant Genetic Resources Institute at Rome. IPGRI has published numerous English-language monographs on (for example) unusual Andean food plants, providing considerable material on their history and uses. This type of technical institutional reference material will provide you with a generally unbiased view into local foods and foodways and may even raise important questions about issues local cultures face in perpetuating their food identity. Those issues may help you formulate further research goals.
4. Go Local: This leads you into the area of regional publications and will require a working knowledge of the language spoken in that place. In the case of Andean cultures, the influence of the Inca Empire (Tawaintinsuyu, "the four united provinces") cannot be ignored, since the empire comprised a geographic area now encompassing several South American nations. It is thus necessary to read works like Calderon Quillatupa's *Cocina en las Naciones Confederadas del Tawaintinsuyo* (1999), which takes up indigenous cookery on a region-by-region basis within the four original provinces of the old empire. The philosophical foundations of the cuisine are discussed, as are the class system and class dietetics that existed under Inca rule. Recipes are given in Spanish but also with their native Quechua names, which

may prove useful during fieldwork. The bibliography will point you in the direction of other cookbooks, especially histories and anthropological studies that offer a cultural context for what exists in this region today. This will also help you ascertain what is meant by "traditional" in any given place and how this may or may not relate to tourism.
5. Confirm the Data: The next step should require fieldwork—actually going to the chosen location to learn, on a first-person basis, about its daily life, its food markets, the types of places where people eat—and then, using the background information gleaned from research, developing a set of questions that you want to answer. Use this questionnaire as a template for interviews, but keep in mind that interviews also reveal unexpected data; flexibility about the type of material you are looking for is therefore advisable. If you are well versed in the background material of a given place, you should be able to develop intelligent questions that will help you approach your research problem from several angles, not the least of which would be local cookbooks, or recordings of oral traditions where cookbooks are not used regularly. This suggests that two of your most indispensable tools will be a tape recorder and camera.
6. Prepare Your Conclusions: The final step is to gather your material together and see what themes emerge. Write a proposal if you want to publish it, and send it to an editor whose journal appears well suited to your type of research. If you believe your work represents a full-length book, create a chapter outline, a summary of the book's contents, and what makes it different from any others in the field. Send this to a publisher who you already know has an interest in the type of topic you have chosen. An editor may give you extremely useful feedback on ways to polish your work or to enhance it with material you had not considered.

The author of seventeen books, **William Woys Weaver** received his PhD from University College Dublin, the first doctorate in food studies to be conferred by that university. He has received many publishing awards and until recently served as an adjunct professor of food studies at Drexel University in Philadelphia. He has four books in progress, all dealing with the issue of food and place.

References

Aduriz, Andoni Luis. 2012. *Mugaritz: A Natural Science of Cooking*. London: Phaidon Press.
Brears, Peter. 1987. *Traditional Food in Yorkshire*. Edinburgh: John Donald.
Buell, Paul, and Eugene Anderson, eds. 2000. *A Soup for the Quan*. London and New York: Kegan Paul International.
Calderon Quillatupa, Francisco. 1999. *Cocina en las Naciones Confederadas del Tawaintinsuyo*. Huancayo (Peru): PAKO.

da Camara Cascudo, Luis. 1983. *História da Alimentação no Brasil.* 2 vols. São Paolo: Editora da Universidade de São Paolo.
Dembińska, Maria. 1999. *Food and Drink in Medieval Poland.* Revised and adapted by William Woys Weaver. Philadelphia: University of Pennsylvania Press.
Glassie, Henry. 1968. *Pattern in the Material Folk Culture of the Eastern United States.* Philadelphia: University of Pennsylvania Press.
Good, Phyllis Pellman, and Rachel Thomas Pellman. 1984. *From Amish and Mennonite Kitchens.* Intercourse, PA: Good Books.
Gutierrez, C. Paige. 1992. *Cajun Foodways.* Jackson: University Press of Mississippi.
Hess, Karen. 1992. *The Carolina Rice Kitchen: The African Connection.* Columbia: University of South Carolina Press.
Hess, Karen, and John Hess. 1977. *The Taste of America.* New York: Grossman.
Lemon, James T. 1972. *The Best Poor Man's Country: A Geographical Study of Early Southeastern Pennsylvania.* Baltimore: Johns Hopkins Press.
Meyzie, Philippe. 2007. *La Table du Sud-Ouest et l'emergence des cuisines régionales (1700–1850).* Rennes: Presses Universitaires de Rennes.
Nilsson, Magnus. 2012. *Fäviken.* London: Phaidon Press.
Petrini, Carlo, and Gigi Padovani. 2006. *Slow Food Revolution: A New Culture for Eating and Living.* New York: Rizzoli.
Psilakis, Maria, and Nikos Psilakis. 1995. *Cretan Cooking.* Iráklion: Karmanor.
Redzepi, René. 2010. *Noma: Time and Place in Nordic Cuisine.* London: Phaidon Press.
Sing, Phia. 1981. *Traditional Recipes of Laos.* London: Prospect Books.
Stern, Jane, and Michael Stern. 2011. *Roadfood: The Coast-to-Coast Guide to 800 of the Best Barbecue Joints, Lobster Shacks, Ice Cream Parlors, Highway Diners.* Rev. ed. New York: Clarkson Potter.
Weaver, William Woys, ed. 2004. *A Quaker Woman's Cookbook: The Domestic Cookery of Elizabeth Ellicott Lea.* Rev. ed. Mechanicsburg, PA: Stackpole Books.
———. 2013. *As American As Shoofly Pie: The Foodlore and Fakelore of Pennsylvania Dutch Cuisine.* Philadelphia: University of Pennsylvania Press.
Wörter und Sachen: Kulturhistorische Zeitschrift für Sprach- und Sachforschung. 1909–1944. Heidelberg: C. Winters Universitätsbuchhandlung.
Yoder, Don. 1971. Historical Sources for American Foodways Research and Plans for an American Foodways Archive, *Ethnologia Scandinavica* 1: 41–55.

CHAPTER 17

Sensory Ethnography
Methods and Research Design for Food Studies Research

Rachel E. Black

Background

If ethnography is about "being there," why are so many anthropologists not more explicit about the sensory experience of fieldwork? The embodied nature of participant observation in particular has caused some discomfort for anthropologists as they tread the fine line between objectivity and subjectivity in their research. The emotive, sensory elements of fieldwork are often cast into the shadows in favor of a seemingly more objective, sterile, "scientific" approach to conveying research findings. Thankfully, sensory ethnography is putting anthropologists back in the field, not only while doing research but in their written work as well (Pink 2009). Anthropologist David Howes (2006: 121) has pointed out that this new branch of ethnography emphasizes "'participant sensation' as opposed to 'observation'" as a way of making sense of the world from an emic orientation.

Sensory ethnography encourages engagement of the ethnographer's entire body as a sensory apparatus for knowing the world. Drawing heavily on phenomenology, anthropologists such as Michael Jackson (1996) and Robert Desjarlais (1997) have brought sensory experience into the mainstream of anthropological practice. Despite this move toward greater sensory engagement in fieldwork, smell and taste have only begun to emerge as senses that can reveal complex social and cultural relations in ethnographic studies. For instance, Paul Stoller's *Taste of Ethnographic Things* (1989: 9) shows how "taste and smell are central ingredients in the recipe of Songhay social relations" as well as in their cooking. This book is a pivotal work in the anthropology of food and sensory ethnography because it not only places food at the center of ethnographic understanding, but also demonstrates how the anthropologist's sensory engagement in fieldwork can provide new insights and understanding. Stoller insists that since "one cannot separate thought from feeling and action" (1989: 5), sensory experience should not be overlooked as unscientific or irrational. Building on C. Nadia Seremetakis's (1994) work on food, the senses and memory, and moving beyond Proust's madeleine, David Sutton's (2001) research on food and memory in Greece demonstrates the ways in which taste and memory play a part in constructing social relations across time and space. This is particularly vivid in his description of banquets that are staged with the purpose of being remembered. Sutton also presents 'thick description' of how the perfume of a basil plant evokes home for a Greek migrant. These are just a few examples of the ways anthropologists are employing their senses and including sensory experience as part of the theoretical underpinning of their work. For a more thorough literature review, see David Sutton's *Annual Review of Anthropology* article "Food and the Senses" (2010).

The Senses and the Anthropology of Food

Historically, there has been a hierarchical privileging of the senses in Western thought. Cartesian dualism imposed a division between the higher and lower senses. Since Aristotle, the higher senses have been sight and sound and the lower senses, olfaction, touch and taste. Although scholars have contested this hierarchy (Jütte 2005: 61–62), there is evidence that sight and sound have been privileged in anthropological studies. Often thought to be more objective because of the direct relation to the mind, accounts of sights and sounds proliferate in ethnographic writing. At the same time, anthropologists have felt that smelling, touching, and tasting the field might be more subjective and potentially dangerous.

Interestingly, sound has remained a relatively under-studied area of the anthropology of food. However, food scientists working for industry spend a great deal of time thinking about the way food sounds when we eat it. There are a number of studies that show that our perception of food quality and freshness depends greatly on the crispness and crunchiness of food when we eat it (Zampini and Spence 2004). Soggy potato chips that fail to crunch when we eat them are incredibly disappointing and unsatisfying, even if they taste good. The cultural construction of beliefs and meanings around the sounds of food preparation and consumption remain marginal in anthropological studies. Perhaps work will be done on the importance of audition in culinary techniques. The baker can tell if the bread is cooked through by knocking on the loaf. How many other culinary techniques depend on sound? How do we learn these auditory cues that are part of culinary technique? Why are we moving away from this sonic sensibility?

In food studies, the visual aesthetic has reigned supreme. French culinary innovator Antoine Câreme's elaborate sugar paste constructions, which were carefully illustrated in his culinary writings, are one example of this long tradition of the elaborate presentation of food in French cuisine. Nowadays, food photography and the proliferation of "food porn" in blogs and social media have once more brought attention to the importance of the visual aspects of food (O'Neill 2003). Although many anthropologists have criticized the privileging of the visual, a strong movement in visual anthropology has also urged a rethinking of the place of sight in fieldwork (Pink 2009; Grasseni 2007. In the introduction to the volume of collected essays *Skilled Visions,* Cristina Grasseni (2007: 5) claims that a new concept of visual anthropology is possible: one where 'visions' is plural—"as local and shared practices, naturally connected to the other senses." Grasseni's work on cattle breeding reminds us that visual training is very much an embodied form of knowledge that takes time and experience to develop (2007). Visual knowledge has an important place in all sorts of areas of food production, from animal husbandry to restaurant criticism.

When we think of visual anthropology, we often recall the ethnographic films we watched in undergraduate anthropology classes, where Masai women talked about milking their cows and fearless warriors frenziedly danced as part of a ceremony marking the rites of passage of a boy to manhood. In more recent ethnographic films, food has become a popular topic of exploration. In 2002, food was the focus for the International Festival of Ethnographic Films. Mainstream films about food have also proliferated. The popular genre of the food documentary took off in the early 2000s with Morgan Spurlock's *Supersize Me* (2004), a one-man exposé of the effects of America's fast food addiction, and *Food, Inc.* (2008), which takes a look at the dynamics of the American agri-food industry. The visual impact of these films has caused many people to think twice about their diets and the political and environmental impact of their food choices. In this sense, the visual is a very powerful medium of communication and has been an important outlet for food activists and educators in North America and Europe.

The visual certainly has the potential to evoke emotive responses and jog the memory. However, when it comes to the senses that are deeply rooted in memory, the most primal is perhaps our sense of smell (Rhind and Hargraves 2011). Its power lies in its ability to transgress social, cultural, and physical boundaries. Martin F. Manalansan (2006) gives the example of the cooking odors of Indian food that permeate the hallways of apartment complexes and clothing of immigrants, marking and altering the space of the migrant body and home. Smells do not stay put: this is one of the reasons they are transgressive and potentially dangerous. At the same time, smell taps into deep-seated emotions and memories. Industry has understood that subtle olfactory cues can be used to manipulate consumer behavior. Applied anthropology focused on consumer research is increasingly putting sensory ethnography to work in understanding what influences consumer choice (Valtonen, Markuksela, and Moisander 2010).

Research in neuroscience has shown the important role that smell plays in the sense of taste—it is nearly impossible to study the sense of taste without considering smell (Shepherd 2012). However, taste is more closely tied to the breaching of bodily boundaries: when food is tasted, it has penetrated the body and entered inside. This action is potentially filled with symbolic and ritual meanings that are meant to enforce categories of purity and pollution (Douglas 1966). Taking food into one's mouth is in some cases a leap of faith. The anthropologist in the field may have no problem smelling the dog meat stew, but when it comes time to taste it there may be hesitation or a bodily aversion. However, to taste and ingest this food is to come closer to the hosts who are offering this gift. To refuse it would be rude and would immediately place the anthropologist further into the category of outsider, working against all the hard-won trust. By tasting the same food, anthropologists come closer to the shared experience of their informants. The culture embodied in cooking has flavors that are unique to a specific people and sometimes even to the individual cook—food may be spicy, bland, mushy, fresh, or even acidic. Certain flavors and tastes might be associated with specific moods, life stages, or magical beliefs. In many cultures, sensations associated with food and eating are classified and used to make sense of the world. Judith Farquhar's (2002) research on post-Maoist China shows how tastes take on specific political meanings. The anthropologist cannot fully understand these meanings until she has tasted them.

These examples of taste have focused on consumption and its meanings; however, taste can be equally important for food preparation and production. How does the baker know if the starter is active? It tastes sour. How does the farmer know his grapes are ready to be picked? He tastes them to see if they are sweet enough for making wine. Sensory experience is critical for the reproduction of embodied knowledge. These types of knowledge are often overlooked in the large-scale production of food because they lack codification and are difficult to reproduce in an exacting way. This embodied sensory knowledge of food is often associated with craft production. Heather Paxson's (2012) work on artisan cheese production in the United States is an excellent demonstration of how ethnographic research can help us understand the social, cultural, and economic implications of small-scale craft production. In particular, Paxson explores the value of human and bodily engagement in the production of food. Lissa Roberts's (2005) exploration of the development of the 'new' chemistry and the death of the sensuous chemist looks at how the human body, once a prized element in laboratory analyses, was displaced in favor of new scientific apparatuses. Eighteenth-century chemists encouraged this distancing of embodied experience in experimentation on the grounds that the new equipment was more rational and objective. A similar move away from hands-on engagement in food production toward production using machinery occurred in farming and food production practices. This sensory shift has made important economies of scale possible. At the same time, though, the loss of embodied knowledge is often considered a loss of cultural heritage. The current craft movement, like other craft movements before it, seeks to reengage embodied knowledge and reconnect production and consumption (Morris 1883).

In the artisanal production of food, touch is an important part of knowing how to grow and prepare food and beverages. If anthropologists want to understand how people in different cultures reproduce traditional knowledge or how they have incorporated new technologies, they might want to try their hand at making bread or building a dry stone wall. They will quickly understand that this type of knowledge is generally not acquired in the matter of an afternoon: embodied knowledge sediments itself in the individual through careful apprenticeship, practice, and a great deal of repetition (Herzfeld 2004; Smith 2004; Black 2012). The hands can say whether the bread dough is properly hydrated and the stones fit well together. This is why doing is so important in ethnographic research. It is hard to understand the weight and skill of labor without engaging in the most menial of daily tasks.

Although long-term fieldwork is not often a reality for most undergraduate or master's students, it is still possible to engage students in culinary and agriculture activities. Amy Trubek and Cynthia Belliveau (2009) demonstrate the utility of culinary labs in their Food and Culture courses. Their students report that the lessons they learned through cooking are the ones that stick with them. Similarly, for my Food and the Senses class I have incorporated activities such as pizza making in order to teach about touch. I prepare three different batches of dough: one is overhydrated, another is underhydrated, and one is just right. Students are invited to touch each dough sample. They pull off chunks and stretch it with both hands, noticing if it is pliant or if it sticks to their fingers. Next, using a fresh batch of dough, I get the students to "roll out" their pizza by hand—they cannot use a rolling pin or any other device. This activity is not only entertaining; it also makes the students aware of the skill and embodied knowledge that it takes to make pizza. As the pizzas cook, the smell envelops the room and the students remark on their rumbling stomachs. When the pizzas are finally pulled from the oven, aesthetic remarks ensue. The final sensory moment is the taste of warm pizza enjoyed by all. As this culinary activity demonstrates, like nearly all senses, touch does not work alone—sight, sound, taste, and smell offer supporting points of reference for the acquisition and application of embodied knowledge.

The senses often work together in unexpected ways. Synesthesia occurs when one form of sensory stimulus leads to the experience of another, involuntary sensory experience, creating a sort of union of the sense. For example, a person will associate a particular smell with a color, combining the olfactory and the visual. Anne Meneley's (2008) research on olive oil suggests that this foodstuff lends itself to a sort of "synaesthetic bundling" that gives this oil unique gustatory and symbolic value. The neurological condition and the cultural construct of synesthesia remind us of the close interrelations between sensory experiences. In addition, as David Sutton (2010) points out, synesthesia calls the Western five-senses model into question.

There are many opportunities to use sensory methods in fieldwork related to food production, preparation, or consumption. The most important point to remember when doing sensory ethnography is to stay aware of sensory experiences. For example, be sure to take notes about what your field smells like. Maybe you are doing participant observation in a bakery. This is a great opportunity to note how workplace smells change during the day. While observing or participating in bakery activities be sure to note the consistency of the dough. Ask your participants how they know when the dough is ready or when the bread is cooked. Ask questions that encourage reflection on sensory experience. Embodied ways of knowing are often taken for granted, but they can reveal interesting findings if given some attention. Field methods should engage the ethnographer's senses as well as fuel curiosity about the sensory experiences of others. Ways of doing, sensing, and knowing can vary widely across cultures. Do not assume that your experience is universal.

Though it may seem obvious that people studying food should engage in experiential forms of learning and consider the senses in their analysis of food systems, it is worth considering some of the methods food scholars can use to raise their awareness of sensory experience and train their sensory apparatus. The following section will outline a series of lab activities and methods that can be used in the classroom and in the field.

Methods

Thick Descriptions

For students who do not have much experience doing fieldwork, a participant observation assignment can be both a good introduction to the field and a sensory approach to ethnography. Taking Geertz's concept of thick description (1973), this exercise asks students to observe with all of their senses, record the sensory experience of the observation, and analyze what is happening inside and around them. This activity encourages students to develop a greater awareness of what it means to "be there" and helps them to develop sensory vocabulary in their writing.

Students are asked to choose a food place. It can be defined very broadly (e.g., any place where food is produced, prepared, or consumed) or it can be given a very specific scope (e.g., a farmers' market). Students are then told to observe their food place for a period of time. This is left to the instructors, but limiting the observation to 15–30 minutes can help the students focus more closely on the sensory experience of fieldwork. Students may submit their field notes and analysis to the instructor for comment. I have also asked students to share their experiences in class, which can also be useful for getting them to consider the subjectivity and cultural nature of sensory experience. For an example of thick descriptions of taste and smell in ethnographic research see Pink's (2008) study of a Welsh town.

Sensory Labs

The field of sensory analysis uses series of sensory labs to statistically evaluate food and drink products. These labs take place in controlled environments, and the assessors are generally part of a trained panel. Sensory analysis is often used to evaluate consumer products. Borrowing from this area of scientific study, I have adapted the lab test model to the classroom. A controlled lab is not necessarily required when the focus of the exercise is sensory engagement and inquiry, rather than statistically valid and unbiased industry testing. Lab activities can be kept simple and do not always require a great deal of preparation and equipment.

One example of a lab activity that was used in an attempt to overcome and question the sense of sight was a blind tasting. A variety of food samples were placed in small cups and delivered to blindfolded students, who were invited to smell, touch, and taste the food. After handling and tasting each sample, they discussed their experiences. At the end of the lab the students were asked to reflect on the importance or insignificance of sight in their experience of food more generally. By asking students to pinch their noses when tasting the samples and then asking them to taste the food normally, a similar lab focused on smell and taste can be created. This is a good exercise to do when studying the physiological and neurological aspects of taste and smell, as it clearly demonstrates the interconnection between the two senses.

A formal wine tasting is another lab experiment that can be used to explore the interconnections between language and sensory experience (Peynaud 1996). Tasting wine as a group is also an excellent exploration of the subjectivity of taste. The vocabulary and professional training of professional wine tasters can also provide an outlet for discussing taste education (Terrio 2000). Wine tastings can be organized to draw into question the concept of *terroir* or the taste of place (Trubek 2008).

Students have created what are perhaps the best labs in my Food and the Senses course. As part of the course, students work in groups to propose a sensory lab. One example includes an investigation of disgust via tastings of various foods that potentially evoke disgust (mealworm lasagna, gelatin, cilantro, etc.). This lab elicited a discussion of cultural taboos, genetic differences, and personal preferences in cultural context. Students have also done molecular gastronomy labs and labs that focus on the linguistic importance of our description of foods. They are also encouraged to develop labs that could be used in educational settings.

Food-Centered Interview Techniques

Anthropologist Carole Counihan coined the term food-centered life histories (2004, 2009). In this interview technique, Counihan asks informants to talk about their lives through food. Often this features informants explaining how to cook certain recipes, and descriptions of the sensory experience of eating and preparing food. In my own research I have prompted informants to offer rich sensory accounts of kitchen work, for example by asking about a recipe and then probing further for details on technique. David Sutton's recent research on home cooking practices and the use of kitchen equipment and utensils is a good example of this kind of ethnographic focus on embodied knowledge (Sutton 2006). Sutton asks his participants to cook familiar dishes while he films their techniques. Sutton discovered that kitchen utensils are not always used in the ways in which manufacturers intended. In addition, many people modify tools to fit their needs. In my own research, looking more closely at culinary practices has helped me to understand the process of apprenticeship in the kitchen and the gender lines that exist as part of a hierarchy of knowledge in professional French kitchens. Ethnographic interviews are important tools, but there is nothing quite like being there in the kitchen. Professional kitchens being busy places with little space for an ethnographer to stand around and observe, I acquired basic culinary skills that allow me to engage in the work of the kitchen. Not only does this allow me to observe up close, but I also take note of my own sensory experiences of the work, which include engagement with touch, taste, smell, sound, and sight. My field journal is littered with notes about the embodied experiences of fatigue at the end of shift, adrenalin rushes during busy moments, and sometimes the panic I experienced when things were not going as planned. After periods of participant observation, I like to conduct interviews with male and female participants to compare my own experiences with those of the people around me. Through my research I have found that sensory experience is culturally informed and has a strong gendered component. Each kitchen has its own unique culture and gender dynamic that would be impossible to understand secondhand.

Conclusion

When studying food it is indispensible to consider the senses. Whether you are eating a plate of pasta with a group of participants or working in a kitchen, your own experience and that of the people around you can tell you a great deal about the cultural meanings and practices that surround all aspects of food. As you engage in ethnographic research, the most important thing to remember is to take note of sensory experience. This chapter has attempted to explain why sensory awareness is important for ethnographic research, and it has suggested a number of methods whose use can help anthropologists engage the senses while in the field.

Rachel E. Black is a Visiting Professor at Connecticut College. She is the former academic coordinator of the Boston University Gastronomy Program. Black has published a number of books and articles including *Porta Palazzo: The Anthropology of an Italian Market* (2012), and she co-edited *Wine and Culture: Vineyard to Glass* (2013). Currently she is doing historic and ethnographic research on women who cook professionally in Lyon, France, and the challenges they face in this profession.

Key Readings

Drobnick, Jim. 2006. *The Smell Culture Reader.* Oxford: Berg.
Howes, David. 2005. *Empire of the Senses: The Sensual Culture Reader.* Oxford and New York: Berg.
Korsmeyer, Carolyn. 2005. *The Taste Culture Reader: Experiencing Food and Drink.* Oxford and New York: Berg.
Stoller, Paul. 1989. *The Taste of Ethnographic Things: The Senses in Anthropology.* Philadelphia, PA: University of Pennsylvania Press.
Sutton, David. E. 2010. Food and the Senses. *Annual Review of Anthropology* 39: 209–223.

Additional Resources

Centre for Sensory Studies: http://www.centreforsensorystudies.org
The Harvard Sensory Ethnography Lab: http://sel.fas.harvard.edu
Neuroanthropology: http://blogs.plos.org/neuroanthropology/
Sense Lab, Concordia University: http://senselab.ca/
Sensing the Unseen, *Sensate Journal:* http://sensatejournal.com/2012/04/sensing-the-unseen-2-0/
Sensory Studies: http://www.sensorystudies.org
The Wine Aroma Wheel: http://winearomawheel.com

References

Black, Rachel. 2012. Wine Memory. *Sensate.* http://sensatejournal.com/2012/06/rachel-black-wine-memory/, accessed Sept. 13, 2016.
Counihan, Carole. 2004. *Around the Tuscan Table: Food, Family, and Gender in Twentieth-Century Florence.* New York: Routledge.
———. 2009. *A Tortilla Is Like Life: Food and Culture in the San Luis Valley of Colorado.* Austin: University of Texas Press.
Desjarlais, Robert. R. 2011. *Shelter Blues: Sanity and Selfhood Among the Homeless.* Philadelphia: University of Pennsylvania Press.
Douglas, Mary. 1966. *Purity and Danger: An Analysis of Concepts of Pollution and Taboo.* New York: Praeger.

Farquhar, Judith. 2002. *Appetites: Food and Sex in Post-socialist China.* Durham, NC: Duke University Press.
Geertz, Clifford. 1973. *The Interpretation of Cultures: Selected Essays.* New York: Basic Books.
Grasseni, Cristina. 2007. *Skilled Visions: Between Apprenticeship And Standards.* Oxford: Berghahn Books.
Herzfeld, Michael. 2004. *The Body Impolitic: Artisans and Artifice in the Global Hierarchy of Value.* Chicago: University of Chicago Press.
Howes, David. 2006. Charting the Sensorial Revolution. *Senses and Society.* Vol. 1(1): 113–128.
Jackson, Michael. 1996. *Things as They Are: New Directions in Phenomenological Anthropology.* Bloomington: Indiana University Press.
Jütte, Robert. 2005. *A History of the Senses: From Antiquity to Cyberspace.* Cambridge, UK, and Malden, MA: Polity.
Kenner, Robert (director). 2008. *Food, Inc.* [motion picture]. United States: Magnolia Pictures.
Manalansan, Martin. F. 2006. Immigrant Lives and the Politics of Olfaction in the Global City. In *The Smell Culture Reader,* ed. J. Drobnick. Berg.
Meneley, Anne. 2008. Oleo-Signs and Quali-Signs: The Qualities of Olive Oil. *Ethnos* 73(3): 303–326. doi:10.1080/00141840802324003
Morris, William. 1883. *The Revival of Handicraft.*
O'Neill, Molly. 2003. Food Porn. *Columbia Journalism Review* 5(September–October): 38–45.
Paxson, Heather. 2013. *The Life of Cheese: Crafting Food and Value in America.* Berkeley: University of California Press.
Peynaud, Émile. 1996. *The Taste of Wine: The Art and Science of Wine Appreciation.* New York: Wiley.
Pink, Sarah. 2008. An Urban Tour: The Sensory Sociality of Ethnographic Place-Making. *Ethnography* 9(2): 175–196. doi:10.1177/1466138108089467
———. 2009. *Doing Sensory Ethnography.* Los Angeles and London: Sage.
Rhind, Jennifer, and Stella Hargraves. 2011. *Meditations on Scent.* http://www.sensorystudies.org/sensorial-investigations/meditations-on-scent/. Accessed 26 June 2013.
Roberts, Lissa. 2004. Death of the Sensuous Chemist: The "New" Chemistry and the Transformation of Sensuous Technology. In *The Empire of the Senses: the Sensual Culture Readers,* ed. D. Howes, 106–127. Berg.
Seremetakis, C. Nadia. 1994. *The Senses Still.* Chicago: University of Chicago Press.
Shepherd, Gordon. 2012. *Neurogastronomy: How the Brain Creates Flavor and Why It Matters.* New York: Columbia University Press.
Smith, Pamela. 2004. *The Body of the Artisan: Art and Experience in the Scientific Revolution.* Chicago: University of Chicago Press.
Spurlock, Morgan. (producer and director). 2004. *Supersize Me* [motion picture]. United States: The Con and Kathbur Pictures.
Stoller, Paul. 1989. *The Taste of Ethnographic Things: The Senses in Anthropology.* University of Pennsylvania Press.
Sutton, David. 2001. *Remembrance of Repasts: An Anthropology of Food and Memory.* Oxford and New York: Berg.
———. 2006. Cooking Skill, the Senses, and Memory: The Fate of Practical Knowledge. In *Sensible Objects: Colonialism, Museums and Material Culture,* ed. Elizabeth Edwards et al. Oxford: Berg.
———. 2010. Food and the Senses. *Annual Review of Anthropology* 39: 209–223.

Terrio, Susan. 2000. *Crafting the Culture and History of French Chocolate.* Berkeley: University of California Press.

Trubek, Amy. 2008. *The Taste of Place: A Cultural Journey into* Terroir. Berkeley: University of California Press.

Trubek, Amy. B., and Cynthia. Belliveau. 2009. Cooking as Pedagogy: Engaging the Senses through Experiential Learning. *Anthropology News* 50(4): 16–16. doi:10.1111/j.1556-3502.2009.50416.x

Valtonen, Anu., Vesa. Markuksela, and Johanna Moisander. 2010. Doing Sensory Ethnography in Consumer Research. *International Journal of Consumer Studies* 34(4): 375–380. doi:10.1111/j.1470-6431.2010.00876.x

Zampini, Massimiliano, and Charles Spence. 2004. The Role of Auditory Cues in Modulating the Perceived Crispness and Staleness of Potato Chips. *Journal of Sensory Studies* 19(5): 347–363. doi:10.1111/j.1745-459x.2004.080403.x

CHAPTER 18

Methods for Examining Food Value Chains in Conventional and Alternative Trade

Catherine M. Tucker

Behind every item of food in a supermarket, restaurant, or your own refrigerator lies a value chain. Most of us would not have access to food without the market and trade relationships that structure how food is produced, transported, processed, distributed, and finally acquired by consumers. Value chains, also known as commodity chains or global commodity chains (GCCs) refer to the set of processes and linkages that connect disparate activities and relationships and create value to culminate in a final product. Examination of GCCs is critical for understanding how people, places, natural resources, and processes are connected in the global economy (Bair 2009), and the implications these evolving connections have for individuals, societies, and the planet. Trade and exchange of food and other goods have existed for millennia, but commodity chains emerged with the political, economic, social, and technological transformations associated with the rise of capitalism and the modern world system (Stringer and Le Heron 2008). Hopkins and Wallerstein coined the term "commodity chain" in 1977. As they explained, "What we mean by such chains is the following: take an ultimate consumable item and trace back the set of inputs that culminated in this item—the prior transformations, the raw materials, the transportation mechanisms, the labor input into each of the material processes, the food inputs into the labor" (1977: 128). Today, most researchers recognize this foundational definition, but many prefer the term "value chain" (or global value chain—GVC) because it goes beyond the concept of an undifferentiated product ("commodity") to recognize the human effort, power relations, governance arrangements, and dynamic processes that create value as goods are produced in the modern global economy (Kaplinsky and Morris 2001; Sturgeon 2009).

Many food-related questions require examination of one or more value chains. For example, understanding food systems and their political, economic, social, environmental, and health ramifications requires consideration of the path that food takes from producers to consumers. A number of studies have considered specific segments or entire value chains to address food-related research questions (e.g., Fischer and Benson 2006; Foster 2008; Pilcher 2006; Pomeranz and Topik 2006). Mintz's *Sweetness and Power* (1986) traced the history of sugar production, showing how sugar production and consumption in the eighteenth century exacerbated the slave trade and linked Africa, the Americas, and Europe while influencing social, economic, and political processes. The work remains an influential example of research on commodity production at a time when the modern world system and value chains were taking shape. Despite recognition of the need to understand value chains for primary and specialty crops, it can be a daunting task to trace all the links in a conventional value chain from the producer to the final consumer (Wallerstein 2009).

In general, food value chains pose challenges for research due to their complexity—entailing a number of nodes or links—and because they can cover great distances across nations and around the world (Ryan and Durning 1997). Alternative trade approaches, such as fair trade and direct trade, simplify value chains as part of an effort to reduce the costs charged by intermediaries, and thus return a larger share of the sale price to the producer (Jaffee 2007). However, the most important commodities for alternative trade include coffee, tea, cocoa, and bananas, which must be transported over great distances from the tropical areas where they grow to reach the majority of their final consumers in the northern hemisphere. Given these contexts, this chapter will explore the approaches for researching food value chains, including methods, practical suggestions, and examples from recent studies.

Special Challenges of Studying Value Chains

How do we study relationships and processes that encompass many different people who may speak different languages, represent a range of cultures and socioeconomic circumstances, live in different countries, and carry out contrasting activities in a specific value chain? Although value chain research encompasses a greater breadth than many anthropological studies, traditional data collection methods remain valid, and find unique adaptations. This chapter, although limited in length, considers participant observation, interviews, surveys, focus groups, and participatory research. The how-to aspects and applications of these methods have been covered extensively elsewhere (e.g., Bernard 2011) as well as in this volume (e.g., chapters by Paxson, Pérez, and Black). Another very useful method is mapping of value chains. Kaplinsky and Morris (2001) offer a useful handbook (available free online) for studying value chains with an economics-oriented perspective, including a particularly helpful guide to value chain mapping. In the specific case of food studies research methods, Miller and Deutsch (2009) provide a primary reference with many practical suggestions and guidelines. This discussion, for its part, will point to useful resources and highlight nuances relevant for research on food value chains.

One of the challenges in value chain research is that researchers may need to develop a different set of research instruments to collect data on each node or segment of a value chain. In the case of coffee, for example, conventional value chains encompass coffee farmers, intermediaries, processors, exporters, roasters, distributors, retailers, and consumers (Tucker 2011). Capturing these different engagements with coffee requires questions designed to fit the varying experiences and perspectives. The procedures and principles for developing a research design, selecting methods, designing data collection protocols, pretesting survey instruments, and analyzing data remain similar to any other social science research, but the work multiplies with each segment of a value chain included in the study.

General Comments on Methods

The methods selected for any type of research depend on the questions asked. As a general rule, investigating food value chains merits a mixed-methods approach, given that any data collection method has limitations as well as advantages. Incorporating both qualitative and quantitative methods allows for "triangulation" of answers to complex questions and for checks on validity. Moreover, the answers to certain questions may benefit from multidisciplinary perspectives and techniques. Projects can gain rigor through collaboration among several researchers who bring different theoretical and methodological strengths to fieldwork and subsequent analysis. The combination of methods that makes sense for investigating your research questions relates to available time, financial resources, and the contexts in which the research will be conducted (Bernard 2011).

Participant Observation

Participant observation has long been the "bread and butter" of data collection in cultural anthropology, and is the foundation for ethnographic research (DeWalt and DeWalt 2010). It is an increasingly popular method of collecting in-depth data on cultural and social contexts across the social sciences. A number of helpful guides and discussions offer insights to the principles, practice, ethics, and challenges of participant observation (e.g., Bernard 2011; DeWalt and DeWalt

2010; DeWalt, DeWalt, and Wayland 1998; Gardner and Hoffman 2006; Hume and Mulcock 2004; Spradley 1980).

Studying food value chains provides opportunities for researchers to apply participant observation in diverse, possibly far-flung places that may include agricultural fields, farmers' markets, processing factories, packing room floors, corporate offices, grocery stores, restaurants, or a neighbor's kitchen. Regardless of the location or the people present, participant observation retains the principle of the researcher genuinely participating in the activities underway while remaining as objective and observant as possible. It is most closely associated with extended fieldwork, which allows for the development of familiarity, rapport, and in-depth understanding with people in a study site. When site visits are brief, as may be the case in a project studying a number of different locations linked in a value chain, it becomes more difficult to develop rapport, or assess the degree to which your presence distorts people's interactions and patterns of behavior. Even so, participant observation can provide insights through the disciplined practice of observation and willingness to engage respectfully with the activities happening around you, whether that means offering to pick coffee beans during the harvest or volunteering to help clean up after an evening meal at a respondent's home.

The diversity of contexts to be studied in value chain fieldwork means that researchers must be able to shift gears, act appropriately in diverse environments, and understand differing expectations. Instead of being familiar with one or several cultural contexts, researchers may need to work in many cultural contexts, establish rapport with contrasting (perhaps competitive) groups, speak several languages fluently, and adapt readily to environmental, dietary, and behavioral differences. Work on food value chains thus fits under the umbrellas of multi-sited ethnography and transnational research (Hannerz 1998, 2012; Marcus 1995). Hannerz observes that "what matters is that some phenomenon or complex of phenomena can be seen as transnationally distributed in a manner that also involves ongoing interconnectedness, interaction, exchange, or mobility" (1998: 237).

Interviews and Questionnaires

Interviews are a highly useful and flexible means of gaining information. Formats for interviews range from unstructured (open-ended) to semi-structured and structured. Open-ended questions are especially suitable when little is known about the topic of interest (Weller 1998). Unstructured interviews are common in ethnographic research, as they allow for free exploration of questions and concepts in a conversational format that can be conducive to building rapport. They also have the clear advantage of allowing informants to provide details that they believe to be important, which the researcher might not otherwise discover.

However, unstructured interviews require significant investment of time to carry out and then analyze the wealth of qualitative data generated. Semi-structured interviews, with more focused questions and basic organization, can facilitate analysis and identification of patterns. Unstructured and semi-structured interviews prove useful for research that includes multiple segments of a value chain, because a researcher with limited knowledge of the contexts of a given segment of the chain can acquire helpful information by asking general questions and listening attentively. Once more knowledge is gained, researchers can more confidently develop structured questionnaires.

Structured interviews, also called surveys or questionnaires, can be administered in four ways: (1) self-administered (handed out or mailed to individuals to complete on their own and return), (2) in person (face-to-face), (3) via telephone or Internet call, or (4) with computer assistance, using a laptop, desktop, or device with Internet access (Bernard 2011). Structured interviews may include open-ended questions, but questions with a set of predefined options (including an "other" option of adding an answer) tend to dominate, as they are more readily entered into databases and analyzed statistically. Online surveys have become increasingly useful and user-friendly; many survey software programs are available free online (e.g., SurveyMonkey, SurveyGizmo, KwikSurvey, Checkbox Survey, and Zoomerang). Certain programs provide formats for question creation and offer descriptive analyses of responses, which can greatly facilitate the research process. Self-administered surveys and questionnaires present many advantages in terms of their ease of use and consistent options for responses, but response rates tend to be low, which may raise questions of sample representativeness. In value chain research, online surveys offer accessibility to widely dispersed individuals who may be difficult to reach in person or by phone, including entrepreneurs and representatives of alternative trade organizations. Small coffee roasters, for example, can be found in many countries around the world, but the cost of face-to-face interviews would be prohibitively high, and telephone or Internet-assisted conference calls (e.g., Skype) tend to encounter scheduling challenges due to time zone differences. Of course, the approach for survey administration should be selected with consideration of the contexts of those you intend to reach, including their educational backgrounds and whether they have easy and reliable access to the Internet.

Group Interviews and Focus Groups

Interviews with groups are an efficient approach to discovering shared understandings, perceptions, and experiences. Focus groups—a specific form of group interview—are generally designed to involve individuals who do not know each other but share attributes relevant to the study. People tend to be more willing to open up when they are unlikely to face subsequent encounters or consequences (Bernard 2011). It is not always possible to meet this criterion; for example, it may be difficult to find individuals who do not know each other when research takes place in small, rural communities or within an organization. In these cases, group interviews may be designed to take place with organized or informal groups. In studies of value chains, it can be very useful to interview people who participate in groups at different nodes in a value chain, such as farmer organizations, fair trade cooperatives, trader associations, food processing establishments, cooking or food-tasting clubs, local food and food justice advocates, and community-supported agriculture associations, among others. The format can reveal a range of variation in perceptions, reveal patterns in experience, shed light on relationships within and beyond the group, and foster exchanges about the group's experiences, local contexts, and conditions that influence decisions and actions (Bryant and Bailey 1991; Trotter and Schensul 1998). Focus groups are often used as a complement to surveys: they can be effective for checking the clarity of survey questions, discussing survey results, or eliciting additional details (Bernard 2011). Furthermore, focus groups offer an efficient way to compare different groups' experiences with, and understanding of, value chains in which they participate.

Group interviews have limitations in that they prove useful only for topics that people are willing to discuss in public (Trotter and Schensul 1998). Furthermore, if there are power differentials or tensions within the group, some members may not be willing to express contrasting or minority views. For guidance on designing and running focus groups, useful resources include *The Focus Group Kit* (Morgan and Krueger 1998), Krueger and Casey (2009), and Stewart, Shamdasani, and Rook (2007).

Participatory Research

While traditional data collection maintains a distinction between the researcher and subjects of a study, participatory research dissolves that barrier. This presents a number of challenges for traditionally trained social and natural scientists. It contradicts the established top-down mode of carrying out research and implementing recommendations. Researchers may lack training for such work, and it may be difficult for them to share control over a research design and procedures (Buruchara 2008; Castellanos et al. 2012; Gonsalves et al. 2005a). Yet participation offers an important alternative to "research as usual" in a world where conventional value chains have contributed to social inequities, environmental problems, and structural violence. Participatory approaches can give a voice to participants in conventional chains. Alternative trade initiatives have aimed to build partnerships between consumers and producers to counter the inequities of conventional markets and value chains. Participatory research therefore offers an approach for studying alternative trade that is coherent with its principles of partnership and goals of counteracting social inequities.

Fortmann (2008) defines participatory research as "doing science together." This approach recognizes that much local and indigenous knowledge is based on observation and experimentation, which aligns it with Western science even if many scientists have yet to realize this (e.g., González 2001). Moreover, interdependent research is a better way to answer some questions (Fortmann 2008). Participatory research is appropriate when projects aim to mitigate social problems, when researchers recognize that local knowledge may help answer research questions, and where research includes the objective of meeting local needs. Results from participatory research show that when local people (as "citizen scientists") help to collect data, test options, and analyze results, they are more likely to adopt promising solutions that fit their needs (Murphee 2008; Chevalier and Buckles 2008).

Working collaboratively with local people has become a prevalent methodology for applied research on economic development initiatives (Chambers 1983; Kumar 2002), public health problems (Israel et al. 2013; Minkler and Wallerstein 2003; Roberts 2013), gender issues (Agrawal and Gibson 2001; Hanson and Terstappen 2009), and conservation projects (Austin 2004; Campbell and Vainio-Mattila 2003; Gonsalves et al. 2005b). This method has promise for studies of value chains, especially when projects aim to mitigate the inequities encountered by rural producers whose labor provides the raw foods for markets. For example, one project with a rural Mexican fishing cooperative trained fishers to collect data on their catch and sales. They used the data to improve fisheries management and were empowered to obtain NGO status and arrange contracts (personal communication, X. Basurto, October 2012). Through partnerships at study sites, participatory research has the potential to empower participants, create shared knowledge, and increase the possibility that research results will be useful for residents of study sites as well as for researchers and policy makers (Murphee 2008).

Using the Internet for Research

The use of the Internet in research extends far beyond providing simple and effective survey tools. It also provides access to public databases, blogs, social media sites, and webpages of organized groups and companies. The specific databases and webpages that a researcher finds useful will depend on the research questions and the desired subjects or partners of the research. Many trade organizations and business journals publish reports and archive issues online, accessible for free or for a fee. The United Nations' Conference on Trade and Development

(UNCTAD) website presents over fifty serial reports and briefs covering commodity prices, trade policy, global investment trends, tariff profiles, and G20 discussions, to name a few topics relevant to value chain research (www.unctad.org). The Consultative Group on International Agricultural Research (CGIAR) (www.cgiar.org) and its consortium of research centers offer numerous publications, blogs, and reports related to major agricultural crops and a wide range of social and environmental issues related to food security, food policy, agricultural productivity, economic processes, and development globally. A selection of relevant organizations and online resources for food and value chain research are listed at the end of this chapter. Publicly traded corporations, which dominate a number of value chains, also publish online reports that cover investments, profits, losses, and projections. Some of these reports are distributed only to shareholders, but access to these reports can be gained by purchasing a single share in the company.

Studying Coffee Producers' Adaptations: An Example of Including Value Chains in Research

Discussing methods in the abstract is simpler than selecting and applying them on the ground. A guiding principle for any research is to ask yourself several questions: What kind of information is needed to answer my research question and test my hypotheses? How may this information be obtained? What are the possible challenges of obtaining the information with a given method? As an example, one of my collaborative research projects explored coffee farmers' adaptations to volatile coffee prices and climate change in Mexico and Central America. My colleagues and I posed several research questions, including: What do farmers perceive as the major economic and climatic impacts on their production and livelihoods? What do they perceive as their options to adapt to these impacts? How do farmers respond, as individuals and organized groups, to reduce risks related to market and climatic shocks? Subsequently, we developed a set of hypotheses for the research questions. We hypothesized, for example, that members of organized groups would have better access to market information, including prices, agricultural techniques, alternative markets, and value chain arrangements.

Our interest in value chains increased during our research, given that farmers' market experiences reflected the institutional arrangements in coffee's global value chain. We sought farmers' qualitative perspectives as well as quantitative evidence of their experiences, so we designed a mixed-methods approach that incorporated individual and group interviews, a household survey, participant observation, value chain mapping, and collection of national and international reports on coffee markets, value chains, and climate records. The household survey, conducted among a sample of primarily smallholder coffee producers in four countries, required several iterations and field tests before we felt confident that our questions were eliciting reliable and comparable answers in each country. We found that several questions had to fit local dialects—"value chain" (*cadena de valor* in Spanish) was rarely part of our respondents' vocabulary. Therefore we asked a series of questions about who bought their coffee and how it was processed. Similarly, the semi-structured interview protocols had to be designed to explore the contrasting kinds of knowledge found among the diverse groups that we wanted to include, with questions appropriate to the stage of the value chain in which they were participating (e.g., members of cooperatives, intermediary coffee buyers, agricultural extension agents, managers of coffee processing plants, representatives of regional and national coffee organizations, fair trade certifiers, and others).

Once analyzed, the survey and interview responses showed that farmers participating in organized groups, particularly cooperatives and coffee producer organizations, appeared to have more awareness of market conditions and crop diversification options (Tucker, Eakin, and Castellanos 2010). Group interviews proved especially helpful in gaining insight to farmers' understanding of the value chains they were participating in. Avoiding use of the term "value chain," we instead asked the farmers to draw a chart showing each person or organization that bought their coffee, from the time it left their farm until a consumer bought it. Independent coffee producers knew the intermediary to whom they sold coffee, but rarely knew anything about subsequent stages in the value chain. By contrast, producers organized in cooperatives were able to map their value chain, including the names of the entities involved at each stage (Castellanos et al. 2012). Through interviews and discussions with intermediaries, managers of coffee processing plants, and representatives of national coffee institutes, we were able to verify and add details to the organization of coffee value chains. This research revealed great interest in fair trade among farmers and coffee organizations, and led to my current research on the experiences that coffee farmers, buyers, traders, and consumers have had with alternative trade (Tucker 2011).

Being Open to the Unexpected

A productive research project builds upon a well-developed research design, interesting questions, an appropriate suite of methods, and disciplined data collection. Even so, some of the most important moments in research result from accidents, mistakes, and serendipitous encounters. You never know when someone in the street, at an office, or on a bus might offer a key insight or become an invaluable contact. On a recent plane ride, I sat beside a quiet man reading a book on coffee. Having read the book myself, I dared to ask him whether he found it interesting. He explained that he was a small coffee roaster from Alabama en route to explore the possibility of direct trade with a coffee cooperative in Honduras. We struck up an animated conversation as I shared my own research on coffee production, and he shared his experiences trying to establish direct trade arrangements. Until that moment, I had had only limited success locating entrepreneurs working with direct trade, but through him, I gained access to information and contacts that had been beyond my grasp. In addition to careful planning and rigorous research methods, successful researchers exercise flexibility, openness, and willingness to learn from anyone who may cross their path.

Concluding Thoughts

The study of food value chains and their ramifications poses notable challenges, but it is necessary to understand the workings of the modern world system, and to consider options for mitigating its numerous problems. As Wallerstein (2009: 89) observes,

> We are measuring indirectly and imperfectly a total phenomenon that we cannot see directly no matter what we do. The point however is to figure out how this total phenomenon operates, what are its rules, what are its trends, what are its coming and inevitable disequilibria and bifurcations. It requires imagination and audacity along with rigor and patience. The only thing we have to fear is looking too narrowly.

Catherine M. Tucker is an ecological and economic anthropologist at the University of Florida. Her research focuses on community-based natural resource management, and impacts of global change processes on livelihoods and natural resources. Most recently, she has been studying coffee production and commodity chains, especially coffee farmers' adaptations to market volatility, alternative trade, and climate change. In a related project, she is studying watershed and forest resource management in coffee-producing areas of Mexico and Central America. She is the author of *Coffee Culture: Local Experiences, Global Connections* (Routledge) and *Changing Forests: Collective Action, Common Property and Coffee in Honduras* (Springer). Her recent work has been published in *Human Ecology, Human Organization, Global Environmental Change, Ecology and Society, Environmental Science and Policy,* and *Environment, Development and Sustainability.*

References

Agrawal, Arun, and Clark C. Gibson, eds. 2001. *Communities and the Environment: Ethnicity, Gender and the State in Community-Based Conservation.* Piscataway, NJ: Rutgers University Press.

Austin, Diane E. 2004. Partnerships, Not Projects! Improving the Environment through Collaborative Research and Action. *Human Organization* 63(4): 419–430.
Bair, Jennifer. 2009. Global Commodity Chains: Genealogy and Review. In Frontiers of Commodity Chain Research, ed. Jennifer Bair, 1–34. Stanford, CA: Stanford University Press.
Bernard, H. Russell. 2011. *Research Methods in Anthropology.* 5th ed. Walnut Creek, CA: AltaMira Press.
Bryant, Carol A., and Doraine F. C. Bailey. 1991. The Use of Focus Group Research in Program Development. In *NAPA Bulletin 10,* ed. John van Willigen and Timothy J. Finan, 24–39. Washington, DC: National Association for the Practice of Anthropology.
Buruchara, Robin. 2008. How Participatory Research Convinced a Skeptic. In *Participatory Research in Conservation and Rural Livelihoods,* ed. Louise Fortmann, 18–25. Hoboken, NJ: Blackwell.
Campbell, Lisa M., and Arja Vainio-Mattila. 2003. Participatory Development and Community-Based Conservation: Opportunities Missed for Lessons Learned? *Human Ecology* 31(3): 417–437.
Castellanos, Edwin J., Catherine M. Tucker, Hallie Eakin, Helda Morales, Juan F. Barrera, and Rafael Díaz. 2012. Assessing The Adaptation Strategies of Farmers Facing Multiple Stressors. *Environmental Science & Policy* 26: 19–28.
Chambers, Robert. 1983. *Rural Development: Putting the Last First.* Essex: Pearson.
Chevalier, Jacques M., and Daniel J. Buckles. 2008. *SAS: A Guide to Collaborative Inquiry and Social Engagement.* Sage: IDRC. http://idl-bnc.idrc.ca/dspace/bitstream/10625/35977/1/IDL-35977.pdf. Accessed 25 July 2014.
DeWalt, Kathleen M., and Billie R. DeWalt. 2010. *Participant Observation.* Lanham, MD: AltaMira Press.
DeWalt, Kathleen M., Billie R. DeWalt, and Coral B. Wayland. 1998. Participant Observation. In *Handbook of Methods in Cultural Anthropology,* ed. H. Russell Bernard, 259–300. Walnut Creek, CA: AltaMira Press.
Fischer, Edward F., and Peter Benson. 2006. *Broccoli and Desire: Global Connections and Maya Struggles in Postwar Guatemala.* Stanford, CA: Stanford University Press.
Fortmann, Louise. 2008. Introduction: Doing Science Together. In *Participatory Research in Conservation and Rural Livelihoods,* ed. Louise Fortmann, 1–17. Chichester: Wiley-Blackwell.
Foster, Robert J. 2008. *Coca-Globalization: Following Soft Drinks from New York to New Guinea.* New York: Palgrave Macmillan.
Gardner, Andrew, and David M. Hoffman, eds. 2006. *Dispatches from the Field: Neophyte Ethnographers in a Changing World.* Long Grove, IL: Waveland.
Gonsalves, Julian, Thomas Becker, Ann Braun, Dindo Campilan, Hidelisa De Chavez, Elizabeth Fajber, Monica Kapiriri, Joy Rivaca-Caminade, and Ronnie Vernooy, eds. 2005a. *Participatory Research and Development for Sustainable Agriculture and Natural Resource Management,* vol. 1, *Understanding Participatory Research and Development.* Ottawa: CIP-UPWARD.
———. 2005b. *Participatory Research and Development for Sustainable Agriculture and Natural Resource Management,* vol. 3, *Doing Participatory Research and Development.* Ottawa: CIP-UPWARD.
González, Roberto J. 2001. *Zapotec Science: Farming and Food in the Northern Sierra of Oaxaca.* Austin: University of Texas Press.

Hannerz, Ulf. 1998. Transnational Research. In *Handbook of Methods in Cultural Anthropology*, ed. H. Russell Bernard, 235–256. Walnut Creek, CA: AltaMira Press.

———. 2012 Being There…and There…and There! Reflections on Multi-Site Ethnography. In *Ethnographic Fieldwork: An Anthropological Reader*, ed. Antonius C. G. M. Robben and Jeffrey A. Sluka, 399–408. Chichester: Wiley-Blackwell.

Hanson, Lori, and Vincent Terstappen. 2009. Collaboration on Contentious Issues: Research Partnerships for Gender Equity in Nicaragua's Fair Trade Coffee Cooperatives. *Journal of Agromedicine* 14(2): 105–111.

Hopkins, Terence K., and Immanuel Wallerstein. 1977. Patterns of Development of the Modern World System. *Review* 1(2): 111–145.

Hume, Lynne, and Jane Mulcock, eds. 2004. *Anthropologists in the Field: Cases in Participant Observation*. New York: Columbia University Press.

Israel, Barbara A., Eugenia Eng, Amy J. Schulz, and Edith A. Parker, eds. 2013. *Methods for Community-Based Participatory Research for Health*. 2nd ed. San Francisco: Jossey-Bass.

Jaffee, Daniel. 2007. *Brewing Justice: Fair Trade Coffee, Sustainability, and Survival*. Berkeley: University of California Press.

Kaplinsky, Raphael, and Mike Morris. 2001. *Handbook for Value Chain Research*. Prepared for the IDRC. URL: http://www.prism.uct.ac.za/Papers/VchNov01.pdf. Accessed 25 July 2014.

Krueger, Richard A., and Mary Anne Casey, eds. 2009. *Focus Groups: A Practical Guide for Applied Research*. Los Angeles: Sage.

Kumar, Somesh. 2002. *Methods for Community Participation*. New Delhi: Practical Action.

Marcus, George E. 1995. Ethnography in/of the World System: The Emergence of Multi-Sited Ethnography. *Annual Review of Anthropology* 24: 95–117.

Miller, Jeff, and Jonathan Deutsch. 2009. *Food Studies: An Introduction to Research Methods*. New York: Berg.

Minkler, Meredith, and Nina Wallerstein, eds. 2003. *Community-Based Participatory Research for Health*. San Francisco: Jossey-Bass.

Mintz, Sidney W. 1986. *Sweetness and Power: The Place of Sugar in Modern History*. New York: Penguin.

Morgan, David L., and Richard Krueger. 1998. *The Focus Group Kit*, volumes 1–6. Thousand Oaks, CA: Sage.

Murphee, Marshall W. 2008. Foreword. In *Participatory Research in Conservation and Rural Livelihoods*, ed. Louise Fortmann, xvi–xxii. Hoboken, NJ: Blackwell.

Pilcher, Jeffrey M. 2006. *Food in World History*. New York: Routledge.

Pomeranz, Kenneth, and Steven Topik. 2006. *The World That Trade Created: Society, Culture, and the World Economy*. Armonk, NY: M. E. Sharpe.

Roberts, Laura Weiss. 2013. *Community-Based Participatory Research for Improved Mental Healthcare*. New York: Springer.

Ryan, John C., and Alan Thein Durning. 1997. *Stuff: The Secret Lives of Everyday Things*. Seattle, WA: Sightline Institute.

Spradley, James P. 1980. *Participant Observation*. New York: Holt, Rinehart & Winston.

Stewart, David W., Prem N. Shamdasani, and Dennis W. Rook. 2007. *Focus Groups: Theory and Practice*. 2nd ed. Thousand Oaks, CA: Sage.

Stringer, Christina, and Richard Le Heron. 2008. Introduction: Mapping the Concept of Globalising Networks. In *Agri-Food Commodity Chains and Globalising Networks*, ed. Christina Stringer and Richard Le Heron, 16–23. Hampshire: Ashgate.

Sturgeon, Timothy J. 2009. From Commodity Chains to Value Chains: Interdisciplinary Theory Building in an Age of Globalization. In *Frontiers of Commodity Chain Research,* ed. Jennifer Bair, 110–135. Stanford, CA: Stanford University Press.
Trotter, Robert T. II, and Jean J. Schensul. 1998. Methods in Applied Anthropology. In *Handbook of Methods in Cultural Anthropology,* ed. H. Russell Bernard, 691–735. Walnut Creek, CA: AltaMira Press.
Tucker, Catherine M. 2011. *Coffee Culture: Local Experiences, Global Consequences.* New York: Routledge.
Tucker, Catherine M., Hallie Eakin, and Edwin J. Castellanos. 2010. Perceptions of Risk and Adaptation: Coffee Producers, Market Shocks, and Extreme Weather in Central America and Mexico. *Global Environmental Change* 20: 23–32.
Wallerstein, Immanuel. 2009. Protection Networks and Commodity Chains in the Capitalist World-Economy. In *Frontiers of Commodity Chain Research,* ed. Jennifer Bair, 83–89. Stanford, CA: Stanford University Press.
Weller, Susan C. 1998. Structured Interviewing and Questionnaire Construction. In *Handbook of Methods in Cultural Anthropology,* ed. H. Russell Bernard, 365–409. Walnut Creek, CA: AltaMira Press.

Relevant Organizations and Websites (Accessed 3 September 2016)

Note: This is a selection of websites that I have found useful in my research. There are numerous websites with relevance to value chain research; the usefulness of any site will depend on your own research.

Consultative Group on International Agricultural Research (CGIAR), http://www.cgiar.org
Fair Trade Federation, http://www.fairtradefederation.org
Fairtrade.net, http://www.fairtrade.net
Fair World Project, http://fairworldproject.org/voices-of-fair-trade/alternative-trade-organizations-and-the-fair-trade-movement/
Food and Agriculture Organization (FAO), www.fao.org
Global Value Chains Initiative, http://www.globalvaluechains.org
IMD Global Value Chain Center, http://www.imd.org/research-knowledge/global-centers/value-chain/#/home/
International Center for Tropical Agriculture (CIAT), http://ciat.cgiar.org
International Coffee Organization (ICO), http://www.ico.org
International Development Research Centre (IDRC) http://www.idrc.ca
International Food Policy Research Institute (IFPRI), http://www.ifpri.org/
International Labor Organization (ILO), www.ilo.org
International Maize and Wheat Improvement Center (CIMMYT), http://www.cimmyt.org/en/
International Potato Center (CIP), www.cipotato.org
Kenya Coffee Traders' Association, http://www.kenyacoffee.co.ke/
National Coffee Association of USA, Inc., http://www.ncausa.org
National Federation of Coffee Growers of Colombia, http://www.juanvaldez.com
Tea and Coffee Trade Journal Online Archives, http://www.teaandcoffee.net/

United Nations Commission on Trade and Development (UNCTAD), http://unctad.org/en/pages/home.aspx

World Coffee Research, https://worldcoffeeresearch.org/news/

Relevant References and Sources Online

Cattaneo, Oliver, Gary Gereffi, and Cornelia Staritz. 2010. Global Value Chains in a Postcrisis World. http://issuu.com/world.bank.publications/docs/9780821384992/1?zoomed=&zoomPercent=&zoomX=&zoomY=&noteText=&noteX=&noteY=&viewMode=magazine. Accessed 2 September 2016.

CIP. 2014 Linking Farmers to Markets—Our Experiences in Developing Sweetpotato Value Chains in East and Central Africa. http://cipotato.org/press-room/blogs/linking-farmers-to-markets-our-experiences-in-developing-sweetpotato-value-chains-in-east-and-central-africa/. Accessed 2 September 2016.

Hellin, Jon, and Madelon Meijer. 2006. Guidelines for Value Chain Analysis. ftp://ftp.fao.org/es/esa/lisfame/guidel_ValueChain.pdf. Accessed 2 September 2016.

Herr, Matthias, and Tapera Muzira. 2011. Development of Value Chains for Decent Work. (Desarrollo de cadenas de valor para el trabajo decente), http://www.ilo.org/empent/areas/value-chain-development-vcd/WCMS_115490/lang--en/index.htm. Accessed 2 September 2016.

Nang'ole E. M., D. Mithöfer, S. Franzel. 2011. Review of Guidelines and Manuels for Value Chain Analysis for Agricultural and Forest Products. ICRAF Occasional Paper No. 17. Nairobi: World Agroforestry Centre. http://www.worldagroforestry.org/downloads/Publications/PDFS/OP11160.pdf. Accessed 2 September 2016.

Nutz, Nadja and Merten Sievers. A Rough Guide to Value Chain Development. 2015. Geneva: International Labour Office. http://www.ilo.org/wcmsp5/groups/public/---ed_emp/---emp_ent/---ifp_seed/documents/publication/wcms_366005.pdf. Accessed 2 September 2016.

Robinson, Phyllis, and Nicholas Reid. n.d. *The History of Authentic Fair Trade.* http://cdn.coverstand.com/29041/177947/cedb1c9a5ab2dd02bb5870c65af7e41f9be5da01.1.pdf. Accessed 2 September 2016.

Trienekens, Jacques H. 2011. Agricultural Value Chains in Developing Countries: A Framework for Analysis. *International Food and Agribusiness Management Review* 14(2). http://ageconsearch.umn.edu/bitstream/103987/2/20100036_Formatted.pdf. Accessed 2 September 2016.

UNCTAD. 2013. *Trade and Development Report, 2013: Adjusting to the Changing Dynamics of the World Economy.* http://unctad.org/en/pages/PublicationWebflyer.aspx?publicationid=636. Accessed 2 September 2016.

UNCTAD. 2013. *World Investment Report 2013: Global Value Chains: Investment and Trade for Development.* http://unctad.org/en/pages/PublicationWebflyer.aspx?publicationid=588. Accessed 2 September 2016.

Webber, Martin. n.d. *Using Value Chain Approaches in Agribusiness and Agriculture in Sub-Saharan Africa: A Methodological Guide.* http://www.technoserve.org/files/downloads/vcguidenov12-2007.pdf. Accessed 2 September 2016.

CHAPTER **19**

The Single Food Approach
A Research Strategy in Nutritional Anthropology
Andrea S. Wiley and Janet Chrzan

Most scholarly analyses of single foods have taken a historical perspective. These texts often take a biographical approach to individual foods, tracing their emergence and human usage, and in many cases considering the social and cultural meanings that develop and change in relation to other social trends. Many are written by scholars in food studies, which has its roots in the social sciences and humanities, with less input from the life sciences. An anthropological approach to single foods encompasses this history, but adds to it a broader evolutionary history and a theoretically informed ethnographic and comparative analysis. Thus the single food approach offers the possibility of closer integration of nutritional anthropology and food studies. As it is amenable to a variety of theoretical perspectives, a single food approach is especially useful in collaborative projects among anthropologists and with scholars in other fields across the academic spectrum. At the very least it provides a way to find common ground for productive exchange among food researchers.

In its broadest form, nutritional anthropology considers the social, ecological, and biological aspects of diet and nutrition, and how these interrelate within and across populations, as well as through our evolutionary and more recent history. A single food focus provides an exemplar of the utility of this biocultural perspective. Foods are complex biological substances that achieve their status as sustenance within fluid cultural milieus that encourage or discourage (or even forbid) their consumption. Culinary practices transform foods' biological characteristics in ways that influence their impact on human physiology. After negotiation of the various social and cultural factors that influence its consumption, food enters the mouth, is subject to further digestive transformations, which have been shaped by our evolutionary history, and ultimately becomes part of our physiology, with short and long-term effects on biology. Our biological experiences with food can then feed back into cultural ideals, policies, and economic supports for foods we find desirable, or proclaim are "good" or "bad" for us.

In this essay we outline the ways that nutritional anthropologists can approach a research project using a single food focus. We then consider the ways in which single food analyses advance some central concerns of the field, including diet and human evolution, cross-cultural variability in food usage and meaning, child feeding and growth, and dietary transitions, especially in the context of globalization. We will use our own research on milk and alcohol as examples of how a focus on one food can bring together these diverse concerns. Nutritional anthropologists typically have focused on food consumption and its biological consequences rather than production, and we will emphasize consumption. Still, there is no inherent reason why such an approach could not be elaborated to include consideration of the political, economic, and ecological factors that shape production and the commodity chain that links production loci to those where consumers can purchase food. It comes as no surprise that the work that is the touchstone for anthropological analysis of food is Sidney Mintz's *Sweetness and Power: The Place of Sugar in Modern History* (1985), which considers the political and economic processes that linked the production of sugar by slaves in the New World with transformations in the diets of the English working class of the nineteenth century. In this case sugar is a food with profound consequences in macro- and micro-level social and cultural domains as well as culinary practices and nutrition.

Research Strategies

Anthropologists take two main approaches to the study of a specific food. One is to consider it as one would any object of ethnographic interest. This method starts with descriptive data that are then used in an analytic framework that locates the food in relation to other aspects of social life. In this case the primary concern is with the food itself. The alternative approach is more deductive, when a particular food turns out to be important with respect to understanding something else that is of primary concern, whether it be the "cause" of food taboos, or biological outcomes such as high rates of obesity, micronutrient deficiencies, or stunted child growth. As is the case with most scientific work, these approaches tend to dovetail and encompass both "thick description" and theoretical considerations, but they represent different starting positions to an anthropological investigation of a particular food. We will emphasize the first approach in this chapter, where interest in the food itself is primary.

Like eating, setting out to study a particular food first requires a choice among many foods. Some foods are more amenable to anthropological field research than others; it is best to start with a food that is well known to many ethnographic informants or survey respondents and central to some forms of cultural discourse. It may well be that this food is widely consumed, but one might also choose a food that is explicitly not eaten because of taboos, or legal or religious prohibitions. A forbidden food is suitable as long as it is in fact available and recognized as food, even if only as one consumed by "others." Indeed, many earlier studies of foods focused on those that were "tabooed" (e.g., Marvin Harris's [1985] analysis of pork taboos among Jews and Muslims, or religious prohibition of cow consumption by Hindus). Thus the main criterion for selecting a food should be the existence of some kind of cultural dialogue about it, and hence this approach requires some baseline observations and knowledge about food consumption and discourse in a particular cultural context.

Non-fieldwork–based, cross-cultural analysis that is based on extant ethnographic material (e.g., that found in the Human Relations Area Files; http://www.yale.edu/hraf) is also facilitated by this approach. With a specific food as the common material, examining existing literature on the different uses of and discourse around the food is relatively straightforward (although the written materials often have uneven coverage of diet), and reveals similarity and difference in cultural meanings ascribed to it as well as consumption patterns. Publicly available survey data can also be mined. In the United States, the National Health and Nutrition Examination Survey (NHANES; http://www.cdc.gov/nchs/nhanes.htm) provides nationally representative data on dietary behavior, including consumption of specific foods, from either 24-hour recalls or food frequency questionnaires, with nutrient analysis based on the USDA National Nutrient Database. While there is little information on beliefs about particular foods, these data can provide baseline information on consumption patterns of specific foods and their association with different biological outcomes. Such surveys are themselves cultural products, and the inclusion of questions about specific foods can provide an indication of their valuation and expectations about their consumption. In either case—through intensive fieldwork or secondary analysis of existing ethnographic and survey data—a single food serves as an anchor for research. Especially in the former, food is a tangible object for focused discussion and provides an entrée into both ethnographic fieldwork among those consuming (or not) the particular food, as well as the organizations that may be promoting, protecting, or otherwise concerned with that particular food.

In some cases it may be better to focus on a group of related foods rather than a single one. For example, specific fruits or vegetables or species of animal may not yield much information if they are not widely consumed. So a focus on chili peppers (*Capsaicin spp.*) might be a more fruitful approach than a particular species, or cruciferous vegetables as a category might be more appropriate than setting out to study broccoli. One might also consider a commercially available processed and packaged food (cf. Errington Gewertz, and Fujikura 2013), a popular food product (such as flap meat in the Pacific Islands; Gewertz and

Errington 2010), or a common food combination or preparation that is widely consumed (cf. the analysis of rice and beans by Wilk and Barbosa 2012). Again, this is something that needs to be ascertained at the outset and based on solid ethnographic or survey data.

Once a food has been established as a focus, the direction taken depends on the anthropologist's interests but at least should be informed by ethnographic fieldwork and framed by a systematic survey of consumption of the food of interest, specifically noting differential patterns among subgroups or within households, and any temporal patterns such as seasonality in consumption. These can be ascertained through food frequency questionnaires, long-term participant-observation, or other methods that are more suitable to the research objectives (see the chapter Dietary Analyses in volume 1 of this set). This should be combined with systematic investigation of how people access the food of interest. If the researcher finds it useful to understand production, markets, and commodity chains, this aspect would be elaborated.

Common to all research questions concerning consumption of a given food is an understanding of the local "emic" meanings of the food. How is it understood in relation to other foods in the diet? What is "special" about this food? What do people think it does to the body? To whom is it recommended for consumption and why? Who is prohibited from eating it and why? How is it prepared and why? Is it highly valued or disdained? How is it situated within local dietary guidance, formal and informal, and how does this demonstrate valuation of different foodstuffs? Elicited from participant-observation and structured interviews, answers to these questions can be confirmed in other cultural domains such as advertisements, subsistence activities, trade networks, prices, ethnomedical systems, public health, and nutrition education efforts, among others. Equally important is the food's biography. Where was it domesticated? How did colonialism affect its distribution? Is it newly introduced? How do current consumption patterns compare to historical trends? How are current political and economic trends impacting local access, consumption patterns, and meanings? What is the current cultural discourse about the food, and do its users have a narrative about the food that agrees or contrasts with the historical biography? If the aim is to understand cross-cultural variation in the usage and/or strongly held beliefs about a food, then this investigation needs to be repeated systematically across cultural contexts, or gleaned from extant materials. Importantly, this analysis should not simply track "usage of food 'X' across space and time" but rather should be informed by theoretical questions that provide meaningful insights into similarity and variability in food use and meaning across human societies.

These emic understandings can be juxtaposed with knowledge of the food based on Western scientific investigation (etic understandings). Its botanical or zoological taxonomic name and placement, nutrient composition, toxicity, phytochemical composition (for plants), and ecological requirements need to be evaluated. Most relevant to nutritional anthropology is how the food has been understood in nutritional terms. Food composition tables can be used to ascertain nutrient components, or if these are not available, laboratory analysis of a food sample may be necessary. Which micro- or macronutrients is the food a rich source of? What are its known effects on human biological function? How has the food been evaluated as a "good" or "bad" food within nutrition science and public health nutrition? The data on nutrient composition are not meant to reify a "nutritionist" approach to food, which scrutinizes food nutrients and bases dietary recommendations on them rather than regarding them as a package within the context of a biologically complex organism (Scrinis 2013). Instead, the intent is to generate a point of intersection with the nutrition literature, especially if the food has an unusual nutrient or biochemical profile, and use a common definition for comparative analysis.

Examples of Single-Food Ethnographic Studies

Anthropologists' explorations of single foods generally arise out of their own ethnographic research, whether sociocultural, biocultural, or even archeological in original training. It is this grounding in anthropological theory and method that guides the single food study and protects the researcher from falling into the trap of the "Oooh, look! Something Shiny!" school of writing. Ethnography also distinguishes such work from that of the journalist (whose focus is usually on the present day as understood through interviews and background research) or the historian, who is more likely to adopt a descriptive trajectory determined by events and processes in the past. While the anthropologist may use some of these methods to contextualize the topic, the core and guiding methodology is that of direct anthropological fieldwork. Anthropologists can then trace connections across space (cross-cultural, commodity chain, and globalization studies), time (archeology and historical records), and network (social structures, food mapping, and food sharing cultural norms) in order to fully pursue both emic and etic understandings of the food's use within or across cultures. The core of such research, though, is ethnography that examines the human utilization of a particular food or food product.

Perhaps the most prominent example of single-food ethnography is Sidney Mintz's (1985) exploration of the history of the sugar industry in Puerto Rico and changes in European sugar intakes as a result of slavery, global trade, and changing wages and work structures. Mintz was a sociocultural anthropologist whose participant-observation research among cane sugar workers in Puerto Rico spanned several decades. He worked in the fields with the cane cutters, lived in their communities, and explored the economy of the plantation system. It was this focus on the social and economic processes that shaped the production of the commodity called sugar that encouraged his additional research into the history of the intertwined economic systems of the Caribbean and Europe and from there, a focus on the social history of the use of sugar in both regions. Through careful examination of historical texts, economic capital flow, and changing social patterns of use he was able to authoritatively argue that the use of sugar united slave, proletariat, and master/capitalist through a globalized economic world system that shaped colonial polities—both the colonized and the colonizer—and created capital structures that created a global working class linked via production and consumption of sugar. He argued that the core alteration of diet brought about by the production of sugar—the substitution of simple carbohydrates for complex grains (ibid.: 198)—shapes current food production and consumption and defines the primary and essential processes adopted by most food manufacturers today, thereby deeply affecting nutriture in current human populations. Such a monograph, reliant upon sociocultural knowledge gained from many years of fieldwork (a thick description) is made possible only by the researcher's ability to trace connections outward from core ethnographic knowledge.

More recently, a similar approach was taken to explore the use of flap meat amongst Pacific Islanders living in the New Guinea archipelago, which is a cheap, fatty cut of lamb or mutton. Gewertz and Errington (2010) connect the dots between the economic poverty, ill health, and obesity of Pacific natives, and the distribution of meat products that are cheap precisely because they are the by-products of a globalized New Zealand and Australia-based lamb trade that exports the more favored muscular parts to first-world nations. They trace the path of flap meat as a commodity through the Pacific, exploring the meanings its use has for producers and consumers, using multiple sites of study in order to link the social, cultural, and economic nodes that connect each part of the chain. Unlike their earlier study of sugar production, which sought to "understand processes of globalization as they have come together in one place" (ibid.: 7) by using participant observation to create a thick description of sugar production, the flap meat study required multiple sites and thus threatened to devolve into a "thin" description. Two strategies for following a commodity chain, they assert, are to either station multiple anthropologists along the chain's nodes or to rely on previous ethnographic experience to inform the exploration of "where the commodity originates, passes through, or is consumed" (ibid.: 8). Because of their long experience in the region, Gewertz and Errington were able to implement the latter strategy, in part by doing fieldwork in places they had previously visited. Their deep knowledge of the region and its multiple cultures allows them to adapt interviewing methods more typical of journalism to the study of commodity chain creation, meanings and use.

Their methods are very neatly outlined in the introduction of their book, but here we present a synopsis. Relying on previous ethnographic work to contextualize their interviews, they moved from New Zealand to Australia and finally to the Pacific Islands, the primary site of consumption. In New Zealand they interviewed people who produced or had an interest in the production of mutton, lamb, and flap meat: farmers, traders, public health officials, and government policy workers. In Australia they interviewed public health specialists and meat traders. In Papua New Guinea they interviewed importers, retailers, health workers and government representatives. They also conducted dietary research about flap meat use in a village where they had already done extensive fieldwork, did "market basket" research with subjects known through a previous study, and had graduate students visit five towns to collect data on attitudes about flap meat. In Fiji they repeated this method and had students interview 185 people about use of flap meat. In Fiji the principle investigators also interviewed health and government officials and meat importers. The interviews and fieldwork were supplemented with library research and historical studies of the economies of the region. Clearly an enormous amount of data to compile on one food subject, this resulted in a robust and indeed quite thick description of the movement, consumption, and health consequences of flap meat throughout the Pacific region. Their use of multiple methods and multiple sites provides a grounded and comprehensive approach, one that is far more robust than most studies of global food chains. They identify their study as one that traces a commodity chain through time and place (see Tucker in this volume for methods used in commodity chain research), but they have situated their research in an examination of the socioeconomic forces that ensure that flap meat is available to Pacific Islanders as surely as New Zealand lamb chops are available at Trader Joe's. And by using interviews and participant observation methods, they were able to understand why Pacific Islanders have come to prefer flap meat, and to view it as a symbol of modernity and economic prosperity rather than the sad castoffs of a global commodity chain that ships the prime cuts to the first world, leaving the trimmings and offal to be eaten by the working class and poor.

Catherine Tucker has used classic sociocultural methods to follow a commodity chain for coffee from producer to consumer. While she begins her narrative in the first world with an examination of coffee culture in relation to food and culture theory, her monograph is anchored by her years of fieldwork amongst coffee producers in Central America. She uses three theoretical approaches to understand how we produce, distribute, and utilize coffee: that of Levi-Strauss, who argued that mental structures shape how human societies assign values and meanings to food; of Bourdieu, who maintained that taste preferences are generated by social class affiliation; and economic world-systems theory, which traces the trade connections within and between cultures/societies to understand the meanings of foods and the structures of global commodity transfer (Tucker 2011: 12). Given that that the volume is designed to introduce undergraduates to anthropological concepts, her exploration of coffee using these theories allows students to understand the theory in relation to production and consumption of coffee—a product that many students use daily. Parts One and Two roughly outline Levi-Strauss's and Bourdieu's theories to discuss coffee use, economics, and national preferences in relation to history, economics, and identity. Each chapter begins with a personalized anecdote—a kind of field note—that encourages the reader to place himself or herself into the text as someone who experiences coffee culture. The core of Tucker's volume begins in Chapter 11, with stories and field notes from her research on coffee production and distribution. Standard participant-observation techniques follow the bean from planting to beverage, and each step is explained using stories from the field. She ends with a section on economic markets and world systems, using coffee as an example of how a boom-and-bust commodity cycle is often invisible to consumers but devastating to the economies and cultures of producing peasant farmers. By linking her field research to history, commodity distribution, and identity consumption, she neatly illustrates the many ways an anthropologist can understand the production, consumption, and belief systems that bring a food product from field to table across national borders, cultures, and time.

Anthropologists, because of their research and lived experiences in two (or even more) cultures, are uniquely qualified to apply world systems theory to the study of food in a global context. A good example of this is provided by Wilk and Barbosa's (2012) edited volume *Rice and Beans: A Unique Dish in a Hundred Places*. The individual authors use a variety of methods to explore how the combination of rice and beans has become a meaningful and staple dish in many cultures around the world. The editors point out that two approaches to the culture and history of foods are most typical: "the first keeps the focus on a particular place and tracks the way foods come and go as a unique local cuisine develops and changes. The second follows a particular foodstuff...as it spreads around the world, moving from place to place" (Wilk and Barbosa, 2012: 1). They loosely label these approaches as "follow that food" and "cuisine = terroir = culture" (ibid.: 4). They also remind us that although single-food books may be immensely popular, they also often miss the very important point that all foods are ingredients that are not usually eaten on their own: they are almost always part of a larger recipe, food association, or cuisine that has health and dietary consequences.

Anthropological theories and methods can provide the contextualization that makes sense of the ingredient as it becomes culturally appropriate food and provide a thick description that anchors the foodstuff in the history, beliefs, and culture of a people. In particular, they indicate that the anthropological approach allows for "tracing the ancestry, distribution and variation in rice and beans in a broad, straight avenue right into the history of the Atlantic world, from the trauma of conquest, to the tragedy of African slavery, and onward into the more recent saga of nation-building and neocolonialism" (ibid.: 5). They thus outline the agenda as one that explicitly links cultural practice to economic and social history and present a series of informational nodes that illuminate how a food can be used to explore cultural processes and historical trajectories.

All of the individual authors in Wilk and Barbosa's volume trace the history of rice and beans in particular countries or cultures, using their particular area of anthropological study to analyze this combination's sociological import for contemporary eaters. To illustrate these methods, we will describe one chapter that uses participant observation and life history to explain how rice and beans have come to hold an important place in the cuisine of Cuba. Using methods similar to those of Ramona Lee Perez (Life History Methods in this volume), Anna Cristina Pertierra (Pertierra 2012) documents how her mother-in-law, a Cuban housewife, "makes do" in her efforts to source and prepare iconic Cuban dishes when faced with rations, differing currencies, and lack of raw ingredients. Using kitchen-table ethnography, Pertierra traces how the Cuban political structure and economy have glorified rice and beans even as they make the ability to source and prepare it problematic. The efforts required to find the basic ingredients for the dish *congri* (the Cuban name for rice and beans) are an essential part of household economy as well as identity. Women pride themselves on being able to find the right ingredients and use them properly to create their particular version of congri. Partierra traces the steps taken to locate and price the beans and the ingredients for the *sofrito* (a garlic, onion, and pepper flavor base), analytically integrating the needs of a household economy with the history of the Cuban economy from the Socialist era through the Special Period (when the Soviets reduced their financial support of Cuba, resulting in widespread shortages of many food staples) to the post-Soviet state with its opportunities to purchase imported goods, but often at inflated prices. By using one cook's story of the efforts needed to cook *congri*, Partierra effectively links the Cuban national economy and history to the daily lived experiences of a citizen.

Another example of how economic processes and structures can be revealed by the study of single foods is Daniel Knight's study of mushroom harvesting in Greece (Knight 2014). Each autumn, village residents who have relocated to other towns and regions to find jobs return to their ancestral village of Kalloni to gather mushrooms. Mushrooms are plentiful in the nearby woods, and the history of hunting for them spans generations. Villagers negotiate knowledge about mushroom gathering areas and share—or fail to share—their harvests. The return to the village unites families who have moved away, providing an embodied reminder of their earlier lives in the village. For the latest generations, the return to Kalloni is an opportunity to spend time with older family members and learn the ways of the village, hearing also about their forebears' peasant economy, which relied on woodland gathering in addition to farming. The farms are no longer functioning, but the familial knowledge of woodland gathering areas and the rituals attached to sharing and hiding this knowledge teach a remembered history of family and place and guarantees that old ties—and old resentments—are remembered and cherished. Mushrooms are both an important cash crop and an iconic dish, and by gathering, cooking, and sharing their harvest, the scattered residents are able to re-create a portion of their shared history as villagers, as well as experience an embodied knowledge of what it means to be a "Kalloniot."

In order to link these various strands of culture and history together, Knight used standard participant observation methods, working with the villagers as they hunted for mushrooms, discussed tips and locations, hashed over old resentments, and shared stories of the past with each other. He states that "in Kalloni, mushrooms signify the struggles of previous generations and define an era when the village was a thriving community" (ibid.: 186). As an ethnographer, he links a collective village identity to the gathering of mushrooms, a ritual that reunites far-flung families and villagers even today. He contrasts the historic memories of mushroom collecting—so wrapped in the memories of the village—with the contemporary social activities associated with the return to the village, the staging of festivals, and the collecting of mushrooms. In doing so he demonstrates how food economy and culture can transcend modern processes of dispersion and disconnect.

Particular foods are undoubtedly tied to collective—and sometimes individual—identities, and they can also function to shape identity. How the use of alcohol contributes to the social and personal identities of college students was one of the questions that one of us, Janet Chrzan, asked when writing the Routledge volume *Alcohol: Social Drinking in Cultural Context* (Chrzan 2013). The ethnographic data relied on students' essays and diaries from a harm-reduction course on the medical anthropology of alcohol use that she taught from 2001 through 2010. Students wrote weekly about their observed experiences with alcohol, wrote essays about alcohol advertising and were also required to attend a college party sober and to write about it as an ethnographic encounter. Grounded theory was used to identify themes in their writings, and Chrzan narrowed the list of topics to sociality (the Drunk Self), negotiating gender, sexuality and sexual response, caretaking and accomplishment behaviors, and "time-out" stress management. In reviewing their writings it became very clear that students used alcohol strategically to manage their public image, their social lives, and their romantic relationships. Alcohol was not merely a drug, it was a near-essential tool used to negotiate the transition into adulthood. Much of the modeling for these behaviors was derived from the advertising industry, since alcohol advertising is widespread and often targets college-age youth. This then led to an analysis of the semiotics of alcohol advertising, a topic that has been covered extensively already; Chrzan was fortunate to be able to examine students' writings about alcohol ads in relation to previous semiotic arguments about advertising provided by sociologists and linguists.

Chrzan also included historical and cross-cultural information derived from primary and secondary sources in order to contextualize the modern-day use of alcohol within the history of European drinking. Using a historical timeline she focused on how past societies thought about alcohol, how (and how much) they drank, and how use and belief changed over time. She was also interested in alcohol as a food item and used historical manifests to calculate the possible caloric contribution of alcohol to the diet. Her goal was to understand when and how alcohol intake—particularly that of beer and wine—could be considered an adaptive strategy for the storage of foods (grapes, grains) that would allow better nutriture during lean agricultural periods. Indeed, until distillation became widespread, drinking beer and/or wine would have provided much-needed calories to farming populations. As food storage became more reliable, non-alcoholic drinks plentiful, and higher proof tipple more popular, alcohol became more a drug and less a food. The book was designed to encourage students to think critically about their alcohol use, and to give them a framework for understanding beliefs about intake. By using primary and secondary sources, social histories, and ethnographic accounts, Chrzan was able to demonstrate that modern drinking cultures are not created de novo by each generation but are deeply embedded in the cultures of Western Europe.

Milk: A Single Food Example for Nutritional Anthropology

The above examples are from anthropologists working on particular foodstuffs without specific analysis of the biological consequences, especially in the domain of nutrition. Here we describe another example of an investigation by one of us (Andrea Wiley) of a single food that speaks to some of the central concerns of nutritional anthropology (most of the material described below can be found in Wiley 2014 and Wiley 2016). As a food with some unique biological properties, milk turns out to be particularly well suited to the single food approach. Milk usage is related to the emergence of human genetic and behavioral adaptations over the course of recent human evolution and likely has important effects on the human life history and biological function. In this case "milk" refers to milk from nonhuman mammalian sources, most often cows. Human breast milk, an equally illustrative example, is the subject of a robust literature by nutritional anthropologists (e.g., Stuart-Macadam and Dettwyler 1995; van Esterik 1989). Milk consumption patterns vary widely both within and across cultures, and these co-occur with differences in strongly held attitudes toward and beliefs and policies about milk and genetic traits related to milk digestion. Some of these attitudes stem from milk's normative status in many contemporary human populations, where milk is seen as a food with especially salutary effects on human bodies, especially those of children.

Wiley's interest in milk stemmed from milk's unusual natural history. It is the only food produced specifically to be consumed, unlike all other foods that are acquired through predation. It is a peculiar biochemical substance, shaped over the course of mammalian evolution to have specific physiological effects on its consumers (infant mammals) through its nutrient content and high density of bioactive molecules. Many humans consume the milk of other species and do so well beyond infancy, which is the only time that other mammals encounter milk in their diets. At the same time, milk figures prominently in popular as well as nutritional discourse about diet in the cultural context of the United States and other countries, and such rhetoric achieved global spread in the early twenty-first century. Furthermore, milk is enmeshed in political, economic, cultural, and health discussions and institutions.

From this starting point Wiley then considered milk in relation to the well-known biological variation in milk digestion across human populations. Although humans have domesticated several mammalian species for milk—goats, sheep, water buffalo, horses, and camels, among others—cows have come to predominate as the primary source of commercial milk (India is an exception, where most milk comes from another large bovine species, the water buffalo). Domestication of cattle and human usage of their milk occurred around 8000 BP (Burger et al. 2007; Craig et al. 2005) and resulted in genetic differences between populations as natural selection shaped allele frequencies among populations utilizing this new foodstuff (Enattah et al. 2008; Enattah et al. 2002; Ingram et al. 2007; Ingram et al. 2009; Itan et al. 2010; Tishkoff et al. 2007). Variation in milk digestion in adulthood (i.e., lactase persistence or impersistence) is one of the key examples of human biological variation that is clearly the result of natural selection, and there are various candidates for the selective force that resulted in some populations having high frequencies of the allele that allows for lifelong milk digestion. One thing is clear from population comparisons: all populations with high frequencies share a history of dairying, although not all dairying populations have high frequencies of lactase persistence, suggesting some coevolutionary interactions between culture and biology. Dairying and milk usage are necessary but not sufficient to understand the evolution of lactase persistence in some human populations.

Human biological variation in relation to milk centers on ability to digest the milk sugar lactose beyond childhood. Lactose is unique to mammalian milk and is a double sugar (a disaccharide) made up of glucose and galactose. Lactose cannot be absorbed in the small intestine directly but must be cleaved into its component sugars, which can then be absorbed, enter the body's circulatory system, and used for energy. This process requires a specialized enzyme called lactase, which is found along the cells that line the upper small intestine. In general, infant mammals produce lactase in order to digest the lactose they are ingesting while nursing. However, lactase production diminishes over time and eventually stops all together, usually around the time of weaning. Mammals living in the wild never consume milk again after they are weaned; since the lactase appears to have no other function in the gut, it would be wasteful of scarce energy and nutrients to continue to produce it. Those mammals whose milk does not contain lactose (i.e., the marine mammals) also do not produce lactase, suggesting that if the enzyme was not needed, it was eliminated by natural selection.

Population variation in adult lactase activity historically maps onto cultural variation in dairy production and consumption as well as differences in the valuation of milk and milk products. Wiley began her investigation of this variable cultural discourse about milk in the United States, first in relation to the well-known biological variation in milk digestion. To this end she considered the scientific and biomedical literature's usage of terminology in relation to this variation (i.e., the use of medicalized terms such as "lactose maldigestion" or "lactase deficiency"); government policies that promoted milk consumption for all Americans, regardless of ancestry (e.g., the Dietary Guidelines for Americans); advertisements from the dairy industry; and interviews with individuals about their understandings of and attitudes toward milk. In addition, to get a systematic understanding of milk consumption patterns she analyzed data from the NHANES database, as well as other U.S. Department of Agriculture databases on milk production and the overall milk supply available for consumption (USDA/Economic Research Service 2016).

Milk's biochemical components are important to understand, as they underlie not only the evolution of lactase persistence in some dairying populations, but also some of the emic and etic understandings of milk. Cow's milk is, for example, high in calcium, and this underlies many claims (both scientific and popular) that are made about why individuals should consume milk in the United States, even though other dietary guidelines highlight milk's protein or vitamins as the most important. Meanwhile, although milk fat is a highly valued commodity economically, in public health nutrition it stands out as something to be minimized in the diet. Milk's biochemical makeup is relevant to many other topics, including how it is altered in the processing of milk into yogurt or cheese and the relationship between cow's milk consumption and child growth.

The most common culinary techniques used with milk involve fermentation and/or separation of the solids from the liquids. Heating milk and allowing it to ferment in a warm, moist environment allows lactophilic bacteria (such as *Lactobacillus*) to break down the lactose into lactic acid, thereby producing yogurt. Or, adding strong acid or special enzymes such as rennet to heated milk will cause its proteins to aggregate. This curdling separates the milk solids from the liquid whey. Lactose is primarily found in the whey portion, while the solids include milk proteins and fat. This basic process produces cheese. After separation the curds can be pressed to remove more liquid and aged to produce the wide range and distinct flavors and textures of cheeses traditionally crafted in Europe.

In both of these processes—neither of which is technologically at all complex—the biochemical properties of milk are significantly altered (as is milk's status as a "food" vs. "drink", although yogurt can be both). In both cases the lactose content is diminished—either converted to lactic acid or drained off in whey; the more extensive the fermentation or the more aged the cheese, the less lactose. Thus in the gastrointestinal system, the consequences of milk ingestion are quite different from those caused by consuming other dairy products. Widespread use of these techniques, especially fermentation, may help explain why lactase persistence rates are low in the Mediterranean and also in South Asia, a region with a long-standing dairy tradition that relies heavily on fermented products (although not cheese).

Milk's components are also pertinent to both emic beliefs about milk as a particularly important food for child growth and the scientific literature that evaluates the relationship between milk consumption and various measures of growth. If milk is produced by mammalian mothers to support the rapid growth of their infants, it seems plausible that milk would also contribute meaningfully to later child growth, especially when the milk comes from another, much larger mammalian species. The connection between milk and growth in body size seems to underlie the current global spread of milk consumption, including among populations with low rates of lactase persistence (e.g., East and Southeast Asia). For example, China's population has embraced milk, and China's dairy industry is the fastest growing in the world. Milk is in the Chinese recommended "food pagoda" and is distributed in child feeding programs and widely promoted to allow the Chinese to make up for past "growth deficits." Whether increasing milk consumption will contribute to greater body size among Chinese citizens remains to be seen, but milk's "specialness" as a food—inherent in its biochemical makeup—allows it to be associated with growth in body size. The meanings of larger body sizes and the ways milk is deployed metaphorically to reference growth and power connect the biological to the social and engage with discussions of the globalization and symbolism of food more generally (Wiley 2011).

These investigations provided insight into emic understandings of milk and the assumptions and biases people with different knowledge bases, experiences, and agendas make about milk. It was then possible to consider these understandings in relation to some key anthropological concerns. For example, describing bodies that digest milk throughout life as the norm (both in the sense of it being the most common and in the sense of it being "normal," healthy, and hence normative, i.e., how the body "should" be) has led to what Wiley terms "ethnobiocentrism"—an elaboration of the more familiar anthropological term ethnocentrism to include the interpretation of other peoples' bodies and behavior only in relation to those of one's own body and culture, generally with the view that one's own is "better" than the other, or that one's own is "normal" and others are somehow "abnormal" (Wiley 2004, 2016).

Milk consumption and its relation to ideas of "biological normalcy" are also relevant to how we understand child growth in relation to a set of growth standards. Standards are normative—they indicate how children "should" grow (WHO Multicentre Growth Reference Study Group 2006). For example, the new World Health Organization growth standards demonstrate that healthy breastfed infants from seven different populations all grow similarly, up through age five years (de Onis et al. 2007a). Beyond age five, though, there is no such normative standard, and the 1977 U.S. National Center for Health Statistics growth data are used as a reference population for evaluating the growth of children and adolescents (de Onis, et al. 2007b). Given the normative status of milk in the diet of U.S. children, the fact that there was no attempt to ascertain the milk-drinking status of children aged 2–5 years in the WHO standard, and the evidence suggesting that milk drinking may result in greater height (de Beer 2012; Wiley 2012), questions arise about what constitutes our understanding of "normal" child growth. That is, growth standards reflect the growth of children who consume milk. What "healthy" child growth looks like in the absence of milk is not clear, and nutritional anthropologists have long been interested in the relationship between diet and child growth.

Conclusion

In sum, the single food approach holds much promise in nutritional anthropological research. The examples demonstrate the ways in which interrogating a single food can address central concerns in nutritional anthropology and the broader field of food anthropology, particularly by addressing how food processing, distribution, and consumption are entwined in larger, often more visible cultural systems. Eating is clearly a process with profound effects at all levels of biological organization (i.e., molecular, cellular, physiological, organismal, and population). But ingestion is also a moral, economic and political act demonstrated by the cultural complexity of producing, preparing, sharing, and eventually consuming an item seemingly as simple as a single type of food.

Andrea S. Wiley is Professor of Anthropology and Director of the Human Biology Program at Indiana University, Bloomington. She received her PhD in medical anthropology from University of California, Berkeley and San Francisco, an MA in demography from UC Berkeley, and a BA in the biological basis of behavior at University of Pennsylvania. She is the author of four books: *Cultures of Milk: The Biology and Culture of Dairy Consumption in India and the United States* (Harvard University Press, 2014), *Re-imagining Milk* (Routledge, 2011 [2nd ed. 2016]), *Medical Anthropology: A Biocultural Perspective* (Oxford University Press; with John S. Allen, 3rd ed. 2017), and *An Ecology of High-Altitude Infancy* (Cambridge University Press, 2004). Her current research focuses on the relationship between milk consumption and child health in the United States and in India.

The two countries make an apt comparison as both are major producers of milk and both have cultural and/or religious traditions that privilege milk, yet the cultural and biological contexts in which milk is promoted and consumed are very different. Milk is designed to facilitate the growth and survival of juveniles within a particular mammalian species, yet cow's milk is now widely consumed by humans of all ages. Thus the question is how ongoing consumption of milk alters human life history trajectories. There is also well-described variation in the digestive physiology necessary to consume milk after infancy, yet milk is increasingly consumed in populations with little culinary history of milk. The causes and consequences of such dietary changes are a focus of my research.

Janet Chrzan is Adjunct Assistant Professor of Nutrition at the University of Pennsylvania and received her PhD in physical/nutritional anthropology from the University of Pennsylvania. Her research explores the connections between social activities, nutritional intakes, and maternal and child health outcomes in pregnant teens. She is also interested in the dietary consequences of culinary tourism and the social and nutritional contexts of alcohol intake.

References

Burger, J., et al. 2007. Absence of the Lactase-Persistence-Associated Allele in early Neolithic Europeans. *Proceedings of the National Academy of Sciences* 104(10): 3736–3741.
Craig, O. E., et al. 2005. Did the First Farmers of Central and Eastern Europe Produce Dairy Foods? *Antiquity* 79(306): 882–894.
Chrzan, Janet. 2013. *Alcohol: Social Drinking in Cultural Context*. New York: Routledge.
de Beer, Hans. 2012. Dairy Products and Physical Stature: A Systematic Review and Meta-analysis of Controlled Trials. *Economics & Human Biology* 10(3): 299–309.
de Onis, M., et al. 2007a. Comparison of the WHO Child Growth Standards and the CDC 2000 Growth Charts. *Journal of Nutrition* 137(1): 144–148.
de Onis, M., et al. 2007b. Development of a WHO Growth Reference for School-Aged Children and Adolescents. *Bulletin of the World Health Organization* 85(9): 660–667.
Enattah, Nabil Sabri, et al. 2002. Identification of a Variant Associated with Adult-Type Hypolactasia. *Nature Genetics* 30: 233–237.
Enattah, Nabil Sabri, et al. 2008. Independent Introduction of Two Lactase-Persistence Alleles into Human Populations Reflects Different History of Adaptation to Milk Culture. *The American Journal of Human Genetics* 82(1): 57–72.
Errington, Frederick, Deborah Gewertz, and Tatsuro Fujikura. 2013. *The Noodle Narratives: The Global Rise of an Industrial Food Into the Twenty-first Century*. Berkeley: University of California Press.
Gewertz, Deborah B., and Frederick K. Errington. 2010 *Cheap Meat: Flap Food Nations in the Pacific Islands*. Berkeley: University of California Press.
Harris, Marvin. 1985. *Good to Eat: Riddles of Food and Culture*. Prospect Heights, IL: Waveland Press.

Ingram, C. J., et al. 2007. A Novel Polymorphism Associated with Lactose Tolerance in Africa: Multiple Causes for Lactase Persistence? *Human Genetics* 120(6): 779–788.

Ingram, C. J., et al. 2009. Lactose Digestion and the Evolutionary Genetics of Lactase Persistence. *Human Genetics* 124(6): 579–591.

Itan, Yuval, et al. 2010. A Worldwide Correlation of Lactase Persistence Phenotype and Genotypes. *BMC Evolutionary Biology* 10(1): 36.

Knight, Daniel M. 2014. Mushrooms, Knowledge Exchange and Polytemporality in Kalloni. Greek Macedonia. *Food Culture and Society* 17(2): 183–201.

Mintz, Sidney. 1985. *Sweetness and Power: The Place of Sugar in Modern History.* New York: Viking.

Pertierra, Anna Cristina. 2012. The More Things Change, the More they Stay the Same: Rice and Beans in Modern Cuba. In *Rice and Beans: A Unique Dish in a Hundred Places,* ed. Richard Wilk and Lívia Barbosa. New York: Berg. 35–60.

Scrinis, Gyorgy. 2013. *Nutritionism: The Science and Politics of Dietary Advice.* New York: Columbia University Press.

Stuart-Macadam, Patricia, and Katherine A. Dettwyler, eds. 1995. *Breastfeeding: Biocultural Perspectives.* New York: Aldine de Gruyter.

Tishkoff, S. A., et al. 2007. *Convergent Adaptation of Human Lactase Persistence in Africa and Europe.* Nature Genetics 39(1): 31–40.

Tucker, Catherine M. 2011. *Coffee Culture: Local Experiences, Global Connections.* New York: Routledge.

USDA/Economic Research Service. 2016. *Food Availability (per capita) Data System.* http://www.ers.usda.gov/data-products/food-availability-%28per-capita%29-data-system/.aspx#.Ukml7FNEMyY. Accessed 18 September 2016.

van Esterik, Penny. 1989. *Beyond the Breast-Bottle Controversy.* New Brunswick, NJ: Rutgers University Press.

WHO Multicentre Growth Reference Study Group. 2006. WHO Child Growth Standards: Length/Height-for-Age, Weight-for-Age, Weight-for-Length, Weight-for-Height and Body Mass Index-for-age; Methods and Development. http://www.who.int/childgrowth/standards/technical_report/en/index.html.

Wiley, Andrea S. 2004. "Drink Milk for Fitness": The Cultural Politics of Human Biological Variation and Milk Consumption in the United States. *American Anthropologist* 106(3): 506–517.

———. 2011. Milk for "Growth": Global and Local Meanings of Milk Consumption in China, India, and the U.S. *Food and Foodways* 19(1): 11–33.

———. 2012. Cow Milk Consumption, Insulin-Like Growth Factor-I, and Human Biology: A Life History Approach. *American Journal Of Human Biology* 24(2): 130–138.

———. 2014. *Cultures of Milk: The Biology and Meaning of Dairy Products in India and the United States.* Cambridge, MA: Harvard University Press.

———. 2016. *Re-Imagining Milk: Cultural and Biological Perspectives,* 2nd edition.

Wilk, Richard, and Lívia Barbosa. 2012. *Rice and Beans: A Unique Dish in a Hundred Places.* New York: Berg.

Wilk, Richard, and Lívia Barbosa. 2012. A Unique Dish in a Hundred Places (Introduction). In *Rice and Beans: A Unique Dish in a Hundred Places,* ed. Richard Wilk and Lívia Barbosa, 1–17. New York: Berg.

Index

activism, 119, 175-177
advertisement/advertising, 58, 62-63, 72, 131, 134, 150, 169, 171, 183, 189, 208, 255, 261, 264
agriculture, 43, 105, 153-154, 159, 165, 170-171, 184, 196, 217, 222, 224, 231, 243, 264
agronomy, 197
alcohol, 14, 87, 189, 253, 261-262, 267
American Anthropological Association code of ethics, 124
American food, 188, 205, 207, 209, 215
anonymity, 76, 97
aphorism, 170
archaeology, 31, 132, 139, 153, 183, 221
art, 70, 73-74, 171, 186, 189, 191, 215, 218
audio-recording, 11, 138
autoethnography, 117, 121, 124

banquet management, 186
Belmont Report, 20, 23, 27
biocultural anthropology, 33, 43
biological anthropology, 31-32, 132
biological normalcy, 265
blog(s), 131, 134, 137-138, 150-151, 170, 182, 190, 229, 244-245
body image, 8, 18, 24, 41, 58-67
body mass index, 24, 43, 66-67
Bourdieu, 54, 132, 171, 258-259

cartoon, 150, 169-171
catering, 186
Central America, 246, 248, 259
cheesemaking, 97
citizen scientists, 244
climate change, 246, 248
cognitive analysis, 131
cognitive anthropology, 158
Collaborative Institutional Training Initiative (CITI), 115
Committee on Nutritional Anthropology (CNA), 32
commodity chain, 14, 200, 238, 247, 253, 255-258
communicative competence, 133
consent form, 52, 114, 122
construction, 8, 72, 98, 102, 134, 173, 205, 208, 210-211, 228
Consultative Group on International Agricultural Research (CGIAR), 246
content analysis, 33, 177
conversation analysis, 134
cookbooks, 72, 131, 137-138, 170, 182-183, 185-188, 190-191, 215, 219-220, 222-223, 225
cooking tools, 116
corporate archives, 188
cross-cultural analysis, 254
culinary chats, 36, 52-53, 116, 144
cultural anthropology, 8, 31, 34, 92, 99, 134, 139, 153, 177, 204, 240

Cultural Domain Analysis (CDA), 10-11, 138, 158, 160, 162, 164-165
culture hearths, 222
dairy industry, 264-265
dairying, 263-264
data analysis software, 135, 175, 177
data collection, 2, 9-11, 22, 33, 40, 42, 41, 62, 65, 74-75, 83-85, 89, 114, 151, 160, 175, 199, 240-241, 244, 247
data mining, 175
data report, 118, 121-122, 125
Declaration of Helsinki, 19-20, 28
demography, 266
diaries, 41, 65-66, 85, 117, 137, 184-185, 198, 208, 220, 261
diet and human evolution, 253
dietary changes, 267
Dietary Guidelines for Americans, 264
dietary literature, 188
dietary patterns, 104-105, 189
direct observation, 8-9, 41-42, 81-89, 164
direct trade, 240, 248
  and alternative trade, 238, 241, 244-245, 247-248
discourse, 10-12, 54, 60-61, 126, 131, 133-135, 137-138, 147, 150, 152, 154, 173-174, 254-255, 263-264
discourse, 10-12, 54, 60-61, 126, 131, 133-135, 137-138, 147, 150, 152, 154, 173-174, 254-255, 263-264
discourse analysis, 131, 154
discursive psychology, 131, 134
domains, 11, 23, 61, 70, 113, 131, 138, 158-159, 164, 200-201, 204, 253, 255

eating disorders, 18, 59
eating heuristic, 147
economic development, 244
edible, 38, 86, 161, 164, 208-209
embodiment, 40, 113
emic, 11-12, 158, 214, 227, 255-256, 264-265
encyclopedia, 154, 182, 191, 215
entextualization, 172
epistemology, 39, 47, 49, 51, 53-55
ethics, 3, 7-9, 15-17, 19-21, 23, 25, 42, 53, 64, 75-76, 113-115, 120, 122, 124, 175-177, 189, 198, 240

fieldwork ethics, 114
  research ethics, 7, 15, 17, 19, 21, 23, 25, 75, 114, 120, 122, 177
ethnobotany, 35, 165
ethnographic fieldwork, 120
ethnography, 8, 11, 34, 37, 41-42, 47-48, 53-55, 74, 77, 83, 99, 112-120, 123-125, 131, 133, 139, 146-147, 154, 197-198, 203-204, 208-214, 221, 227-230, 232, 234, 241, 256, 260
  using participant observation, 11, 257
ethnography, 8, 11, 34, 37, 41-42, 47-48, 53-55, 74, 77, 83, 99, 112-120, 123-125, 131, 133, 139, 146-147, 154, 197-198, 203-204, 208-214, 221, 227-230, 232, 234, 241, 256, 260
  of communication, 11, 133, 139, 146
  of Speaking, 139, 147, 210
ethnohistory, 134
ethnosemantics, 133
etic, 255-256, 264
etiquette manual, 170-171, 175
etymology, 170
explicit meaning, 209, 213

fair trade, 153, 240, 244, 247
fermentation, 86, 95, 264-265
festival, 94, 101, 171, 229, 261
fieldnotes, 99
fieldwork, 99, 114, 120, 124
fieldwork ethics, 114
fiestas, 101
fife, wayne, 99
film, 71, 229
focus groups, 8-11, 34, 42, 59-66, 101-110, 122, 135-137, 143-145, 152, 154, 176, 239, 242-243
  advantages, 81-82, 240, 242
  with children, 73, 105, 132
  construction, 8, 72, 98, 102, 134, 173, 205, 208, 210-211, 228
  formal, 32, 35, 47, 93-94, 96, 136, 187, 203, 233, 255
  group composition, 102
  informal, 49, 53-54, 65, 94, 101-103, 115-116, 136, 203-204, 243, 255
  international setting, 103

272 Index

limitations, 10, 22, 42, 48, 82, 102, 107, 159, 240, 243
timing, 85
folktale, 171
food
    anthropology, 31, 33, 35, 37, 39, 41, 43, 112, 119, 266

food (continued)
    art, 70, 73-74, 171, 186, 189, 191, 215, 218
    consumption, 40, 58-63, 65, 67, 77, 85, 105, 135, 161, 197, 224, 253-254
    deserts, 117
    ethnography, 8, 112-114, 117, 119-120, 123, 125, 197, 256
    event, 133, 147, 211, 213
    film, 71, 229
    ideologies, 134
    images, 63, 72, 75-76, 145, 169
    journals, 144, 146
    magazine, 62, 171, 187, 219
    mapping, 36, 256
    music, 183, 186
    production, 8, 14, 40, 82, 86, 116, 143, 148, 151-152, 197, 199, 201, 229-230, 232, 257
    radio, 150, 183, 189
    scale, 38, 67, 134, 151-152, 163, 173, 186, 197, 199, 230
    studies, 1-3, 7, 9-15, 17-19, 21, 23, 25, 32, 36, 47-48, 52, 54, 71-72, 74, 112, 121, 165, 191, 194, 196-200, 203-204, 206, 208, 210, 212-214, 221, 225, 227-228, 240, 252
    taboos, 253
    talk, 10-11, 129, 131, 137, 143-155, 171-173
    TV, 138, 150, 170, 189
food and meaning, 200, 203-204, 212
food composition tables, 256
food frequency questionnaire, 254-255
food value chains, 240-242, 248
    challenges of studying, 239
food voice, 48-49, 116, 121, 124, 139, 144, 154
food-and-talk events, 143, 146-147, 150, 154
food-based life history, 47, 51, 213
food-centered life histories, 48, 53, 116, 144, 234
foodscape, 121, 124, 171
foodways, 10, 14, 49, 56, 93, 113, 119, 121, 125, 131-135, 138, 143, 145-146, 149, 152, 154, 171, 173, 183-184, 186, 189, 191, 207-208, 210-215, 222-224
free lists, 10-11, 158, 160-165

garbage, 38
gastroaesthetics, 171
gastronomy, 112, 119, 187, 191, 233, 235
gender, 23, 34, 36, 43, 48, 56, 60, 62, 64-67, 72, 77, 82, 84, 88, 93, 99, 102, 108, 119, 125-126, 139, 147, 153, 163-164, 170, 185, 188, 198, 210, 234, 244, 261
gender issues, 244
genres, 131, 147-148, 174
global commodity chains (gccs), 238
globalization, 59, 198, 201, 253, 256-257, 265
grounded theory, 39-40, 173, 212, 261
group interviews
    advantages, 81-82, 240, 242
    limitations, 10, 22, 42, 48, 82, 102, 107, 159, 240, 243
    utility, 117, 231, 252
growth, 38, 89, 253, 264-267
growth standards, 266

HIPAA, 23, 25, 27
household income, 183
household management, 184
human biology, 200, 266
human relations area files, 254
human research protections, 127
human subject, 15, 18-22, 36, 115, 120, 176
    human subjects review, 115
Hymes, Dell, 139, 154

identity, 18, 24, 36, 40, 48-49, 51, 58, 60-61, 110, 126, 134-135, 139, 145, 147-148, 153, 170, 177, 186, 198, 204-206, 208, 210-213, 217, 219, 221-224, 259-261
implicit meaning, 209

informal working groups, 101
informant documentation, 42, 115, 117-118, 120, 122, 124
informed consent, 7, 16-17, 19, 21, 25, 53, 97, 115, 176
ingredients, 101, 104-105, 117, 133-134, 136, 147-148, 185-188, 190, 210, 212, 219, 227, 259-260
Institutional Review Board (IRB), 10, 20-21, 24-25, 114-115, 120-122, 124, 176
International Commission on the Anthropology of Food (ICAF), 35
Internet
   online resources, 144, 151-153, 175, 177, 245
interpretive analysis, 198
intertextuality, 150
interview/interviewing, 8-9, 11, 17, 34-36, 40-42, 47-54, 59-66, 72, 74, 76, 82, 84, 88, 93-94, 96-99, 107-108, 113, 115-117, 120, 122-124, 135-137, 143-144, 148, 152, 154, 164, 169, 171, 173-174, 176, 208, 220, 223, 225, 234, 239, 241-243, 245-246, 255-258, 264
   semi-structured, 35, 59, 61, 92, 95-96, 116, 136, 241-242, 246
   structured, 9, 34-35, 47, 54, 59, 61, 81-85, 88, 92, 95-96, 116, 136, 160, 241-242, 246, 255
   unstructured, 81, 95, 97, 241-242
   open-ended, 241

justice, 7, 20, 22-23, 25-26, 74, 176, 180, 244, 250

key informant interviews, 59, 61
kitchen, 8, 41, 47, 51, 53-55, 94, 101, 104, 113, 116-117, 120, 133, 136, 138, 144, 148, 183, 185-186, 217, 220, 222, 234, 241, 260
kitchen table ethnography, 8, 41, 47, 53-55, 116

label, 136, 152, 160, 170, 259
lactase/lactose, 263-265
land tenure, 184

language, 10-11, 14, 51, 53, 81, 109, 131-140, 143-154, 170, 174, 177, 186, 219, 224, 233, 239, 241
language ideologies, 134, 139, 153
language socialization, 11, 139, 148-149, 152-154, 177
legal proceedings, 188
Levi-Strauss, 132, 170-171, 209-210, 258-259
linguistic anthropology, 3, 10, 131, 133, 135, 137, 139, 153-154, 177
linguistic ethnography, 131
linguistic repertoires, 134
listening, 9, 47, 50, 55, 242
literary criticism, 53, 138
local food, 43, 54-55, 112, 118, 217, 223-224, 243

manners, 11, 187, 205
manuscripts, 218
market information
   in research, 15, 20, 23, 42, 63, 73-75, 113, 118, 207, 244-246
materiality, 10, 139, 153
meaningfulness, 207, 211, 214
media, 9, 11, 35, 58-59, 63, 70-72, 74, 76-77, 99, 117, 121, 131, 138, 145, 150-152, 189-190, 208, 229, 244
mediated food interactions, 150, 154
menus, 116-117, 137, 158, 170, 187, 208, 211, 224
metacommunication, 173
metatext, 12, 169-171, 173, 175-176
methodology, 14, 33-34, 36, 39, 51-52, 55, 59, 72-74, 107, 109-110, 114, 123, 134, 144, 148, 158-160, 164-165, 182-183, 190, 200-201, 204, 212, 221, 244, 256
Mexico, 8, 47, 54, 56, 101, 110, 145, 160, 165, 245, 247
milk, 14, 95, 99, 104, 160, 198, 200, 253, 262-267
   consumption, 200, 262, 264-266
   digestion, 262-264
   See also lactose/lactase
Mintz, Sidney, 182, 197, 199-200, 253, 256
mixed-methods, 9, 34, 84, 101, 103, 105, 107, 109, 197, 199, 240, 245

mixed method approach, 34, 41
moderator, 65, 106-107, 109-110
multiple methods, 198, 258
multisensory, 169
mushrooms, 260-261

National Health and Nutrition Examination Survey, 254
Network of Food Data Base Systems, 105
Nuremberg Code, 18-20
nutrition, 1-2, 7-8, 31-33, 35, 39-40, 88-89, 103-104, 108, 110, 134, 152, 159-160, 162, 165, 183-184, 197-198, 201, 252-256, 262, 264, 267
nutritional anthropology, 1, 3, 9, 32-36, 81-83, 89, 93, 252, 256, 262, 266-267

obesity, 18, 24, 43, 59-60, 65-67, 153, 170, 253, 257
observer, 9, 83, 106-109, 182
orality, 131
    oral history, 48, 52, 136, 139
    oral presentation, 10, 118, 120-123

palatable, 104, 208-209
Paleoanthropology, 132
participant observation, 2, 9-11, 34-36, 41-42, 59-63, 66, 81-85, 87, 92-96, 99, 115, 117, 120, 124, 133, 135, 139, 143, 146, 148, 151, 164, 200, 227, 232, 234, 239-241, 245, 257-258, 260-261
    advantages, 81-82, 240, 242
    considerations, 2, 9, 23, 75, 116, 150, 199, 212, 253
participant sensation, 200, 227
participatory research, 24, 70, 75, 239, 243-244
patents, 188
performance, 40, 50, 148, 171, 210-211, 213, 219
pets, 208
photo elicitation, 72, 77, 144, 146
photography, 9, 35, 42, 49, 70-72, 75-76, 115, 117, 120, 124, 219-220, 229
photovoice, 72, 75, 77
pile sorts, 10-11, 158, 162-163, 165
plague, 185

poem, 42, 170, 189
policy, 43, 50, 76, 95, 123, 134, 153-154, 165, 171, 174, 176-177, 201, 244-245, 247, 253, 258, 262, 264
primary source, 138, 182-184, 186, 188, 190-191, 198, 263
processing, 14, 82, 84-86, 184, 188, 241, 243, 246, 264, 266
propaganda, 189
pseudonyms, 97, 135

qualitative data, 42, 81-82, 84, 96, 132, 135, 140, 173-175, 177, 242
    qualitative data analysis programs, 140
    qualitative methods, 32, 34, 108, 121
    qualitative research, 40, 47, 99, 102, 107, 174-175, 201, 203
quantitative methods, 35, 82, 198-199, 240
    quantitative research, 34, 40
    quantitative surveys, 59, 66

rabbit, 208-209
rapport, 40, 47, 51-52, 60-62, 64-65, 83, 93, 106, 108-109, 241
    importance, 41, 47, 58, 60, 64, 84-87, 106, 108
recipe, 10, 55, 73, 92, 117-118, 123, 170, 184-186, 190-191, 211, 213, 215, 221-224, 227, 234, 259
reference, 1-2, 9, 13, 16, 34, 62, 93, 97, 122-123, 137, 139, 172, 183, 200, 204-206, 209, 224, 231, 240, 265-266
regional cuisine, 220, 222
research design, 1-3, 7-8, 10, 15, 37, 39, 41, 62-63, 66, 103, 106-107, 114, 116, 118-122, 124, 212, 227, 240, 243, 246
research ethics, 7, 15, 17, 19, 21, 23, 25, 27, 75, 80, 114, 120, 122, 178, 271
research question, 2, 8, 13, 22, 37-38, 40-42, 50, 66, 75-76, 82-85, 89, 95, 114, 123, 143-144, 182, 239-240, 244-245, 255
researcher-elicited talk, 143-144, 154
respect for persons, 7, 20-22, 24-25
restaurants, 38, 84, 117, 148, 160, 187, 190, 207, 217, 223, 241
    restaurant reviews, 187

rice and beans, 255, 259-260
rituals, 206, 213, 260

sampling
    convenience, 84, 116, 145, 199
    random, 19, 104, 116
    reality, 35, 76, 105, 116, 124, 199-201, 217, 220-221, 231
    serendipity, 116
    snowball, 51, 94, 116
schools, 43, 152, 176
seasoning, 185
semi-structured open-ended interviews, 59, 61
semiotics, 10-11, 139, 153-154, 177, 204, 261
senses, 14, 56, 70, 73-74, 94, 113, 200, 227-229, 231-235
sensory analysis, 233
sensory ethnography, 74, 113, 120, 227-230, 232, 234
sensory labs, 233
single food approach, 252, 254, 256, 258, 260, 262, 264, 266
social history, 136, 144, 184, 186, 257, 262
social media, 150-151, 190, 229, 244
social science, 16, 43, 99, 102, 200, 203-204, 240, 252
socialization, 11, 132, 137, 139, 144, 148-149, 152-154, 177
Society for the Anthropology of Food and Nutrition (SAFN), 32
sociolinguistics, 131, 139
soup kitchen, 94, 113, 120
speaking
    heuristic, 147
speech events, 133, 147, 149
Spradley, James, 99
story, 8, 37, 47-49, 52, 54-55, 65, 71, 94, 97-98, 116, 144, 189, 259-261
storytelling, 2, 41, 74, 148
study design, 7, 21-22, 37, 64
sugar, 104, 186, 189, 191, 197, 199, 228, 239, 253, 256-257, 263
Surveys
    constraints, 145

household, 55, 85, 87-88, 96, 108, 116, 183-186, 221-222, 245, 255, 260
Kwiksurvey, 242
online, 41, 67, 71, 144, 151-153, 175, 177, 186, 224, 240, 242, 244-245
SurveyMonkey, 242
utility, 117, 231, 252
Zoomerang, 242
Sweetness and Power, 198, 200-201, 240, 254
symbols, 12, 204-208, 211

taboos, 189, 233, 253-254
talk, 10-11, 38, 48-49, 52, 54-55, 59-61, 63-64, 67, 92, 96, 114, 129, 131-133, 135-138, 143-155, 171-173, 190, 206, 234
taste, 14, 35, 37, 56, 73-74, 77, 82-84, 86, 94, 104-105, 133-134, 145, 147, 150, 170-171, 186-187, 191, 201, 205, 208, 220, 223, 227-231, 233-234, 258
television program, 42
testimonios, 55, 116, 124
textual analysis, 42, 131, 172, 174
Thanksgiving, 125
Theoretical approach, 37, 40-41, 258
theory, 1, 3, 9-10, 12-13, 17, 31-32, 37, 39-41, 48-49, 54-55, 73, 114, 124, 169, 173-174, 197, 199, 203, 210, 212, 214-215, 256, 258-259, 261
thick description, 14, 40, 93, 135, 228, 232-233, 253, 257-259
time allocation, 82
toast, 104, 150, 171
trade, 17, 137, 153, 217, 238-239, 242-247, 255-258
transcript, 48, 50, 98, 137, 149, 152, 171, 173-174, 178
transcription, 11, 50, 53, 98, 107-109, 137, 140, 143, 149, 151-152, 154, 173, 178
triads, 163
Turkey, 209

University of Gastronomic Sciences, 112, 119
USDA National Nutrient Database, 254

value chains, 237-246
    value chain mapping, 240, 245
video-recording, 11
visual aids, 59, 62, 123
visual anthropology, 8-9, 41, 70-73, 75, 77, 229

white paper, 171
world-systems theory, 258

www.ingramcontent.com/pod-product-compliance
Lightning Source LLC
Chambersburg PA
CBHW070914030426
42336CB00014BA/2409